AUSTRALIAN

GAY AND LESBIAN

WRITING

AUSTRALIAN

GAY AND LESBIAN

WRITING

An Anthology

Edited by

Robert Dessaix

Melbourne

OXFORD UNIVERSITY PRESS

Oxford   Auckland   New York

OXFORD UNIVERSITY PRESS AUSTRALIA

Oxford   New York   Toronto
Delhi   Bombay   Calcutta   Madras   Karachi
Kuala Lumpur   Singapore   Hong Kong   Tokyo
Nairobi   Dar es Salaam   Cape Town
Melbourne   Auckland   Madrid

and associated companies in
Berlin   Ibadan

OXFORD is a trade mark of Oxford University Press

National Library of Australia
Cataloguing-in-Publication data:

Australian gay and lesbian writing.

Includes index.
ISBN 0 19 553457 3.

1. Homosexuality—Literary collections. 2. Lesbianism—Literary
collections. 3. Gays' writing, Australian. 4. Lesbians' writings,
Australian. 5. Australian literature. I. Dessaix, Robert, 1944– .

A820.80353

Publication of this title was assisted by the
Commonwealth Government through the Australia Council,
its arts funding and advisory body.

Typeset by Solo Typesetting, South Australia
Printed by McPherson's Printing Group
Published by Oxford University Press,
253 Normanby Road, South Melbourne, Australia

CONTENTS

EDITOR'S ACKNOWLEDGEMENTS

For their generous advice and interest I would like to thank Tom Shapcott, Gary Simes, Michael Hurley, Gary Dunne, Garry Wotherspoon, Laurin McKinnon, Tom Thompson and Nicholas Pounder. I am grateful to the staff of the English Department at the University of Melbourne for the Fellowship enabling me to carry out research as well as for the stimulating conversations and guidance they offered me. For their unflagging support, wise direction and enthusiastic encouragement at every stage in the project I especially thank Peter Rose and Helen Daniel.

INTRODUCTION

A music hall BAWD *appears*

Chorus

A remarkable deception, a sensational career
An extraordinary case of personation
Concealment of her sex, a woman's milit'ry career
Masquerading as a man. Abomination!

In Heathcote in Victoria it's 1873
They've nabbed a person wearing pants
they say that he's a she
I can't abide that sort of thing
it almost makes me sick
For a woman must be pretty
and a man should have a . . .
(*Boom, Boom*)
         . . . good suit for Sunday!

Repeat Chorus

On Saturday they found a chap
in the bush near Ballarat
He was naked as a baby
all except for his cork hat
Now everyone could see quite plain
the measure of his . . .
(*Boom, Boom*)
         . . . hand
Which only shows that it ain't the clothes
that always makes the man!

Repeat Chorus

Now when a country's young like ours
one has to make quite sure
that womanhood and manliness
are governed by the law
For what is going to come
of a nation bright as this

> If a woman breaks the horsies
> and a man sits down to . . .
> (*Boom, boom*)
>   . . . mend his trousers!
>
> *Final chorus*
> [BAWD exits]

To thunderous applause, no doubt. This entertaining musical interlude is from a play called *Poor Johanna* (1991) by Robin Archer and
Judith Rodriguez and it captures with almost insulting vigour a deep-
seated perception of Australia as a land where, on the whole, women
are women and men are men and Blind Freddy can tell the difference.
The Bawd, speaking almost certainly for millions of ordinary Australians, is celebrating here the notion that in a young, healthy land
such as Australia social order depends upon keeping sex rigorously
identified with gender. People whose behaviour suggests a different
kind of meshing of gender with sex make the Bawd—and millions of
decent Australians—sick: women who masquerade as men, of course,
women who aren't softly beautiful, inviting possession, men who
don't see their penis as their primary signifier and people who carry
out tasks usually assigned to the other sex. The Bawd has no need to
include derisive remarks about homosexuals in her musical interlude—
the ultimate abomination is lurking unnamed in every line of her
song. Yet the very bravado of the Bawd's delivery should make us
suspicious. Such bravado is only called for when the assumptions it is
based on are in fact under threat.

To judge from Australia's literary heritage, the threat has taken
many forms over the past one hundred years or so, from intensely
romantic same-sex attachments to the creation of a homosexual
subculture, from scandalous cross-dressing to the conscious cultivation
of homoerotic sensibilities. Earlier in Australia's colonial history the
threat was scarcely alluded to in fiction or poetry, although in various
official documents and in memoirs homosexual practices amongst the
male and female convict populations were discussed. By and large,
however, in these pre-Freudian, pre-Jungian, pre-Wildean days, few
seem to have doubted that sex and gender were the same thing—men
were masculine, women were feminine—and sexuality in the sense
of a genital orientation either towards or away from the opposite sex
was to all intents and purposes simply not discussed within the polite
confines of the literary arts. In the twentieth century, particularly
after the First World War, sex and gender began to refuse to line up
obediently one behind the other, even in mainstream fiction and
poetry, populating Australian writing with a growing number of

male and female characters displaying gender characteristics from all points in the masculine-feminine spectrum. Our Bawd would have been horrified—women wearing trousers and breaking in the horses would have been the least of her worries.

In the popular mind, of course, whenever sex and gender start to slide apart the possibility of homosexuality at least raises its head. In fact, the merest sign of any dislocation is still enough to cause suspicion: the footballer (sex: male) who reads poetry (gender: feminine), the business executive (sex: female) who is competitive or wears a tie (gender: masculine), the father of four (sex: male) who enjoys housework (gender: feminine). In any gap between sex and gender the popular mind has a nasty feeling that homosexuality may be breeding like a fungus. (And so it may, of course, but it just as easily may not.) Indeed, to this day, Australian parents, except in the more bohemian quarters of the larger cities, spend a lot of time monitoring any slippage in their children.

In literary terms the widening gap between sex and gender led to more overt discussion of sexuality and the 1960s saw a small but powerful explosion of works dealing directly with questions of sexual orientation. In fact, sexuality itself has now become a leading theme in Australian fiction, poetry and drama, to the point where some writers have made literary careers writing about nothing else. By comparison with other national literatures, the number of prominent Australian writers who have explored aspects of homosexuality in their mainstream work is quite extraordinary. As a measure of the acceptance of homosexual themes in Australian fiction, for example, it is worth considering that of the twenty-four writers represented in *The Faber Book of Contemporary Australian Short Stories* (1988), edited by Murray Bail, presumably without any thought to the sexual orientation of either the writers or their fiction, almost half have at some time written on homosexual themes and indeed almost a third of them are included in this present collection.

The Colonial Period

Farewell Tasmania's isle!
  I bid adieu
The possum and the kangaroo.
Farmers' Glory! Prisoners' Hell!
  Land of Buggers!
  Fare ye well.

'Farewell to Tasmania' Frank the
Poet (Francis MacNamara),
early 1850s

Some contemporary cultural historians, ensconced comfortably inside linguistic models of reality, claim that since the word *homosexuality* did not exist until the late nineteenth century homosexuality as such did not exist until then. The Irish convict Frank the Poet (shepherd, popular rhymster and rascal) would have been astonished to hear this, once it had been explained to him what the modern term referred to. Homosexuality may not have existed *as such*, but practices we would now call homosexual certainly did exist in colonial Australia— indeed, they certainly existed in pre-colonial Australia, if such a term makes any sense—and are well documented. The prevalence of sodomy and other 'unnatural crimes and unnameable offences', including lesbian sexual assault, under the notorious Probation System of convict discipline in Van Diemen's Land (Tasmania) between 1839 and 1846 was one of the reasons that the system was eventually abandoned and the Lieutenant-Governor, Sir John Eardley-Wilmot, recalled. In his 1847 report on the Probation System to the Secretary of State in London, Charles La Trobe, eventually Lieutenant-Governor of Victoria, adopted a curiously modern stance, despite his abhorrence of 'moral pollution': homosexual behaviour, he concluded, was the result of social conditioning, not of innate propensities—remove the conditions (construct partitions between prisoners' bunks, supervise prisoners' movements, particularly in the bush, close down certain 'hotbeds' of vice) and the behaviour would disappear. And indeed, according to official accounts, it did. Those who favour the social construct theory of homosexuality might care to ponder the oppressive uses to which it was put in mid-nineteenth century Tasmania.

Lesbian practices amongst female convicts in Van Diemen's Land were of as much concern to the authorities in both Hobart and London as were male homosexual practices. According to the 1843 report of the committee of inquiry into conditions at the Female Factory in Hobart, lesbianism was brazenly rife. Some women went so far as to arouse each other's passions during divine service. As in the men's penitentiaries, social structures which reflected hetero-sexual structures were set up in the Female Factories, replete with fancy-women, passionately romantic attachments, coupling, rape and domination. Although the local press showed some interest in homo-sexual practices amongst the convict population (partly for convoluted political reasons, as it might today), there is almost no reflection in literary works of the period of a phenomenon that was by all accounts widespread. Even in Marcus Clarke's classic novel *For the Term of His Natural Life*, which was largely set in Tasmania, there is little direct reference to homosexual behaviour despite the fact that

one of the novel's main characters, the brutal commandant on Maria
Island Maurice Frere, was based on a man called John Giles Price
(1808–57) whom many believed to be homosexual. Much like the
authors of official reports, Marcus Clarke preferred to allude to
homosexuality in terms which positioned it outside any natural
human framework: 'In the factory—a prison for females—the vilest
abuses were committed, while the infamies current, as matters of
course, in chain gangs and penal settlements, were of too horrible a
nature to be more than hinted at here. All that the vilest and most
bestial of human creatures could invent and practise, was in this
unhappy country invented and practised without restraint and without shame.'[1] Later in the novel the Reverend James North writes in
his diary for 14 May 1846 about lights-out after evening muster on the
prison island of Norfolk: '. . . the ruffians are left to their own
devices until morning. Knowing what I know of the customs of
convicts, my heart sickens when I in imagination put myself in the
place of a newly-transported man, plunged from six at night until
daybreak into that foetid den of worse than wild beasts.'[2]

In the mainland colony of New South Wales homosexuality was
common, according to the historian A.G.L. Shaw, who tosses caution
to the wind and simply gives an ancient practice its modern name,
'particularly in the ironed gangs and penal settlements'. It is impossible now to know, as he puts it, 'how unusual this was in other
circumstances'. Certainly, in his memoirs entitled *The Exile's
Lamentations*, the English convict Thomas Cook manages to give the
impression that 'this horrid contagion', these 'horrible propensities',
this 'filth' had 'reached a great part of [his] fellow prisoners here' at
Mt Victoria in the early 1830s.[3] 'So far advanced were these wretched
men in depravity, that they appeared to have entirely lost the feelings
of men,' he tells us, presumably meaning 'real' or 'natural' men.[4]
Indeed, if any man made so bold as to 'persist in publicly deprecating
their horrible propensities, he would be struck, kicked and otherwise
abused.'[5] Homosexual favours, he makes quite clear, were a form of
currency with overseers and prisoners alike and could save a convict
from a flogging on the triangles. Cook was especially outraged that
some convicts should show open pleasure and delight in their practices,
but 'sad experience . . . taught me the uselessness of any attempt to
check the progress of their Sinful abominations, and thus . . . I
remained a Silent observer . . .' of these 'characters altogether unfit
to be classed with human beings'.[6] Thomas Cook's revulsion, like
many Australians' before and since, was ostensibly based on moral
considerations and a sense of what is 'natural', but it doesn't take

much scratching at words like 'moral' and 'natural' to reveal concerns of a more political nature: by 'moral' and 'natural' he really means a hierarchical social order based on Christianity and a strict division of power between male and female. To this day, whether it means to or not, homosexuality undermines this kind of social order.

In some ways the association of male and female homosexuality with the convict system in nineteenth-century Australia has had important reverberations, both in public ideas about homosexuality and in its literary representations. By locating homosexuality within a separate microcosm, only tangentially related to the 'real world' outside, the public was able to reclassify homosexuals as either real men or real women and put its mind at rest. In this sense Zimmer, the narrator of Robert Adamson and Bruce Hanford's novel *Zimmer's Essay* (1974), hits the nail on the head when he says: 'It is untrue to say that the prison culture of New South Wales is a homosexual culture. It is a culture that is strictly heterosexual, and that rigidly enforces two separate codes of conduct upon its members, who are either masculine or feminine.'[7] Nor is there any hint of 'homosexuality' in this sense in Jim McNeil's prison play *How Does Your Garden Grow* (also 1974): the three main characters are male (Mick, 'Brenda' and Sam) and the sexual arrangements down to the last courtesy and inflection in the voice mirror a conventional working-class world where sex and gender eclipse each other entirely. Sam lusts after fat German frauleins, as he puts it, *and* after 'Brenda', Mick after 'Brenda' and his wife, and everyone feels perfectly comfortable with the arrangement. None of the characters is thought of as 'homosexual'.

This literary association of homosexuality with an abnormal closed social system has given Australian writers the freedom to explore homosexuality by locating it inside other kinds of microcosms — in particular prisons, boarding-schools, ships, the armed services and hospitals. In a sexually abnormal world such as a boarding-school or the crew's quarters on board ship, readers presumably find it easier to accept the 'normalcy' of what would be considered shockingly abnormal in the world at large and, to reassure them, some sort of equivalent of the normal male/female masculine/feminine binary lineup is usually in operation. As early as 1937 Kenneth 'Seaforth' Mackenzie could write a novel focussing, often with great physical explicitness, on a schoolmaster's homosexual passion for one of his pupils in a Western Australian boys' boarding-school. No howls of outrage seem to have greeted the publication of the novel — on the contrary, it was awarded a prestigious literary prize. If the equivalent of the normal male/female, masculine/feminine lineup is *not* in operation (as in much contemporary gay and lesbian writing, such as Mary Fallon's, Susan Hampton's, Gary Dunne's, Ian MacNeill's, Michael Hurley's and many others') the general reader's tolerance drops markedly—and in prison, as Zimmer observes, it can have violent repercussions. 'The big losers in the prison sexual politik are the "cats", who will not accept feminine status, but who are weak and so are raped, or coerced into cock-sucking. They do not receive the chivalry accorded to queens.'[8]

Another kind of permissive closed system in evidence in Australian literature is the microcosm of same-sex bonding, more or less overtly sexual in nature. The nineteenth-century bushranging gang was always a likely site for this kind of bonding, and indeed several well-known gangs have been eroticised in this sense both in the popular imagination and historians' discussions. In 1880 the bushranger Andrew Scott (Captain Moonlight), for example, spoke and wrote in deeply emotional terms of his friendship for his fellow gang-member Jim Nesbit. 'Nesbit and I were united by *every* tie which could bind human friendship, we were one in *hopes*, one in *heart* and *soul* and this unity lasted until he died in my arms,' he wrote. 'When he died my heart was crushed . . . my fondest hope is to be with him in Eternity.'[9] Many authoritative commentators on the Kelly gang, including historians Manning Clark, John Molony and Garry Wotherspoon, have raised the question of homosexual bonding within the gang, particularly between Aaron Sherritt and Joe Byrne. Sidney J. Baker, in *The Australian Language*, goes further: 'After examining all the relevant evidence, I have little doubt that they were a group of homosexuals'.[10] Later in the century a number of Australian writers celebrated 'friendships' of such emotional intensity that the modern reader cannot avoid reading sexual feelings into them, despite the lack of explicit evidence. In the 1890s John Le Gay Brereton and other poets in the circle now dubbed the Whitmanites because of Walt Whitman's influence on their lives and work (Francis Adams, for example, and Bernard O'Dowd) openly celebrated male friendships in terms usually reserved for heterosexual attachments. Around the turn of the century there seems to have been a growing appreciation among the aesthetic élite of the sexual possibilities only half-hidden by something vaguely defined as decadence—in a character such as the scandalously attractive poet Esmé Colquhoun in Rosa Praed's novel *Affinities* (1886), or in 1910 amongst the music students in Leipzig in Henry Handel Richardson's *Maurice Guest*, for example. Just before and during the First World War Lesbia Harford wrote love poems growing out of a sexual attachment to a woman. In fact, according to Girlie in Barbara Hanrahan's novel of truly gothic sexuality *The Frangipani Gardens* (1980), in Adelaide as the First World War ended 'it was all right for Boy [her brother] to love a man— quite the done thing, in fact, Queer Street being a fashion of the moment. But you did it lightly—with an ironic smile and lots of back-chat. You didn't say "I loved him" with tears in yours eyes' (as Boy had in fact just shamefully done about his wartime mate Jim).[11] Sex and gender, in other words, must stay rigidly aligned.

For all the tentative questioning of whom one might properly 'love'—and I use the word conscious of its ambiguity—there's little, if any, indication in published Australian writing before the First World War of any serious questioning of our Bawd's common-sense premise that men must be men and women must be women, little evidence of any serious argument with the proposition that sex and gender were naturally aligned. Despite the fact, for example, that several gay historians have referred vaguely to writers such as Catherine Helen Spence, Rosa Praed and Ada Cambridge (all born around the .niddle of the nineteenth century) as precursors in the field of gay fiction, it is difficult to see in what way that is true, except in the sense that they questioned, sometimes radically, the effect of traditional institutions such as marriage on the lives of women. Given the lack of any gap between sex and gender, homosexuality as a behaviour remained quite literally unnameable, despite the existence of a homosexual subculture in Sydney and in other cities by the end of the century. No Australian Oscar Wilde, if any was lurking in the growing suburbs or on a country estate, poked his head, or was permitted to poke his head, above the literary horizon.

Between the Wars

Eldred had a soothing deference which made every woman conscious of her sex, and every boy vaguely surprised that he was not a girl.

The Picnic (1937), Martin Boyd

But then Eldred, a disreputable Bloomsbury type of person who dabbled in the publishing of pornography, *had* read Swinburne and Wilde in his youth and was not unacquainted with Rossetti and Burne-Jones. And whatever Eldred's notion of his own sexuality, the narrator's sexual consciousness is clearly now a modern one: not only is 'every boy' aware of Eldred's sexual attractiveness *as a male* to himself (and therefore of his own 'female' possibilities), but elsewhere in the novel the male narrator joyfully eroticises the male body, if in rather unimaginative terms: Christopher Westlake, a young Australian in England, is described over and over again as a 'young colt', 'a magnificent blond beast', 'my sunburst, my golden bull', even, rather mystifyingly, as 'a congested boar'. (Unfit or too fit 'to be classed with human beings', to hark back for one disconcerting moment to Thomas Cook's damnation of homosexual practices?) Christopher Westlake's body is in 'the splendour of late spring . . . there was no spot of weakness or decay in his body . . . he had met no match for his physical magnificence'. Indeed, an embrace from this Australian barbarian would, according to the simmering Sylvia Rounsefell, 'combine an innocent but extreme African sensuality with a strange spiritual return to classic sunlight'. Of course, by exoticising the Australian's sexual attractiveness, turning it into something African or Greek rather than simply Australian, Boyd was resorting to a well-tried ploy of a coyer age: don't worry, he was in effect saying, I'm not describing here a common-or-garden Australian boy, your son, your father, you—I'm describing an exotic flower. (Boyd was briefly much more daring ten years later, after the war, in his novel *Lucinda Brayford*: the heroine, watching 'two sprawling sunburnt boys', Tony and Bill, fooling around together on a hot Australian beach, not only recognizes 'the impulse of sensuality' in what she calls 'the ragging', but considers it 'a thing to be accepted naturally, and . . . an enrichment of life . . . to contain some dim promise of a deeper relationship between Tony and herself . . .'[12] Lucinda Brayford is not remotely fazed by any slippage between gender and sex and sees sexuality—homosexuality, in this case—as merely an aspect of gender. A very modern woman, Lucinda.) There are numerous examples of this ploy being used in Australian writing to deflect panic, from Henry Handel Richardson's descriptions of bisexuality amongst the decadent German protagonists of *Maurice Guest* to the Dutch hero of Australia's first truly gay novel, *No End to the Way* (1965).

Interestingly enough, even in Kenneth 'Seaforth' Mackenzie's ground-breaking novel *The Young Desire It* (1937), the schoolmaster, whose growing passion for a schoolboy forms the backbone of the novel, is English, while the schoolboy, whose sexual proclivities after a bit of dithering about turn out to be conventional in the extreme, is Australian. And even the Englishman feels obliged to make sense of his feelings in terms of exotic Greek models.

During the war the now increasingly admired writer Eve Langley published *The Pea-Pickers* (1942), a novel about two sisters, Steve and Blue, who dressed and behaved as men in order to find work on farms in Eastern and Northern Victoria. Lesbian desire is stifled in the novel (but at least it's there) and heterosexuality, if not exactly heterosexual desire, moves rather dully to centre stage. The story 'The Daughter of Ixion' (unpublished), set in 1933 in a Girls' Friendly Society hostel in Wanganui, New Zealand, is more overtly lesbian in tone, but curiously, although Eve Langley eventually changed her name to Oscar Wilde, it is clear from the vicious autobiographical piece 'Last, Loveliest, Loneliest' (unpublished, 1938) that she was deeply hostile to male homosexuality, seeing it as a degenerate and culpable threat to the stability of her marriage to the painter Hilary Clarke. Between 1929 and 1933 one of Australia's most celebrated writers, Henry Handel Richardson, wrote a series of stories called 'Growing Pains: Sketches of Girlhood', two of which are reproduced here. They are utterly modern in their exploration of sex and gender and assumptions about the sexuality of female characters in traditional fiction. In her stories the male sex (although not necessarily the masculine gender) is regarded with distaste by young women, who start experimenting with other ways of living fulfilling lives apart from as female appendages to biological males. Her novel *The Young Cosima* (1939), about Liszt's daughter and her marriage to Richard Wagner, also touches on themes of bisexuality.

Still, for all the progress made by writers such as Langley, Mackenzie and Richardson in questioning the identification of sex with gender, it was not until the post-war years that published writing in Australia began to explore homosexual relationships as merely a variety of human relationships in general. *The Young Desire It* may indeed merit the title of First Australian Homosexual Novel in the sense that it appears to have been the first novel by an Australian writer to address itself to a homosexually motivated attachment as an aspect of its main theme (the growing sexual self-awareness of its teenaged protagonist), but in post-war Australian literature an altogether new kind of writing was floating to the surface: writing about a subculture, a subculture which we now know from books such as *Being Different* (edited by Garry Wotherspoon, 1986) and Sumner Locke Elliott's novel *Fairyland* (1991) had been flowering colourfully for decades in Australia's largest cities. What began to emerge, hesitantly and hedged about with delicate euphemisms, was a gay literature.

The Second World War and the Immediate Post-War Years

A fat little man sat down beside me and said in a patronizing voice, 'I'm so glad that you are mixing with "the right people" now.'

I looked at him before saying 'What do you mean, the right people?'

At the Cross: Growing up in King's Cross, Sydney's Soho,
Jon Rose (1961)

What the fat little man meant, as the sixteen-year-old Jon Rose knew perfectly well, despite the air of the feckless *ingénu* he affected, was that in the bohemian quarter of Kings Cross during the war there was a certain artistic 'crowd' who viewed sexual relations between men—and between women—with tolerance and even amusement and that young Jon did not seem averse to mixing with it. When it transpired that Jon was happy to mix with it but choosy about whom he went to bed with, the fat little man, quite rightly in his terms, called Jon 'common'.

At the Cross, published in 1961, was one of the first post-war books for a general readership which described in positive tones what was in a sense a gay culture in Sydney during the Second World War. Jon's sexual experience as a teenager from Melbourne trying to survive on the streets of Kings Cross was not very different from that of teenagers from out of town doing the same thing almost half a century later: his body was a commodity desired by both males and females, there were opportunities for prostitution, there were established networks of homosexuals, bisexuals and people with a wide range of sexual tastes who cross-dressed, went to drag balls and behaved with flamboyant disregard of society's rigid notions of sex and gender. Jon is coy about how he actually fitted in with this 'crowd', but he documents life in this quarter of Sydney during the war with great frankness. We know from other sources that in Sydney during the war (and no doubt Brisbane, Melbourne and other cities) there was a loosening of attitudes towards sexual behaviour, a willingness to experiment sexually, at least in certain circles. Networks formed, certain bars and cafés became known meeting-places, and openly homosexual behaviour became possible at beaches and in inner city locales in a way that seems almost shocking now, when homosexual behaviour has been licenced in certain places—on certain streets, in certain suburbs and professions—but is as exotic elsewhere as it ever was, if not more so.

Little of this shift in attitudes was immediately visible in published Australian writing—Sumner Locke Elliott wrote about it in *Fairyland*, which was published half a century after the events it describes, Thea Astley wrote about it in *It's Raining in Mango* at a similar distance. Reminiscences are slowly appearing, but at the time, in the 1940s and 1950s, it did not seem a suitable subject for literary works. This is partly because of Australia's political and social conservatism at the time, well-documented elsewhere, as in Garry Wotherspoon's *City of the Plain: History of a Gay Sub-culture* (1991), but also because, by and large, even men and women with homosexual inclinations tended to see gender as synonymous with sex: there were men and there were women—some men pretended to be women and some women pretended to be men, and these people were 'homosexual', but basically there were only two kinds of human beings. It's true that in the work of a few writers, such as Hal Porter (in stories such as 'The Dream', 'Along the Ridge' and 'The Jetty'), Patrick White (in 'The Cockatoos') and Martin Boyd (in *Lucinda Brayford*), strangely and not always pleasantly ambiguous male adolescents do appear (and in 'The Cockatoos' one female character has a sudden lesbian fantasy about another), but little if any early post-war fiction or poetry seems to have sought to explore homosexuality as a normal variety of human sexual experience. As in Hollywood films today, and like the fat little man who importuned Jon Rose, characters displaying homosexual tendencies tended to be either sinister or buffoons or possibly both. In Colin MacInnes's 'Australian' novel *June in Her Spring* (1952), for example—published in England but 'Australian' because it was set in Australia and based on his years in Australia in the 1920s—the homosexual 'Uncle' Henry, who is clearly sodomising his 'nephew' on a regular basis, is portrayed as an effete, manipulative dissembler standing in the way of his 'nephew's' becoming 'normal', and connections are artfully made between homosexuality and madness. Still, at least the subject was given an airing. Lesbianism, of course, remained invisible. Not having a penis, the pole by which all orientations were measured, women might do anything with their fingers and tongues, from scraping plates and eating an ice-cream to inducing an orgasm in a friend, without changing anything very much.

In the 1960s the shift in attitudes towards sexuality, as towards many other things, was sudden and immense. The outside world was sending messages about less binary possibilities in films such as *Sunday, Bloody Sunday, A Taste of Honey, Boys in the Band* and *The Killing of Sister*

George, and, of course, in the perceived androgyny of such pop groups as The Beatles and The Doors. There was an immediate reflection of this change in Australian fiction and poetry. The difference in tone between Jon Rose's shyly tolerant *At the Cross*, published in a hardcover edition by André Deutsch in 1961, and Neville Jackson's *No End to the Way*, published in a Corgi paperback edition in 1965 with a provocative cover and the subtitle 'The classic novel of a homosexual marriage', is astounding. In a real sense *No End to the Way* was the first Australian gay novel and it was available not just to the *cognoscenti* or to prowlers in the library stacks, but to fathers of three stopping off at a railway kiosk on the way home from work, to men in the suburbs curious about their own sexual inclinations—in other words, to ordinary Australian readers.

At first glance *No End to the Way* appeared to be a voice in the wilderness. A more or less ordinary Perth suburbanite (at least he was not a schoolteacher or artist or sleek uncle with a private income) meets a bisexual Dutch migrant in a gay bar (the word 'gay' is used in the novel), falls passionately in love with him, has a reasonably long-lasting sexual relationship with him, then dramatically loses him. Many readers were astonished to learn that in Perth in the mid-1960s a gay culture existed, with bars, dinner parties, 'marriages' and social networks, and that many men even in Perth during that period lived more or less satisfying lives predicated on a homosexual orientation. A closer reading of this remarkable novel (written, by the way, teasingly in the second person) reveals a less liberated narrative viewpoint than the basic storyline suggests. In fact the object of desire, the young Dutchman Cor, is described in stereotyped masculine terms: 'anyone, camp or square, would swear it was all man and had nothing else on its mind but women'. It has 'big shoulders, big hands, and hips so narrow they wouldn't even know how to sway . . . No tizzy jewellery or anything like that.' He has a 'firm forehead', short-cropped hair, 'deeply entrenched' eyes, a 'long and straight' nose, a 'chiselled' mouth, a 'firm and well-shaped' chin with a cleft in it. He is, in effect, phallic—cutting, shear, hard—from top to toe— 'perfectly normal', as the narrator tells us.[13] Of course, in gender terms, this description *is* an act of liberation, at least in one sense: it says that you can be 'all man' and still enjoy sex with men. You don't have to be an effeminate Latin master or a retired colonel who likes showing his stamp collection to young lads on their way home from football. In another sense it simply reinforces the notion that to be 'normal' you must be either conventionally masculine or convention- ally feminine ('effeminate', if you're a male). The narrator himself is horrified when at one point Cor sobs uncontrollably, threatening to turn into 'the usual little nancy'. And, in the end, the narrator loses Cor to the normal heterosexual world and is left with what he calls his 'maladjustment'. All that a gay man can hope for, really, is to be 'adjusted to your maladjustment'.[14] This sort of stuff is no longer very heady.

It was also in the early 1960s that poets like David Malouf and Don Maynard were able to publish poems that, in a concealed way, spoke of homosexual feelings and Stuart Lauder was able to publish, in London, his extraordinary novel *Winger's Landfall* (1962) whose homosexual protagonist penetrates a steamy network of passion, betrayal and coercion amongst the crew of a passenger liner on a voyage from Australia to England. While he himself seems to regard sex with other men as just part of a seaman's life in the microcosm of the crew's quarters, sexual life on board ship in fact reflects heterosexual patterns fairly closely, with some men acting out traditional male roles and some acting out traditional female roles (dressing in women's clothing, calling each other by women's names, parodying female mannerisms and speech patterns and so on—so-called 'screamers'). On another level, homosexuality is linked throughout the novel with a sinister, secret religious cult.

The sudden opening up of homosexuality as a leading theme in fiction is well illustrated in the novel *Shake the Golden Bough* (1963) by Tom Hungerford, a writer who by no stretch of the imagination could be co-opted into a gay writers' camp. Given that the main character, a twenty-five-year-old Australian boxer in New York, is constantly described as 'verr-ee prett-ee', 'good-looking', 'one of the most beautiful people I've ever seen', 'Tab Hunter half as big again' and 'attractive to men or women' (this by a straight man),[15] it's no wonder the novel is full of sexual tensions revolving around the availability or non-availability of the boxer to men, including one overtly gay character. 'Ya like girls,' his trainer Barney says to him. 'I prefer them to boys,' Charlie comes back at him, 'given the choice.' ''At's show-business,' says Barney, who walks around him, studying him 'like a pasha buying a slave girl'.[16] It certainly is in the 1960s. Charlie complains that he's had to fight faggots off all over the world.[17]

In this era of unparalleled turbulence in society, at least on the literary front, progress was certainly made towards speaking openly about male homosexuality and towards considering it to be a variant on 'normal' sexual behaviour—to that extent gender (the construction of masculinity and femininity) was coming adrift from sex (biological maleness and femaleness) and the drift was being written about. A gay culture was in the making. The era of *sexuality* as an accepted literary theme, however, was yet to come.

The Modern Period

I'll be a woman or a man
I'll be a double-decker tram
I'll be anything you want me to be
I'm pretty weak at seven
Stronger by eleven
But when I'm drunk at twelve I'm me

> *Rock-n-Roll Sally*, by Sasha Soldatow, a
> burlesque performed by the author in
> nightclubs, art galleries, restaurants,
> bookshops, theatres and other venues
> between 1976 and 1983

It's the double-decker tram that catches the attention. This is modern. This would not have occurred to Neville Jackson or Stuart Lauder, let alone to earlier writers. After Stonewall, after the formation of gay liberation groups in Australia, after the softening up of public opinion during the 1960s, gender and sex have come completely unstuck and sexuality is very much in the sights of a new breed of avowedly 'gay' writers. Sasha Soldatow's burlesque is also modern in that it seeks to document rather than to probe or explain a current sexual sensibility. It's cynical and sleazy, recognizing no taboos and making no excuses for itself—it takes a sympathetic audience for granted. This is all very sudden. But a decade and a half later not dozens or scores but hundreds of writers of both sexes were following Soldatow's lead (if he *was* leading), although in the vast majority of cases without his flair.

An important feature of the 1970s (apart from the popularity of the television soap opera, 'Number 96', with its sympathetic portrayal of the homosexual character, Don) was the number of books published by mainstream writers, none of whom would have identified themselves as 'gay', dealing more or less openly with homosexuality, both male and female: Frank Moorhouse (*The Americans, Baby*, 1972), the poet Robert Adamson (with Bruce Hanford in *Zimmer's Essay*, 1974), Louis Nowra (*The Misery of Beauty*, 1976) and Patrick White (*The Twyborn Affair*, 1979), with Elizabeth Jolley's *Palomino* being published in 1980, along with Beverley Farmer's first novel *Alone*, Barbara Hanrahan's *The Frangipani Tree* and Nicholas Jose's short-story collection *The Possession of Amber*. There was poetry from David Malouf, Michael Dransfield and Tom Shapcott. On the fringes, Lee Cataldi published her *Invitation to a Marxist Lesbian Party* (1978) and writers such as Pamela Brown, Margaret Bradstock, Joanne Burns, Mary Fallon, Rae Desmond Jones and Don Maynard began to publish poetry or short fiction on gay and lesbian themes. Sometimes the stance was more or less separatist—'I'm gay, I'm going to record gay sensibilities and experiences, if you're not interested, read something else'—and sometimes, as in the case of the more mainstream writers, the stance was more 'I want to incorporate this kind of sensibility and experience into the tale I'm weaving'.

In the 1980s and 1990s the focus has shifted once again. Sexuality is not a matter for doubt or questioning, it is *the* leading signifier in anyone's sense of self—anyone, at least, who is culturally aware. In the wake of the liberalisation of laws on homosexuality in most Australian States, the rolling back of virtually all censorship restrictions, the establishment of SBS (Australia's equivalent of Channel 4 in the United Kingdom), the arrival of BlackWattle Press in Sydney (specialising in publishing gay writing for a gay readership), the flourishing of the Sydney Mardi Gras and the introduction of courses in gay studies on several Australian campuses, writing on gay and lesbian topics has proliferated. Mainstream writers such as Moorhouse, Jolley, Shapcott, Krauth, Jessica Anderson and others have felt even freer to write on this theme than before, and specifically gay writers with gay audiences in mind have published their short stories, novels, poetry collections and plays and contributed to anthologies such as *Edge City on Two Different Plans* (1983), *The Exploding Frangipani: Lesbian Writing from Australia and New Zealand* (1990), *Pink Ink* (1991), and *Travelling on Love in a Time of Uncertainty* (1991).

In the face of such an avalanche of writing it is dangerous to come to general conclusions about its directions and quality. However, certain generalisations are tempting. One of the most striking characteristics of gay and lesbian writing in Australia in the 1990s is its brevity. Although David Malouf has written a number of novels with homoerotic overtones, tying in with the mateship theme in Australian writing in a provocative way, and several lesbian writers have written fine detective novels with strong lesbian elements (Finola Moorhead and Jan McKemmish, for example), and even a whole series of detective novels with a lesbian detective (Clair McNab), only Dennis Altman, Australia's best-known gay activist and commentator, has actually written a full-length, more or less traditional novel focussing on homosexuality (*The Comfort of Men*, 1993). Gay men and women seem to opt for the short-story form, the poem, the reminiscence, the performance piece, the prose poem, the passing reference in a longer work, the memoir. Gary Dunne, one of Australia's best-known gay writers and perhaps our closest equivalent to Armistead Maupin, has published a novel (*Shadows on the Dance Floor*, 1993) about a man dying of AIDS, but it too is short and severely episodic, as are Benedict Ciantar's novel *Distractions* (1991) and Ian MacNeill's *Beaches and Billabongs* (1993). It is an intriguing fact that the sustained narrative on homosexual themes in Australia remains overwhelmingly the province of heterosexual writers born before the middle of the century. It is difficult to avoid at least asking the question as to whether or not the traditional novel is a form inherently 'heterosexual', unconsciously based on heterosexual paradigms about the generation of meaning through heterosexual coupling and reproduction—indeed, inherently phallic in its structure, and therefore, by implication, masculine and heterosexual.

It is also intriguing to note that stylistically lesbian writers have proved much more adventurous, playful and subversive on the whole than male gay writers. Feminism has no doubt made many women writers more aware than their male counterparts of the relationship between language and power, but in some ways male writers simply seem to be writing fiction that is true to gender stereotypes: it is reportage (it transmits recognisable pictures of certain social realities) with a camp edge. Of course, there are many exceptions to this generalisation—names such as Michael Hurley, Javant Biarujia, Benedict Ciantar, Paul Radley and Tim Herbert come to mind—but on the whole I believe it to be true.

This particular collection presents the reader with a variety of texts exemplifying a homosexual sensibility from different periods in Australian literary history. This sensibility is only sometimes 'gay' in any strict sense and the term has been adopted in the book's title more as a convenient shorthand. The selection has been arranged thematic-ally in order to break down expectations about some supposed development from repression to freedom or silence to noisy celeb-ration. No consideration was given in choosing the texts to the sexuality of the writer, although it is perhaps worth noting that less than half of those represented would be expected to identify as 'gay' or 'lesbian'. The primary consideration was always pleasure for the reader, although some account was taken of the historical importance of certain works. The convict's letter which opens the collection has, for example, little literary merit, but as the earliest unequivocal testimony to an Australian writer's homosexual feelings it has an honoured place here.

I trust the collection will shed a new light on some well-known writing, bring some little-known writing to the fore, and enrich the reader's sense of the literary culture of an exuberantly literary corner of the English-speaking world: Australia.

Robert Dessaix
February 1993

Notes

1 Marcus Clarke, *For the Term of His Natural Life*, Collins/Angus & Robertson, Sydney, 1992, 101.

2 Ibid., 355–6.

3 Thomas Cook, *The Exile's Lamentations*, Library of Australian History, Sydney, 1978, 19.

4 Loc. cit.

5 Ibid., 20.

6 Ibid., 28.

7 Robert Adamson & Bruce Hanford, *Zimmer's Essay*, Wild and Woolley, Sydney, 1974, 31.

8 Loc. cit.

9 See Wotherspoon, Garry, 'Moonlight and . . . Romance? The death-cell letters of Captain Moonlight and some of their implications', *Journal of the Royal Australian Historical Society*, vol. 78, parts 3 and 4, 1992.

10 Sidney J. Baker, *The Australian Language*, Currawong, Melbourne, 1966, 94.

11 Barbara Hanrahan, *The Frangipani Gardens*, UQP, St Lucia, 1980, 18.

12 Martin Boyd, *Lucinda Brayford*, Cresset, London, 1947, 56.

13 These references are on pages 15 and 22 of the 1958 Corgi edition.

14 Ibid., 21.

15 These references are on pages 33 and 36 of the 1963 Angus & Robertson edition.

16 Ibid., 80–1.

17 Ibid., 151

NOTE TO READERS

It should be noted that where ellipses (. . .) appear centred on a new line or in square brackets an editorial cut has been made. An original break in the text is indicated by three bullet points (• • •) on a separate line.

The unbracketed dates at the end of each piece refer to the date of publication as a separate work or in a collection rather than in journals or magazines. Bracketed dates refer to the date the work was written.

F o r e w o r d s

Anonymous

A Convict's Letter 1846

Dear Lover,
I hope you wont forget me when i am far away and all my bones is
moldered away I have not closed an eye since i have lost sight of you
your precious sight was always a welcome and loving charming spectacle.
Dear Jack I value Death nothing but it is in leaving you my dear behind
and no one to look after you But I hope you will beware of the delusive
of man. the only thing that grieves me love is when i think of the pleasant
nights we have had together. I hope you wont fall in love with no other
man when i am dead I remain your True and loving affectionate Lover.

John Le Gay Brereton

Rouge et Noir

Why should I be thus shaken by a dream,
Than which a baby's babble has more meaning,
Unless the tedious thoughts that I have traced
Of late to where they lose themselves in the sea
Have wronged my sense? And that my friendship, too,
Should lay the spell on me. To think that love
Like mine should send a clap of misery
To cling upon me like a shadowy plague
That baffles grappling!
                                    Under a sloping roof
Of twining branches, as I thought, I lay
And read, and in among the perfect green
Of new-burst leaves the sunlight pierced and threw
Round splashes of lilac colour on the book,
Twinned circles wavering to the sleepy sigh

Of noontide, and the gladioles were stirred
To half-heard rustlings in their yellowing blades
And light seed-bearing wands; the lizard sunned
His grace of bronze beside the crisping leaves
That the last storm had torn from the trees; afar
The steam-boat panted on the river. While
I lay with fettered senses, lazily
Following Gautama's golden words and deeds,
I heard a sound of slowly-wending feet
Approaching, so I rose and thrust apart
The boughs and looked; a sad-faced company
Of men and maids and children walked adown
The hillside with its rust of perished ferns,
And each of them was clad in spotless white
And crowned with faded leaves, and in their midst
Four young men bare a coffin, over which
Was spread a blood-red pall. There as they went
The shrubs and flowers drooped behind them. Then
With reverent head I stood, and while they passed
I plucked the hindmost by the sleeve to ask
Whose body lay beneath yon crimson pall;
For answer came two whispered words that struck
My soul to dulness, but I watched them go,
With one thought in my heart, and on my lips
One single phrase—'He was my friend, my friend!'
Before the words had died away, the bush
Had vanished, but the thought remained unchanged.

Now I was in my sleeping-room, and there
With a keen knife I pierced a purple vein
Within my arm, and lay awaiting death,
And listening to the dripping of the blood
That redly marked the passing time. I heard
The bees at work in the blossoming tree before
My window, and I heard a lumbering cart
Toil up the road with picnickers, and still
My blood flowed and my strength ebbed, but I thought
Of him, the boy I loved, and was content
To die, for we might meet beyond the bourne,
Or, though we met not, dreamless sleep were better
Than waking misery. A distant clock
Tolled out the hour, and a cow lowed far away,
And farther still it seemed to me, my ears
Being blunted so that the sound of ruddy drops
Scarce entered, and my strength was almost null;
All will or power to move had faded out,

Till I was ripe for the end. Then suddenly
Before the darkness fell I heard a laugh
Out in the sunshine, and my name was cried
In joyous tones; his foot scattered the gravel
As he ran through the garden, but I lay
Powerless, and the horror beats amain
At my temples as I write; I crushed my force
Into a single knot for one last cry,
To shout his name, and, with the effort, woke.

1896

LESBIA HARFORD

I can't feel the sunshine

I can't feel the sunshine
Or see the stars aright
For thinking of her beauty
And her kisses bright.

She would let me kiss her
Once and not again.
Deeming soul essential,
Sense doth she disdain.

If I should once kiss her,
I would never rest
Till I had lain hour long
Pillowed on her breast.

Lying so, I'd tell her
Many a secret thing
God has whispered to me
When my soul took wing.

Would that I were Sappho,
Greece my land, not this!
There the noblest women,
When they loved, would kiss.

(1915)

Lie-a-bed

My darling lies down in her soft white bed,
And she laughs at me.
Her laughter has flushed her pale cheeks with red.
Her eyes dance with glee.

My darling lies close in her warm white bed,
And she will not rise.
I will shower kisses down on her sleepyhead
Till she close her eyes.

Gioja's no happier fresh from the South.
But my kisses free
Will straiten the curves of this teasing mouth,
If it laughs at me.

(1915)

THOMAS SHAPCOTT

Elegy for a Bachelor Uncle

We knew too much about him, and too little,
our mother's only brother, our fat, apologetic uncle,
who had always lived at home, at our grandmother's house,
because of habit, or the drift of a few years too many,
or because, as he said, she needed him.
His room was fringed with the dead shells of his hobbies
and the few books he was always intending to finish.

Growing up we took it for granted that he should be
textbook illustration of a popular theory,
complete with selfish possessive mother, security,
and mannerisms too dull, too ingrown, to be borne
at close quarters. On the occasions when we called
we always left early, brazen with excuses.

He was not fifty when he died, leaving only my grandmother
shocked and unprepared, groping for a handkerchief.
We knew too much about him, and too little,
        because now that he is dead
I think of a day shortly before the end
when he put a record on for me and my new bride
it was a dance-thing old as the thick shellac disc
its sound had been scored into and there
on the scratched veranda he asked her to dance,
spinning her round and round effortlessly. I was
        embarrassed—
but he smiled, and was unfamiliar
and at ease, and I saw a drowned young man,
my uncle, urging through the mediocre decades,
groping up to the last rim of Possible, yet,
forgetting the mirror and all the intractable measurements.

But the record lasted only three minutes;
and I took her away quickly. Now I must live
among acts not known and words too long unsaid.
I knew too little; and he found me out.
I wish I could believe him wholly dead.

(1962)

GWEN HARWOOD

Ganymede

Springtime: the eye once, scaling alps of blossom
might have traced in curdling cloud the foolproof shine
of a god's descent, a god's claws lifting the lissom
sweetness of mortal youth from sure decline —

the Phrygian mode. Light poking past his nose
compelled Professor Eisenbart to witness
spring's lyric conquest of his room. He rose,
thought of his mistress and her tiresome sweetness,

and turning from his work to earth's green text
by flowers' sharp asterisks found himself drawn
to footnotes of unwelcome longing, vexed
to see below him on the hotel lawn

the cause of his unrest: a boy whose wealth
of beauty, gathered now beneath the tragic
green of a cypress, had seduced by stealth
since their first meeting, Eisenbart from his magic

formulae. Descending by the stairs
(he feared the lift's steel cage), passing a room
where idle women nursed their lapdog cares,
he reached the formal garden, with its gloom

of cypress and tormented hedge enfolding
the boy's still-life repose. And if the women
saw them ascend the stairs, Eisenbart holding
the boy's hand in his own, it was a human

fabric that drew their sighs: youth's gold warp threading
its joy through darker woof. His rented heaven
enclosed them both at last. Eisenbart treading
the orbit of his hope felt a warm leaven

lighten his bones, nerves, arteries; expand
the burden of his breath until he choked
and tasted his own panic, shocked, unmanned:
smiling assent that could not be revoked

the boy, bred in the slippery city, stared
with childhood's cunning at a future come
too soon. His graceful ivory body, bared,
spoke of itself alone. Corruption, dumb,

winked, a sour beggar, through his perfect eyes
miming its own deceit in flesh and feature.
Eisenbart, who might upon that prize
have dropped as the hawk swoops to serve its nature,

felt, softer than snow on water or on snow,
a winter's delicate absences reclaim him.
Ganymede, with crude mockery, chose to go.
Eisenbart took his pen; let sunset frame him

a city fringed with water and cold light,
restless with growing life; and turned to live,
to work in his own world, where symbols might
speak to him their sublime affirmative.

1963

JAVANT BIARUJIA

Hamid

where is my sultry Java nefandous light and thunder now that it is the
wet season mad with *ketoprak* lords Shiva Vishnu and Brahma are crazy
with lexicons of secret words

he traces his finger from clavicle thru nipple to *linea alba* he whispers
bulu against biceps grazing soles unto his mouth a leaping tongue a
silken tongue glides on mine a tongue curled between the teeth takes it
in the heat our teeth grinding in the lubricious brunt of maduran bulls
at loggerheads his spine sprung as taut as Arjunas bow hearts pounding
under the veiled sun the *panas terik* the stifling trick of noon sweat
trickling down the bulge of buttocks to perinaeum pink and reptilian
the perorations of his tongue stir the scent as after rain on a dusty road

the ink soon dries crustily in a curl of hair and on my leg *black sweet* he
says as he places my hand on his powerful brown thighs

(1987)

SUSAN HAMPTON

From *Surly Girls*

Back Cover Blurb

What is heterosexuality? Why does a certain percentage of the population feel attracted to the opposite sex? Is it curable? Experts in the field file their reports.

Experts in the field file their reports on the phenomenon of heterosexuality

JORDAN: I see a lot of it, from a great height. I think it's a form of insecurity. When you watch it, their body language is pretty depressing.

JANICE: I saw a lot of it with my parents. It . . . you know . . . I couldn't see it working.

BELLE: Het culture is stuffed. And lesos and poofters are stuffed, too.

NATALIE: She always talks like that. I think the only real problem is that heterosexual parents aren't fit to be raising people like us. They don't know anything about us and they keep doing the wrong things.

ALLI: You know it's the full macho thing in Nicaragua. But the revolution's liberating women willy-nilly. Then their feminism's a by-product that'll get funnelled off after the war, it'll be contained.

BELLE: That's what I mean.

NATALIE: Belle, you've spoken.

BELLE: Sorry, I'll try and be good, OK?

KAREN: I get into trouble, you know, for painting women fucking. Not from people against pornography, but from interested critics who try to like it because they assume the viewpoint will be theirs, the voyeur, the man with two women. But the women's glances lock out the male viewer, and they hate that. It's not pornographic enough.

ANGY: Men find it difficult to get over the trauma of being weaned, they eroticise the site of the breast with the fervour of a two year old.

ALICE: I do that, I'm sure. Oh goodness. Maybe I'm straight.

SANDRA: Brenda turned me off heterosexuals, I mean, she's gay but she's incorporated the romantic mythology, she failed in the fight against her conditioning, I reckon. I hope she doesn't mind me saying this. Is she going to read this? I mean any radical change in the way lovers relate, has to come from lesbians. All the classic het stories about lovers, soul mates, end in death. Romeo and Juliet. Heloise and Abelard. *Fatal Attraction*, did they die at the end of that? You have to go to *Hiroshima Mon Amour* to get love as a transcending force. Duras knew what alternatives there were. It becomes a spiritual quest, it concerns the inner life.

BELLE: You think lesos are the people of the future. That womyn-loving wommin will work it all out up at the land? Carrying water from the creek and studying astrology and building their own houses. Ay? And taking heaps of drugs and staying out of it, eh.

KAREN: Like the rest of Western culture.

NATALIE: Belle, you've already spoken.

BELLE: Sorry, I wasn't good, was I.

NATALIE: No.

BELLE: Sorry.

ELIZABETH: Have I spoken? I can't remember. What's the subject?

BRENDA: I've read what Sandra said and she's wrong. Monogamy is not the prerogative of heterosexuals. Some people prefer it.

LINA: Take the money and run.

SALA: Well I'm delivering flowers now. What I see is that so much heterosexual behaviour's either sentimental or violent. Do you know what I mean? The unsaid is never at one with the said. Valentine's Day cards and Interflora, then it's a Hitchcock movie. An interviewer asked Hitchcock what was his main idea for successful movies. He said, 'Terrorise the women.' But so what. Do you have less love troubles with the relevant gender? It's a comedy, right?

ELIZABETH: Wash your mouth, girl.

SALA: Human behaviour I mean, you could say, 'Why do humans feel attracted to sex? Is it curable?'

ALICE: OMMMMMMMMMM.

ANGY: Alice, I love you when your lips vibrate.

ALICE: Happy nuns.

ANGY: I bet they fucked themselves silly in those abbeys.

BELLE: Violette would like to say, ravaged by time, in her considered opinion, she will—

Temptation

The temptation is always to include the bizarre. Because it is so ingrained in us from childhood that lesbians are bizarre. So when we sit down to write we think of ourselves in this way. Because we are thinking of ourselves speaking to the public. And they think we are bizarre. And so we surround ourselves, fictionally or not, with the periphery, the carnival world, junkies and migrants and prostitutes and koories. Poems to the mentally insane. To write about the ordinary life of a lesbian, what is she doing, going to work, buying some flowers at the edge of the street, eating a meal, kissing her lover, making a documentary, going to the shops in her four-wheel-drive—but here we have the bizarre already, the image of a lesbian in this sort of vehicle, and yet my sister drives one, my straight sister, and it is consumed by the normal, her image. So it's not the four-wheel drive in the sentence, but the word lesbian which carries the connotation bizarre. She will draw to her, because of the word that describes her, every cliché connection—in language, in thought. She must be butch to be driving this car. Sometimes she is, or looks this way, as well. And sometimes not at all, but it is a word which will encapsulate her every time, whether she's living in the suburbs and having breakfast with her mother, or washing a window, or speaking to her child. No amount of normalising surrounds will release her from the peripheral world: she always feels that her life is both normal (to her) and bizarre (to them); she is already because of her attraction to women part of the carnival world, and though the fact that she works as a stiltwalker may be temporary and incidental, it seems apt once we know she's a lesbian, though there are many more of her working in offices and going home at night to a regular hot meal.

The lesbian feels aligned to the carnival world because her sexuality is masked and relegated there. And yet the masks the straight world employs never cover so completely their real actions. The mask the lesbian wears, at work, say, has the force of the complicity of everyone around them, to the point where the joy in the carnival, the opposite of its suppression, becomes foremost and she dresses like Radclyffe Hall in a Chinese silk smoking-jacket, making overt the code which calls up another world. Or now she will have a certain kind of haircut, the mask of visibility, so she'll be recognised by kindred spirits, and by the world as someone who has chosen to be carnival, since she cannot avoid both the pleasure and the significance of that world remaining.

1989

Desiring

In the lives of many homosexuals desire plays a role it does not need to play in well-narrated heterosexual lives. Popular culture, including popular gay culture, parodies the centrality of homosexual desire in everything from situation comedies ('Are You Being Served?', 'Terry and Julian') to standing jokes of the 'backs to the wall' variety. Homosexuals, and particularly male homosexuals, are portrayed as endlessly, indefatigably and indiscriminately libidinous. In reality, of course, desire is a much more profound, nuanced and contradictory emotion.

Desire fulfils an important function for the homosexual: in the face of socially enforced deferral of sexual and emotional satisfaction, desire at least keeps open the channels of communication with fulfilling experience. The homosexual is usually aware of his or her 'otherness' from well before adulthood. For many the only way to explore that 'otherness' is through desire.

In these poems, extracts from novels and one short story the male writers have tended towards recording both the desirability of the male body and the need to defer enjoyment of it. Indeed, the eroticism of the poems in particular seems to grow out of the suspension of desire. Whether the desiring male lives in colonial Ceylon (as in Donald Friend's novel *Save Me from the Shark*) or in contemporary inner-city settings (as in Rae Desmond Jones' or Tony Page's poems), the desiring is thwarted and the thwarting becomes virtually the point of the narrative.

Elizabeth Riley, Jenny Pausacker and even Mary Fallon, on the other hand, seem less intent on recording the desirability of the female body than the desirability of lesbian experience. In their writing, too, deferral is an important leitmotif, but the effect is often comic rather than harrowing, leading not to a suspension of the narrative, but to its continuation.

Desire is present in almost all the works in this anthology, but the following selection reflects the pivotal part it plays in homosexual experience.

THOMAS SHAPCOTT

Young Men's Bodies

So out of reach. Yet the wish to reach. What for?
Towards, perhaps. *Perhaps* is what answer?
The only answer is out of reach, perhaps further
than any young body could reach toward. Sure
of itself (that is the condition), let the sweat pour
as if the boy did not even heed his odour
(what for?) (why are you searching?): let the youngster
steer his body simply. Let your jaw

screw tight, then, provide applause. You provide envy.
No, not that, dream you provide lust. Why not
admire the body, muscle, prick and sweat
of the living body, why not? The young man's body
veers, leers (it is himself), draws towards something to learn.
So out of reach. You reach. You did not learn.

(1979)

ELIZABETH RILEY

From *All That False Instruction*

I went up to University with unrivalled childish optimism—a rare thing
except perhaps in working-class families. The star in the ascendant, a
great academic future, a niche even in the civilized comfortable classes.
Not to mention the bracing air of free and ranging thought which I
anticipated. Hearing the notorious Menshinski, a White Russian philosophy professor of no mean sophistry, I applauded his laudable
demolition of the grounds of accepted sexual ethics. What fun!

No wooden-headed headmistress would draw my mother aside and
warn her of incipient socialism, revolutionary tendencies, unrealistic
idealisms. The atmosphere indulged my dreams, offered exotic stimulation. Everything was dynamic. The sun of late summer poured down
on the college gardens, the brickwork pavements, the big stone chapel.
My room, narrow and cell-like, was nevertheless my own. I rearranged
the furniture around its edge to create a token space on the rug. Outside,
the creosoted-wood fire escape mixed with branches and sky. The
college bell rang out the orderly hours; at six-thirty we donned our
academic gowns and forgathered in the big dining-room with its
polished wood chairs and tables. On these academic and cultivated
bagatelles I throve the first months; single-minded, clear-sighted,
untrammelled . . .

. . .

Emma Brightfort came into college for three weeks while someone was sick. She wanted to read my poetry. I'd been pouring out the sunset reveries on mortality and ephemeral beauty for years and came to Emma with little to show. She inspired the confidence that her judgements were sound and worthwhile. A blonde big-nosed compelling face with every lineament of determination; but something locked up about it, as if will ruled the affections and might have crippled them.

'You've got the gift of the gab,' says Emma.

'Have I?' I ask.

'Yes, but you've got to get rid of this self-pity, you know.'

'Have I?' I ask. 'But Shelley is just like that.'

'Yes,' says Emma, 'that's exactly right. Shelley is a wallower.'

'Oh.'

Emma reads so avidly, believes, does she? that she's found a poet. Glimmerings of self-faith. She tells me when she thinks it's good; again if necessary. She doesn't baulk at reassurance.

She has an unfailing eye and ear. Sees the florid nothings, hears the lagging rhythms. And she tells lucidly. I begin, painfully and nostalgically, to abandon my superstition that the poet's inspired word is immutable, stands. I start to work with words, hack out dead wood and burn it. Emma, who insists that she is neither poet nor creator—just critic— places her finger on the strengths of my writing, gives me my poetry. Which, in these next years, will be much the same as giving me my sanity. She is hard on sentimentality, murderous about self-pity; and if detachment has with her the status of a moral imperative, it is not one that I'm any the worse for contemplating.

There was, too, a splash of something like hero-worship in Emma's attitude; surprising in a woman so self-assured, so categorical. An illicit attraction for the daring and original. Emma probably didn't know that I went to those dozens of student parties only to sit around in terror of the milling drinking strangers—and I didn't admit it. Rather, I hinted at unspeakable exploits, cracked myself up as something of a seasoned drinker, gay and worldly, a youngster ranging through her experiences with the artist's absorption.

A Paddington party. 'Why don't you come, Emma. It'll be great.' In an upstairs balcony room people tripped over one another, hid their beer in corners or carried it about with them, and a girl who might have been the hostess tried to clear bodies from the centre-floor to start some dancing.

'What would you like to drink, Emma?'

'Oh lemonade.'

'Come on.'

'A bit of vodka perhaps.'

'I'll see.'

I threaded through the press, found the kitchen, pinched a nip of vodka from an unattended bottle, opened my Cinzano and headed back. On the stairs a boy asked me for a swig. I poured some. He slopped it over and I filled it up again.

'Good grief Maureen, have you drunk all that already?'
I passed it off brilliantly. 'Oh well, feeling pretty thirsty, you know. Here's a vodka and orange—pinched.'

Just as I slumped back with studied ease into the armchair a reeling dancer crashed back into my lap grinding my ankle with his boot. I went white; Emma helped me out into the air and took me back to college. We drank coffee all night, a luminous warmth between us. Finally, fearing the moment she'd get up and leave, I said, falsely, 'I'm tired. Must get to sleep.' Throw her out. Get in first. Yet I'd have liked to spend all my time with this sympathetic, encouraging girl. Which I admitted neither to myself nor to her.

One night, late, after a session on my poems—she didn't get tired of the fantastic output—she climbed into bed and asked to be tucked in. Craig embarrassed. I strode to the bedside and heaved the mattress like some sort of super-muscular nurse, slapped the blankets under and stood back. Not just Craig clumsiness; she wanted me close and I, wanting to be close, recoiled.

'You tuck in like a ditch-digger,' she mumbled, and there was hurt in her voice. For an instant I wanted passionately to lean over and reverently kiss her forehead, but I gave the laconic adolescent grin, said good night and was gone.

After a film the others went back in the bus and I walked up through the city alone. Ripple-soled desert boots creeping along the pavements, crossing at red lights, green lights, amongst many-coloured lights. Cars stopping. 'No. I like the night and walking, thank you.' Tongue whipped across dry lips. A tense heroic figure in the streets. Running the imaginary gauntlet of a neon underworld; feeling tall, muscular, equal to any tough who might slip out of an alley, knife drawn. Across the wide asphalt of Railway Square. All this, but a posture walking it. Playing cool, a game with no rules, one player.

Next Sunday, in chapel. Split second collapse of this whole religion. One instant I seem to be Maureen Craig in the presence of the Lord. The next obliterates me. I feel the tense agonized face-muscles, register the forehead's dented frown and the head's Rollande-Clagge angle of devotion. Straining at the attitudes of sanctity; manifest constipated godliness. Craig shoots up to the chapel vaulting, sees holy-Craig; titters. I look around expecting an audience, observers of holy-Craig. But there are none. The priest is still handing out wafers, the rest of the congregation is praying. And Craig, unobserved, unverified, melts into the wooden pew.

With staggering rapidity I identified dozens of Craigs, each playing its appointed role to perfection—Craig the Moody, Craig the Gay, Craig the Detached, Craig the Witty, Gritty, Lovely. Leaving only a thunderous vacuous consciousness of nobody.

College seemed tomb-empty when Emma left. I borrowed a book I didn't need from Jules Vernon and returned it late one night, happening to be carrying a sheaf of poems (mine) on my clipboard. How to write verse and influence people. Motives hopelessly confused. Loneliness? Solve the enigmatic computer mind? Get even with the oneupmanship which plagues my attempts to star in the Steve tutorials? Make friends with her?—anyone can see she's lonely. Everyone makes excuses for being friends with her, as if it's a minor scandal. Why join her against the rest? Some kind of deep-set fellow-feeling? Or . . . someone who'll need me so much I can ask the earth? But I do not ask myself these things.

'Oh, come on in, Maureen, do.' Accent of St Agatha, but I skip it. 'Stay and have a coffee.'

'OK.'

She fusses with her sugar basin and super-nice chipless mugs. She makes nervous gestures which are stage-sweeps of the arm, but interrupted, arrested. She drops it half-way, can't carry it through.

We sat down, she sprawled on the bed, me tensed in the armchair, and started sipping the coffee which she made in a stylish china coffee-filter. She grilled me harmlessly about progress in History I.

'You're awful in English tuts, Jules.'

'What?'

'Oh, you know, nasty—clever. It's hard on us real first years.'

'Whatever do you mean?'

'Oh I dunno. You admitted you hadn't read that Eliot, but you kept saying my ideas were shit.'

'I didn't agree with you, Maureen.'

'But you hadn't read it.'

She pursed her lips and beamed. Then I dropped the bombshell.

'You know Julia, y'shouldn't do that kind of thing. Makes people hate you.'

Shock registered; real horror.

'Who?' came out like an explosion.

'Oh just Abigail and Erif and me.'

'You mean just the girls in that tut?' There was a trace of relief.

'Oh yeah, and everyone else too.' Jesus, her face was starting to crumble. Was I doing this for her? or for me? or why the hell was I doing this? 'Oh yeah, lots of people. Not just classes. Y'do it all the time. Even talking about the bloody weather. Y'always think you know the answers. People hate it . . .' I trailed off, but she was tense and said nothing. 'Oh you know, just that you're always right about everything. And shit you are brighter than most of us, probably, but sometimes you could be wrong, y'know.' Floundering here. And the stricken face in front of me wasn't what I expected or even wanted of the confident Jules. 'Oh it's not that bad, Julia, just y'could think before y'say things sometimes and people mightn't put you down as such a Smart Alec, such a bloody know-all. You know I think you're all right, I just get hurt when you pick my ideas to pieces when you haven't even read the stuff. That's all really.' Capitulating, but to no visible effect. I was scared she'd start crying any minute, I wouldn't have had the first clue about comforting anyone. I didn't touch people.

But she didn't cry—as if it was worse than crying.

'And you? You hate me too?'

Cornered. 'Shit no. I just hate what you do to me in classes. I like you.' A lie. But I had no alternative. The honesty-bit had gone much too far. I escaped after I'd downed the coffee, saying I'd see her tomorrow and show her the poems.

The beginning of those nights we stayed up talking forever until dawn, breakfasting bleary-eyed. Her family was academic and upper class, she the eldest child when old Vernon evidently thought it proper to have a son heading the family; Julia out of step, wrong sex from the start. It crossed my mind that my mother, too, might have preferred an eldest boy. Julia had had to labour hard in every arena to compensate for being female, to fulfil the sky-high expectations of her parents—a first-rank economist and a reader in sociology, both of them straining to the top of their fields with the children in tow. Scarcely knowing, I had hit the weakest link in her confidence. For a long time she dropped her everyday sparring and listened to me. I confessed the story of how-I-nearly-drowned-Ken-and-got-away-with-it. To admit simply, to anybody, that it had been my fault. A mere fact. Dead and harmless. A nothing—eating away my skull for six years. Julia got the lurid, humourless life-story. The patience of her, the warmth, the sheer sympathy; I was believed, good Christ, believed on my own terms. Someone agreed it must have been tough. She sat, nightslong, listening, listening. Finally, and this felt odd to the point of embarrassment, she offered physical comfort, an arm around the shoulder, a hug, a brief clasp of my hand. How could I have seen Julia except as the epitome of goodness.

I was wearing cheap floral pyjamas. I scuttled around the corridors to see Julia before I went to bed, to swap our days. Her existence was priceless. It was cold in her room and she said I might crawl in under the blankets. Shyly I agreed, aware with a flash of misgiving of her huge breasts under flannelette. Her arms around me, I felt the touch of hand on flesh with panic. I stayed there frozen. Gently she stroked my back; gently she moved her hands around my waist and began touching my breasts. Every muscle went as stiff as bone, the flesh across my stomach like a board. The word lesbian flashed through my petrified mind. Why, I wondered, wasn't I beating an instantaneous retreat? But nothing permitted escape. I heard those vehement denials to the man in the car turn antique inside my head. The schoolboy who kissed me at twelve; that prick at the cricket; the driver's bafflement at my non-response. Not that I cared for Julia's rubbing either. My flesh crept with the embarrassment and shame of it. People had much better leave their bodies alone—the body will do its stuff—needs no attention; the stench of thin shit, the ignominious lump of bloodied cotton-wool between the legs—these were the body's perpetual realities. I wanted no dealings with bodies. I said my good nights in a hurry and fled.

I avoided her for three days—three helpless days, knowing I wouldn't be able to do without her much longer. No choice to be made. I simply procrastinated the inevitable. She came one morning before breakfast.

'Hello,' she said, anxious.

'Er. Hullo.'

'I'll make some coffee if you like.'

'Tea?' I was able to suggest.

'If you'd rather.'

She sat on the bed and took my hand in both of hers.

'I've been . . . er . . . working hard on Luther.' An inexact truth.

'Good,' she answered readily. 'I've been busy too.'

As if by common consent we both avoided any reference either to the night in both our minds or to my days in hiding.

After that first-flesh encounter Julia simply waited for me to catch up to her own radical stage of ability to touch naked skin. By hair-breadth degrees we grew accustomed to each other. Without, however, removing our clothes. Fractional reticent lovers—the closed-lips kiss, the audacious fumbling with breast and back, the automatic mutual abstention from any move below the belt. The word—the awful slimy word, lesbian— was a continuous discord at the back of my mind.

'Isn't this a lesbian way to behave?' I asked her a few weeks later.

'I suppose it is,' she said. 'That's what the psychology books would say.'

Two highly intelligent young women gingering in total darkness. Both of us needing desperately a physical warmth which seemed to have nothing to do with such a loaded and nasty idea as lesbianism. Yet the label pushed itself forward. We knew we had to hide though no-one had ever told either of us. Unspoken rules overshadowed the present and threw doubt on the tangible affection between us. How unnatural that neither of us could trust her own feelings.

From the fire-escape came a girl's dulcet voice.

'Do let me in, Maureen.'

Julia sprang up off the bed as if there'd been an almighty thunderclap. I, actor since five, rose from her arms studying calm, my heart thumping, and answered, 'Sure,' I unbolted the fire-exit and let the girl in. She smiled sweetly and asked if I was having Julia to coffee tonight. I couldn't work out how much she'd seen or inferred.

'Yes.'

'Oh well, I'll invite you round another time.' She smiled.

'Great.'

Julia and I said nothing. When her footsteps had gone, I unbolted the exit again and carefully climbed up and down the fire-escape from roof to landing, assessing what range of vision was possible. It was obvious that, if the girl had cared to lean over the railing, my bed with its guilty activities would have been all too visible. It was bad enough that the rooms couldn't be locked—an ancient deterrent to fornication—but neither of us had dreamed of ladies taking nocturnal strolls on the fire-escape. It looked too much like spying for comfort. With the terrorism of letting us know they knew, thrown in. What expectant little group was waiting somewhere for their agent to report?

A week later, just as we were going to sleep, there was a shuffling and sniggering outside my door. A light tap. Would they come in, maybe? Turn on the lights? Expose us? Call the Principal? Someone thundered on the door. Silence. I felt Julia's body tense up. They were still there. Then the sound of running footsteps and giggling. We stayed awake for hours, Julia afraid to go back around the passages to her room, both of us hearing night-noises magnified by fear.

Always an element of terror. Springing apart when the knock comes on the door; dread of the girl who might just walk in and catch us at it. A secretive subterranean existence—underpinned by my unremitting shame of the body itself. Surrounded by polite deadly spies, animal nervousness when they dropped the slimy ubiquitous word, consciousness raddled with guilt. Guilt sprouting from their malice. And guilt implicit since earliest memory, guilt over every damned impulse.

Julia went often to chapel, though the formal absolutions of the church proved inadequate. Besides, she intended to repeat the sin. Long tortuous discussions about the form and evil of lust—a poor excuse for lust, our feeble solemn gentleness. We applied the idea of lust, the idea of sin, to everything that involved our bodies. Whatever we said, the fact of our guilt remained, and whatever we said reinforced that anyway. Along the line we had both acquired a dislike and mistrust of ourselves which made nonsense of the other idea—the idea of love.

Confusion. It felt good, warm, secure—to be able to speak openly to another person; to be able to give; to feel warm and unjudged. Yet all this was just as surely negated.

Julia went out with a spindly hook-nosed biochemist from one of the men's colleges. I resented that she continued to do so, though he used up little of her time. I craved assurance that he wasn't important, and didn't believe her when she gave it. She insisted that she wasn't in love with him, which afforded marginal security, yet she evidently enjoyed his attentions. I wanted exclusive territorial rights. Whenever she spent an evening with him I plunged into a black and well-enacted despondency.

'Why don't we go to the pictures instead?'

'I've promised to go to the dance with him, Maureen. I like him.'

'You'd prefer to go off with him.'

'But you and I spend most of our time together. You said you have to get that essay written anyway.'

'I can't work when I don't know where you are.'

'But you will.'

'Roughly.'

'Come now, Maureen. A college dance is a college dance.'

'Oh shit it's all right. I'll go for a walk down to the park.'

'You shouldn't go over there at night alone. It could be dangerous.'

'Who cares?'

'You know I care.'

'Oh yeah?'

'Of course.'

Patterns of blackmail.

She came home early, her eyes red and her hands shaking. My satisfaction ill-disguised.

'What's wrong?'

'Christopher.'

'What about him?'

'He loves me.' I winced inside, a falling premonition of loss.

'Isn't that what you're after?' A shade of sarcasm.

'No. No. No.' Her voice was tense and her eyes bitterly afraid.

'What happened?'

'I don't know.'

'Did he want to make love to you?' Scared out of a more usual timidity.

'No. Not that. He was very understanding.'

'What then?'

'He wants me to love him.'

'Well?'

'I can't.' Buoyancy again. She couldn't be lying in this state.

'You've got me, Julia.'

'It's different.' Doubt crept back.

'How?'

'Oh you know. We've agreed. We'll need men in the end.'

'I dunno.'

Silence.

'He was so good to me, it was awful. Because I couldn't. He even asked if I'd like him to fetch you.'

'Fetch me?'

'Yes. He thought it might be you I was in need of.'

'It wasn't?'

'I couldn't have told him anyway. So I had to stay. I was just afraid. And upset that he should think you're more important than he is.'

'I suppose it'll be all over the college.'

'He's not like that, Maureen, shut up.'

'Why don't you go back to him then?'

'I can't, I can't, I can't.'

I depended with rapacity—as thoroughly as once on my mother, but Julia was complaisant and rarely frustrated me. A visit to her room if she happened to be out landed me in acute depression pointed up by pique. I checked her common resorts in these moods, ferreted for her. Eventually my check on her movements was total. Her consideration for me amounted to reporting departures, arrivals, destinations. Julia liked being so jealously guarded; her strongest need was to lavish, spend, exhaust herself with giving away: 'It is good to see you happy, Maureen—so good.' While I leant on her she saw lonely Craig made happy and secure, saw that it was her doing and that it was good—the heavier I leaned the better. She had her proof of indispensability, again and again.

In between the days of sunny security there were slippery times when the inured loneliness of earlier years seemed to have been a lucid pool of freedom and uncomplicated joy.

. . .

Emma Brightfort was allotted the room next door to mine. A unique experience, to live awhile in a women's hall of residence—or so the legend went. Proximity to the university was the big argument in favour, but the college students, with their meals provided, avoided the campus and were drawn back by the dubious magnetism of their colleges to the familiar corridors and faces. Emma, anyway, was no victim of the prevailing insularity. Having spent two years living at home and having passed her university days in the university, she wasn't so susceptible to the ghetto-mentality of the majority. I, spending most of my time with Julia, was no exception to the climatic rule. I came back like the rest every lunchtime, even between lectures. Many only left to go home to their parents. Bizarre stultification.

I was faintly nervous of Emma. Of course we'd be able to resume those invaluable discussions of my poetry and everyone else's—a mine of stimulus to my reading and writing; but her personal approval was obscurely necessary to me and I shrank from her detecting the Julia affair. The information was at large amongst the students; the curious stare, the voices that dropped when we passed. Somebody would tell Emma—or she might innocently walk in. Julia and I had been placed in the same wing as requested. No fire-escape spy-holes and a readier reason for being in each other's company. But still no locks. Might not Emma, or Libby Stace, or any of the freshers simply knock and enter?

'Perhaps the best thing would be to stop,' Julia suggested.

'What? Stop sleeping together?'

'Stop making love. Just be friends.'

'That's impossible.'

'But it makes you so guilty, Maureen.'

'It also makes me happy.'

'Sometimes. But it can't go on forever, anyway. It's dangerous. It'll have to end somewhere.'

'I don't see why.'

'Because, well, women can't spend their entire lives together.'

'Why not? I like sharing your life.'

'Can't you imagine what it'd be like living your whole life in secret? Always afraid it'll leak out?'

'I'm not going to let other people run my life. Anyway we could escape.'

'Nonsense, Maureen. You don't want to escape from people like Emma. You're an extrovert.'

'Bullshit. I'm very contemplative.'

She laughed. 'That too of course. But seriously now, you need people. It's silly to go on living in a way that cuts you off from them.'

'It can't be helped, Julia. I'm in love with you. It's you I want.'

'But that's so naïve. The longer you go on like this, the harder it's going to be to branch out, to meet men.'

'I don't like men. And they don't like me. And anyway you talk as if I'm the only one in danger. Aren't you in love with me?'

'No.' Something of a shock.

'What do you mean?'

'I love you—dearly. But no, I'm not in love with you. And I'm thinking of your best interests.'

'You're my best interest, bugger it.'

'You won't always think so.'

'I think so now.'

Julia made it clear that for her this would not be going on much longer, that only her weakness and sinfulness made her unable to take a firm stand. When she talked of our friendship as ruining our lives I understood what to expect. Cut loose, I said to myself each day. Cut loose and stand alone. Before the trouble. Cut loose, I muttered as I looped the day's knots. It seemed that something was quite wrong with me; absence of spine, I defined it. The thought of imminent loneliness hurled me into blank panic. Cut loose, I commanded, bombarding myself with resolutions not to seek Julia out, to get myself used to the idea. I was living all the time with an undertow where I was scared and horrified that this was what love came to. How did I get like this? I asked myself, certain that I must've been better off in my isolation on Strackard Hill, apostrophizing the sunset and eulogizing the earth. I simply could not understand how I came to be the way I was—I wondered if I'd been born with a fatal flaw.

Nor could I change myself. If I could get to be isolated again, I thought, really cut off from all of them . . . so I didn't need them, didn't love them, didn't mind one way or the other about any bloody thing . . . If I could only get tough, detached like Emma. I wanted to grow a shell as if that might somehow be the answer—I suspected, vaguely, that it couldn't be. How did it come about that I was almost incapable of doing anything without someone's approval. Mother's or Julia's or whoever? How did I come to have no centre, no certainty, no will of my own? I read a bitter quip somewhere: There is a rat in my bed at night; that rat is me. I was impressed and copied it down on my desk calendar. I am not even as tough as a rat, I thought. Rats are hardy.

Julia was reading in the Library when I dragged her out for company.

'Maureen, I really mustn't stay long. I've got an essay to do.'

'But I'm feeling lonely, miserable.'

'I'm sorry my dear. I'm sorry. But everyone's alone.'

'Oh sure.'

'No, Maureen, don't shrug me off like that. You really don't seem to accept that at all.'

'I didn't say I didn't accept it. It's just I don't like it.'

'And you want it different?'

I scowled.

'Because it's a fundamental of the human condition. We're all born alone; we all die alone; basically we're alone.'

'Yeah but we can get close to each other.'

'But never identical.'

'Shit, Julia, I don't want to be identical. I just want to be with you.'

'There's a limit.'

'Well why is it so much harder for me apparently? Why am I so bloody spineless and gutless and helpless?'

'I don't know, Maureen. But you must know I've done my best to help.'

'Oh sure.'

'Anyway,' I continued after a moment, 'what about marriage? Do you reckon that married people are still utterly alone?'

'In a way.'

'Argh. Sophistry—they've got company, someone to sleep with, someone to talk to, someone who cares.'

'Sometimes.'

'Well, Jesus, it's up to them to make it work, isn't it?'

'Some people are really together I suppose.'

'All right then. Why not us?'

'Maureen. Two women do not get married.'

'Not formally. But that doesn't matter, does it?'

'It wouldn't work. It couldn't.'

'I just don't see why not. If there's affection, sympathy, communication—I think it'd work.'

'You should try to meet men, Maureen.'

Every exchange with Julia confirmed the panic. Only occasionally would she let me get into bed with her and even then threw me out before morning. Scandal-scare and self-scare. I started thinking about marriage. Obviously the exit from the impasse. I couldn't tolerate the isolation I ought to have embraced; I imagined a husband instead—soul-mate and lover. But Julia was the only person I'd ever known who approximated to the image. I couldn't see too many husbands in the offing.

In her anguish, disguised as usual as a concern for my normality and future, Julia wrote to the Student Counsellor to see if he could help us put a stop to the lesbian bondage.

'Do you want to stop?' he asked us.

'Yes,' said Julia loudly.

'I don't know,' I muttered.

'Why?' he asked.

'We think it's bad for us. It makes things difficult in college, and we are afraid of becoming homosexuals.' She spoke quickly, nervously; and she spoke for both of us. Why, I thought murderously, did she let it all get under way if she was going to back out at this stage? But she insisted to the Counsellor that my welfare was her central concern. My objections to her corrective course seemed churlish, even to me.

When he suggested that we might see less of each other and masturbate instead of making love, I nearly fell off my chair. The word, which had much the same slimy quality as lesbian, was a shocker. And perhaps he was, indeed, only trying to point out the absurdity of Julia's project for purity.

'I wouldn't get anything out of that,' I blurted out.

'No?'

'No.'

'I shouldn't think I would, either,' Julia added quietly.

Evidently he overestimated the sexual content of the whole affair—or wanted to let us know that we did.

Our visits to him must have assuaged Julia's guilt—we drifted on as before, in a spirit of tenuous truce.

The discovery of Shakespeare's sonnets cheered me—a lucky ident-ification.

'Did you know, Emma, that Shakespeare had homosexual tendencies?' Bull at a gate.

'Nonsense. He can't have had.'

'Why not?'

'There's nothing in the plays.'

'I've been reading the sonnets. They're written for a young man.'

'What about the famous dark lady?'

'Oh yeah, there's her, but that's only the last thirty or so.'

She was interested, but sceptical.

'Listen to this—number twenty:

> "And for a woman wert thou first created,
> Till nature as she wrought thee fell a-doting,
> And by addition me of thee defeated

> By adding one thing to my purpose nothing.
> And since she pricked thee out for women's pleasure,
> Mine be thy love, and thy love's use their treasure."'

She took the book and bent over it frowning.

'There's only one interpretation,' I said. 'And I've just read the rest. It's all intense. He gets jealous of his friend's adventures with women. In one he's waiting up for him. It's a love-affair.'

'I suppose so,' she murmured, thumbing the pages.

'And anyway, people who think they're for a woman read them as love-lyrics.'

'Yes. I've read about the idea somewhere, but I assumed it was crackpot. People are always trying to prove artists are homosexual.'

'Some are, I suppose.' I was taking care to speak casually. With Emma—indeed with everyone—I pretended that the matter had nothing to do with me. A game of tactful silence.

'Undoubtedly.' She let it rest, delicately, without reference back to me, made no sign that I might have a self-interest in the interpretation— though my love poems could have had no conceivable object but Julia. Emma never asked. What she guessed she kept to herself. We skirted the realities.

Yet, from Shakespeare's apparent passion for a fellow-male, I drew some sort of strength, a fleeting fellowship with the great and the maligned. They might dismiss Wilde as *fin de siècle* and febrile; no one dared blackball the Bard.

. . .

The vacation might have gone off well enough, on the tenterhooks of my best behaviour, if I'd had the sense to receive my voluminous mail at another place—though [my mother's] hawk-eyed watch on my movements and the tiniest reason for each might have found me out anyway. By the time Julia's fourth fat letter arrived her suspicious curiosity could no longer be contained.

'Maureen, I've got to talk to you.'

'Yeah?'

'What's going on?'

'Whattayamean what's going on?'

'What's going on with Julia Vernon?'

I looked blank, trying non-comprehension at base one.

'Julia?'

'Yes. Julia.'

'There's a couple of letters if that's what you mean . . .'

'And what kind of letters would they be, eh? I notice you don't leave them lying around with your other letters.'

'Have you been sniffing through my letters now?' A nauseating thought. She ignored the query.

'Maureen, it's unnatural.'

'What's unnatural?' I knew what she was talking about. How she knew, though, puzzled me.

'All these letters. You carry on as if you're in love with the girl.'

Could I have said well I am? Not likely. But I must have jumped.

'Yes,' she snarled. 'Caught you there!'

'What?' said I feebly.

'There's no bloody use denying it, Maureen. It's a shock to me and I don't know what it'll do to your father when I tell him and as for your old Granny . . .'

'What the hell are you talking about Mother?' False calm.

'You know bloody well what I'm talking about. I brought you up to be a decent clean-living girl; that's all I've ever wanted from you, and now—this.' She was starting to weep, a look of real anguish. To my halting assertions of innocence she replied, through sobs, 'There's no point in denying it Maureen. I'm not bloody well blind.'

'You're just a suspicious bitch.'

'And it's just as well, isn't it? At least I can put a stop to it now. To think my own daughter . . .'

'For Christ's sake what are you talking about?' It was clear that this tack was exhausted, but I could not think of another.

'Oh my God, anything but this. This . . . this . . . unnatural . . . anything but this . . .'

'Anything but what?'

Her face was mad with disgust, horror deeper than anger, a vast loathing. What it must have cost her to say that word.

'This . . . this . . . this lesbian business.'

The word. That word. Still shocking, even to me.

'I am not a lesbian. I am not.' A child of maybe five, redhot in the face, guilty in the eyes, half-tearful, trapped, denying its mother's accusation. 'I am not.' I looked down at the chessboard tiling of the big kitchen; our voices high-pitched, matched, vehement. For a moment I understood that her suspicion was certainty. I saw that she (somehow) knew. All my retreats were cut off.

'What's so unnatural about it anyway?' I'd defined my defensive. Tacitly admitted. She broke down. Hysterical, unbearable sobbing.

'My God . . . my daughter . . . unnatural . . . you ask what's unnatural . . . oh my God . . .'

I knew I should walk out. Leave a shred of doubt. I knew that nothing either of us said could make the slightest difference. That I would not give Julia up nor she accept it. Despite myself the truth was out and the truth admitted of no resolution between us. But I stood still, tears starting in my eyes, stood still and waited. She kept muttering about her God and her daughter through the sobs. 'To think it'd come to this . . . my God . . . this business . . .' Finally she quieted and looked at me.

I stood, swimming in a maelstrom of black and white checks, drowning and unable to move. Although I knew she was gathering for the counterattack. She took a weighty breath and said, as if it pained her, 'This is going to have to stop, you know.'

'This is *not* going to have to stop.'

'I won't have my daughter indulging in this kind of filth.'

'This is *not* filth.'

'Oh, and what is it then? Eh?'

'I love Julia.' As if that'd be any defence.

She sneered. 'Love? You've never known what love is. You've always been too selfish. Look at you now.'

'What about me?'

'Standing there in your jeans with your thumbs in your belt like some sort of boy.'

'What's that got to do with it?'

'Do you think that's normal?'

'I don't give a stuff whether it's normal.'

'And your language.'

'Stuff my language.'

'Maureen, for God's sake . . .'

'I don't believe in your bloody God.'

'Maureen, please, you've got to be reasonable.'

'You can talk.'

'Well you can't expect me to take this sort of thing lightly. Your whole life's at stake.'

'It's my life.'

'Oh my God, if only you were pregnant I'd at least be able to talk to my friends. But this . . .' So much easier, pregnancy. A respectable scandal.

'You'd like to see me knocked up, would you?'

'You know I don't want to see you in *any* sort of trouble.'

'Bullshit. You've been making trouble for me ever since I can remember.'

'I've been making trouble have I? I give you music lessons, speech lessons. I leave Looe Marsh and all my friends so you can go to a good school . . .'

'It was a lousy school.'

'We didn't know that then. I make sure you get a good education, get you to University . . .'

'You wanted board when I was saving to study.'

'We were never well-off, Maureen, you know that as well as I do. We had to scrape and scratch year-in year-out for you and Ken to have all the things we missed out on.'

'Oh shit yes, I appreciate all that.'

'You never showed it.'

'How did you expect me to when you hated me the whole bloody time?'

'Don't talk nonsense, Maureen.'

Suddenly the possibility of making her understand.

'I'll tell you something Mother. It's about time you knew. Sure you gave me speech lessons—and showed me off to those precious friends you had to leave behind. Sure you left, and every argument since you've rubbed in your great sacrifice and my ingratitude, when I hated that bloody school—full of snobs and half-wits. On top of that you blamed me for Ken turning into a juvenile delinquent. Little Kenny-boy wouldn't've had that sort of thing in him, now, would he? And all the bloody time I was slaving my guts out doing your cooking, your house-work, your shopping, at your beck and call, and always under your thumb. Shit, I wasn't even allowed to go out with other girls because you thought something might happen to me. Lose your little slave.'

'You always grumbled . . .'

'Yeah. But I always did it—and you hardly ever said a word of thanks. *You* talk about ingratitude. Yours stinks to the high heaven. And all that time you favoured Ken as if he was the one helping you out.'

'He's a boy.'

'Yeah, and I wish I'd been one. You believed him when he lied, the little bastard, you belted the shit out of me for the things he did and made out I'd done. You were blind to everything he did because he was a boy and boys get away with everything. The way he came in the other night—and laughed at you—and you still make all the allowances for him. You never made any for me. You even belted me once for trying to get away to see Granny.'

'You're making it up.'

'No, Mother, I'm not bloody well making it up. You caught me at the back-fence by the gums, dragged me back inside, locked me up in the bathroom and took to me with that bloody great canvas belt you used to have. I suppose it's not the kind of thing you like to remember. I wouldn't like to have treated a kid like that.'

'But why would I have done a thing like that?'

'Search me. How should I know? You said Granny was spoiling me and wouldn't let me visit her for months.'

'Well she did spoil you.'

'Yeah. Look how spoiled I am now, eh?'

'It's no laughing matter.'

'If you loved me, you bitch . . .'

'Maureen!'

'. . . if you loved me you kept it a bloody dark secret.'

'No, no, Maureen. NO. You've got it all wrong. Of course I loved you. No other girl would see it like this.'

'That's how I see it. That's how I feel it. That's how it was.'

'I wasn't to know you felt like that . . .'

I sniggered through my tears.

'Maureen, please . . . if you feel like this I'm sorry, really sorry . . .'

'Thanks.'

My throat felt lacerated, my eyes hot as if I had suffered the attack myself. I would have liked to be able to put my arms around her and make peace. I couldn't do that any more than leave her. No peace and no exit.

She cornered me at the end of my tirade.

'I want to help you.'

'I do not need your help.'

'Come on now, Maureen. You must be worried yourself. It's no way to live.'

'It's my business.'

'You need help.'

'I do not.'

'A psychiatrist then, if you won't let me . . .'

'There's nothing you or any headshrinker or anyone else can do. It's my business.'

'There's your family to think of. Do you want to be known as one of those all your life?'

'I don't give a shit.'

'I'll have to take drastic steps if you won't do something about this yourself.'

Fleetingly I wished I could humorously promise to be good, as Ken would have done, and leave jovially. I stood. Defiant.

'If this doesn't stop I'll contact Mrs Vernon—I'm sure she wouldn't be too pleased.'

'She's in Melbourne.'

'She'll be back.'

'Anyway, she's enlightened I bet. Not everyone's living in the nineteenth century still.'

'It's got nothing to do with being old-fashioned, Maureen. It's a simple question of morals.'

'Bullshit.'

'What's more I should think the College Principal would be anxious to put a stop to your carryings-on.'

'Jesus mother, you can't go telling the college.'

'We'll see.'

'You wouldn't.'

She raised her eyebrows with an air of despair.

'I might be forced to.'

Visions of Julia's mother clouting me with a lecture-board—yet surely a sociologist might have some tolerance . . . And college . . . Maureen Craig, expelled 1965, for lesbian practices. An awful warning. A public affair it'd be: there Emma stands smiling wanly, there Libby Stace and her fresher-cronies tittering. Dr Heath appears in full academic regalia—ermine and red velvet—wielding a mace, as the college music students strike up the Funeral March and the tutors file past in black, each signing the expulsion warrant with a flourish. Craig shivers in a bath-towel. 'Who put you in?' Emma inquires in a stage whisper. 'My mother.' The assembly gets their laugh out of it, great waves of swelling hilarity. A couple of hefty seniors step forward for the public flogging and Craig is finally carted out to the nature-strip, dumped in the big bad world, while students aim pebbles from upstairs windows.

Through the panic and desperation I couldn't follow my mother's torrent of propositions for my immediate relief from sin.

'You can't do this to me,' I screamed. 'You can't.'

'Just promise me you'll stop.'

'I can't. And I won't.'

'Well you're not staying under my roof then. We've always been respectable people. Your grandmother'd die of shame . . .'

'I don't want to stay here. You begged me to come home. I never wanted it. I'll be gone by morning.'

'Maureen. Please. I only want to help you.'

'All you're worried about is the scandal—and your old-hat morals. I'm not interested in your morals—they never did you any good, that's for sure. And I don't give a stuff what you try. I hate your moral guts.'

As I clattered down the steps she yelled after me.

'These aren't idle threats, Maureen. I'll take action. I'll stop you. I'll have to help you if you won't help yourself.'

I emptied all my change out in the telephone box and shakily dialled trunks. Get through to Julia. Get help.

'That'll be eighteen shillings for three minutes.'

'I've only got twelve.'

'That won't be enough, I'm sorry.' Frenzy.

'Please, please give me two minutes—it's a matter of life and death.'

He connected me; must've enjoyed the situation that was life and death to me—he didn't cut us off. I babbled on for an hour. Julia agreed to sound out her mother and suggested I try the Vice-Principal, who knew and liked me.

'Come back soon,' I begged foolishly.

'Saturday.'

'I'll be back in college.'

'I love you, Maureen. Don't worry. We'll find a way through.'

I packed my suitcase and went to sleep in the armchair for an hour or so. Terrified of meeting my mother I got up at dawn, wandered the drizzling Harwich streets until nine, had my mail redirected and caught the train to Central. I'd lasted eight days with the family. This looked like the end.

1975

JENNY PAUSACKER

Graffiti

1

Still hard to believe that a kid called Cathy Sidiropoulos can be wandering along these arched grey cloisters. Though the university's not all arched grey cloisters, by any means. Plenty of glass towers crammed into the remaining spaces—some sleek and gleaming, others more like an academic high rise. It's a maze, a place where you can easily get lost.

So Cathy's relieved when she pops out into a quadrangle and comes face to face with some low-slung sandstone. Inside it, there's a window-less room where she goes for lectures, which means she can now locate a toilet without having to ask anyone. She shoves at glass doors and swing doors, clatters across patterned tiles, bites her lip at a row of closed wooden doors. Backs away to the mirror and pretends she came in to push her hair about.

Not the only mane of bushy hair on campus. Not the only arched dark eyebrows, olive skin, narrow nose. Then why is she still scared of being spotted as an outsider? Dunno. Try again. Okay, why is she still waiting for those stimulating discussions and people who understand? Why can't she accept that it's just lecturers droning on and tutors asking questions with set answers, same as school?

And more importantly, why has no one flushed a toilet and quit their fucking cubicle? Cathy clatters, Cathy slams at the door with the heel of her hand. It flies open. Tricked again—the whole row's probably vacant. Even the toilets in this dump automatically shut you out.

Jerking irritably at her pantyhose, relaxing and reading the graffiti. 'HERE I SIT, ALL BROKEN-HEARTED, CAME TO SHIT AND ONLY FARTED.' Real intellectual, that is. 'HOW MANY THERAPISTS DOES IT TAKE TO CHANGE A LIGHT GLOBE? ONE, BUT THE LIGHT GLOBE HAS TO WANT TO CHANGE.' Don't get it. 'THE STANDARD OF GRAFFITI IN THIS TOILET IS APPALLING. WHAT DO WE PAY TAXES FOR?' Hey, someone agrees with me.

A debate about student taxes meanders down the rest of the wall. Cathy turns away to wrest sheets of paper from the dispenser. 'LESBIANS RULE, OK?' Blink. Blink again. 'NOT BY ME. LESBIANS ARE CUNTS.' Blink, blink, 'YEAH, AND THAT'S ONLY ONE OF THE GREAT THINGS ABOUT US.'

Paper flutters to the floor. Cathy twitches out a second batch, hesitates, wipes quick and light. Pantyhose covers her like chainmail. Mirror reflects a reddened face. Us, she shudders. Us. There are lesbians here.

2

Watching 'Zorba the Greek'

Maybe I should've gone on watching *Zorba the Greek*. Many people that I admire have admired it—that's why I tuned in when it appeared on SBS, having missed it the first time around. But within minutes it became clear to me that this was another of those scenarios where an uptight Anglo male is taught to relax and see life more clearly by a Greek/Italian/black/streetkid/prostitute/drag queen/ageing actress/homosexual thief—anyone, in short, who hasn't been crushed by the heavy privileges of being an Anglo male.

Only this time the story wasn't written by E.M. Forster or Ernest Hemingway—it was written by a Greek. Maybe I should've gone on watching but, with an instant sense of betrayal, I switched channels, contemplated an exchange in an American sit com and turned off the TV.

The trouble is, as a lesbian feminist I've never managed to locate myself in my own culture. I'm not part of 'the norm'—an elusive phenomenon including live in the suburbs, coke-sniffing in New York and anything else that a large enough number of people feel comfortably familiar with. On the other hand, I don't feel solidly established as part of 'the other'—an equally elusive phenomenon including groups which aren't currently crushed by heavy privileges, countries which haven't recently been world dominators and anything else that a large enough number of people can be led to consider exotic. I mean, can you imagine a bestseller where an uptight Anglo male is taught to relax and see life more clearly by a lesbian feminist? No, you can't, and neither can I.

Mind you, lesbian feminists have a small niche in the culture, all the same. Let's take a few thoroughly random examples. I buy a new comedy magazine and find that it's stacked with jokes about lesbian feminists—you know, overalls, hairy legs, health food, hatred of men and especially boy children. I browse through the paper and learn that the police searched the room of a guy in a recent murder case and discovered, among other things, a feminist magazine with comments written on it, saying that the magazine was for and about lesbians. Later in the same paper an argument against the ordination of women is based on the fact that some feminist theologians support equal rights for gays.

Given all of this, I suppose I'd have to say that lesbian feminists definitely come under the heading of 'the other': it's just that we haven't yet attracted an appropriate publicity machine to convince people that we're warmer, wiser, more peace-loving, better tap-dancers or whatever. But times change and anything's possible. I'm almost able to imagine a bestseller where an uptight Anglo *woman* is taught to relax and see life more clearly by a lesbian feminist. (*The Kiss of the Spiderwoman* with Olivia Newton-John and Meryl Streep, maybe.)

Not that I want to be Zorba the Gay, myself. I'd rather get away from the whole business of insiders and outsiders and see us all as dots on a continuum. Reading Doris Lessing's *Diaries of Jane Somers*, I was rapt to find she'd included a lesbian feminist character, not to make a particular point but simply because some of the people in the world are lesbian feminists. After all, most of the time I'm a lesbian feminist not to make a particular point but simply because I am.

Though if it's so simple, how come I've spent such a lot of time thinking about it?

3

This Sunday three of the aunts visit at once. So many comments about her old T-shirt that her mother shoos her off to change. Now Cathy's a good Greek girl in a party frock, dreaming about the kid who sat next to her in the politics lecture. Zap—and the kid materializes in the lounge room, six silver earrings glinting against her bright red spikes, three jumpers of different lengths over heavy black tights, pointy shoes with angular buckles. Get the aunts' faces.

'So, Cathy, you're meeting lots of nice boys at the university? Politics, that's a good subject. You could be getting to know our next prime minister.'

Not fair, Cathy thinks sullenly. You want to marry me off like a peasant, but you know everything a city person knows. Mama had it easier. No, scrub that. Mama didn't have it easier.

'I'm never going to get married.'

Disapproving clicks from Thea Lella, but Thea Maria can take it. 'That's right, Cathy. You work for a while, maybe buy a little flat, and then it's time to think about getting married.'

Cathy slips her hand up her sleeve and pinchs hard while she forces a smile. What's the point? Can't go on repeating the same thing over and over. They can, but you can't. Easier to stuff your face with cake and hate the kilos afterwards. Better to hate the kilos than your family.

'Well, look who's here. Peter—what a surprise.'

'You told me to come, Mum,' Peter points out. 'I got other things to do with my time, y'know.'

'Aren't you going to say hello to your cousin Cathy? Eh, you look nice together, like a picture.'

Now she understands the party frock. Now she's herded out to the back yard, to pick tomatoes for Thea Maria. Peter grumbles that they've got heaps of bloody tomatoes at home—thank you, Peter—but inevitably Thea Maria insists that their bushes aren't half as good. So away they go, Peter slouching ahead, Cathy stumbling as her high heels dig into the earth.

He looms over the tomatoes, chest and upper arms bulging disdainfully, and mumbles words she can't catch. Cathy smiles brightly, knows she's somehow blown it already. She starts to babble, tells Peter about the essay she's writing, paragraph by paragraph. Feels like a puppet on jerky strings, with a squeaky voice mouthing away in the distance. Watches him yawn and turn on his heel.

Handfuls of warm red globes, carried back to the house with a sense of relief and doom.

4
Thinking About Rock'n'Roll

I spent a lot of time thinking about why lesbian feminists like rock'n'roll. The most unlikely of my friends can give you all the words to 'Tan Shoes and Pink Shoelaces' or differentiate without missing a beat between the Crystals and the Shangri-Las. So many times during the early days of Women's Liberation there'd be a group of us crammed into someone's kitchen or lounge room after a meeting/dance/spraypainting session, and after we'd worked our way through a bracket of feminist songs, someone would go, 'One, two, three o'clock, four o'clock — rock!' and the rest of the night would belong to the fifties.

The fifties! High heels and girdles and skirts that blew up around your waist at the slightest breeze. A hundred tips on making the perfect pav and raising the perfect baby. Ads of women smiling at the kitchen sink while square-jawed hubby strode in, taking off his hat. Why would lesbian feminists want to recapture, even for a night, the feeling of the fifties?

Listen to the songs, though, and you won't hear much about square jaws and smiling aprons. There are the cute numbers about young love, I admit. There are the raunchy numbers about rocking round the clock and twisting the night away, certainly. But above all there is heartbreak and torment, the lonely crying great pretenders making anguish sound like ecstasy.

You can see the appeal of that for a bunch of young women who've just gone through the hard slog of deciding they're lesbian.

I stuck to that theory for ten years, and then I went to a party in a house with a piano. A young woman got out her music and started to play. The Seekers, early Dylan, Carol King's 'Tapestry' — all the songs of the sixties that I played continually in my London bedsitter. Great songs but not songs to sing along to, or so I'd always said, except that the young women around the piano were doing precisely that.

Death of a theory. Forget about any natural affinity between lesbian feminists and rock'n'roll. My generation sings the songs that were around before we were teenagers, and the next generation sings the songs that were round before they were teenagers. It's all part of a broader generalization about how everyone feels nostalgic for the sights and sounds of their childhood.

And it shook me, I can tell you. I realized that I couldn't even generalize about my own community, not without a battery of sociologists and statisticians to provide me with the proper data, the control groups and the comparative studies. Okay, I can offer my impressions, contribute to the oral history of the world, but it's not the same.

Of course I'm part of a lesbian feminist community, nonetheless, made up of people I know well and people I know slightly and people I've only heard about and people I don't know at all, just like any other community. Whether I can or can't make authoritative statements about it, I still know it's there . . .

5

Cathy Sidiropoulos hurries back to uni on Monday to look at men. Peter's not a fair test, after all. What can essays and neatly flounced dresses and scribbled thoughts in a diary say to the disco and the gym, nights with the boys and days painting houses? Not a fair test.

So she prowls around, examining guys like clowns and guys like stockbrokers. This one fingers his acne, this one smooths his bald spot. This one's hard to get talking, that one's impossible to stop. They lumber, they stride, they posture nervously—okay, there are lots of different men, but where does that get you?

Other women seem to know the answer. Twining tightly to his side. Hovering desperately at his elbow. Laughing and joking in the group, then catching his eye at the critical moment. Paired with a guy who almost seems their twin, paired with a guy who appears to be their polar opposite. Staying away from one guy, flocking around the next.

Cathy feels it all. The triumph, the heartbreak, the boredom, the contentment. Watching the women, she lives a hundred loves in a morning. Only one problem. She still can't work out how the women decide to direct their love towards one guy rather than another.

Finally, exhausted, she hides in the toilets. Here, at least, she won't have to think about the puzzle of men and women. Wrong. At one handbasin, an excited babble about the weekend's progress from Connor to Ziggy to Tony. At the other handbasin, a young woman weeps quietly over John.

Cathy stops her peaceful combing. Adds herself onto the queue. Stands back politely once and then twice. Walks into the same cubicle as before. Settles down with a sigh, as though she's getting ready for her favourite TV series.

The dialogue continues. With a biro that peels the paint, someone has written 'WHAT'S SO GREAT ABOUT BEING A LESBIAN THEY JUST CAN'T GET A MAN.' Cathy's eyes flinch shut and everything's black. Then through blurred eyelashes she reads 'WHO WANTS A MAN?' Her muscles relax, but the biro stabs on. 'WELL I DO.' 'AND I DON'T,' answers a green texta. 'SO WE'RE BOTH HAPPY, RIGHT?'

I'm not happy, thinks Cathy. Never have been. Never will be.

6
Addressing the RSL

I have a recurrent fantasy, which goes like this. I'm walking into a large church hall, filled to capacity with rows of wooden seats. I stride up the steps to the stage and turn with a flourish to address the audience: representatives of the RSL, Women Who Want to be Women, the Concerned Parents Association, the Festival of Light and other organizations whose pronouncements on homosexuality I have noted from time to time.

'What do lesbians really do?' I begin.

Shoulders jerk back and heads flick upright as I go on to explain that we eat, sleep, own dogs, like football, watch videos, raise kids, pay taxes, buy takeaway, hate football, live alone, read books, own cats, go to work by bus—in short, we lead thoroughly recognizable lives, in the same streets and blocks of flats as everyone else.

Before the audience becomes too restive, I agree that there is, however, another view of lesbianism. From this perspective the lesbian life is so overwhelmingly attractive that anyone who hears about it will automatically want to experience it: consequently all non-condemnatory accounts of homosexuality have to be suppressed if heterosexuality is to continue. 'Flattering,' I say with a smile. 'But a bit over-glamorous.'

Glancing occasionally at my notes, I go on to combine history, sociology and biology in an erudite argument which proves that lesbians exist. I indicate that I consider debate about whether lesbianism is natural to be on a par with the proceedings of the Flat Earth Society. Tactfully, I suggest that my audience could in time learn to feel comfortable with their own choices, even while other people are making other choices.

Then I step back through the curtains and make a dash for the exit and my getaway car.

I've had that fantasy for years. Except last time I tried it, I walked onto the stage, turned with a flourish, shrugged and said, 'Ah, forget it.' You can get tired of explaining your existence. These days I just want to get on with my life. I am, therefore I am.

Unfortunately, that's a fantasy as well. There are people I've never met who nonetheless spend time thinking about what I mean to them. Inevitably they become part of my life, just as I feel part of the lives of all the women who have been harassed and attacked, cut off from showing ordinary affection, banned from the bedsides of their ill or dying lovers; who have had their dances and bars raided, lost their jobs, lost custody of their kids, sat through routine denigration of their way of life; who have been barred from information they needed and civil rights others take for granted, told they don't exist, turned into a ready target for legislation or agitation, raped or murdered—because they were lesbian.

If I sit here now, with the leisure to choose words to write on a blank sheet of paper, it's only because for the moment history permits me to do so, not because I've triumphed over history. Like all people from groups which have been systematically denied, I take nothing for granted.

This can create problems. It can also create a special pleasure as you eat, sleep, watch videos, pay taxes, go to work by bus. When you have to explain yourself, you learn to understand yourself.

7

The alarm shakes Cathy out of sleep. The shower drills at her skin, stimulating nerve ends of memory. The clothes lying ready on her chair.

Don't stop to think. Get dressed. Now, the mirror. Skirt chopped off above the knee, heavy tights. Scarlet jumper baggy over violet jumper. They clash. Cathy nods approval. Though the flat morning light outlines her in grey, she looks just as great as when she practised the night before.

Sure hands loop a multicoloured ribbon through her hair and round the bow mockingly. She nods again and walks into the kitchen.

'Cathy, your skirt! Your hair! You can't go out looking like that.'

'Yes, I can,' and to prove it, out she goes. Okay, she'll cop it when she gets home this evening, but by then she'll have flown her colours half-way across the city. She'll have something to defend.

She doesn't expect anything to change except her, but she's wrong. An old man at the bus stop winks and says, 'Haven't seen a bow like that since Shirley Temple.' The kid in her politics lecture comes to sit beside her again and they arrange to swap text books. In the caf people move back to let her pass with her tray. She's visible. By the time she joins the kids waiting outside the tutorial room, it seems quite easy to ask questions and give answers. She even continues on once she's inside the room.

Afterwards she makes her way to the low-slung sandstone building. Selects the right wooden door. Pushes it open. Looks at the long column of graffiti. Across it, someone has scrawled in red 'YOU'RE ALL A BUNCH OF PERVERTS,' and someone else has added in fine neat lettering 'LESBIANISM GOES AGAINST NATURE.'

Cathy's heart is thumping. Cathy's texta is ready. Cathy thinks for a moment. Cathy writes 'LAY OFF, CAN'T YOU? LESBIANS ARE ALL RIGHT.'

She steps back to study her handiwork and her smile radiates through her whole body. Though it takes another year before she can test the truth of her words for herself.

1990

RAE DESMOND JONES

Dawn

before dawn a soft carbon film
shifts on the surface
of the ground
        the paper barrows
        squeak along the lanes
        & the old men start to
        walk slowly out of the parks
        & cough phlegm off
        their chests
behind plate glass an old woman
squeezes a mop & on the paths
men walk heavily & carry overnight bags
& do not speak
        in concord there is
        an all night florist which
        has its doors closed &
        yellow flowers wilting in
        the windows
i am suspicious & look unsuccessfully
for wreaths
        thoughtful at
        the possibilities i begin
        to walk past an italian in
        dusty steel toe boots
three yards away he looks up
& his eyes hit through me like a hammer
into an old brick wall & i pass close
enough to smell the morning
on his skin
        with the sense of him
        at the bottom of my
        belly two car sales later
        i am still caught in
        the broken question
        of my breath
diplomacy i decide.
i don't often see the dawn

1977

The El Paso Restaurant

the radio playing country & western
 on the first floor of the el paso restaurant
the air conditioner snoring
 & down on the street gary cooper hitches
up his stockings & checks the clock

the waiter hobbles in boots &
 a red cowboy shirt because he's not used
to high heels & he leaves us the menu
 the plastic seat sweaty & you angling
the light onto your chrome sheriff's badge
 & a tear in the creases of your scarred old
elephant arse of a face
 & the filaments of our souls
touching & joining & even though the waiter
 ignored you i could not go on to the fort
without you & i am thirty-five & breaking apart

now amigo we are both pegged back
 the apaches squat in a ring of painted faces
& their cocks hard against their loin cloths
 the wet rawhide tightening in the sun &
no distant bugle & colonel custer's long
 yellow hair was not taken on the little big
horn

the greasy cards fanned out &
 the naked joker upward on the table my
shuffle & you john wayne archetypal cocksucker
 leave your guns at the door
the horses wait outside & four ugly drag queens
 lean against the hitching rail & it's almost
noon & the meat is curling on the grill
 downstairs

1977

PETER ROSE

Aviator

A portrait of him standing there
would be enough now —
easeful and sleek, despite
bitters of another year
less cogent than the last,
which he relates,
stroking an agile neck.
Evening on his skin
is subtle and chemical,
furtive as a connoisseur
not yet emboldened, plotting
future carnivals of touch,
but critical, vigilant,
appraising the several strokes
of his casual beauty —
olive skin, alien cross,
teak glint of languid eyes
that appraise, too,
in their franker way,
asking weighted questions:
avocation, destination,
how I like to spend my nights.
A portrait of him standing there
would be enough now.

1993

Obscure Figure

Perhaps it was Patroclus I dreamt of.
Perhaps it was him I watched,
wearily shedding his bloody armour
then leaning, enigmatic,
over a low-slung spartan bed,
naked, brown-skinned, alone,
until the moment of Achilles' return.

1990

TONY PAGE

Passion at Byron Bay

Hang-gliders over the lighthouse,
Passion briefly out of harm's way.
Da Vinci's charcoal sketches
Sprout technicolour wings
Along the arms of gods who float
On the waves of my desire.

Summers punch below the belt.
The beaches burst with groin.
One urge jumps on top of the other.
Watching the gliders numbs my hunger
Because I can nearly pretend
They are not human at all.

Passion grabs the wheel again
And here I am, driven too fast
On the wrong side of the road
By last night's pick-up
Who will never learn to fly.
The headlights not working
On this road snaking to the sea,
Lurching with every corner

    All cliff edges
    And no wings

1992

Monster in the Park

The sun's vice squad turns off
Its spotlight in the west.
There are fewer citizens
To hunt me down once it's dark.

Over there strolls a childless couple
Who shower too much affection on their dogs.
They distract these birds from
The sweets I throw at their feet.
The sparrows rise like a handful
Of jewels tossed in the air.
Even they do not trust me.

My arms have grown thin
Because they make no contact
With the people I'm forbidden to love.
This tree lets me stroke its trunk
Without fearing my warmth,
But it is not enough.
Let me out of the dark.

1992

Dialogue

Your coffee's cold.
I pour it down the sink.
Who sang in the shower
If it wasn't you?

Ring me at work. How can
I keep up the story
If no one phones?
It's not asking too much.

Isn't it time you paid
Your share of the food?
You'll get too thin
If you never eat what I cook.

I bump into the day
From every angle possible.
But you never take shape
Or step into flesh.

Maybe I've forgotten
What you look like.
When I toss and turn
Trying to perfect our rhythm
Will you hold me still?

1992

DAVID HERKT

Satires

I

That Protestant bitch has faked tears once too often
    and why, one asks, when she got the boy?
I wanted him. She hadn't even noticed him.
    Then over drinks my tongue ran free on what I'd do
if I had him or let him have me;
    I must've started her cunt to itch.

Then last night when she got him, she cried on the phone,
    'But it wasn't me.'
Meaning it was him who'd taken her, not she lured him to her bed.
    Lying feminist!
The only time she credits a male and she gets it wrong.
    He was just a vacant body;
it was the poet in me that made alluring what she could not see.

II

So his circumcised prick has found a vacancy to fill.
    With all the arrogance of youth, he assumes his little toy
is what they want.
    Not in my case. I'd cut him down to size.
He's the vacancy I'd like to fill
    and from what she said
a few lessons in how to take it might improve his skill.

III

Even if narcotics were finally to render me completely impotent,
    i.e. unable to screw tomorrow,
those two would still construct me as the desiring one,
    for their whole relationship depends on it;
she wants him because I refused her and I want him
    and he needs her because he's afraid that he wants me.
I wish they'd sort it out because an hour ago with someone else
    I really had to work to come.

IV

The plot she came up with the other night
    continues to amaze me.
The idea was, she said, swearing me to secrecy,
    as he was only in it for our mutual flattery,
we should withdraw it altogether and leave him stranded,
    Narcissus without a mirror.

I couldn't. I want him far too much.
      And besides I wouldn't ally
with that conniving bitch in any scheme.
      I mean I don't mind someone playing with me
as long as it's with my prick. And then what of him
      when he consoles her night on night?
I can't tell what was given me in confidence
      though it could win me what I want;
I at least have morals.

V

We got home and as is my need
      I had to go into the bathroom.
He asked to watch with natural curiosity.
      'Sure,' I said, holding my syringe,
'This is the spoon and this is the heroin and this,'
      screwing round my shirtsleeve tight,
'This is the torniquet. This is the blood and I ease it in.
      It's not here yet. Yes it is. It's here right now.'
I did it very neatly for him
      though there are other things I'd rather show
and I'd rather watch as he rolls upon his stomach;
      I'd ease it in so slow and gentle
and just as neatly for the same effect.

VI

Now what the fuck did he mean today?
      I was listing the books he'd borrowed from me
when we came to C.P. Cavafy.
      'I've been meaning to ask,' he said,
'There was one poem about a young man wanting to study
      with all his books spread round him
and the next line implied he was getting screwed.
      I even remember the page number, one-two-four.'
What could I do?
      I talked of Cavafy's themes as one poet on another
to a student who was about to leave me for the library.
      Surely no-one's that unconscious anymore?

VII

I was told she lunched today at Slattery's in King Street.
      She had duck-liver entree and a well-hung steak for main.
Her ex-boyfriend had ravioli followed by the roasted lamb.
      They were celebrating a fraudulent insurance claim
and were holding hands all through desert.

If that is all he means to her
    that she forgets him for a well-hung steak,
I wish she'd clear the field for me.
    I like my meat as fresh and rare as possible.
Size is of no consequence at all.
    I also like it unstuffed;
she, on the other hand, is stuffing it up
    as much as possible and all that she can.

VIII

Well maybe that's that.
    I might show him these poems tomorrow
and tell him though they might appear all true
    there's a little poetic licence,
that I love him and I once liked her,
    and I hope, like all good poets, that he will smile
which means I'll get my poet's laurels
    and doubly so if he should turn his back on me.

IX

So I showed him these and he pleaded for a copy.
    I guess they appealed to his vanity
because, sure as hell, he didn't mind the slander of the girl
    he'd taken pains to tell me that he loved.
But he didn't come through with the goods.
    'I'm stubborn,' he repeated drunkenly,
though he didn't stop the game,
    and when I was kissed goodbye in front of her,
he forced his tongue into my mouth again.

X

I had returned to the country for a month or two
    committing them to each other, a sentence worse than death,
when after two weeks of silence I received his telegram:
    'Envoy love me don't take umbrage letter follows.'
I wired back: 'I do I don't returning Friday night.'
    and he met me off the plane.

It turned out she'd got bored with him,
    unable to taunt me with her prize,
and in no uncertain terms she told him it was over.
    Today when I was idly comparing dates,
I found he telegrammed the day she pissed him off.
    You've got to admire him;
there's one who does not wish to spend a minute undesired.

1988

Mary Fallon

From *Working Hot*

Peaches — Peaches and Cream

'. . . you could cry like that every day'
said Freda Peach cold
'. . . do you mean ME — do you mean I could or one
could' asked Toto
'. . . anyone could we could all cry like that every day if
we wanted to if we didn't stop ourselves . . . come to me'
she said
now how many people can say that without it sounding
ridiculous but she can Freda can Freda Peach

that body that Vienna loaf that Camembert that
avocado that glacé fruit that marzipan-iced fruit-cake

you come over and over
so many times so quick
I'm thunderstruck
I'm flabbergasted
I'm in awe of my fingers
(the tips tingle if we haven't fucked for a few days)

'come and give me a kiss' said Toto
'here and here and here and one here'

'I can't get enough of your mouth' said Freda Peach and
she couldn't

I was a mouse running along a live wire between
two terminals
your hands
you ran me back and forth
back and forth I ran

going to sleep with you holding me saying 'I love you
because . . .' over and over
and you even had reasons
reasons like a contract

'the girl with the magic mouth' said Freda
and I was

waking up arms around your neck and breasts thinking
'oh shit the washing pay the rent buy the wood for the
table' and you wake up and we're kissing and it's so
warm and drowsy and I say 'no no today we won't

spend all day in bed today I must do the washing pay
the rent get the wood for the table ring about the
paint ...'
'what about the washing'
'it won't get washed'
'what about the rent'
'it won't get paid'
what about the table it won't get made
what about the paint it won't get bought
passion and excess (yum yum)

'how comforting for you that there will always be the
big soft warm bed to come back to you sloth you
lounge lizard little forays in the mind that's all you
want to stimulate you titillate you
not go too far
impotent flourishes at language
mind you carve those words well now use words to
carve carve up words with words
it's Scrabble and the word is lunch
to you the word is lunch' Toto Rampant

'you are one of the only people I know who knows
how to love profoundly
you are a lover's lover' said Freda Subdued

'you just want me to fit into your cosiness just the last
little bit but necessary part to complete your total
comfort to give you the illusion of change challenge
passion' Toto Stillrampant

'yes I suppose one of the main reasons (but I do love
you) for being with you is the being-seen-with/being-
seen-to-be and I have refused any deep personal
commitment you're right—goodnight' Freda Unsubdued

'deep personal commitment? I respect you? wedlock
warlock' Toto cursed to the shut black door 'you say
there are barriers you feel barriers between us that I am
not responding to you sexually but it is precisely when I
am responding to youjustyou in your hands on the end of
your ten pin fingers (you bitch you had me on the end of
a pin—escargot) and it was just you you youjustyou
I was responding to I wanted lover lover lover with eyes
on you and just the usual burn of your fingers you get
so excited saying "I can feel it I can feel it ohyesyes yes
that's it that's the nerve that's the muscle hi chi g spot
there just feel it moan for me" you want me to you say

"moanmoreforme" and I do down there where I have
fallensafely to an extent off the wire down under your
two taw eyes the weight of covers blankets
ceilings skies and there are words flying up words
wording myself from this
beginning from
this unworded beginning
this unworded beginning'

snail's trail
you make me as sweet and juicy
as a chewed stick of sugar cane
and you the kanaka with the machete
and the breath from your mouth
as sweet and sticky as syrup during the crushing
licking your molassas lips
white juice on your jaws

the tide must have risen and fallen
during the night
leaving silvery saltwash lacetrails
around my mouth and on my
fingers

'keep your creepy crawly squashy maggots—your ten
white curled fingers off me
keep your sticky honeyheart away from my hands
your lovecrumbs in my bed sugar on the floor chalk
and cheese grating across a blackboard' said Toto
(sometimes called Offensive Hair)
'watch the theatrics Toto they'll land you in trouble'
'the pleasure of you on my tongue' replied Offensive Hair
as the guy said as he went to the electric chair 'this is
the first time in my life I've got what I wanted'

'. . . too much meaning you place too much meaning
around sex fucking Toto' said Freda
'no it's just that I know you go crazy when you lose
access to a loving woman's loving body you'll see'

bereft stranded beached

image
a woman with her legs apart masturbating furiously
under floodlights in an empty stadium
image
a swamp being drained
image
you deliberately sopping up gravy with chunks of bread
image
you treadling determinedly and mechanically
on an old Singer sewing machine
the needle stabbing in and out of the material under
your keen eye
image
the mystery as tight as a pearl milked from me

realising you're just lazy
'you're just lazy Freda just a fucking lazy lover'
'yes I know—it's true—I am'
Toto masturbates
a voyeur rubs her breasts and belly

saying to herself
'it means too much
divest it
it means too much
divest it
it means too much
divest it'

oh I am bereft stranded beached
your body is sometimes
such a honeycomb
then
such a Canberra rock

I am suddenly
breaking
my
teeth
and
fall back
off you
humiliated

'we desire to be desired' says that bitch
Freda Peach 'chew me'
no stamina no straight answers
she whispered hoarsely 'chew me'

the oyster eaters
and
in my mouth full
my imagination and
imagining full of
a flesh flower

a fat marzipan rose
an intricate radish rose

a sex salad
a lucky muff diver
what a lucky licker
muff diver dyke
sportswoman chewer
glutton to some
you say
'you'll never have enough'
or
'you'd come at anything'

to be full of you
is to be full of myself
like a fat shadow

you fall asleep like a kid with a bellyful
apple cores and passionfruit skins
composting at the bottom of the bed

at the bottom of the bed
is where your head was

I found a tongue twister
engorged in the tuft of your muff
I stuffed

OK now you try it

a pleasure of a poem
a bliss on paper
you make me
wake
and waking me a mess
of white puff balls
exploding (poof)
into the blue mist of a dawn
(didIsaybluemistofadawn
ofcourse ohyes I meant
pinkskyoverthecity)

so crying so crying again
there at your feet
struggling beside you
with you know what
and so much of it too

and sometimes it's worth it
sometimes it clears away
everything clears and there you are
real in a real world
sometimes it is just suddenly so very there
so very me so very nice so very
scrunched up wound up sprung open
burst forth
sometimes it's so ohyes worth it all
all the straining after
hanging on
hanging in there
to explode white puff balls
handfuls of daddy christmas thistle
dandelion clocks
into a bluedawn of pinksky
is worth the effort uphill
after the carrot
and you
what about you then
you beaut
you beauty
choking out
you you you Tommy Gun
you you you April Fool
you you you Jack-be-Nimble
you you you Jack-in-the-Box

oh you castrate me fret me
you make me make out with myself
you make me lie wanting you
I wait for some sign
you are still
monolithic
(you are the golden phallus
the Easter Island statue)
it's such femfetish

you castrate me fret me
you tell me what to do with you
it was never like this before
you stop me
you start me
you make me wait for you to want me
(yet it was you who dreamt your two
front teeth were knocked out how come)

you say you don't understand when
I love you
say I love you and fuck you
you say the loving has nothing much
to do with the feeling fucking
you say I don't realise how violent
and degraded your sexuality is
I say it is this sexuality I have
handled for thirty years now
and it's this and your
saying this and then my love and running
between these three
that create the tension friction frustration
excitement orgasm in the end

my heart plops down sinker weight
like a lead moon
into dark water
plumbs depths and
jerks back into its pocket
locket on a chain

you are still
I am a moth batting a bulb
how we women can flap
around and around our desires
all night if necessary and wake
rampant jackbooted ugly
a terror in the office

you say you want me to just
fuck you poke and poke and poke
into you hard

and still waking wound around
our dawn bodies
'your dawn body' you said

and still we can play ping pong
all night with these contradictions
fears even a terror or two

and still we have danced and danced and
danced on glass on hot coals on booby-
trapped ground and come and come close
to coming and not come and it's still to come
done such juggling feats with a ball of bliss
a beanbagful of heartseedpeel
fingered and palmed down and balled so
much it's made a circus it's made us
make a circus of a night

what can be said—
only
pleasure leads us on
by the nose
pleasure brum brums our stomach
kicks the starter motor
is attached to the starter motor
is the starter motor
still
thirty years on
pleasure   erusaelp
pleasure   erusaelp
pleasure   erusaelp
and this is an everyday miracle of course
'and'
a conjunction
'and'
a word a bliss to say sometimes
'and'
a handful
'and'
a clenched hand
'and'
a cupped hand
'and'
a poofed breath

and p l e a s u r e

p l e a s u r e

'what a performance' said Freda Peach

I heard on last night's news that unexplained red
fireballs were reported hurtling at tremendous speed
across the Blue Mountains and I heard on this
morning's news that somewhere in America a woman
spontaneously combusted while crossing at the traffic
lights even her small change had melted together in
the intensity of the heat

I've lost my nerve
skiing across pages
my stomach turns at the thought
of the velocity

1989

DONALD FRIEND

From *Save Me from the Shark*

Colonel Blaring's kindness furnished me with strong recommendations
to his brother, the Governor of Shri Langka. More—he urged the
amiable Sir Launcelot to find me some harmless employment that would
leave leisure for painting. A post as manager of the Government
Experimental Plantation in the hills was available. I was glad of the
chance.

'Our last man there got amazing results from cross-pollinating papaiia
trees. Suicided in the end, poor chap. Took himself too seriously. The
bungalow is very comfortable. Wonderful view,' said Sir Launcelot at
luncheon. 'Does no good to believe all you hear about the place. A lot of
nonsense is talked.'

'What *was* it they were saying about it the other day?' wondered Lady
Blaring. 'Riots?—agitators?'

'Independence demonstrations,' said her son Gerald.

'Independence!—the poor dears don't know what they're letting
themselves in for. Look what happened to England when the Romans
marched out.'

'Look what happened when we kicked the Stuarts out!' I agreed
enthusiastically. Gerald kicked my ankle.

Sir Launcelot's eyes briefly sought the dull decency of George V's
likeness over the mantelpiece. 'H'm. Reminds me of our earlier talk.
Diplomatic usage.'

In a moment the Governor was well away on his favourite subject.
'. . . fascinating anomalies. No one has satisfactorily solved some of the
trickier ones that come up when dealing with modern royalty.

'Take an example. A princess of the House of Hanover takes leave of a Governor with the words *"See you later, Alligator"*. Now should he reply *"In a while, Crocodile"*, or "At your Highness's pleasure"? A Minister in this quandary must make a lightning appreciation of the delicate balance between royal wit and protocol. Dare he ignore the impish informality of the imperial "crocodile" for the conventional but tricky safety of "Highness"? Royalty has been so sparing of wit in the last two centuries that it does not care for its rare sallies to go unappreciated. The Minister must avoid dangerous temptations to be facetious. How fatal it might prove to his future career, for instance, were he to say, "Your Highness's humble alligator awaits the Royal Crocodile's pleasure". Royalty is touchy. Having tossed off its jest, it may be in no mood for further persiflage. Its temper is notoriously saurian.'

Brief acquaintance with this pleasant hospitable family (I had been their guest since my arrival on the island a few days previously), had inspired an admiration for their son, Gerald, a young man of my own age whose affection for his parents in no way mitigated a vein of mysticism strongly marked in his character, which they seemed at pains to pass over without recognition.

His devotion to the teachings of a Bulgarian *guru* — Swami Vladimir — had checked only a few months previously when the master, attended by Gerald, lay dying.

'Give me a word to light my path,' Gerald had implored the expiring sage.

'Go take a bucket of water. Stir till solid.'

These had been the Swami's last words: they pierced Gerald's heart with a thousand cutting doubts.

'Diplomatic usage suppresses the use of the first person singular to such a degree that in time a diplomat loses his sense of personal identity. He may come to confuse himself with national abstractions,' observed his Excellency, looking vaguely at smooth lawns and exultant bougainvillaea blazing beyond the windows.

'Selflessness — or humility — whatever it does for orientals, is not an ornament, let alone a virtue, of the English language. Nor of English thinking. Selfless English is unexceptionably dreary.

'*Mourn Ego no longer than the sullen surly bell*', he experimentally murmured.

Gerald looked amused. 'It's not so much Ego in prose style as Ego in itself that bothers my thoughts,' he said.

'I was afraid so, my boy.'

'Unselfish people seem so . . . so *unformed*,' said Lady Blaring.

This slow-moving quiet meal would have appeared peculiar to one unaccustomed to the eccentricities of the English.

Other guests who had been expected — Laura Lavere, Vivienne, Kosta and Tony — had not turned up: their yacht had put in to port the previous day.

'Laura is ageless,' remarked Sir Launcelot.

Gerald struck the odd note. No word took cognizance of his shaven head. And he wore the yellow robe of a Buddhist monk.

'Do you see much of your friend lately, the mystic philosopher?' asked Lady Blaring with oblique kindliness.

'You know he's dead, Mother,' Gerald answered.

The Experimental Plantation was seventy miles upcountry. I soon settled in to its routine. Hints, echoes of recent events, trembled on the cool air of the verdant hillsides. It was a lonely place. Time passed quietly, slowly, among dripping mists.

My predecessor had developed strains of vegetable carnivora. Witness to his skill was an acre of giant lilies that looked like beef-steaks. They ate frogs, and had to be fed twice daily. The coolies detested, were nervous of them. The whole place crawled with monstrous flora of freakish design, never an honest flower among them.

But it was the section devoted to giant papaiias that had led to major disturbances. Huge fruit had been developed to secrete concentrated pepsine, used commercially as a meat-softener.

Trouble followed the disappearance of a Departmental Inspector. The man had gone out alone one morning and was never seen again. Searchers discovered his false teeth, a zip-fastener and some small coins. It was believed that one of the heavy fruit had fallen on his head as he strolled through the plantation. It must have stunned and then digested him. The labourers, primitive superstitious folk, rioted and cut down the trees. The office staff barely escaped with their lives.

My new work largely concerned the proliferation of ant-eating orchids. High hopes centred on these attractive, mauve plants which had tremendous potential as a termite-exterminator.

Faint regrets for Hortense faded with new interests. My solitary situation in those dank and misty hills would not have aroused anyone's envy, yet loneliness acted as a stimulant to my painting.

I was not much dismayed by moans and bumps in the night emanating from the ghost of my predecessor, or perhaps from the tenderized inspector. Yet it was undeniably a melancholy place after dark. I worked till late by lamplight. Bundles of drawings remitted to London sold readily.

Things continued like this for months before I began to hunger for company. I began then to frequent the nearby village. I drove down in the evenings in the Department van, taking along a bottle of gin.

The inhabitants brought a table and chair for me and placed it beneath a huge tree in the heart of the settlement. They gathered there at the end of each day like a casual council or club, and discussed the affairs of their community with informal seriousness.

When they had got over their initial shyness I too was welcome to add a voice to their councils. They did not however respond at all to curiosity about events prior to my coming to work at the Plantation. Nor would they comment on references made to ghosts in my bungalow.

What most aroused their interest, was the peculiarity and interpretation of dreams.

As they became used to me and I began to separate personalities and appearances from the brown anonymous mass of grave faces, a gradual apperception took place of one who was seen but fleetingly on the periphery of shadows beyond our circle, who drifted occasionally and only momentarily into the light of dim lamps lit when the last daylight faded, one whose face evoked half-memory and a pang of desire.

I came to look forward to another glimpse, sustained a twinge of deprivation when a glance was not vouchsafed; it was as though I were becoming addicted to a pleasing narcotic whose source was not known, yet whose withdrawal inflicted the pain of deprivation. Once or twice our glances met. It was like a message thrown over a dark abyss: a disconnected word or two legible before it fluttered down into darkness eluding hopes of clarification.

It was the custom for anyone who had dreamed anything out of the ordinary to tell it to the informal council beneath the holy *waringin* tree at evening. Their corporate experience seldom failed to discover the significance of portents for the benefit of all.

The elders sensibly exploited this custom to confirm patriarchal authority. The dreamer, or sometimes the subject of a dream, was obliged to heed the findings of the interpretation, which was couched occasionally in terms of definite instruction.

Thus:

'The widow will travel on foot to Sailabimbaramaya temple and offer the priest there a bowl of milk-rice, a cucumber and a parcel of saffron dye. Then on her return home it will be seen she has ceased to covet her neighbour's cattle.'

And:

'The tailor should marry the virtuous but amenable woman in his dream. She is undoubtedly his landlord's daughter. The landlord will benefit in the gaining of a hardworking son-in-law if he and his family whitewash the neglected forefront of his house where it faces the bazaar.'

When a dream warned of danger to the community the whole village joined in prescribed activities to protect itself. Everyone gave something towards the expense of exorcist rituals, which were bizarre and costly, but apparently effectual.

The effect of the custom was admirable. It gave them unity and strength even in the secrets of their sleeping minds.

Their greatest fear was of witchcraft, a species of psychic anarchy that threatened their combined spiritual force. It was guarded against by punishments consisting of curses that could be lifted only by the working out of severe penances. Physical affliction was never resorted to.

The often-glimpsed but as yet never-completely-seen face had now grown into a force dominating my imagination.

In a Western environment where phenomena are subject to crude and matter-of-fact definitions, one would not be caught infatuatedly ogling a football coach under the fanciful supposition that he was a naiad of the rockpool.

However, in the orient, distinctions blur in the drifting smoke of dim lanterns and evening fires. Brown and lissom graces, liquid eyes and the smooth skins of both sexes lose the edges of difference. And so do attitudes of mind. And so do climates of emotion.

It came without surprise that the face I admired belonged to a youth of about nineteen years. Too wary to risk becoming a laughing-stock by pursuing him before all-too-observant eyes, my problem was to induce the council to make a gift of him. I knew enough of their ways to believe it possible.

Chance brought us face to face on a path in the plantation. The unexpectedness threw me into confusion. Then I saw what should have been clear before. He had a cast in one eye — too slight a displacement to add more than strangeness to the serious harmonies of his features, yet enough to splinter a perfection otherwise tediously regular. There is nothing more chilling to the sensitive admirer than the painful vacancy of perfected beauty. It is an ocean of emptiness.

We were both startled. We stared at one another on the path between ranks of botanical monstrosities. He averted his head shyly. The movement betrayed not only the chance displacement of his eyes but a curious resemblance to Hortense and to even yet another face from long ago on Thursday Island.

All this was seen in a second. He stood politely aside to let me pass.

'Were you looking for me?' I asked.

'I came with a message for one of the labourers.'

Then he walked on round a bend of the path out of sight. I stood undecided, then turned and quickly followed.

But beyond the turn of the track there was no one to be seen.

'You are well aware,' I told the village elders one night soon after, 'though you choose not to discuss with me, of the business of ghosts that disturb my house. However, I now appeal for your help in the matter of a dream that has been repeated for three nights running. It deals with serious questions I would like answered.'

'Command us, *Mahatmaya.*'

'I entreat the wisdom of your wisest men.'

'Speak on. Your words cause fruit to ripen.'

'In the dream I see this *waringin* tree. A great golden snake comes out of the tree. It is a God. It speaks to me. It says, "There is a person in the village whose eyes are crossed. Waking or sleeping, in laughter or tears, walking or sitting down, this person must tend your every need until the next full eclipse of the moon!"'

They listened at first in consternation, then in astonishment into which came relief, until at last a gale of joy and mutual congratulation swept over them. They laughed, they shouted, they embraced one another until as one man they turned on me and showered me with shared rejoicing.

'The God has spoken!' cried the headman. 'All is clear. Tomorrow it shall be arranged.'

Impatience ate up every moment until I went down to the village next evening. I found the atmosphere charged with jubilation. As I got out of the van, friendly hands seized, patted and caressed me, led me excitedly into the headman's house.

From then on helpless amusement rendered me unresisting to their ministrations. I found myself stripped of all my clothes, stood in a pottery tub and ritually—and a trifle embarrassingly—bathed in sweet-scented water. Soon clothes of the finest linen were draped on me: a gold sash, a silver dagger, turban of silk. I realized then that I was being clad in the gala raiment of a bridegroom.

Protest was impossible. It had gone too far. My hilarious astonishment pondered the incredible implications of their arch and bawdy remarks. Delighted laughter and affectionate—almost impertinent—familiarities of handling frankly advertised the amorous humour of my village friends. Such groping and goosing bordered on indecency.

I was a doll in their charge, arrayed in the community's goodwill, being prepared for a marriage ceremony with the handsome youth of my choice: the handsome youth, dismay struck chill with the realization, of a pretended dream.

I wondered under what dispensation of their flexible religion the ceremony would be sanctified. I had never had any indulgence for blasphemy in others. Too late to worry. An ecstacy of expectancy made me a too eager groom. I was rushed from one sensation to the next on the impetus of so much warmth, touched everywhere at once on my body by quick silky hands skilled in the play of swift caresses.

There had been no time to wonder what the Colonial Department of Agriculture might say about their employee's unusual nuptials. Still . . . odder couplings went on amongst the plants, did they not?—the noise immediately surrounding me chopped further thought into fragments.

The dishonesty implicit in the trick I had played on the villagers was the only bad patch. My sponsor, the headman, was urgently murmuring instructions on how to behave in the ensuing ceremony as I was brought out of the house to more jovial acclamations, laughter, dizzier noises. I was led to where two kitchen chairs, thrones for the occasion, were placed in the shade of the spreading tree. A canopy of scarlet cloth gave them dramatic importance.

A procession approached in the crowded street. Drums and tabors: urchins darting scattered petals. Showers of flowers exploded among fireworks drowning the piercing roulades of flute and clarinet, loud as the colours of the curtained litter borne towards me.

I stumbled to approach it. The curtains trembled, parted slightly. A pair of slim brown hands appeared, to be clasped in mine.

This moment, the moment when the elated groom joyously takes hands, drawing his betrothed to join him, is in essence the solemnization of the marriage.

From that there is no going back.

'Come out, fair one!—Come out, O rival of the moon: the bridegroom waits!' shouted the crowd.

'Come,' I said, thrilling at the feel of those hands, lying in mine quiescent—but ready, I knew, to grasp the wild abandonments of lovers' frenzies with a fevered response once we were in the darkened room of ardours and satiations.

'Come,' I repeated. 'Are you afraid to grasp at happiness?'

With an abrupt movement of decision and courage the curtains were shouldered aside, and the bride, hands still held firmly, emerged from the litter.

O God!—*who* the devil was this cross-eyed middle-aged hag?—and what right had *she* to weep?

The mob set no boundary to their expressions of mad exhilaration. Half-fainting with horror, I was carried beside that sobbing bundle of ugliness back to the chairs. She—the monstrous substitute for all my desires, whom I had never previously set eyes on—wept heartily as we sat there, a tearsodden cross-eyed lump, insultingly distressed.

All around the populace rowdily surged and pranced. Kneeling, they offered us platters of nauseous pink cakes crowned with marigolds. They plied us with sherbets dyed virulent green. Shock cut me off from the noise as though a sound-track had been severed, and the evening continued in silent horror as I estimated the consequences of my folly.

The misery of the next few years wonderfully benefited my art. Every wearisome domestic frustration, each day's despair, scarred my agonized canvases, brewed a black bile from my talent, sending ideas like carrion to tear the stained veils of appearance. As a result I came to be seriously esteemed in the art world. Critics respect above all a sourness of the spiritual breath, believing it to be the odour of tragic sincerity.

It shames me to look back on that time. The martyrdom I valued as the distinction of my own life was nothing to what I imposed on Veenah, my cross-eyed wife. She suffered, with what appeared to be loving devotion, my petulant and ungrateful demands. She tended the bruises and sore places on my ego. I had no pity to spare her. I conceded her the privilege to lavish attention on me, irritating as it was. The only gift I had for her was this boon—to see to my comfort. It was the best I could do. God knows it cost an effort. Of her patience under pain, of her noble endurance, I knew nothing until she was dead.

The end came without warning on the fourth anniversary of our wedding. I, who had counted the days like a man in gaol, had marked off the beginning of that day also. I was standing at my easel in the village square, at work on a canvas of the great *waringin* tree.

Evidently another wedding was in preparation, for although as yet there were few people, the scarlet wedding-litter with its white curtains stood in readiness beneath the tree, lighting the shadow with a flame of colour just where my picture needed it.

It was hot. The air was still. A light linen hat to which I was much attached protected my head from sunstroke. Veenah as usual stood by passing tubes of colour as I needed them.

'The blue.'

'The *cobalt* blue, clot. Will you never learn.'

A stirring filled the air. Before we knew what had happened a whirlwind swooped from the sky. It snatched my hat. It whisked it aloft and hooked it to a twig on the very apex of the *waringin* tree.

'Don't stand there like a ninny,' I told Veenah. 'Think of some way to get it down. You *know* I'll get a headache if I work without it.'

Without saying anything, she went to the tree and began climbing. Some people appeared to stare wordlessly. Halfway up she paused to rest on a big branch. We on-lookers saw the uncoiling of the great hamadryad, the King-cobra who embodied the God of the tree, saw him rear from his place and strike her on the breast.

'Fate,' the headman consoled. 'Today is the eclipse of the moon: the term of Veenah's penance.'

'Penance?'

'Her marriage to you. Do not sorrow. Think only she has completed the terrible punishment ordered by the God in your dream. The God has accepted the expiation of her crime and released her from further misery.'

'But what *was* her crime, that was so terrible?' I was more flabbergasted than griefstricken. Indeed, it would be hypocritical to describe my state of mind as more than '*seriously* inconvenienced'.

'When she was young,' said the headman, 'Veenah was the prettiest girl in our village, though there was a cast in her eye, a small fault then that later became exaggerated.

'Your predecessor at the Experimental Farm fell under her spell. He loved her to distraction. She was his mistress for years. He never noticed her growing ugliness. His passion continued until he destroyed himself on her account. That was after she had grown weary of him and was herself the victim of a consuming unrequited passion for the Departmental Inspector who was a regular guest at the bungalow.

'One day, she waylaid the Inspector in the plantation. She confessed her infatuation. He thought it a great joke and laughed brutally at her, turned from her and walked away. In blind rage she picked up a stake and struck him on the head. This was witnessed—every leaf has eyes here—by a labourer, who saw her drag the unconscious Inspector to a giant papaiia tree. The labourer fled in terror and for fear of blame said nothing to our village council until the next day. Then it was too late.'

'But that was *murder*!—nobody warned me. I might have been killed myself!'

'You were quite safe,' said the headman. 'You see, you were her penance. The God chose you in a dream. Have you not thought, that *you* might be part of one of *our* dreams?'

At Government House, the Blarings were forbearing.

It was Gerald who insisted I stayed with them again until I shipped home. Gerald's erstwhile shaven skull now flowed with curly locks. He no longer wore the yellow robe, yet looked more charmingly ascetic than ever. He asked no questions but in the end I told him everything.

'That sort of thing—it might be what the teacher meant when he said "*Stir till solid*"?—or perhaps not,' he mused.

Lady Blaring's tact and kindliness cast me as someone who'd been very very sick for a long time with an ailment not nicely mentioned. In convalescence it was no longer catching.

'One has heard such encouraging things about your termite-exterminating orchids,' she said.

She did however add, 'This climate does not suit everybody.'

'So you're leaving us. Well, well,' remarked his Excellency. 'I daresay there'll be a war soon. That man Hitler.'

'Quite a boon. They attacked the Chippendale escritoire last week. *Chinoiserie* is so prone, alas.'

'Who are you talking about, dear?' She ignored him, fearing to lose her trend.

'Nasty creatures. So *clever* really. They send a spy first to sniff out the land. If it's all right they're all there in a trice, creeping soundlessly. Before you know anything, thousands are munching away.'

'Mother!'

'. . . Poor Lettice Loveday, a goose of a woman, left her reticule on the verandah. Next day they'd eaten a hole in the bottom and were all sitting inside, calm as you please, chewing her lipstick!'

'I insist on being told who these people are.'

Lady Blaring gave her husband a look of affectionate patience.

'Mr Hughes's orchids, Launcelot. You should pay more attention. They will benefit mankind. Science can be a wonderful thing when put to proper use.

'You may think me fanciful, Mr Hughes,' she smiled at me, 'yet who knows?—when they have disposed of the termite problem, your orchids might develop a taste for the death-watch beetle!—Herbert writes they've caused *havoc* at Blaring. Anne Boleyn's bed was found to be infested. They gave the Bishop of Ely a sleepless night, poor man.'

Accompanying me to the ship, Gerald said 'I wonder if you understand the gist of Mother's meanderings? She seldom makes a direct point. She hesitated to warn you. She fears you might develop like Charteris, who once married Hortense. They were both a bit too much for one another. Nowadays he flits about Asia a few steps ahead of his misdeeds, poor fellow.'

'I'd like to meet him some day.'

'Not if you take Mother's advice.'

We said goodbye on the wharf.

1973

Initiating

The first approach, the first realisation, the first seduction, the first sense of moving into another world—these are memorably exciting, and occasionally fetishised, events in any homosexual narrative.

For some—particularly writers from an older generation—initiation is often connected with an institution of some kind: the single-sex school (for example, in Elizabeth Jolley's novel *Miss Peabody's Inheritance*), the army (in the stories by David Malouf and Sumner Locke Elliott) or prison. For others (in this selection Kate Walker, Henry Handel Richardson and Dennis Altman) the excitement lies less in a ritual of seduction than in a switch in self-awareness, the growing pressure to explore other sexual identities apart from the one our culture takes for granted.

In both kinds of writing initiation may be welcomed or resisted, overt or disguised, sudden or gradual, erotic or simply confusing. It can range from brutal rape (in *Zimmer's Essay*, for example, elsewhere in this collection) to sensuous wonderment (in Dorothy Porter's poem 'Sauce'). Someone in a position of power may take pleasure in initiating someone in a weaker position (as in Frank Moorhouse's classic, and still shocking, novella *The Everlasting Secret Family*) or, in more contemporary writing, a young man or woman may virtually take the matter into his or her own hands and initiate the initiation, as it were. Kate Walker's remarkable novel for teenage readers (and their parents) *Peter*, takes this modern, self-determining approach. Whatever form initiation takes, however—ritualised, coy, romantic, violent—it remains one of the most central themes in Australian homosexual writing.

Henry Handel Richardson

Two Hanged Women

Hand in hand the youthful lovers sauntered along the esplanade. It was a night in midsummer; a wispy moon had set, and the stars glittered. The dark mass of the sea, at flood, lay tranquil, slothfully lapping the shingle.

'Come on, let's make for the usual,' said the boy.

But on nearing their favourite seat they found it occupied. In the velvety shade of the overhanging sea-wall, the outlines of two figures were visible.

'Oh blast!' said the lad. 'That's torn it. What now, Baby?'

'Why, let's stop here, Pincher, right close up, till we frighten 'em off.'

And very soon loud, smacking kisses, amatory pinches and ticklings, and skittish squeals of pleasure did their work. Silently the intruders rose and moved away.

But the boy stood gaping after them, open-mouthed.

'Well, I'm *damned!* If it wasn't just two hanged women!'

Retreating before a salvo of derisive laughter, the elder of the girls said: 'We'll go out on the breakwater.' She was tall and thin, and walked with a long stride.

Her companion, shorter than she by a bobbed head of straight flaxen hair, was hard put to it to keep pace. As she pegged along she said doubtfully, as if in self-excuse: 'Though I really ought to go home. It's getting late. Mother will be angry.'

They walked with finger-tips lightly in contact; and at her words she felt what was like an attempt to get free, on the part of the fingers crooked in hers. But she was prepared for this, and held fast, gradually working her own up till she had a good half of the other hand in her grip.

For a moment neither spoke. Then, in a low, muffled voice, came the question: 'Was she angry last night, too?'

The little fair girl's reply had an unlooked-for vehemence. 'You know she wasn't!' And, mildly despairing: 'But you never *will* understand. Oh, what's the good of . . . of anything!'

And on sitting down she let the prisoned hand go, even putting it from her with a kind of push. There it lay, palm upwards, the fingers still curved from her hold, looking like a thing with a separate life of its own; but a life that was ebbing.

On this remote seat, with their backs turned on lovers, lights, the town, the two girls sat and gazed wordlessly at the dark sea, over which great Jupiter was flinging a thin gold line. There was no sound but the lapping, sucking, sighing, of the ripples at the edge of the breakwater, and the occasional screech of an owl in the tall trees on the hillside.

But after a time, having stolen more than one side-glance at her companion, the younger seemed to take heart of grace. With a childish toss of the head that set her loose hair swaying, she said, in a tone of meaning emphasis: 'I like Fred.'

The only answer was a faint, contemptuous shrug.

'I tell you I *like* him!'

'Fred? Rats!'

'No it isn't ... that's just where you're wrong, Betty. But you think you're so wise. Always.'

'I know what I know.'

'Or imagine you do! But it doesn't matter. Nothing you can say makes any difference. I like him, and always shall. In heaps of ways. He's so big and strong, for one thing: it gives you such a safe sort of feeling to be with him ... as if nothing could happen while you were. Yes, it's ... it's ... well, I can't help it, Betty, there's something *comfy* in having a boy to go about with—like other girls do. One they'd eat their hats to get, too! I can see it in their eyes when we pass; Fred with his great long legs and broad shoulders—I don't nearly come up to them—and his blue eyes with the black lashes, and his shiny black hair. And I like his tweeds, the Harris smell of them, and his dirty old pipe, and the way he shows his teeth—he's got *topping* teeth—when he laughs and says 'ra-*ther!*' And other people, when they see us, look ... well I don't quite know how to say it, but they look sort of pleased; and they make room for us and let us into the dark corner-seats at the pictures, just as if we'd a right to them. And they never laugh. (Oh, I can't *stick* being laughed at!—and that's the truth.) Yes, it's so comfy, Betty darling ... such a warm cosy comfy feeling. Oh, *won't* you understand?'

'Gawd! why not make a song of it?' But a moment later, very fiercely: 'And who is it's taught you to think all this? Who's hinted it and suggested it till you've come to believe it? ... believe it's what you really feel.'

'She hasn't! Mother's never said a word ... about Fred.'

'Words?—why waste words? ... when she can do it with a cock of the eye. For your Fred, that!' and the girl called Betty held her fingers aloft and snapped them viciously. 'But your mother's a different proposition.'

'I think you're simply horrid.'

To this there was no reply.

'*Why* have you such a down on her? What's she ever done to you? ... except not get ratty when I stay out late with Fred. And I don't see how you can expect ... being what she is ... and with nobody but me—after all she *is* my mother ... you can't alter that. I know very well—and you know, too—I'm not *too* putrid-looking. But'—beseechingly—'I'm *nearly* twenty-five now, Betty. And other girls ... well, she sees them, every one of them, with a boy of their own, even though they're ugly, or fat, or have legs like sausages—they've only got to ogle them a bit—the girls, I mean ... and there they are. And Fred's a good sort—he is, really!—and he dances well, and doesn't drink, and so ... so why *shouldn't* I like him?

... and off my own bat ... without it having to be all Mother's fault, and me nothing but a parrot, and without any will of my own?'

'Why? Because I know her too well, my child! I can read her as you'd never dare to ... even if you could. She's sly, your mother is, so sly there's no coming to grips with her ... one might as well try to fill one's hand with cobwebs. But she's got a hold on you, a stranglehold, that nothing'll loosen. Oh! mothers aren't fair—I mean it's not fair of nature to weigh us down with them and yet expect us to be our own true selves. The handicap's too great. All those months, when the same blood's running through two sets of veins—there's no getting away from that, ever after. Take yours. As I say, does she need to open her mouth? Not she! She's only got to let it hang at the corners, and you reek, you drip with guilt.'

Something in these words seemed to sting the younger girl. She hit back. 'I know what it is, you're jealous, that's what you are! ... and you've no other way of letting it out. But I tell you this. If ever I marry—yes, *marry!*—it'll be to please myself, and nobody else. Can you imagine me doing it to oblige her?'

Again silence.

'If I only think what it would be like to be fixed up and settled, and able to live in peace, without this eternal dragging two ways ... just as if I was being torn in half. And see Mother smiling and happy again, like she used to be. Between the two of you I'm nothing but a punch-ball. Oh, I'm fed up with it! ... fed up to the neck. As for you ... And yet you can sit there as if you were made of stone! Why don't you *say* something? *Betty!* Why won't you speak?'

But no words came.

'I can *feel* you sneering. And when you sneer I hate you more than any one on earth. If only I'd never seen you!'

'Marry your Fred, and you'll never need to again.'

'I will, too! I'll marry him, and have a proper wedding like other girls, with a veil and bridesmaids and bushels of flowers. And I'll live in a house of my own, where I can do as I like, and be left in peace, and there'll be no one to badger and bully me—Fred wouldn't ... ever! Besides, he'll be away all day. And when he came back at night, he'd ... I'd ... I mean I'd——' But here the flying words gave out; there came a stormy breath and a cry of: 'Oh, Betty, Betty! ... I couldn't, no, I couldn't! It's when I think of *that* ... Yes, it's quite true! I like him all right, I do indeed, but only as long as he doesn't come too near. If he even sits too close, I have to screw myself up to bear it'—and flinging herself down over her companion's lap, she hid her face. 'And if he tries to touch me, Betty, or even takes my arm or puts his round me ... And then his face ... when it looks like it does sometimes ... all wrong ...as if it had gone all wrong—oh! then I feel I shall have to scream—out loud. I'm afraid of him ... when he looks like that. Once ... when he kissed me ... I could have died with the horror of it. His breath ... his breath ... and his mouth—like fruit pulp—and the black hairs on his wrists ... and the way he looked—and ... and everything! No, I can't, I can't ... nothing will make me ... I'd rather die twice over. But what am I to do? Mother'll *never* understand. Oh, why has it got to be like this? I want to be happy, like other girls, and to make her happy, too ... and everything's all wrong. You tell me, Betty darling, you help me, you're older ... you *know* ... and you can help me, if you will ... if you only will!' And locking her arms round her friend she drove her face deeper into the warmth and darkness, as if, from the very fervour of her clasp, she could draw the aid and strength she needed.

Betty had sat silent, unyielding, her sole movement being to loosen her own arms from her sides and point her elbows outwards, to hinder them touching the arms that lay round her. But at this last appeal she melted; and gathering the young girl to her breast, she held her fast.—And so for long she continued to sit, her chin resting lightly on the fair hair, that was silky and downy as an infant's, and gazing with sombre eyes over the stealthily heaving sea.

1934

The Wrong Turning

The way he helped her into the boat was delicious, simply delicious: it made her feel like a grown-up lady to be taken so much care of—usually, people didn't mind how you got in and out of things, as you were only thirteen. And before he let her step off the landing he took her strap of books from her—those wretched schoolbooks, which stamped her, but which she hadn't known how to get rid of: her one chance of going for a row was secretly, on her way home from school. But he seemed to understand, without being told, how she despised them, and he put them somewhere in the boat where they wouldn't get wet, and yet she didn't need to see them. (She wondered what he had done with his own.)

He was so *nice*; everything about him was nice: his velvety brown eyes and white teeth; his pink cheeks and fair hair. And when he took his coat off and sat down, and rolled up his sleeves and spanned his wrists on the oars, she liked him better still: he looked so strong ... almost as if he could have picked the boat up and carried it. He wasn't at all forward either (she hated cheeky boys:) when he had to touch her hand he went brick red, and jumped his own hand away as quick as he could.

With one stroke they were off and gliding downstream ... oh, so smoothly! It made her think of floating in milk ... though the water was *really* brown and muddy-looking. Soon they would be quite away from the houses and the little back-gardens and allotments that ran down to the water, and out among the woods, where the river twisted like a snake, and the trees hung over the edge and dipped their branches in ... most romantically. Then perhaps he would say something. He hadn't spoken yet; he was too busy rowing, making great sweeps with the oars, and not looking at her ... or only taking a peep now and then, to see if she saw. Which she did, and her heart thumped with pleasure. Perhaps, as he was so clever at it, he'd be a sailor when he was a man and go to sea. But that would mean him travelling far away, and she might never see him again. And though she'd only known him for a fortnight, and at first he hadn't liked to speak, but had just stood and made eyes at her when they met going home from school, she felt she simply couldn't bear it if he did.

To hide her feelings, she hung one hand over the side of the boat and let it trail through the water—keeping it there long after it was stone cold, in the hope that he would notice it and say something. But he didn't.

The Boy was thinking: I wonder if I dare tell her not to ... her little hand ... all wet like that, and cold. I should like to take it in both mine, and rub it dry, and warm it. *How* pretty she is, with all that fuzzy-wuzzy hair, and the little curls on her forehead. And how long her eyelashes are when she looks down. I wish I could make her look up ... look at me. But how? Why, say something, of course. But what? Oh, if *only* I could think of something! What does one? What would Jim say, if he wanted to make his girl look at him?

But nothing came.

Here, however, the hand was jerked from the water to kill a gnat that had settled on the other.

This was his cue. He parted hastily with his saliva.

'I say! Did it sting?'

She suppressed the no that was on her lips. 'Well ... yes ... I think it did, rather.' And doubling her bony little schoolgirl fingers into her palm, she held out the back of the hand for his inspection.

Steadying the oars, the Boy leant forward to look, leant so far that, for a wild moment, she believed he was going to kiss the place, and half instinctively, half from an equally strong impulse to 'play him,' drew it away. But he did not follow it up: at the thought of a kiss, which *had* occurred to him, shyness lamed him anew. So nothing came of this either.

And we've only half an hour, thought the Girl distractedly. If he doesn't say something ... soon ... there won't be any time left. And then it will all have been for nothing.

She, too, beat her brains. 'The trees ... aren't they pretty?—the way they hang right down in the water.' (Other couples stopped under these trees, she'd seen them, and lay there in their boats; or even went right in behind the weeping willows.)

But his sole response was: 'Good enough.' And another block followed.

Oh, he saw quite well what she was aiming at: she wanted him to pull in to the bank and ship his oars, so that they could do a bit of spooning, she lying lazy in the stern. But at the picture a mild panic seized him.

For, if he couldn't find anything to say even when he was rowing, it would be ten times harder when he sat with his hands before him and nothing to do. His tongue would stick to the roof of his mouth, dry as a bone, and then she'd see for sure how dull he was. And never want to go out with him again. No, thank you, not for him!

But talk wasn't everything — by gum, it wasn't! He might be a rotten hand at speechifying, but what he could *do*, that he'd jolly well show her! And under this urge to display his strength, his skill, he now fell to work in earnest. Forward swung the oars, cleanly carving the water, or lightly feathering the surface; on flew the boat, he driving to and fro with his jaws grimly set and a heightened colour, the muscles standing out like pencils on his arms. Oh, it was a fine thing to be able to row so well, and have a girl, *the* girl, sitting watching you. For now her eyes hung on him, mutely adoring, spurring him on to ever bolder strokes.

And then a sheerly dreadful thing happened. So lost was he in showing his mastery, in feeding on her looks, that he failed to keep his wits about him. And, coming to a place where the river forked, he took the wrong turning, and before he knew it they were in a part where you were not supposed to go — a bathing-place for men, much frequented by soldiers.

A squeal from the Girl roused him; but then it was too late: they had shot in among a score of bathers, whose heads bobbed about on the surface like so many floating footballs. And instantly her shrill cry was taken up and echoed and re-echoed by shouts, and laughter, and rude hullos, as the swimmers scattered before the oars. Coarse jokes were bandied, too, at the unwarranted intrusion. Hi! wasn't there nowhere else he could take his girl? Or was she coming in, too? Off with her togs then!

Crimson with mortification at his blunder, at the fool he had made of himself (before her), the Boy savagely strove to turn the boat and escape. But the heads — there seemed to be hundreds of them — deliberately blocked his way. And while he manœuvred, the sweat trickling down his forehead, a pair of arms and shoulders reared themselves from the water, and two hands grasped the side of the boat. It rocked; and the Girl squealed anew, shrinking sideways from the nearness of the dripping, sunburnt flesh.

'Come on, missie, pay toll!'

The Boy swore aloud.

But even worse was to come. On one bank, a square of wooden palisades had been built out round a stretch of water and a wooden bath-house, where there were cabins for the men to strip in, platforms to jump from, ropes strung for those who could not swim. But in this fence was a great gap, where some of the palings had fallen down. And in his rage and confusion the Boy had the misfortune to bring the boat right alongside it; and then ... then. ... Inside the enclosure, out of the cabins, down the steps, men were running, jumping, chasing, leap-frogging ... every one of them as naked as on the day he was born.

For one instant the Girl raised her eyes—one only ... but it was enough. She saw. And he saw that she saw.

And now, to these two young creatures, it seemed as if the whole visible world—themselves, boat, river, trees and sky—caught fire, and blazed up in one gigantic blush. Nothing existed for them any more but this burning redness. Nor could they escape; there they had to sit, knee to knee, face to face, and scorch, and suffocate; the blood filling their eyes till they could scarcely see, mounting to their hair-roots, making even their finger-tips throb and tingle.

Gritting his teeth, the Boy rowed like a machine that had been wound up and was not to be stopped. The Girl sat with drooped head—it seemed to have grown strangely heavy—and but a single wish: to get out and away ... where he could not see her. For all was over between them—both felt that. Something catastrophic had happened, rudely shattering their frail young dreams; breaking down his boyish privacy, pitching her headlong into a reality for which she was in no wise prepared.

If it had been hard beforehand to find things to say, it was now impossible. And on the way home no sound was to be heard but the dip of the oars, the water's cluck and gurgle round the boat. At the landing-place, she got out by herself, took from him, without looking up, her strap of books, and said a brief good-bye; keeping to a walking pace till she had turned the corner, then breaking into a run, and running for dear life ... as if chased by some grotesque nightmare-shape which she must leave far, far behind her ... even in thought.

1934

DOROTHY PORTER

Sauce

My love said to me
'Now I know what
a woman tastes like'

she prowled over
to me like a queen
temple cat

'the sea'

I ran my knuckles
slowly down her face
my naughty
my sauce-for-the-goose
Nefertiti

I asked her what they'd
talked about

'Our children!'

Did she recognise you?

'No. And she faked
an orgasm for me.
Very touching
she made so much noise!'

Did you come?

'Oh, she would have
made Osiris come!'

What did she do to you?

'She stroked me with ebony
she sucked me like an oyster
so professional.'

Then my wife
with her white hands
drew for me
in the air
the room
and the whore's ornaments.

Did she get many women clients?

Nefertiti laughed.

'I was her first.'

1992

KATE WALKER

From *Peter*

Friday

David was holding me up so I wouldn't fall off the stool. He pulled a wad
of tissues from the box on the bench, wet them under the tap, and held
them against my forehead, really gently. I was as hot as fire and the
tissues were icy.

'You're sure you don't feel sick?' he asked.

I'd made myself look idiotic enough for one day; I was too afraid to
talk in case I cried. When he took the tissues away to wet them again,

my head fell forward and touched his chest. He didn't push me away. He let me lean there.

'Are you *sure* you're all right?'

He stroked my hair, touching the back of my neck with his fingers now and then. It was the nicest thing anyone had ever done for me. And the softest. He cared—that I might be hurt, that I might fall off the stool.

He put his arm around my shoulders. I put my arms around him and hugged him, pressed my face against his chest and listened to his heartbeat through his shirt.

It was like coming home, like finding the place you've always wanted to be, and I could have stayed there forever holding on to him.

Except I heard Mrs Minslow gasp, 'Oh, my God!' and felt David tighten. Slowly he pushed me away. She stood in the doorway, X-raying us with her eyes. Vince must have told her we were there.

David said calmly, 'Now you're here, Mrs Minslow, I'll leave him with you.' He pressed one of my hands on the edge of the bench, giving me something to hold on to.

She stumbled back to let him out the door, watched him go, then shuffled back in.

'What's he done to you?' Her hands raced at me. 'I warned your mother about him.'

Things flew off the bench—trays, tongs, plastic bottles. And someone—I think it was me—was yelling the same thing over and over: 'You fuckin' old bitch! You fuckin' old bitch!'

She disappeared, and I knew where to. She was going to tell the world everything she'd seen. And everyone would believe her.

David's car was gone, the drive was empty, and I didn't want to be there any more either.

My bike made so much racket under the garage ceiling that I was sure it was going to bring the whole house crashing down on top of me.

I roared down Valley View. The houses were a blur. The wind whipped my hair into my eyes, making them sting. *No helmet, see.*

At the intersection, I crossed the highway against the lights. Horns blared. I roared up the embankment on the other side and down into the Westfield bush.

It closed over me. I found a trail and followed it through brown scrub. Where it went, I went, past dead cars on their lids, past split garbage bags, down gullies, up hills. I didn't watch my gas gauge or my speedo. I just rode, getting faster all the time.

I won't say I went there to wipe myself out purposely, but on my millionth gully, not a particularly steep one, the front wheel slid from under me, the bike went over, and I went down. No earthquake, no crash: just me and the bike, rattling down the slope, skating over stones. No great pain either, just a sick feeling of being out of control, and my shirt tearing up my back. *Mum's gunna kill me*, I thought. Stupid, isn't it, the things you think of?

Halfway down we slid to a halt under this huge leaning gum tree, and I thought: a place to rest, finally! The bush was quiet, the bike was dead, the only thing to annoy me was bits of gravel trickling into my collar. I could close my eyes and go to sleep.

I smelt the burning before I felt it. There was a split second's difference, and I sat up screaming. The bike was on my leg and the exhaust was burning its way through my jeans. I saw pain in fifteen different colours. Kicked the bike seat, kicked the petrol tank. Started moving again, slithering down the slope with the bike. Eventually it came off me, skinning my ankle as it went. *No boots either.*

I wasn't in the shade any more and my leg felt like someone was holding a blowtorch against it. I wrapped my arms around it and hugged it without actually touching it, rocked back and forth, listening to myself taking huge breaths.

Under the circumstances, anyone would have cried. I didn't bawl, just soaked the knees of my jeans. Why not? I was scratched, burnt, my bike was probably a write-off, and I was probably gay. A girl had kissed me and I'd pushed her away, but a bloke had stroked my hair, and I'd melted all over him. I could have ridden round for a week and never got away from that one.

The boys had seen it. Vince had seen it. I was the only dumb bunny who'd taken fifteen years to notice.

So what did I do now?

Leave school. Leave home. I couldn't stay. Mum'd have a field day trying out her fancy counselling on me. Vince'd think it was hilarious. And when my father tracked me down, he'd murder me for being a 'failed' man.

You did this to me, you bastards! I don't know who I was throwing stones at. Anyone. David. He'd seen it in me from the start, that's why he hadn't pushed me away.

He knew I was like him.

Peak hour traffic was six lanes thick along the highway when I finally got out of the bush. The patrol cars were out in force with their big white eyes, and I had to walk the bike home, two kilometres along the verge.

There was nowhere to go but home.

Dad's car was parked out the front. Mum's car wasn't in the garage when I wheeled the bike in, but she was, at the bottom of the stairs, wearing a crushed uniform and a face like poured concrete.

'Leave that there,' she said, meaning the bike, expecting me to drop it on the floor.

She does this when we hurt ourselves, goes into super-efficient nursing mode. I must have looked a mess, limping in with my shirt in pieces.

Dad stomped down the stairs in his bare legs. He'd come straight from Life Savers and was wearing only Speedos and a sweatshirt. He took the bike from me.

'And he's never to get on it again,' Mum said, pushing me up the stairs ahead of her. 'Get rid of it.' It was Dad who had bought the bike for me. In the bathroom she pushed me down on to the edge of the bath and checked the lump on my head. So she knew about the fight.

'Have you been sick?' she asked.

'I'm fine,' I said, shocked that my voice sounded normal. I didn't *feel* normal. I felt I'd come home a stranger.

'I'm not asking you how you are!' she snapped. 'Have you been vomiting?'

'No.'

She pushed my head back and peeled my eyelids open. Dirt fell out of my hair, spattering into the bath behind me. Staring into my eyes seemed to convince her that I wasn't dead, and after that she settled down a bit.

'Where else have you hurt yourself?' she asked.

I avoided looking at her. 'I burnt my leg,' I said.

I started to roll up my jeans.

'Leave it,' she said. 'I'll do that.' She cut away my jeans with a pair of scissors, and didn't bat an eyelid at the sight of the burn. It made my stomach heave. It was raw meat with pukey white wrinkles. She ran water in the handbasin and fussed around, getting out creams and stuff.

Vince couldn't have been home, otherwise he'd have been there: *Only one leg, Ace? Not really trying?*

Dad appeared, plugging up the doorway with his bulk. His bright red Speedos peeked from under his sweatshirt and when he raised his hand to grasp the back of his neck I thought: *He knows, and he's going to kill me.*

'All right, son, what happened?'

Good God, I was still his son?

'Not now, Bob,' Mum said.

'I pranged the bike,' I told him.

'I said, not now!'

Dad stepped closer. The smallest room in the house, and he had me trapped in it. 'Mrs Minslow told us what happened.' *I knew she would.* 'She said he had his arms around you.'

Mum was kneeling on the tiles in front of me. 'This is going to hurt,' she said, and it did. The cottonwool she used to clean around the burn could have doubled as sandpaper.

'I want to know what he did,' Dad said.

They were blaming David, not me. The coward in me almost cried with relief.

'He didn't do anything,' I said, feeble as a plucked chicken.

'You knew he was a bloody poof?'

I nodded.

'Why'd you let him touch you?'

'He was helping me,' I said. 'I couldn't stand up. I'd have fallen over.'

'He was helping his bloody self. Mrs Minslow saw him. She said he had his hands all over you.'

'Don't bully him, Bob,' Mum said.

'Why'd you take off on your bike like you did, without your helmet?'

'I must have forgot,' I mumbled.

'It's not like you to forget. Why'd you swear at Mrs Minslow?'

'I didn't swear at her.' I couldn't think fast enough to do anything but deny whatever he threw at me.

'She said you did.'

'Why do we have to have her in the house?' I said. 'I hate her. She's a rotten old busybody.'

'Thank God she was here,' Dad said. 'Lord only knows what that pervert would have done to you.'

'Bob! Peter told you, nothing happened!' Mum said. 'Don't you believe him?'

'The way you've raised these boys, they wouldn't know if they'd been molested or not. You've taught them nothing.'

She's taught us everything: what to do in case of stranger danger! ringworm! shark attack!

'Can't you see he's hurt? He doesn't need you bellowing at him!' She was the one bellowing now.

'A few scratches? You're carrying on about a few scratches when that mongrel could have given him AIDS! You let him into this house! You put your own son at risk!'

Vince's voice sounded ridiculous as he came into the room, it was so calm. 'I see you found him.'

Dad spun around. 'And where have you been?'

'Looking for him,' Vince said. 'How is he?'

'He'll be fine when your father leaves,' Mum said.

'I'll be leaving soon,' Dad said. 'Where is he?'

'Who?' Vince asked.

'You're sicko mate.'

'If you mean David, he's at home.'

'Good. You know he was caught trying to molest your brother?'

Vince knew everything. 'Yes, I heard the highly colourful Minslow version,' he said.

'He had his arms around him. Cuddling him,' Dad said. 'That doesn't need too much colouring in.'

'David wouldn't molest Peter,' Vince said. 'He wouldn't molest anyone.'

'How do you know?'

'I know him. He wouldn't do it. It's not his style.'

'And what is his style?'

'If he's interested, he asks,' Vince said.

'How do you know? Has he ever asked you?'

'That's my business,' Vince said.

'Ha! D'you hear that, Lynn?' Dad laughed. 'He's tried it on with Vince as well.'

'He didn't *try it on*,' Vince said. 'He didn't know if I was gay or not when he first met me, so he asked. I told him it wasn't my thing, and that was that. He's never asked again.'

'You mean he put the hard word on you months ago and you're still knocking round with him?'

'Yeah, why shouldn't I? He's a nice bloke, I like him. He's got a right to ask. Everyone's got a right to ask. You do, don't you?'

'Not blokes!' Dad said.

'That's your affair,' Vince said. 'David's choice of partners is up to him.'

'Not when he tries it on with Peter.'

'He didn't try anything, Dad,' I said.

'He would have if he'd had the bloody chance. But he won't get it again.'

'Bob, where are you going?' Mum stood up.

'If you go down there and accuse David Rutherford of sexual assault,' Vince said, 'his parents will sue you.'

'I'm not gunna bother accusing him,' Dad said. 'I'm gunna wring his bloody neck.'

'And what if one of your own sons was gay?' Mum said. 'Would you wring his neck too?'

Mum, don't tell him!

'You'd love to throw that one in my face, wouldn't you, Lynn?'

'I'm asking you, Bob, what would you do?'

'Get him away from you for a start,' Dad said. 'And help him get over it. Tell him what's what! Tell him exactly what's expected of him. Get him into sports. Healthy exercise. All the things you haven't done for these boys.'

'What about accepting him as he was?' Mum said. 'Couldn't you love him simply because he was your son?'

'No, a man shouldn't have to accept that, being made a laughing stock by his own children. A man shouldn't have to accept that. And that sicko's father down there should have fixed *him* long ago, and not left it for someone else to do.'

'If you hurt that boy, neither of your sons will ever speak to you again,' Mum said.

'That'd be no great loss with him,' Dad said. He waved a paw at Vince. 'You can have him. You've ruined him. At least this one's still got some feeling for his father.' He reached for my shoulder and I nearly fell in the bath. I didn't mean to pull away. It's just that he's so big, and whatever he was thinking of doing to David, he'd do a thousand times worse to me, because I was his son and I'd let him down.

'I think I'm gunna throw up!' I said.

Everyone scattered, except Mum. She held on to me while I heaved into the bath.

Saturday

On Saturday Mum cooked cakes and biscuits, all the stuff we've missed out on with her being a working mum.

I stayed in bed mostly, and acted sick. She'd come and sit on my bed and act concerned about my head.

'How are you feeling now, honey?' she'd ask, and I'd say, 'OK.'

Possibly she'd guessed what was worrying me and wanted me to talk about it. Much as I loved her, I couldn't. Not my mother, not about this.

We talked about Dad. 'You know your father loves you,' she said.

'I don't think so.'

'He does, honey. That's why he was so unreasonable last night. He thought you'd been . . .' She cornered herself there, but didn't try to get out of it. 'You know what he thought.'

'He was only worried about himself,' I said, 'and what his friends would say.'

'I hope you don't believe that.'

'Well, it was part of it,' I said. 'A big part.'

'I know your father can be overbearing at times, but he's still your father. Don't turn your back on him. It's not your place to make judgements about him. He'd never turn his back on you. Look at him and Vince—they don't always see eye to eye, but your father's never withdrawn his support from Vince.'

Dad pays Vince's way through law school. And if that was supposed to convince me I could tell my father I was gay and live through the experience, it didn't.

I know Mum was trying to help, but after that I pretended to be asleep whenever I heard her coming. It was easier on both of us.

Monday

On Monday I caught a bus into town. I took my Building Society passbook with me, and toyed with the idea of never coming back. But just being on the bus was good enough. It gave me a direction, a place to go.

Town was packed: perfect. It meant I was able to walk around, just one of the crowd. It also meant I could check *them* out without being noticed.

Tony told me once that poofters wear blue socks. I don't know who's the bigger dickhead, him for coming up with such a lamebrain idea, or me for actually believing it. Half the blokes in the world wear blue socks!

Maybe there was no one hundred per cent certain way of telling if someone was gay.

Then I saw this young bloke come out of a record shop, and he was as camp as they come. You'd have picked it three blocks away, just from the way he walked—kind of wiggling his bum. He was only about my age, too. Did I walk like that and not know it? If I did, all the people behind me in the street would have seen, and they'd know about me, and if they saw this bloke up ahead of me, tripping along, naturally they'd think I was following him, hoping for a pick-up!

I stopped dead in the middle of the pedestrian traffic, did an about-face, and walked back the way I'd come.

No, I ran. I ran the length of the block, then down an arcade, past rows of plateglass windows, watching myself ripple from one to the next. Tony says you can tell poofters by the way they run.

How do they run? Like me?

I kept my arms in close and tried to run in a macho way. Probably I was only exaggerating whatever it was I was trying to hide. People were staring.

At the end of the arcade I ducked into the men's toilets and locked myself in a cubicle. I sat on the bowl, panting, my heart pounding inside my chest like two fists on glass. The graffiti on the door in front of me pressed itself against my eyes: JACKO'S GAY. WHACKA SUX ANYONE.

How did they know Jacko was gay?

There was nothing about being gay in our dictionary at home, or in the encyclopaedia. I know, because I'd looked. And there was no one I could talk to.

I'd have loved to talk to David. Everything I needed to know, he knew. But how do you ask about these things? You don't! You can't!

. . .

I drew some money out of my Building Society account and roamed around the back streets until I found a second-hand bookshop. Inside, I browsed until I'd spotted what I wanted. Then I picked out a bike magazine and a comic and brought them up to the bloke at the counter. I was the only one in the shop, so I asked, loudly, on purpose, 'Do you have any of those gay men's magazines? It's my mate's birthday, I wanna give him one as a joke.' So what if he'd heard the line before? He didn't know if it was for real or not this time. And he was getting paid for it.

The gay mags were on a rack behind him.

'Any one'll do,' I said. 'Doesn't matter.' He placed one on top of my comic. 'How much?' I'd drawn out twenty dollars; he charged me two.

I ran again.

Boy, was I careful crossing streets after that. Imagine getting hit by a bus with something like this in your hands! I ducked into another public toilet, locked myself in another cubicle. This one had walls daubed with three different colours of paint, a stainless steel bowl and a light bulb covered with wire mesh. The light was weaker than it had been in the first loo, and the smell of urine was stronger.

I was going downhill.

I sat on the bowl, my hands shaking so much I couldn't hold the magazine. I had to rest it on my knees. My fingers felt like putty, opening the cover. It was stiff and new. Only the bottom right-hand corner was creased, where someone else had done this before me, sat in the half dark with shaking fingers, perving on pictures of naked men. Or two men together.

The photography was great and they were all good-looking blokes with terrific bodies. Mostly they were naked, or they wore scraps of leather or torn singlets. There were no strategically placed pot plants. You got the lot, full on, balls and all.

I've seen this kind of stuff before. There's always a porno mag floating round at school somewhere. But it's different when you're on your own, and you don't have to stage a reaction or pretend you're not looking that hard.

There was no one watching me except the blokes on the pages. I could look for as long as I liked, and react for real.

My arms felt weak turning the pages and my knees shivered. I looked at the next and the next and the next. And yeah, I was interested. Not to the point where it got me horny. The state I was in, I don't think anything could have done that. But I got the *stirrings*, perving on naked men. I went through the whole magazine with my heart racing and my eyes getting grittier.

One of the blokes reminded me of David. He was really lean and athletic looking, and he was smiling in a 'come on' sort of way. I touched his face and let my fingers creep down the page, seeing how far I could go. Seeing what it did for me.

So now you know.

So now I knew.

And I wished I didn't.

It was OK for them, but I didn't want it for me. I didn't want to be a poofter joke, a social outcast, a candidate for AIDS. They had each other; I was on my own.

You could die of this.

I was already dying of it. I was turning hollow inside, draining away. Slowly. Losing myself. Everything I'd thought I was, I wasn't any more.

I tried to flush the magazine down the toilet, to get rid of the evidence, but the water swirled around it and it wouldn't go past the first U-bend. Now it was soggy, and it was going to swell up and get bigger. And no way was I going to put my hand in there and pull it out, not soaked in everyone else's shit-water.

Except if I left it there, it was going to seize up the city's plumbing and I'd be to blame. It'd be all my fault, because I was gay.

I turned around and pressed my face into the corner of the cubicle, I was so ashamed. I didn't know what to do. How was I going to live with this? How was I going to hide it?

Take up body-building and make myself look macho. Go out with girls as a cover—ones who didn't want sex—there's plenty of them out there. Drop Tony.

Drop photography. Become a light-house keeper. A Catholic priest. Give up everything I'd ever wanted. I couldn't have friends any more. It'd be just too risky. Because no one must know. Ever.

I couldn't bear the thought of people knowing about me. I could never let anyone get close to me again.

God, I was going to be lonely. How was I going to live with this? How was I going to get home? How was I going to get out of this toilet even? I didn't know.

I pressed my whole body into the corner of the cubicle. *Hurt?* I hadn't known what pain was till I'd run into this. Living hurt, breathing hurt.

I wished I'd never looked. Wished I'd never lifted the lid. But the damn thing was out now, and it was crawling all over me.

Tuesday

I took up smoking on Tuesday—a pathetic attempt to commit suicide, and an excuse to talk to Vince. Everything I did was either pathetic or an excuse.

He was at the computer, typing in a programme and listening to the cricket on the radio at the same time. I asked if I could bludge a smoke and he said, 'No.'

I hung around anyway, rolled up my jeans and showed him the burn on my leg.

'Aw, for Chrissake, put your poor sore leg away and have one.' He shoved the packet at me. 'But if Mum smells it on your breath, you thieved it, OK?'

That was OK. I could steal, I could sneak, I could do anything. I stood close to the window and blew the evidence out through the flyscreen.

'Do you know if Mum's been on to Dad about the bike?' I said.

'I don't know anything about your bike.' He kept his green eyes on the green screen. Vince is a master at ignoring people.

'I though maybe she'd been at him again to get rid of it,' I said. 'She doesn't want me riding any more.'

'There's your excuse, then. If anyone asks why you've given it up, you can say your mother made you.'

'I'm not giving it up!'

'Well, I'm not talking to her for you, if that's what you want. I'm sick of trying to help you.'

'I don't want you to talk to her,' I said. 'I'll do it myself, when she's had time to get over it. Next week. Or the week after.'

'Or the week after that,' he mumbled.

I must have been getting used to his snipes. They didn't hurt so much any more.

Someone hit a six at the cricket ground and Vince cheered them. He can't stand people doing things half right or half well. He only likes people who are experts, or heroes. And I've never done anything heroic in my brother's eyes.

So be a hero now!

'Um . . . David,' I said. Just getting his name out was hard enough.

'What about him?' Vince's gelled spikes bristled up the back of his neck.

'Did Dad go down to see him?'

'No. No thanks to you.'

'He wasn't cuddling me in the darkroom,' I said.

'I know.'

'Did you ask him?'

'I didn't have to. I know him, he's not interested in little boys.'

'Thanks a lot!' I ground my cigarette into the ashtray.

'Running away again, Ace? If you hadn't taken off on your bike like you did the other day, nothing would have happened. No one would have thought anything about it. But you had to run. You're always running.'

'So did David,' I said. 'He took off too.'

'Not in a blaze of glory like you did. You made it look sus, Ace! And you made *him* look guilty.'

'You weren't there. You didn't see the way she looked at us.'

'Aw, who gives a stuff about the way she looked at ya?'

'I do!'

'Well, you're the only bloody one. No one else takes any notice of her.'

'I had other problems that day,' I said.

'You've always got problems. You're riddled with them. And I'm getting sick of them. You're always laying your shit on everyone else.'

'Like who?'

'Like me! How do you think I feel about what happened? He's my mate and you made him look a creep. How do you think *he* feels? You don't know what he's been through, Ace. He didn't need that.'

I didn't know what he'd been through?

'You and Mum and Dad at each other's throats. If you've got problems, do something about them. Sort yourself out.'

'I did!' I said. 'I phoned a telephone counsellor.'

'What've you got to phone a counsellor about?'

'That's my business.'

He saved what was on the computer. 'Were you thinking of bumping yourself off?'

'Don't be stupid.'

'What'd you phone about?' He took two cigarettes from the pack, lit them, and put one in the ashtray for me.

'All right, it was about girls,' I said, and sat down.

'*A* girl?'

'Sort of.'

'Have you got someone pregnant?'

'No.'

He switched off the radio. 'What's the problem?'

'This girl offered me sex the other day,' I said, 'and I knocked her back.'

'And?'

'Blokes aren't supposed to knock girls back.'

'You can if you like.'

'But she's gunna spread it round now that I'm a freak, that I didn't want it, and you know how that's gunna look.'

'Get in first. *You* spread it round that she's got VD.'

'No!'

'Why not?'

'It's not that simple,' I said.

'It's not that complicated, Ace.'

He makes me feel like I'm the only person in the world who can't handle things.

'Why'd you knock her back? Any reason?'

'Yeah, because she's gross, and a sleaze-bag, and I hate her.'

'Then you'd have been a jerk to take her on.'

The cigarette was making my head feel gluggy, but I kept on smoking it. 'There's this other girl too,' I said. 'Tony reckons I could have her if I wanted. It's his sister.'

'Bianca?'

'No, Sophie.'

'Wouldn't have thought she was your type.'

'She's nice. She's got big boobs.'

'If that's all you're into—who you can knock off and how big their boobs are—then you're a sleaze-bag yourself.'

'No I'm not! That's the point. I don't wanna screw anyone yet. But everyone's telling me I should!'

'Everyone? Or just your over-sexed Italian mate?'

'All the boys are the same. It's all they ever talk about—sex.'

'Because they're not getting any. You can always tell the ones who are missing out, they talk the most.'

'I don't wanna talk about it,' I said.

'Then don't.'

'And I don't wanna do it just yet either. Not with any of the girls I know at the moment, anyway.'

'How about any of the blokes?'

'I know you *think* I'm gay.'

'Ace, I don't think anything! Your sex drive is your own hangup. Do with it as you wish.'

'Bullshit. You're the worst of the lot,' I said. 'You're always telling me what to do.'

'I make suggestions. You don't have to listen.'

'Aw sure! Everyone's on my back, telling me this, telling me that, and I know they're gunna heap ten tonnes of shit on me if I don't do exactly what they say.'

'Stuff everyone else. Make up your own mind.'

'It's not that easy.'

'No, it takes guts, and you've either got them or you haven't.'

'And you think I haven't.'

'I think you're fartin' around looking for them.'

He wants me to be like him. Like Mum wants me to be like her! And Dad wants me to be like him!

We didn't end up bosom buddies as a result of our chat, Vince and I, but for some odd reason I was glad we'd had it.

With my head still woozy from the cigarette, I went down to the darkroom and locked the door. I'd developed the negatives for David's pictures the day before. Now I threaded the strip into the enlarger and drew it along, watching frame after frame of his car beam down on to the board, then his face.

The telephoto lens had caught him, head and shoulders, looking at me, squinting slightly as if expecting something—expecting me not to take his photograph, I suppose, when I'd already done it.

I was glad now that I had, even if it had embarrassed him at the time. It gave me something to hold on to. I printed the picture and sat with it dripping in my hands. The one blond hair in his fringe glowed white and the lines running back from his eyes were trenches. I knew where he'd got them from now. I was developing similar ones myself, lying awake at night, wondering: was I or wasn't I? That business with the magazine hadn't proved a thing. Everyone looks; naked bodies of any sort are interesting, and give you a bit of a buzz.

My putting my arms around him meant more. I'd done it totally without thinking, so I figured that was more likely to be the *real* me, as opposed to the *unreal* me, the one I'd been play-acting for fifteen years. Possibly I only liked girls because everyone had told me I was supposed to. I hadn't liked Gloria.

But David was the nicest person I knew. I liked him, I liked talking to him, I liked his hand stroking my hair.

I touched my own neck, trying to bring back the feeling of his fingers there. He'd been gentle, he'd cared, and I'd never got that from any girl.

I touched his face in the photograph, the dark shadow of his jawline, his lips. And yeah, I could imagine being kissed by him. Just thinking about it made my pulse rate pick up.

I'd thought about these things before—a bit. Never in detail, though, and never with myself in the picture. But now, well ... *What would it be like with a bloke?*

The idea of sex with girls had always frightened me. This couldn't be that much more scary. At least with a bloke you'd know what to do, having practised on yourself.

Before, when I'd been lying in bed staring at the walls, staring at the ceiling, going round the bend, I'd thought: I might *be* it, but I'd never *do* it! But now ... It wasn't totally out of the question. If I could hug a man, and imagine being kissed by him, why not the rest?

I didn't want to go through the rest of my life alone. I wanted to be loved and cared about like everyone else. And I didn't want to die without having done it, either. Sex is part of living, part of being close to someone. Why should I miss out?

The AIDS thing worried me, but that was going to be a problem no matter who I had sex with. Knowing David, I couldn't imagine he'd be into anything other than safe sex. And, thanks to Mum, we had a houseful of condoms and pamphlets on the subject.

There'd be hassles with parents, especially with his. I was under age, and they didn't like me, but if *he* liked me, what else mattered? At least I wouldn't be alone with it any more.

Until I actually did it, I'd never really know, and I had to know. *Not knowing* was driving me insane.

And if you think I was sitting there running this through my head calmly, you're wrong. I had the hot sweats and the cold shivers, and David's photograph shook in my hands.

1991

ELIZABETH JOLLEY

From *Miss Peabody's Inheritance*

The nights belonged to the novelist.

I have a Headmistress in mind, you know, a tremendously responsible sort of woman, the novelist's large handwriting was black on large sheets of paper. The name of the Headmistress is Dr Arabella Thorne; she is known as Miss Thorne. Every afternoon she walks down from the School House through the warm fragrance of a small pine plantation.

She always forgets about the pines and then suddenly she is in the middle of the sandy pine-needly place, walking on a little beaten path. She feels refreshed by the dry lightness of the air and the clean comforting scent from the sun-warmed trees.

It is surprising that she forgets because the school is called Pine Heights.

When Miss Thorne walks alone all kinds of things go through her head. Sometimes it is a line of poetry or a phrase from a piano concerto. Sometimes it is something wise to do with her policy in her school. She wants her students to study for pleasure and she wants them to cultivate an incredible hunger for books. She remembers something Samuel Johnson said in 1728:

> *The flesh of animals who feed excursively is allowed to have a higher flavour than that of those who are cooped up. May there not be the same difference between men who read as their taste prompts, and men who are confined in cells and colleges to stated tasks . . .*

Perhaps it was Boswell who actually said this, Miss Thorne is not sure but she resolves to speak to Miss Edgely about it and ask her to type a memo for the notice board. She will have to check the memo as Edgely is inclined now to make silly little mistakes. Not so long ago she put a *c* where a *p* should have been and left out an *l* and an *e*: '*. . . the copulation in the pubic schools is increasing at an alarming rat*'. The article, to be supplied by Miss Thorne to a journal for higher education, was entirely ruined.

Sometimes, when she walks, she thinks about the girls: the new one called Debbie in her clinging jersey dress, her hair cut long over her eyes and the way she has of throwing her head forward, suddenly, and then her shoulders, first one and then the other and then, with a curious wriggle, alternates these movements, matching them with a jerky swinging of her extraordinarily suggestive but childish hips, first to one side, then to the other; soundlessly, yet as if there is, somewhere inside her, a pulsing music, an irresistible beat, a music to which the girl responds with a rhythm so full of intense feeling that the dance to this outwardly unheard music takes all her concentration and all her energy.

She is a thin girl. I'll tell you more about her later.

. . .

Often Miss Thorne, at the end of afternoon school, pauses to watch the girls dancing. She has never, in all her years of experience, seen a girl dance as Debbie Frome, the new girl dances. She seems to give off a ferocious sensuality. Some of the girls do not dance. Gwendaline Manners, a large fair skinned girl who has been a boarder since she was eight years old, never dances. She looks as if she would like to but is too shy. She is overweight and very tall for her age and is very quiet. Miss Thorne has invited Gwenda to accompany her to Europe during the vacation in May. Though she has not mentioned this to Miss Edgely yet, she has told her life-long friend and travelling companion, Miss Snowdon. Miss Snowdon is matron of the Queens Hospital and a constant visitor to Miss Thorne's apartment, which she shares with Miss Edgely, on the upper floor of the Boarding House.

Both Miss Snowdon and Miss Thorne have the same kind of figure; a portliness brought on by years of responsibility, plenty of money, comfortable accommodation and good meals. Both women have the education, the background and the capabilities required for their positions. Neither of them cares too deeply for other human beings and they are not dangerously touched or moved by the human predicament.

Miss Edgely shares some of the qualities but, by contrast, is small. She has no taste and far less money.

. . .

Miss Thorne looks back to a solemn moment in the shower, in a newly built motel in a remote township in the wheat.

'Edgely's gorn for a walk,' she says stripping off her nightdress, 'so why don't we . . .'

'Oh Super! Prickles!' Miss Snowdon often adopts schoolgirl language when she is with Miss Thorne. (Normally Snowdon speaks in a kind of medical jargon and you will notice that she and Thorne say 'gel' and 'orf' instead of 'girl' and 'off', it's an affectation, but I don't think they are aware of this themselves. Excuse the brackets.)

'Oh Super! Prickles! A water fight! Oh rather! Come on! Race you!'

'This bathroom is very nicely tiled. Good strong jets of water too.'

'Mmm yes. Erotic. Rather. My deah this is madness!'

'Madness! But do go on!'

'Let's have the water just a bit warmer. Ah! that's more like it. Oh wicked! Prickles! Shall I soap you?'

'Of course you may do that again. As often as you like. You exquisite naughty. Oh indecently exquisite.'

'Prickles! This is Bigger than both of us!'

'We'd better hurry deah, I think Edgely might be coming back, it was only a little health walk, to settle her insides after being cramped up in the car. She's been drinking hot water. No deah! nothing in it. Just plain, for the insides . . .'

Miss Peabody in her airless and virginal bedroom tried to make sense out of the letter which was scrawled in red and blue ink. She tried to piece together something of the lives of Miss Thorne and Miss Snowdon. There was a lack of sequence and she realized she must take each letter as it came and hope that in the end she would reach some sort of understanding.

Miss Peabody did not touch alcohol but on this occasion she had a little of her mother's medicinal brandy in a cup of hot milk. It was soothing. The water fight had disturbed rather.

. . .

Smiling brightly all day at the office and being endlessly patient with her mother every evening Miss Peabody began to suffer. She longed for a letter from [the novelist]. She lay in bed shivering on the long bleak cold evenings after the bleak cold days. She withered. She made mistakes at work and could not concentrate.

Unable to go on waiting she wrote to the novelist just a short note asking about Dr Thorne and Gwendaline Manners. Did they leave for Europe or did Miss Thorne change her mind?

Yes they do go to Europe, the novelist replied in a letter which came quickly, and the schoolgirl too, but I am not up to that part yet. If you remember I sent a fragment some time ago, Miss Thorne and Miss Snowdon having a shower. At present the three of them, Thorne, Snowdon and Edgely, are having a three day break driving through the wheat belt. Naturally Gwendaline is not with them; the shower part fits in on this trip. I do not always write everything in the order in which things appear in a finished book. There is too a thin line between truth and fiction and there are moments in the writing of fantasy and imagination where truth is suddenly revealed.

Miss Peabody felt warm again, she glowed somewhere inside herself; here was a wonderful letter. She was reading too quickly, she would go back and reread slowly.

. . .

The reason for Thorne being so tired, the novelist wrote, is not simply the preparation for the beginning of the new term. It is not the *Othello* lectures and the production of the play. Thorne loves literature and she revels in lecturing and she adores producing Shakespeare. She enjoys exciting hitherto unknown, as she thinks, passions in the breasts of young girls while remaining calm and dignified herself, in charge, as it were, of their passions. She watches, with pleasure, the feelings which begin to grow in the youthful girlish Othello, *All's well now sweeting; come away to bed*, and makes them rehearse the scene till eyes sparkle and cheeks are flushed.

The tiredness is something else, a mixture of things partly relating to Miss Edgely who is not handling her menopause at all well and is highly emotional and more unreliable and muddle-headed than usual; and partly to having, on an impulse, invited the shy, unsophisticated Gwendaline Manners to accompany them on the short holiday to Europe in May; and there is something else too, an unpleasantly disturbing little incident which took place soon after the beginning of the term.

As Headmistress Ella Thorne is used to all sorts of difficulties, hysterical girls, angry cooks, bullying or demented parents and in-experienced unqualified staff. It is not so much the actual incident; it is more what the incident implied and its continued implication.

One night, very late, Miss Thorne is in bed reading. In her hand, a heavy tumbler of Scotch. She is enjoying the energy and the majesty of the writing in *Rasselas*, rumbling phrases aloud to herself and hicupping from time to time. It does not suit her digestion to read in bed ... *the spritely kid was bounding on the rocks, the subtle monkey frolicking in the trees, and the solemn elephant reposing in the shade.*

She reads and sips and rumbles and suddenly the Boarding House, on the same floor as her own house, resounds with music. The girls have music every day in their sitting room in the School House but this is at eleven thirty and everyone supposedly in bed and asleep. With the music, which is very loud, there is a remarkable rhythm and a penetrating beat; a girl with a thin mournful voice is singing; someone is dancing in the passage.

Miss Thorne sips her Scotch and waits. Matron is sure to be out there at once to silence whatever revolution is now taking place. Matron has been having her share of troubles; there having been a series of nocturnal raids on the staff supper table lately. It has taken a mustering of good manners to be able to sit down to the meagre leavings following the raids and not to complain, with disgust, at blancmanges and trifles which bear the signs of hands trying to grab what is best handled with a spoon. Miss Edgely, found by Matron on one occasion, has not been able to recall how she came to be bound and gagged and left in the pantry.

The music and the dancing continue so there is nothing to do but go out there. There is a door from Miss Thorne's apartment directly through to the Boarding House.

The girl with the long fringe over her eyes is dancing. Her shoulders, angular in a spangled dress, move alternately with her moving hips as she moves along the wooden boards of the passage towards Miss Thorne who stands sturdily in her doorway. She is amazed at the spectacle. At the far end a group of excited girls in nightdresses and pyjamas are watching. They disappear silently in various directions as the enormous figure of the Headmistress advances slowly. The music beats on.

The girl Debbie, whatever her name is, Debbie Frome, is dancing with that strange internal ceaseless energy. She dances a few steps forwards a few steps backwards a few steps to one side a few steps to the other side her head nods and turns as her body moves forward in a jerky rhythm and a purposeful beat propelling the dancer forward two-three *and* back two-three *and* left two-three *and* right two-three *and* back two-three *and* forward *and* forward. She dances as if she does not know anyone is there. Her expression is one of concentration and her whole body belongs in the fantastic rhythm. The uneven hem of her dress has seductive qualities.

'Turn orf that noise and send that gel to my room,' Miss Thorne's voice rises above the music. 'And see that she takes orf that frock.'

She waits for Debbie Frome in her room. She has thrown some wood onto the dying fire, a little blaze is springing on the hearth. She sits making a few notes about *Othello* at her writing table.

'The irony of the play,' she writes, 'is that the audience know before Othello himself knows what is happening to him.'

There is a knock on the door.

'Come in,' Miss Thorne calls in her most musical voice. The girl, Debbie Frome, enters. For want of something to replace the immodest dress Matron has tied a domestic science apron tightly round the slender body.

Miss Thorne looks up, smiling, from her notes. Her dressing gown is crossed over and tied securely with a magnificent cord bearing two coloured fringed tassles. It is reminiscent of what Othello might have worn when celebrating his nuptials. Miss Thorne has already made a note to remember to lend the cord for the dress rehearsal.

'Come in to the fire, child,' she says pointing to the armchair, a big chintzy thing which she does not like but which makes parents feel safe as does the wallpaper which is covered with pink cabbage roses.

'Would you like some hot milk?' she asks crossing graciously to the bell, forgetting there would be no one to answer at this late hour.

'Nope!' Debbie sits down crossing her legs one over the other, the stiff apron, cracking starch, pulled tight round her and slipping to one side to show her long straight legs.

'No?'

'Nah! I mean, no thank you.'

'And what is the dance Debbie?'

'It's disco Miss Thorne, it's disco. Do you know disco? I'll show you disco. It's easy once you know how. Here! I'll show you.' She stands up and starts to step forward two three, 'I'll show you the camel kick huh?' She sings and dances.

'I don't know where you come from—
Heaven must have sent you/
You held my hand/ You held my hand/
When you needed me you needed me . . .'

'No. No thank you Debbie. I'm too old for that sort of thing.' Miss Thorne smiles kindly. She's thinking that the apron suits the gel. The aprons should be used more often; there was something virginal and attractive about them especially when worn next to the skin like this. The gels would make the most of themselves in the aprons. Well, the ones like Debbie. Not Gwenda unfortunately.

'You're not too old. You're not too old Miss Thorne,' Debbie dances up to her Headmistress, 'I like you as you are,' she sings. She dances round and round and Miss Thorne is obliged to turn and turn.

'Turn!' Debbie says. 'Turn and turn and step but don't touch! Not yet!' She's laughing. 'It's disco Miss Thorne. It's disco!' The girl is singing softly and dancing round and round her.

'Come on Miss Thorne, Miss Arabella Thorne, I can teach you. I can teach you a lot of things. I can teach you what to do with your hands.'

The girl is close to the woman and as she dances she is even closer but does not touch.

'In disco there's no touching,' she says, 'you turn me on I'll have to come,' she sings, looking up at her Headmistress through the ragged, long fringe of hair. Her eyes through the fringe have a teasing look in them. 'Are you turned on Miss Thorne? You like this Miss Thorne Huh? Huh! Huh! Huh! Would you like to touch me now,' she sings, dancing up and back, 'Would you like to touch me now.'

'No thank you Debbie,' Miss Thorne replies quietly, looking down from her immense height. 'And now I think it is time for bed,' she looks at her watch. 'Good gracious! it's well after midnight. What about our Beauty Sleep? Part of the night is for sleep, especially for you young gels with examinations ahead. So goodnight Debbie, orf you go now, orf into bed!'

'Miss Thorne, I want to stay with you all night. Can I stay please?'

'I am afraid that's not possible Debbie. I do however completely understand your feelings,' Miss Thorne speaks kindly in a low voice, lowered on purpose in kindness and to hide any trembling in her voice. 'Everyone has disturbed nights at some time or another Debbie. Sometimes it's homesickness, sometimes it's worry over school work, sometimes the disturbing feelings are sexual, but whatever the reason, it is now time for sleeping. And here at Pine Heights we all sleep in our own beds. Goodnight Debbie. Sleep Tight!'

The girl is sullen but goes towards the door.

'Goodnight Miss Thorne.'

Miss Thorne, alone in her room, shyly but quickly admits to herself that she has been tempted. 'What a delicious yet terrible thing temptation is,' she says to herself, 'especially for someone in my kind of position!' There is no one with whom she can discuss it. Slowly she paces up and down in front of her dying fire. For a moment she thinks how charming it would be to take young Debbie to Europe in place of Gwenda; but quite rightly she cannot do that. Gwenda is already invited.

. . .

The Pension Eppelseimer, under the shadow of the Stepansdom, is quietly in readiness for the travellers. Miss Thorne has altered her usual reservation and, for the first two days, has asked for one double room without bath for Miss Snowdon and Miss Edgely, and for two single rooms also without bath for herself and Gwenda. Without bath is an economy.

'We don't travel so far simply to take showers or baths. Oh! everything smells of lilac!' She snorts and sniffs her pleasure and stoutly mounts the stairs to the rooms explaining to Miss Edgely that, in a few days, they will move into the spacious room with three beds, the one they usually have.

The two elderly ladies Lotte and Liselotte Eppelseimer, who keep the establishment, lead the way, bowing and smiling, turning back several times to show their pleasure at seeing Miss Thorne again. All are carrying separate pieces of luggage.

The floor boards are polished and the late afternoon sun lights up the porcelain panels and the hand painted cherubs in the entrance hall. All the rooms look down into a tiny enclosed garden where there are arbours covered in white and purple lilac. 'To get into the garden,' Miss Thorne explains to Gwenda, 'you simply walk downstairs and there is a stone flagged passage which passes by the shop and office on the ground floor. A door at the end of this passage leads directly into the charming and secluded garden. You will love it! May is the best time for this part of the world.' Miss Thorne, within sight of the profusion of tossing lilac flowers, feels light and full of youthful enthusiasm.

Miss Snowdon, who has arrived a day before, is waiting at the dinner table.

'How was Munich?' she asks.

'Splended deah. How was Basle?'

'Lucerne, Prickles!'

'Oh rather! Lucerne of course. Sorry! How silly of me! Gwenda deah, this is Miss Snowden, Snow deah this is Gwendaline Manners from Pine Heights. Oh! What a journey! And how did "The Placenta"? Well received I hope? Good discussion?'

'Edgely's not coming in to dinner,' Miss Snowdon says, 'I've arranged for her to have something on a tray.'

'That's a good idea, Snow, she's pretty tired.' Miss Thorne, with both fists on the lace tablecloth, European fashion, waits for her evening soup which she takes from the tip of the continental soup spoon.

'Soup soons heah, deah, are not round,' quietly she explains to Gwenda, 'and we do not put our hand in our laps while eating.'

With the coffee and some undefined little sweets wrapped in yellow cellophane, Miss Thorne tells Miss Snowdon about the saint. They are alone together. Gwenda having said 'good night', politely, has gone to bed.

'But it takes at least four hundred years for the evolution, or whatever it's called, for a saint.'

'How d'you mean?'

'Well, I mean saints don't just come over night.'

'Mine,' Miss Thorne unwraps a second sweet, 'Mine occurred in about two minutes during a tunnel.'

While sitting with Miss Snowdon a little longer and smoking one of her black cigars, Miss Thorne confides that she has not had it in her to send the little Manners gel back to school.

'I mean, I haven't told the little gel yet that this is the end of her holiday.'

'She's hardly a little gel Prickles,' Snowdon, with difficulty, unfastens the hooks on her skirt. 'Ah! that's better! I must get on to a diet again. She's hardly little. She's very well developed for her age.'

'She's sixteen.'

'Oh well, what d'you expect? She'll be wanting boy friends and dancing and Lord knows what.'

'No, the trouble is, she doesn't seem to want that sort of thing.'

'No?'

'And, what I mean is, I can't really send her orf out on her own while we do the rounds, Grinzing and all that.'

'I do see the point. Well, pack her orf back to school then.'

'That's not so easy either.'

'Well best sleep on it Prickles. Tomorrow is also a day as they say here in Vienna.'

I have no pain, Miss Thorne tells herself. The bed is clean and soft and yet she is unable to sleep. She lies quite comfortably and suddenly knows that she is not asleep and will not be able to sleep. Possibly it is the long journey and the oppressive atmosphere accompanied by the rumbling of thunder. She has no headache as Miss Edgely has and as Miss Snowdon, before going to bed, admits to having. Possibly it is the sleeping arrangements; instead of the spacious room with three lilac blessed windows, three beds and comfortable substantial furniture, Miss Thorne feels as if her little room is like an airless cupboard. They are used to being together on holidays and often conduct long and profound conversations on the edge of sleep, conversations which affect all three deeply but are entirely forgotten in the morning.

Miss Thorne knows that, through Gwenda, she has upset everyone.

'It's just a temporary arrangement,' Miss Thorne, bestowing aspirin and a glass of water, promises Miss Edgely, 'when Gwendaline is gone we are to have our usual room.'

The thunder rumbles. Summer, in Europe, is the time for thunder storms. The clocks of the city chime during the night and Miss Thorne's little travelling clock ticks away the minutes in a hysteria of time passing. Without wanting them to, thoughts of school come into her mind. The three friends, the three junior mistresses, White, Crane and Fortune, Jannice, Penny and the one who dresses like Electra, all of them so eager, and in their individual ways, good little mothers. And all their children too, all those sturdy little boy children bursting to grow up, unknowing, into the harsh world. In any case, Miss Thorne reflects, she only takes little boys in the kindergarten as Pine Heights is a school for girls. The little boys could not stay for long for this reason. She thinks too about the three young women, how, not so very long ago all of them must have been pleased, excited, delighted to be loved and chosen and to be married. And all three have, more than once, for love and other mysterious reasons, gone through the bearing of their children. In the first place the months of carrying the child and then the giving birth to the child, and, even more arduous perhaps, the task of caring and feeding and other additional burdens attached in general to the bringing up of children. It is not the first time that Miss Thorne has been confronted by this apparent paradox of human behaviour. And here she was stout and well fed, able to travel twice a year as a rule, as cheaply as possible of course but comfortably; here she was lying in bed contemplating the terminating of their employment. Perhaps ending, if only temporarily, their livelihood.

Miss Thorne, not liking to do it, always sacks people quickly. She tells them they can leave the next day or on the same night if preferred as there is an awkwardness, she feels, in sitting at meals with people you have sacked.

She reasons with herself turning her large well-cared-for body over in the narrow bed; that is part of the trouble this narrow bed. She is accustomed to a double bed to herself. She reasons that her school will not be able to continue to make ends meet. One mistress can do what these three are doing at present and, for a time, all must be dispensed with. She will teach the French and the self expression dancing herself and do the bedtime duty. Edge should be able, though it is doubtful, to do turns of evening duties. And though she is unable to teach she could supervise silent reading and study periods and piano practice.

As the night progresses Miss Thorne feels less able about the dancing and the French, beginners and advanced, as well as the maths, Latin and literature she is doing in addition to all the administrative duties. There is too the standard of the quality of Pine Heights. The girl, Debbie Frome, is not exactly suitable material for Pine Heights; Miss Thorne knows that she must cultivate the material; consideration must be given to the cheques from Mr Frome. This is even more important in the light of the fact that Mr Manners' recently written one was not honoured by the bank.

Turning over in the little bed again Miss Thorne is completely honest with herself as she considers her problems and knows where she is not being entirely straightforward. Miss Edgely should go really. Even if discouraged brutally Miss Edgely would never leave. For one thing she has simply nowhere in the world where she can go. Facing, this, Miss Thorne knows that, without Edgely, she herself has no one. There is Miss Snowdon, but Miss Snowdon, living and working in a different situation, could suddenly surprise everyone and marry, a wealthy surgeon perhaps. Such things were not unknown.

The thunder comes closer and lightning flashes light up the small room. It is impossible to sleep; the room is simply a cupboard.

The thunder crashes; it is overhead and seems to split the house. Nothing has split, Miss Thorne's bedroom door is open, that is all. Someone has opened it. In the next flash of lightning Miss Thorne sees Gwendaline in her white nightdress standing just inside the doorway. She is sobbing.

Miss Thorne sits up, the bed creaks violently as if it will give way.

'Why Gwenda! What is the matter deah?'

Gwendaline closes the door and rushes over to the bedside and, falling on her knees, flings both arms over the white counterpane. In the next lightning flash her hair shines as if with a light of its own. Thunder rolls. Miss Thorne pats the girl's shoulder,

'It's all right Gwenda, it's only a storm.'

'I know, I'm scared. I'm silly to be so frightened.'

'Come along, I'll take you back to your own bed,' Miss Thorne throws off her covers and gets up from her bed.

'Please, oh Please let me stay with you.'

'You will be perfectly all right, Gwenda, in your own bed.'

Miss Thorne gently guides the frightened girl back to her own little room. Ennobling thoughts and feelings rise in her breast as she realizes that she can explain to Gwenda that fear is a perfectly natural feeling but there is absolutely no need to be frightened of anything, especially not of thunder.

In Gwendaline's room there is another terrific crash and, after it, a downpour of rain; the heavy pattering of the rain on the leaves and on the roofs of the arbours is a relief. From outside, through the partly open window, there is the smell of the rain. The scent from the soaked lilac is intoxicating.

Miss Thorne, with an arm round the shoulders of the trembling girl, leads her towards the rumpled bed. Sitting down into the middle of the bed, she opens her arms to the girl, embracing her and drawing her close.

'Tell me about Wagner,' Miss Thorne says to Gwenda, 'Tell me how you feel about Wagner and his music. Did you like his music? Did you Gwenda?'

Music would be appropriate, Miss Thorne, taking up most of the mattress, is thinking. The dawn is filled with birds even though they are in the city of Vienna. Well there is music, she thinks, after all, birds are singing in the lilac trees and in a nearby park; their song transcends the sounds of the big city as it comes to life after the night. Even if it is not the *Siegfried Idyll* it is a sweet sweet music, this bird song.

The night was idyllic, tender, hilarious and ludicrous. There was the laughing and the trying not to laugh; it would not have done to disturb everyone in the Pension.

After the storm the night was tranquil. Then suddenly the bed gave way, not the whole bed, but simply, with a slight but prolonged jangling, all the springs fell, littering the oiled boards of the floor. Miss Thorne and Gwenda, their bodies sagging together through the widening space, were resting on the floor.

'Better go to my room,' Miss Thorne managed to gasp. She had laughed till her face was wet with tears. Gwenda, surprisingly, had more sense. It is better to break only one bed, hers. Why not finish the night on the mattress on the floor.

'There would be more room to turn over if we want to.'

'Yes you are quite right, deah.'

. . .

Like Thorne, the novelist wrote to Miss Peabody, I would not mind at all hanging the Edgelys of this world by their necks like fowls before they are plucked.

Miss Thorne feels that Miss Edgely will hold her back from doing things which are useful and good as well as pleasing. Edgely is becoming an obstacle.

Miss Thorne's motives towards Gwenda are developing along lines which I had not envisaged. Miss Thorne is showing a side to her nature which I did not know existed.

'Tomorrow Gwenda,' Miss Thorne pauses on the landing outside Gwenda's little room, 'Miss Snowdon, Miss Edgely and I shall be visiting the central cemetery and a few other places deserving our study and devotion to research.' She watches Snowdon and Edgely as they move on together down the passage to the large room at the end.

'I shall return in a few moments, if I may, Gwenda, to say good night,' she adds graciously.

'Thank you Miss Thorne.'

'It's Grinzing tomorrow or isn't it,' Miss Edgely says to Miss Thorne when they are all three together in their room.

'Oh rather!' Miss Thorne says after an awkward little silence.

'But what about the gel?' Miss Snowden asks.

'Yes, you did promise to send her back to school and she's still here.' Edgely is indignant; 'How can we take her to the Wine Festival! What would they think at school!'

Miss Thorne does not say that she is the one who does the thinking at school.

'Now Edge!' she says, 'everything's all right. All right, Edge! Yes we are going to Grinzing tomorrow, let's no more of this!'

'Ah! Shakespeare!' Miss Snowdon is getting undressed.

'Misquoted, I'm afraid,' Miss Thorne says.

'May I come in Gwenda?'

'Of course Miss Thorne.'

The girl is already in her nightgown, her clothes neatly folded, Pine Heights fashion, over the back of her chair. She smiles at the Headmistress.

'Perhaps you would like to write your letters and postcards tomorrow Gwenda. You could spend the day sitting in one of those charming little arbours in the garden. Just now the lilac is heavenly after the rain.'

'Yes, Miss Thorne,' Gwenda stands and smiles.

Miss Thorne has not forgotten the holidays at Pine Heights with Gwenda, sometimes three times in a year, in a sensible routine of walks and study, not too much study, a translation or two and some drawing, still life perhaps, enduring the loneliness of the empty school, receiving from time to time picture postcards covered all over with neat, round handwriting bearing incredibly dull news from self-absorbed girls who were travelling, or staying happily, with mothers and fathers, aunts, grandmothers or older sisters. Sterile postcards.

Miss Thorne feels an hour of revenge is near. She would like to join Gwenda in the writing of these postcards. It would be nice, she thinks, to have a new biro and squeeze into the small spaces available meaningless words and uninteresting messages to be received by those who had sent them to Gwenda when she badly needed the companionship of a living letter.

'You will enjoy writing your letters Gwenda,' Miss Thorne gives the girl a searching look. 'I want you to have a nice day tomorrow, deah.'

'Can I stay with you, still?' Gwenda asks. 'Please?' Miss Thorne is not sure how to reply.

'I intended to offer you an explanation Gwenda,' she says, 'I think we should not discuss now, simply speak our "good night" only. It is time for sleep now.'

'Good night Miss Thorne,' Gwenda says, stepping forward at the same time as Miss Thorne.

'Good night Gwenda,' for a moment Miss Thorne feels the clinging girl in her embrace. Gently she disentangles herself, holding Gwenda by the shoulders at arms' length.

'Good night deah,' she says with a little laugh, aware of the shakiness of her own voice.

Miss Thorne makes her way slowly along the passage to the end room. She thinks the best thing would be to write a calm and cheerful letter to the girl. She remembers the touchingly innocent things Gwenda is wishing for in her life, a kind husband, her own house with a garden and four, or was it five, babies. She twists her mouth into a wry little smile. All those years with the intellectual and musical background of Pine Heights . . . and the gel wants simply the kitchen, the ironing board and the baby bath.

All the same, it is the way in which Gwenda confided her wishes which has moved Miss Thorne. She does not want to send Gwenda back to school, but she must because of Edgely. Miss Snowdon too deserves her holiday on the terms they have always agreed upon.

Miss Edgely is sitting on the side of her bed.

'I'm cold,' she complains.

'But Edge, it's summer over heah, you can't be cold!' Miss Thorne prepares for bed skillfully.

'I am so! Warm me!'

Miss Thorne who has a half written letter to Gwenda in her head is unwilling. Miss Snowdon's corner of the room is in darkness.

'Oh well,' Miss Thorne says, switching off the remaining lights, 'Oh well, I'll come in for a few minutes then.'

'Not if you don't want to.'

'Now Edge, don't be difficult and sulky! Move over a bit, I've said I'll come in.'

It takes considerable time to soothe Miss Edgely. When at last she is asleep, Miss Thorne is free to write her letter. Putting on the small lamp by her own bed, she writes,

Dear Gwenda,

No doubt you will find it strange to receive a letter from your Headmistress especially since we are travelling together and seeing each other every day. It is because we are not really seeing each other every day that I am writing to you. I want to explain to you, Gwenda, that the Night of the Thunderstorm was in a sense a night on its own. The night can be treasured but, at the same time it is something to be put away, tucked safely in the memory as something belonging to those things which are not within the power of repetition.

I have known you, Gwenda, for several years and I am very fond of you. I have commitments in all sorts of directions, as you will know, from being at school. I have personal involvements too which do not leave me entirely free. That is my side of it.

Now for your side.

You are very young and you are pretty. Yes pretty, even though you yourself don't think so; you have a sweet smile. When you smile, as you did on the Kahlenberg, your whole face lights up. Remember this and remember to smile often.

You must look forward with happiness to the future. Be patient. A nice true friend, as you told me you wished for, will come along for you. Remember that all people go through lonely times at some time or another.

You must enjoy your day in the garden. I shall try to come back early in order to take you to the famous amusement park, the Prater.

Before you go back to school Gwenda, and quite firmly I do have to despatch you, (I have appointments to keep in Paris and in London) I shall take you to the cemetery here to see the graves of Beethoven and Brahms, Schubert, Johann Strauss, Von Suppe and Hugo Wolf—all these famous musicians are buried close to one another. And, nearby is a memorial to Mozart!

Here I am starting to give you a lecture on these beautiful yet simple grave stones when I really want to write that it has given me pleasure to see you enjoying yourself on our little tour. I want to write too that I am perfectly calm about your going back to school the day after tomorrow. I think it advisable for you to be calm too.

Miss Thorne stops writing her letter. She realizes she is far from calm. She has a strong wish to go from the big room along the passage to the little room. She supposes Gwenda is sweetly asleep and she smiles as she thinks of this.

Reading through her letter, correcting the punctuation, Miss Thorne feels it is a mixture of a cheap fortune teller, a salacious correspondent addressing 'Anxious Blue Eyes' or 'Deserted' in the back pages of a popular magazine and a paid museum guide. She knows, however, that hidden behind the carefully measured tread of her letter are real feelings and real passion. And, who should know better than an avid scholar of literature exactly what kind of warning was in the thunder storm.

She knows that it will not do to give Gwenda the letter. She must talk to her instead. She slips the pages under the embroidered dressing table cover to hide it for the time being.

•   •   •

Miss Thorne has not had much wine and is in danger of being out of favour with Miss Edgely and Miss Snowdon. The crowded wine houses and the tubs of flowers, the sentimental songs and the strolling, laughing, accordion players irritate Miss Thorne. She is trying not to show her irritation. She reasons that it is perfectly natural for Miss Edgely to want her holiday to include things she likes. During the slow hours Miss Thorne finds herself thinking of Gwenda alone at the Pension. It will be a long day even if spent in the garden.

The pleasure of the day for Miss Thorne will be to see Gwenda's pleasure when she experiences, for the first time, the extraordinary Viennese entertainment, the carnival and the Prater. Because Miss Thorne did not give her letter to Gwenda, she, Gwenda, does not know of Miss Thorne's intention. The idea of surprising the girl adds to Miss Thorne's private pleasure and excitement.

As well as caring deeply for Gwenda, Miss Thorne finds herself thinking of Debbie Frome and the way she has of peering through her long fringe. She has not lost, in migration, her north of England accent and direct way of speaking. Even after some weeks at Pine Heights she has not lost the way she has of moving her shoulders. Miss Thorne thinks about the bony shoulders moving, shrugging forward in a provocative manner, first one and then the other, so different from Gwenda's slow-moving, massive body. A reflection on the carbohydrates at Pine Heights? Miss Thorne raises her eyebrows. Possibly.

Gwenda so badly needs some of the Frome girl's self-confidence and some of that look of security in the knowledge of the expectation of happiness which brings happiness or which is happiness. There are possibilities ahead for Gwenda if only she can learn to lean forward in the Frome manner and take them.

Miss Thorne sees immense possibilities for her girls at all times, but mostly on Sundays when they enter the school chapel like swans in their white dresses. These dresses seem to stand out and float round the strong, young, solid, girlish bodies.

Immense possibilities. Miss Thorne always stands watching with pleasure and approval as the girls go to their places.

Immensitie cloystered in thy deare womb. She knows the quotation is not quite right for this stage of their development but she likes the words. Poetic references pass through her mind. She changes the quotation to suit present day needs.

'Immensitie cloystered in their hearts,' she says to herself in the porch of the chapel, 'many of these gels have no intention of devoting themselves to motherhood.'

It is typical, significant, that Debbie Frome's dress is not of the same material as the other white frocks. Hers is of some kind of expensive Italian knitted cotton and clings in a revealing, and at the same time, attractive way to her spirited body. The gel, Miss Thorne notices, dances disco rhythm to her pew in chapel.

If only the two gels could become friends. She might then invite them both to accompany her to Europe next May. Together they might even visit the sophisticated night clubs in Vienna where there would be music and dancing to enliven Gwenda. Miss Thorne thinks of the Wagner Festival in Bayreuth. It would be splendid to see the effect Wagner would have on Debbie Frome. Perhaps some time. Miss Thorne smiles.

'Pensive Prickles?' Miss Snowdon is returning with Miss Edgely along the flower laden path from the wine house.

'*Ein Viertel* Dear?' Miss Edgely carries two quarter litre mugs of cold white wine. Miss Snowdon also carries two.

'First one down the hatch has the extra!' she sits on the ornamental bench next to Miss Thorne. Miss Edgely sits on the other side.

'Dawdling, Dreaming and Drinking,' Miss Snowdon sighs. 'Penny for your thoughts Prickles?'

'Oh! she's ah thinking of ah someone beginning with ah *G*.' Miss Edgely takes her wine, in gulps; 'You need more wine dear,' Miss Edgely says, 'you do know, don't you, it doesn't shoot you not to have enough.' She giggles, 'there's plenty more where that came from. I mean, that's what a wine festival's all about isn't it. So drink and be merry!'

Miss Thorne looks at Miss Edgely's flushed face and tries not to associate Miss Edgely's once new and unusual experience many years ago, which pleased Miss Thorne very much then, with the present pleasure of caring for Gwenda and the introduction, the initiation, to new experience to which Miss Thorne is looking forward.

'Say gels!' Miss Thorne makes an effort to put her little plan forward. 'Say gels!' Miss Edgely and Miss Snowdon are not able to hear. An American girl, surrounded by an admiring group of Viennese young men, is singing.

'Wien! Wien! shtatt ob my dreems. Wien! Wien Leeber Wien! Ole!'

Her accent is appalling, nauseating is the word Miss Thorne uses inside her head.

'Say gels,' Miss Thorne tries again, 'what say yew we go try the Prater this evo? My shout!' the simulated Australian accent betrays anxiety.

'Good Grief Prickles!' Miss Snowdon is tipping half the extra *Viertel* into Edgely's glass. 'We always stay late here Prickles! We always stay till the witching hour!' she says in surprise.

'I am thinking,' Miss Thorne says too calmly for the other two, 'that I would like to get back to the Pension. I think we should, all of us, go out for a nice meal somewhere and then on to the Prater. Meals too, interesting ones, are part of a holiday. Cream of mushroom soup? or perhaps, *Suppe mit Griessnockerl* and a tender *Wiener Schnitzel*,' Miss Thorne warms to her subject, 'tiny new potatoes with parsley and butter and a salad plate of those lovely little tomatoes and to finish, you remember, the omelettes served with heaps of jam and sprinkled with sugar, what were they called? *Kaiserschmarren! Kaiserschmarren* and then on to the Prater. It would be an experience for Gwenda to take back to school. An experience I would like her to have.'

'Oh Gwenda! Gwendah! Gwendah!' Miss Edgely interrupts.

'Now Edge,' Miss Thorne raises her voice. 'No Tantrums in the park!' A group of students, passing, laugh with the good nature which is prevalent in the gardens.

'Oh, it's like having to tell Mr Frome that you don't need to learn the language to play French cricket,' Miss Thorne turns away. The others, not understanding, follow her as she walks with purpose through the park. Both her way of walking and her travelling costume, an ample jacket and skirt in blue denim (it has an accompanying set of white drip dry blouses) are out of place.

The day at Grinzing has never ended abruptly like this before.

'I said all along it would be a mistake to bring a schoolgirl on the trip. We never have in the past.' Miss Edgely tells anyone passing, that is anyone who can understand English. 'I said all along it would be a mistake to bring a schoolgirl . . .' Tourists thus accosted are soon running in all directions.

During the long tram ride back Miss Snowdon feels peace should be restored.

'I for one Prickles,' she says, 'rather like the idea of that delicious meal. I'd like to take you up on the invitation. I could demolish easily, I think, a *Tafelspitz*. And count me in on the *Kaiserschmarren*.'

'Good!' says Miss Thorne. 'Come on Edge be a sport!'

Miss Edgely is staring out of the window lurching with every little lurch of the tram. Miss Thorne knowing that she put on the new tartan polyester suit for the first time that day noticed, earlier, Edgely's obvious sense of elation and freedom, as if the trouser suit emancipated her; now, in her dejected state, Edgely draws pity from Miss Thorne.

'Edge!' Miss Thorne says in a voice as low as she can make it, but loud enough to be heard by Edgely over the noise of the tram. 'Remind me when we are near a suitable place, I must send a wire to Bales. Before we left I saw a mouse in the Visitors' Room. If it gets into the Edible Art cabinet, the whole display will be ruined. You'll remind me. All right?'

'All right,' Miss Edgely says.

'Then it's all settled. Shall we eat at the Hotel Graben?'

They sit in silence. Miss Thorne gives herself up to the swaying movement of the tram,

But jealous souls will not be answered so;
They are not ever jealous for the cause,
But jealous for they are jealous . . .

'Pensive Prickles?'

'Not really Snow, just at work in my head.'

Miss Thorne, smiling to herself, thinks of the moment when, after climbing the stairs, she will knock at the door of Gwenda's little room.

1983

SUMNER LOCKE ELLIOTT

From *Fairyland*

He hadn't revealed to her the fact that he had never danced. As they stood up, he put the wrong arm around her but she calmly corrected him and immediately took the lead. As in everything she did, she led with an utter confidence and precision that made it seem as though he were leading her, ludicrous as they must somehow look, Seaton in his shrieking jacket (all she had said about him was 'You certainly look startling, darling') and Camilla a good inch and a half taller. But she insinuated otherwise and cleverly turned him this way and that, gazing down at him with a wholly devoted look of complete surrender while holding him in an iron grip of possession, and it occurred to him that she probably would control the sexual act in the same manner, ravishing the man but appearing utterly submissive in doing so, and as gradually their bodies merged in the rhythm under her direction so did they appear to be in a physical rapture, and then to his embarrassment she began to croon softly in his ear, in a little-girl voice. 'I'm a dreamer, aren't we all?' she confessed to him lovingly and that she didn't want to walk without him, baby, and that she wanted him to stay the way he looked tonight. Her hand gripped his so fiercely that it hurt and from time to time in his anguish he was forced to smile happily at passing couples (the floor, thank God, was now bustling with couples all intent on their own transposition of sex to inoffensiveness) and to applaud the band between numbers. In the little breaks he glanced hopefully at the chairs around the walls, but Camilla stood impatiently and tapped her foot, waiting for the band to begin again and immediately took him again into her embrace. On and on they danced, around and around the dance floor, his aching back, his hands and feet wet with exertion, they circled and circled. Ceaselessly she crooned; she must have learned the lyric of every song ever written in America and the little voice had a plaintive note in it, a nuance of weeping that didn't go with her momentous self-will. It was almost midnight before, to his exultant ears and mutilated feet, the band stomped away at 'God Save the King' and the orange lights dimmed.

At the door of her room, Camilla bent slightly and, caressing him with one arm, said, 'Just give me five minutes and then tap on the door. I've got some Johnnie Walker scotch.'

Now then.

Well, it had to be faced, there was no escaping into any fantasy he may have clung to that nothing more was expected of him than companionship. But for what was she preparing that would only take five minutes? The thought of terrifying (to him) unknown precautionary measures? The memory of reading in some novel that the heroine had anointed her breasts prior to the lovemaking with some fragrant unguent. Is that what she might be doing? A vision of Camilla's orgiastic breasts arose in Technicolor and he sat down on his bed, actually quaking. There could not be the slightest doubt in Camilla's mind of his virginity, but neither was there any doubt that she could handle the situation with her inevitable command and with the teacher's rod in hand (an unfortunate simile at which he almost had the courage to smile). But in actuality, what would happen. What would *she* do while he undressed? Watch? Read a magazine? Would she comment perhaps with joy, perhaps with disappointment, on the dimensions of his precious part? Who would get into bed first? Would he be chided if he put out the light, thus curtailing her enjoyment of watching the performance? What if? What if he were totally unable to perform? He knew that women could and sometimes did falsify the joy of consummation, pretending the climax (it looked to him like white flowers bursting open), but God pity the poor male member unable to rise to the occasion.

He sat for five, ten, fifteen minutes and then, taking off the loud jacket and his tie, prepared for the execution, walked in dragging steps along the corridor to the electric chair and knocked more softly than his heart was beating.

She was in a snow white negligee and barefoot and held open the door. On the dressing table was scotch, glasses, and a siphon; sandwiches lay under a discreet napkin.

Impossibility blacked out the room, screened her out.

'Look—' he said, gulping. 'I'm suddenly all in, just beat. Look, I'm awfully sorry, Camilla, but I can hardly keep my eyes open so if you'll excu—'

'I *see*,' she said.

The slam of the door must have shaken the whole corridor and been heard in every room; the violence of it nearly knocked him over. Certainly the middle-aged man and blonde who might be posing as his daughter glanced curiously at him in passing. But without shame he fell into a deep dreamless sleep the moment he got into bed.

Jittery nevertheless in the morning, he faced the prospect of breakfast with her either in icy silence or taut with mountainous hurt feelings. Passing through the lobby on his way to the dining room, he was summoned to the desk where he was handed a small package addressed simply to 'Mr S. Daly.'

Wrapped in tissue paper was a golden fountain pen from Proud's Jewelers. What on earth? Then he remembered. His drunken exaltation at her dinner party. 'But she could only have been written with a golden pen.' On the crushed plain white card she had written in her bold executive handwriting, 'From a fool who thought you loved her.'

He held he pen in his hand for a long time, then turned to the desk and inquired. Was she already down to breakfast, then? Mrs Dick had checked out at seven that morning. The clerks were busy, could hardly spend time commiserating with this twitchy-faced boy. What? Yes, she took her car. Anything they could do? He stood there stunned for a moment or two and then, realizing his plight, asked at what time he could get a train. Being Sunday, he was told, there was no train to Sydney until four-thirty-five in the afternoon. The courtesy charabanc would take him down to the Rooty Hill Railway station.

. . .

Seaton was so drenched in the downpour that had been going on all day that when Rat Ratcliffe opened the door, Rat said, 'My dear, you look like a little salmon swimming upstream to breed.' Though the invitation had read that it was to be a small dinner party, nobody else had yet arrived at the once splendid Victorian house in Yarmouth Road. It was some time before Rat conceded that the small dinner party was to consist of 'just us.' Seaton was dried off and told to leave his wet raincoat in the bathroom. Passing through Rat's bedroom with the outsize double bed in maroon burlap, he was drawn to the phalanx of photographs framed and hung around the gilded angels on the headboard of male Hollywood movie stars, some whose careers had faded like the photographs themselves, the standard studio portraits that usually were sent in reply to fan letters, but these, incredibly, were all inscribed in wildly diverse handwritings with loving salutations to Rat. Thus Ronald Colman had scrawled, 'To my dear dear friend Rat,' Warner Baxter had asserted he was Rat's 'best pal.' Expansively, Otto Kruger had confessed to 'much affection.' But was it possible to accept Conrad Nagel's affirmation of being 'yours forever'?

Possibly the limits of credulity had been stretched to the utmost when Mr Gable had merely slashed the word 'Clark' across his chest. The little duplicity was made the sadder by the mere fact that it had been intended to deceive. Even harder was it to reconcile with Rat's almost perpetually bright and often witty personality. 'What a darling you are to have come through the flood tonight. I would have phoned to let you off the hook but cunningly you are not phonable and besides I was being self-indulgent.'

Perfect drinks were served in Waterford crystal, the fire bubbled in the hearth, scattered around on the coffee table were fairly recent copies of *Harper's Bazaar* and *The New Yorker*. Great trouble had been taken with delicate hors d'oeuvres and the arrangements of flowers in the room; wine had been set to breathe on the table, candles lit, and Ravel's *'Alborada del gracioso'* put on the record player. But the most perfect of all was Rat's performance of himself, dry, entertaining, changing from one moment to the next in a kaleidoscope of imitations (the Prime Minister's nasal Christmas greetings, Eleanor Roosevelt, Mussolini), and all the time contriving to promote a sense of gracious distance between them, the assurance that no crafty preparations for seduction were under way, no hand was going to be laid on the knee. They sat apart in this gratifying unitedness of two casual friends and gradually Seaton was, with support from several mild gin and tonics, prompted to confide in Rat the full story of Camilla and the disgrace leading to his being fired. Rat's long peeled-banana face stayed placid.

'Got the Spindles treatment, did you?'

It was almost a tradition, then.

'Oh, it was all worked out, my dear, probably from the moment she met you. She has instincts that rarely fail her in that direction. Oh, you're not the first by a long chalk. It's got to be the running joke at her office as to who will be next.'

'But why? Why would she humiliate *herself* into the bargain?'

'Oh, it's all part of the lead-up to her eventual redemption through her forgiveness, that's her orgasm. Do try a dab of horseradish with the oysters, they're a tiny bit bland. Didn't she recommend you for this job at 2XY?'

'Oh yes, I was stunned.'

'There, you see?'

He couldn't see.

'Unless you know about her mania about people like us, you couldn't see, my pet. She has been on a sort of antiquated anti-queer crusade for years.'

Just wait now until he fetched the cream of leek soup.

'But Rat, why?'

'In a nutshell, then, her mum died when she was eight, leaving her with daddy and an older brother, both of whom she adored. One day when she was seventeen, she opened a door. She was not expected. She found her beloved daddy and brother in bed together. See? Well, my dear, when you've caught your father and brother *in flagrante delicto*, shall we say, it makes it awkward for all of you to sit down together in the evening to enjoy egg and bacon pie, so she lit out then and there and went down onto the dark Bondi beach with the first boy she could pick up and they did it eight times. More likely only five, I think, her memory's somewhat epileptic. Anyway, from then on it all became truly tenth-rate Dickens for poor little Sophie Laye, which was her name then, Sophie the Surfer's Delight. She would do it for the price of a meal and a bed at the five-bob-a-night Montana Moon Hotel, which was only two inches up from being a bordello, and for the next year or so her life was something over which, as we say, we draw a veil until, of all people, minty Milton Dick found her working in a fish-and-chips place and took a girlish fancy to her and more or less adopted her and made her over into the lady he would have liked to be, out of the salmon-coloured ankle-strap shoes and satin dresses. She learned *tout de suite*, my dear, and blossomed into the lovely Medusa we know today. It took years, but as the song goes, look at her now. Or, you might call it out of the frying pan into the *pansies*. Wait a sec, now, while I frisk up the mint sauce for the lamb.'

So, that was Camilla, but write her story with a golden pen.

When it came time to leave, Seaton blustered with polite remonstrances about Rat's getting into yellow oilskins to see him to the tram. Nonsense, dear boy, the bird's-eyes twinkled behind the gold-rimmed glasses perched on the beak nose, but there was about Rat the glinting triumph of having maintained once again the architecture of celibacy. Or had he retired from any meanderings years ago when he was still young? Had the lone life been mandated? He seemed purposely without obligation.

So they went out into the weeping night, Rat holding the umbrella, to the tram stop, not trying to speak against the wind and rain. The tram bore down on them through the torrents more like a lighted juggernaut, the conductor hanging on for dear life to the narrow footboard, his whistle in his mouth.

'—such a lovely even—'

'Get on, dear boy. Good night, dear boy.'

Got the little sliding doors open and inside he was the only person on the tram save one man in a compartment further down. The conductor, under his streaming waterproof hat and oilskins, was young and somewhat dark-skinned, good-looking. After he had presented Seaton with the dampened ticket he went off along the narrow footboard of the swaying juggernaut and was seen to take refuge inside one of the forward compartments.

'Fez, pleez.'

Seaton had turned to say he already had—

The beaked face at the door was streaming with rain or tears; the yellow slicker ran water.

'Rat.'

'Fez, pleese.'

'Rat, get in, you'll fall of, be killed—'

'I love you.'

'Rat—'

'I love you with all my heart. Just want to know, is there any hope?'

'Rat—'

'Is there a smidgen? Even a smidge of hope for me?'

'Rat, if you'd get *in* and sit down—'

'No, it's written all over your face, darling, there's not the slightest hope. There never is. Well, on with the daaaance—'

The last was singing, skipping. Still hanging on to the tram as it slowed to a stop, Rat sprang off and vanished into the pitch black wet. The tram stopped, someone got on, the tram started again.

But how could one have lied? Said what? I love you? The poor long banana face, the streaming spectacles, all out of a comic film. But ugly, ugly, he knew the fact was the good-looking tram conductor any time, even soaking wet and smelling dreadfully of soaked oilskins, he would rather embrace, hug him than have Rat touch—

Thus began a train of dismal thinking (trudging up to Central Station for the Arncliffe train) about the unsuccessful men, the middle-aged and un-good-looking who had never found anyone. They were somewhat like the unsuccessful girls, the plain unwanted girls, the secretaries and office workers who went around in bunches and had Friday dinners together, bought theatre tickets in groups and giggled a lot, pretending gaiety, the synthetic men were like them except that they dared not form in groups publicly.

But suppose the gradual attenuation was one's own fault? Suppose one never felt the transmutation? Fell? Imagine the poverty of never finding. The waiting and waiting.

And suppose no one ever came?

. . .

Perhaps something was put in the tea they drank, perhaps it was merely the superfluity of male bodies walking naked to the evening shower wearing only untied boots, nothing more useless than the dozens upon dozens of deactivated organs going flip-flop, flip-flop to the showers. No one looked, no one cared. After a period of such mutual abstention it became a virtue, like an oath of chastity. Yet the more they were sexually restrained by some nitrate, the more they exercised their right to copulate by obscenity; fuck him, you, it, they said. Get it up the flaming cook, they said, reviling the food. Up Vince the Vile they chorused when he canceled the Saturday football game for an 'emu' parade.

Get it up! Always up.

At the picture show on Saturday night at the vast open-air screen, where they sat on log seats with their blankets and lolly water, they incited the male star to molest the female (the more that showed of Lana Turner, the wilder the shrieks). 'Do her over,' a voice would yell from the dark, and after a moment another voice, 'Or I will.' This was inevitably followed by such laughter that the usually prudish dialogue was drowned out for several minutes.

Bereft of communion with the flesh, they claimed their long-distance rights to it with feverish abandonment; they were engulfed in nostalgic wantonness, but in the soft lamplight over their evening poker, their faces were like those of innocent children.

Seaton was unable to remember when exactly it was that the old feeling of exclusion had vanished. He had become one of the mob, browned and red-dusted, thin with the daily portions of dry mutton and boiled potato (cold at lunch, hot at supper), gritty with the constant blowing sand, loquacious on beer nights (Thursday and Saturday they were doled two bottles of warm lager), satisfied. Here in this scorched-earth exile, amidst five-foot-high anthills like ancient Inca cities against the sunset, here where only once a week a train whistle was to be heard in the night, reminding them of the outside world, here was a peace. No one knew.

No one cared, he was one of the poor bludgers who'd copped 'the

Creek.' On guard duty one dawn (bad luck to cop the third shift, which started at four A.M.) he watched as the stars faded and the fuzzy yellow light confiscated the eastern night. As the dawn broke he realized the utterly improbable: he was at peace, not happy, but more peaceful than ever so far in his life and being devoid of the precaution constantly forced on him by his sexuality or peculiarity, whichever it was, was as refreshing as early morning rain; the acceptance of him by 'mates' and the continuous serenity of their peculiar brotherhood made it a singular appeasement.

So it was, going to mess, say, that one automatically put an arm around a cobber and he around you; they needed to and that was all there was to it. For a few moments his unutterable desire was for it to continue for life, that he need never again want, and not wanting the dubious pleasures of his left-handedness, the forbidden delights, taken with care, with the blinds down, touching fingers under the table, disguised with girls present and only imploring eyes to imploring eyes to witness, no longer a prey to any of it, would be the awakening of a reality and a trueness of himself. When the guard truck came to relieve him, he put his arm around the driver's shoulder in this new morning joy.

'How are you, mate?'

'Not bad, mate, how's yourself?'

'Fuckin' nice day.'

He kept it a dream, his secret.

'Corporal Daly.'

'SIR.'

To instant attention, iron heels clicking.

'Can you drive a Ute?'

'Yes, sir.' Captain Smollett's little cold blue eyes. Thinking he might as well get something from the army gratis that might be useful in what they jokingly called the After Life, he had signed on for a driving course while at Victoria Barracks and all he'd driven so far had been small trucks. He knew how to handle a Ute.

'My usual driver's got a touch of dysentery and I have to be up at the Katherine camp, they're having a review of the new two-button slicker, which is going to be issued next March, just in time to miss the Wet, of course. Here's your requisition for the Ute. Be in front of the officers' mess at fourteen hundred.'

'Yes, sir.'

Well, a run up to the Katherine was a breather away from the typewriter and the bloody stencils, even if it had to be with Vince. And maybe he could stay on for mess; rumour had it the blokes at Katherine had a superior mess to the Creek. Might even be a movie if Vince stayed overnight. Rumour was the Katherine blokes had already had *Casablanca*, whereas the Creek got Deanna Durbin week in and week out.

'And bring your rifle, Corporal. We might see if we can pick off a bush turkey for the cook.'

'Sir.'

Captain Smollett was waiting outside the mess at two minutes to fourteen hundred, smoking a cigarette.

He climbed in beside Seaton and they rumbled out a little uncertainly (not absolutely at home with the gears) onto the long North-South road and nothing was said. Captain Smollett stared ahead at the monotonous red dust and stunted gums.

'Ever been to the Red Lily Lagoon?' he asked.

'No, sir.'

'Worth a trip, good shooting there. Crocodiles. Big ones. Come out after you like buggery. Got one right in the eye; she threw a fit, landing on her back, but the chaps said don't go near that lashing tail, so we left her there to die in peace.' Captain Smollett chuckled. 'About fifteen feet she was, the bugger.'

'Fancy.'

'Big bitch.'

They drove in silence; the road spun endlessly before them; once an artillery truck passed them going south and tooted its horn.

'Bloody Territory,' Captain Smollett said, 'goes on forever.'

'Yes, sir.'

When they were passing a greener patch of what looked like mulga and wild wattle, the Captain said, 'Drive off here a moment. This looks like possible turkey territory.' They left the road and bumped a few yards into a low sandy basin surrounded by brittle thorn bushes and some abandoned anthills. Big birds hovered in the blue, but there was no sign of turkey.

'Stop here a minute, Corporal.'

'Yes, sir.'

He cut off the engine and they sat there until the Captain, pointing, said, 'Watch over there a minute, something's stirring behind those bushes. Got your rifle?'

'Yes, sir.'

He brought out his rifle and lowered the side window. They waited.

'Watch over there to the right.'

'I am, sir.'

Nothing moved, they sat silent, so close that he could hear the Captain breathing. When nothing moved for endless minutes, he said, 'I don't think there's anything there, sir' and turned back right into the Captain's warm mouth and then arms were around him tightly and he was pressed against the Captain's faultless shirt.

'Drop your bloody gun, Corporal.' The Captain, chuckling, said, 'Relax, sonny boy, it's all right. You know, I had you pegged from the start. And do you know how I got the idea? You buckle your belt the wrong way, from left to right, the ways girls buckle a belt. I never reprimanded you because I was waiting to find out.'

Later the Captain said, 'Lie back a bit,' and then, even later, 'Do you know something? You're a little corker, that's what you are, a bloody little corker. I'll tell you something, corker, I like you. Do you like me a bit?'

'Yes, sir.'

'Don't be formal for a few fucking minutes, it's all we've got, it might be all we'll ever have.'

Holding him down on the seat, legs twisted under the steering wheel, Captain Smollett kissed him lengthily on the mouth and then said hoarsely, 'I don't think I have to tell you that if ever a word of this squeaked out the results would be very serious for you. I don't have to remind you that the word of an officer against a soldier is generally taken without question. Just a word to the wise, corker.' Sitting straight up now the Captain rebuckled his belt and said, 'Drive on, Corporal.'

They drove on.

It was as fleeting as a quick dream during a five-minute nap; he couldn't yet accept it as real, glancing at the Captain's composed face, the bristling military mustache, the cap set at a perfect angle, it was a little snatched dream during an after-lunch nap.

. . .

Not a vestige of anything having happened. In the office, orders were still barked out, typing errors discovered just before stand-down; not by an eyelash did Vince admit anything more than that Corporal Daly's desk was next to his own and hand him orders to be typed in triplicate. Once on an A8 Form of Inquiry into Ullage, he had scribbled 'Four copies X.' The X was tiny and infinitely discreet or could have been meant as a period. The only hint of a possibility of recollection was that Corporal Daly was mysteriously left off the guard duty roster for nearly ten days.

Then 'Bring this report to my tent, Corporal.'

'Sir.'

The order was given at ten minutes to seventeen hundred.

Seaton took his time typing it, annoyed at the silliness of having a noticeable heartbeat.

The flap of the tent had been left wide open as if to minimize suspicion of anything untoward. Captain Smollett was sitting on the cot in stocking feet. His fiancée in the photograph beside him looked more glum than ever, as though she might have suspected something.

'Stand over there, Corporal. Stand easy.'

'Sir.'

Anyone passing the tent would see an officer reading a report while the NCO waited. Captain Smollett read the report, reread it, reread it again in silence while from across the way sounds of the early cocktail hour reverberated in coarse male laughter from the officers' mess.

Eventually Vince said in a low voice, 'Can you hear what I'm saying? I don't want to speak loudly.'

'Yes, sir.'

He spoke without raising his head from the report, knuckling his forehead. 'Something extraordinary and unfortunate, unforeseen has happened. I have fallen in love with you. I realize that this places both of us in an untenable and extremely dangerous situation. Discovery could mean the end for me of my military career, almost certain dishonorable discharge, and possibly six months at hard labor up at Daly Waters Correction Camp, very likely considerably worse for you. On the other hand, the prospect of never once again being close to you even for a few seconds is infinitely worse. Are you hearing me?'

'Yes, sir.'

'I've been informed there's been some breaking in and stealing from sheds at Number Three Sub Depot, and I intend to make some late-night raids there in the hope of discovering the culprits. I intend to make these inspections alone after lights out. I am hardly in the position, nor is it permissible for me, to make this an order, Corporal, but if a certain person were to be there—do I make myself clear?'

'Yes, sir.'

'You know where. A little after lights out.'

'Sir.'

'That's all, thank you, Corporal.'

In the moon shadows behind the grim corrugated iron sheds at Number Three Sub Depot where there was no sign of attempted night ullage, the two spectral figures became quickly merged into one.

'Quick, we don't have long. Keep your eyes peeled. See anything?'

'No.'

'Thought I heard something.' Whispered. 'Over there.'

Waiting.

'I didn't.'

'God, you sweet, you sweet little bugger. Look, would you do something for me? Would you?'

'What?'

'Say something sweet to me, even if you don't mean it.'

Toward August, the winter turning, the long-awaited, plotted transfer came through. Corporal Daly had been accepted as chief writer for the newly created First Commonwealth Broadcast Unit to produce a weekly propaganda radio program titled 'The Army Show' and not only had the approval of the transfer come directly from General Blamey's head-quarters in Melbourne and so was automatically counterapproved by NORFORCE in Darwin and therefore could not be disapproved by anyone, even Colonel Plank, but also specified that Corporal Daly was to be transported by plane from the Larimah transit camp as far as Brisbane. No NCO had ever before been flown out of the Territory.

'Good on yer, matie,' dear old Grudge said in the shower line, he who had not had a day's leave for what would be three years in September. Handshakes and backslaps came all the way down the naked row of boys in only boots in line for their fifteen thousandth tepid shower with the yellow soap tossed about like a football and the only thing they had to look forward to on a non-movie night, God bless their warm generous natures. Seaton felt a glow for them.

'Report to my tent at stand-down,' Captain Smollett said, shifting papers and not looking up.

This time no precautions were taken. He was naked to the waist, washing himself with a sponge out of a tin basin; he merely gestured toward the camp chair and Seaton sat although it was improper for him to be seated while an officer stood. Was there going to be trouble? Could Vince have discovered some arcane loophole in the army manual that could preclude the transfer?

Vince wiped his face and chest with a towel and said, 'So you're going back to a nice safe cozy job at base, are you?'

'Sir.'

'Don't be formal.'

'They need experienced radio scriptwriters. I'm one.'

'I see.'

Captain Smollett smiled glassily, the smile that invariably preceded a verdict of guilty, bringing with it a punishment of draconian severity. Then still smiling he tore the towel he was holding completely down the middle. It was as biblical as the rending of clothes. In a strangled voice he said, 'This place is going to be unthinkable without you,' and as Seaton rose to go to him, barked, 'Sit still. Anyone might come it.' He bent over the tin wash basin as if in pain. 'I shouldn't complain, it's not that bad of a posting for a somewhat uneducated bloke like me. The officer chaps are not bad, they're not my type, but they try, the boys do their best, it's just that'—a very long pause and then in almost no voice at all—'I'm so fucking lonely. Not only here, everywhere. Back in Melbourne. Everywhere. Oh, I shouldn't complain, I've got a good dull job to go back to. I'm engaged to a fine girl. Got my mum and dad. A bonza sister. They all think I'm the berries, poor boobs. I've never told anyone about myself. You're one of the four people on earth who knows. I wanted just to tell you that and to tell you one last time I love you.' He picked up the tin basin and, moving to the flap of the tent, threw out the soapy water onto the dirty sand. For the first time, he looked at Seaton. 'That's all, dismissed!'

On Wednesday morning, the truck waiting to take him down to Larimah in-transit camp, Seaton took his transfer papers from Captain Smollett, who appeared not to be noticing him.

'Good-bye, sir.'

The voice was a live electric wire. 'Corporal.'

'Sir.'

'Your bootlace is untied.'

1990

DAVID MALOUF

Night Training

The day Greg Newsome turned seventeen he joined the University Air Squadron. It was 1951. The memory of one war, which had been in progress all through his childhood, was still strong in him, gathering to it all the appealing mementos and moods of those years, and the Cold War recently had thrown up another conflict, a smaller one, in Korea. War seemed to him, and to others like him, a natural thing. It galvanised people's energies and drew them to a pitch. It clarified meanings. It held you in the line of history. It also cleansed the spirit by offering occasions where mere animal energy and the noblest aspirations could meet at a point of vivid exultation, and mind and body, which at a certain age seem like divergent states of being, were instantly reconciled.

•   •   •

When Greg went to be medically examined he had to wait for more than an hour in a poky enclosure with walls of three-ply and not a picture on the wall. There were a dozen other fellows there, on benches. He didn't know a single one of them. He plunged into a book, a Loeb Classic. When he was called at last he had to strip and sit on a chair to one side of the examiner's desk.

The man was a civilian, but with one of those handlebar moustaches that in those days still evoked the image of a fighter pilot in the war. He looked at Greg's birth date, then at Greg, and was silent. Greg blushed. It was odd to be sitting stark naked on a chair beside a desk with his flesh sticking to varnish. He hung on mentally to his Plato.

'So,' the doctor said, 'we've got around to you lot.' His face expressed a profound weariness.

•   •   •

On their first camp three months later he was assigned to an Intelligence unit and shared a hut with the other 'baby' of the squadron, a country boy from Harrisville, Cam Brierly. They were so much the youngest that they took it in turns, on official mess nights, when all the officers of the station were assembled, to be Mister Vice: that is, to reply to toasts and initiate the passing of the port. It was a role in which you appeared to be the centre of the occasion, but only in the clownish sense of being a king of fools.

They stuck together, he and Cam. Not because they had anything in common but to conceal from others their appalling innocence.

Their task by day was to catalogue and reshelve the station library, under the eye of the Chief Education Officer, David Kitchener, a cynical fellow who did nothing himself but lounge behind his desk and was by turns a bully and a tease. He resented having them fobbed off on him.

At night, after dinner, while other fellows got drunk, played darts or snooker or sang round the piano in true Air Force style, they tried, one after another, a series of exotic liqueurs of lurid colour and with enticing names: *Curaçao, Crème de Menthe, Parfait d'Amour.* They were sickly every one.

The mess late at night got rowdy, then out of hand. Understanding, though they never admitted it, that if they hung around they would very likely become butts, for their youth was in itself ridiculous, they slipped away before eleven and were soon asleep.

• • •

One of the wildest figures at these nightly gatherings was Dave Kitchener, the officer who gave them such a hard time by day. A bit of an outsider with his fellow officers, he was always looking for trouble. When he got a few drinks under his belt he turned sarcastic, then aggressive, and went on the prowl. They had, more than once, caught him glaring in their direction, and understood that if he once got up and came across it would be to lash them with his tongue. They knew him already: he couldn't be trusted to keep the rules. He passed muster in the office, and on official parade, but in the mess at night his uniform was loosened at the neck, and his hair, which was longer than was permitted, fell uncombed over his brow. He had a sodden look. Six or seven years back—Greg had the story from a fellow who had known him at Charters Towers—he had been a master at All Souls. He was caught climbing into the window of a woman from the sister school, Blackheath, and they were both dismissed. One night when there were women in the mess, Air Force nurses, he went up to one of them and threw a glass of beer in her face.

They had been in camp for two weeks when Dave Kitchener appeared for the first time in their hut.

• • •

It must have been between one and two in the morning. Greg stirred, aware of a presence in the room that registered itself first as a slight pressure on his consciousness, then on the mattress beside him. He woke and there he was, sitting on the edge of the bed. Just sitting. Quietly absorbed, as if he had come in tired to his own room and was too sleepy to undress.

He's made a mistake, Greg thought.

His cap was off, his tie loose, and there was a bottle in his hand.

Greg lay quiet. Nothing like this had ever happened to him, he didn't know what to do. When the man realised at last that he was being watched, he turned, fixed his eyes on Greg, made a little contemptuous sound, deep in this throat, and laughed. He lifted the bottle in ironic salute. Then, reaching for his cap, which he had tossed carelessly on the bed, he set it on his head, got to his feet and took a stance.

'All right, cadet,' he said. 'Get out of there.'

Greg was astonished.

'Didn't you hear? That was an order.' His nails flicked the stripes on his sleeve. 'Get your mate up. I said, *get up!*'

Greg rolled out of bed. He was out before he properly realised it. This must be a dream, he thought, till the cold struck him. Skirting the officer, who stood in a patch of moonlight in the centre of the room, he crossed to Cam's bed and hung there in a kind of limbo, looking down at his friend. He still couldn't believe this was happening.

'Go on,' the man told him.

Cam was sound asleep, and Greg, still lightly touched by a state that seems commonplace till you are unnaturally hauled out of it, was struck by something he had never felt till now: the mystery, a light and awesome barrier, that surrounds a sleeping man; which is meant to be his protection, and which another, for reasons too deep to be experienced as more than a slight tingling at the hair-roots, is unwilling to violate. Cam's head rested on the upper part of his arm, which was thrust out over the edge of the mattress. Under the covers his legs were moving, as if he were slowly running from something in there, or burrowing deeper into the dark.

Greg glanced across his shoulder at the officer, hoping, before this new breach was made, that he would reconsider and go away. But the man only nodded and made an impatient sound. Greg put his hand out. Gingerly, with just the tips of his fingers, he touched Cam's shoulder, then clasped it and shook.

But Cam was difficult. He put up a floppy arm and pushed Greg off. Even when Greg had got him at last into a sitting position he wasn't fully awake. Sleep was like a membrane he was wrapped in that would not break. It made everything about him hazy yet bright: his cheeks, his eyes when they jerked open. Greg began to be impatient, 'Come on, Cam, get up,' he whispered. 'Stop mucking about.'

The man, standing with the cap far back on his head, laughed and took a swig from his bottle.

'Wasser matter?' Cam muttered. The words were bubbly. ''S' middle a' the night.'

Greg hauled him up, cursing, and propped him there. He kept giggling like a child and going loose. 'Cut it out,' Greg hissed, staggering a little in the attempt to hold him. He hadn't realised before what a spindly, overgrown fellow he was. But at least he was on his feet, if not yet fully present. Greg turned to the officer.

Dave Kitchener had been watching his struggles with a mixture of amusement and contempt. He now seated himself, as before, on the edge of Greg's bunk, his legs apart, the cap on the back of his head, his feet firmly planted, the bottle in his fist.

'Right,' he said. 'Now. Get stripped.'

Greg was outraged. So, after all his exertions with Cam, it still wasn't finished.

This is wrong, he told himself as he started on the buttons of his pyjama jacket. *All of it. He shouldn't be wearing his cap that way. He shouldn't be sitting on my bed.* He wrenched at the buttons in a hopeless rage, the rage a child feels at being unjustly punished, feeling it prickle in his throat. Tears, that meant—if he wasn't careful he would burst into tears. His concern now was to save himself from that last humiliation. He lifted his singlet over his head, undid the cord of his pants. They were in winter flannels. In the mornings here, when you skipped out barefoot to take a piss, the ground was crunchy with frost.

Cam was still dazed. He stood but was reeling. Greg looked towards the officer, then, with deliberate roughness, began to undo the buttons on Cam's jacket. 'We've got to take them off,' he explained as to a three-year-old.

When they were naked Dave Kitchener had them drill, using a couple of ink-stained rulers. He kept them at it for nearly an hour.

• • •

He did not come every night. Three or four might pass and they would be left undisturbed, then Greg would be aware again of that change of pressure in the room.

After the first occasion there was no need of commands. As soon as Greg was awake, Dave Kitchener would rise, stand aside for him to pass, and Greg would go obediently to Cam's bed and begin the difficult exercise of getting him to his feet. It was always the same. Cam had to be dragged to the occasion. He resisted, he pushed Greg off. Laughing in his sleep in a silly manner and muttering sentences or syllables from a dialogue of which only the one side could be heard, he reeled and clung on.

Dave Kitchener showed no interest in these proceedings. They were Greg's affair. He left him to it. And because the officer no longer made himself responsible, Greg found all this intimate busines of getting Cam out of bed and awake and stripped more repugnant than ever. Damn him! he thought—meaning Cam. He had come to see this peculiarity in the other boy, his reluctance to come awake, as a form of stubborn innocence. It set his own easy wakefulness in a shameful light. He resented it, and his resentment carried over into their dealings in the library as well. They began to avoid one another.

Meanwhile the waking and drilling went on. And afterwards, while they stood naked and shivering but at ease, the lectures.

• • •

Each morning the squadron was broken up into specialist units, but in the afternoons, after mess, they came together for a series of pep talks that were intended to develop a spirit of solidarity in them as well as providing an introduction to the realities of war. Some of these talks were given by men, bluff self-conscious fellows not much older than themselves, who were just back from the fighting in Korea. They made everything, even the rough stuff, sound like Red Rover or some other game where getting a bloody knee, or your shirt torn, was the risk you took for being in it. One fellow told them that his liaison officers up there had been called Cum Suk and Bum Suk, then went on to describe the effects of napalm.

In the break between lectures they stood about smoking, or formed circles and tossed a medicine ball.

•   •   •

Dave Kitchener's lectures were of a different sort, and they came, after a time, to signify for Greg the real point of these midnight sessions, for which the rest, the dreamlike ritual of ordering and presenting arms, of turning left, right, about face, coming to attention, standing at ease and easy, was a mere preliminary, a means of breaking them down so that they could not resist. They drilled. Then they stood at ease, they stood easy, and Dave Kitchener began.

After the formal hectoring of the bull-ring, the roars of official rage and insult that were a regular thing out there, Dave Kitchener's voice, which seldom rose above a whisper in the room, was unnerving. They felt his breath at moments on the backs of their necks. Then too, there was their nakedness. They were like plucked chooks—that's how Greg felt it. Goosepimpled with cold and half asleep on their feet, they stood, while the voice wove round and around them.

'What I'm trying to do is wake you up to things. You're so wet behind the ears, both of you, you're pitiful! Have you got any idea how pitiful you look? Because your mothers love you, and you've been to nice little private schools, you think you've got it made. That nothing can touch you. That you're covered by the rules. Well, let me tell you, lad, there *are* no rules. There's a war on out there, you're heading right for it, and there are *no rules*. Oh, I know that's not what they tell you in those jolly little pep talks they give you. What I'm talking about is something different. The *real* war. The one that's going on all the time. Right here, now, in this room.' He laughed. Greg heard the spittle bubble on his tongue. 'The one where they've already got you by the balls.' He stood back, looked them over, turned away in disgust. 'You poor little bastards. You don't even know what I'm talking about, do you? You should see yourselves. You're pitiful. You're bloody pitiful. I'm wasting my time on you.'

He would go on like that for the best part of an hour, a mixture of taunts, threats, insults, concern and a blistering anger at the quality in them that most offended him, their naïve confidence in things; which he was determined to relieve them of, and which they were unable to give up—it belonged too deeply to the power they felt in themselves, the buoyancy and resistance of youth. Greg discovered after a time how to handle it. You did just what you were ordered to do down to the last detail, with scrupulous precision, as you never did it out there on the bull-ring. Not in mockery of the thing itself; that would have been to enter into collusion with *him*, for whom this was already a mockery, but to mock his authority with its limits. Your body obeyed to the letter. The rest of you stayed away.

•   •   •

Their last day in camp was a passing out parade. Several of the older fellows were to get commissions, which would entitle them to wear their caps without the virginal white band; three of them got wings. The bull-ring dazzled in the sun; they sweated in their heavy uniforms. A band played. The voices of the drill sergeants leapt out and they responded: *Stand at ease, stand easy.* Dave Kitchener was there, his cap straight, his collar fastened. He saluted when the others did.

Watching from his company in the ranks, Greg was puzzled by a kind of emptiness in himself, a lack of connection with all this. Something in him had moved away, and might have been lounging off there in the shade of one of the huts, with it spine against a wall and the curl of a smile on its lips, bored now with the whole show: these movements that were so fixed and refined that the order they embodied seemed like another nature, the swing of their arms that brought the rifles down, the clunk of boots, their bodies aligned and responding as one to snapped commands. His own body was too constant for him not to remember that he had performed these movements more smartly elsewhere. He had an impulse to make some deliberate error and break the line. He closed his lids and swallowed. *Eyes right!* The image that fixed itself in his head was of the bull-ring empty, lit only by the moon, with the bluish shadow of the flagpole, also empty, falling far across it.

•   •   •

He saw Cam Brierly only once in the next year. They were no longer the youngest, and since that had been the only thing in common between them, they were free to keep apart. They never spoke of Dave Kitchener or made any mention of the night training—which took on, in time, a quality of unreality that belonged to the hours, somewhere between one and three in the morning, when it had taken place: the hours of regulated dark when they, like all those others laid out in officers' huts and barracks, should have been safe under the blankets pursuing innocuous dreams. It was almost, in the end, as if they *had* been. Greg's anger faded in him. So did the sense of injury he felt. When he thought of Dave Kitchener he understood, from the midst of the war he had spoken of, what it was that had fired and frustrated him. He pitied the man.

It was about this time that he had a dream.

He was standing once again beside Cam Brierly's bed, looking down at the sleeping figure from a height, a distance of years, and with a

mixture of tenderness and awe that arrested every possibility of movement in him; he could no more have leaned down and broken the other's
sleep at that moment than woken himself. Some powerful interdiction
was on him. He looked across his shoulder and said firmly: 'No'.

But the one who had been there in his dream was not there to hear it.
He was staring into darkness, fully awake.

1987

DENNIS ALTMAN

From *The Comfort of Men*

Gerald

Gerald grew up in a small country town in the Midlands, in a family that
was both poor and took its poverty for granted. Until he went to school
he never had shoes of his own, and his feet retained their grainy
toughness from walking barefoot, even fifteen years later. His mother
died when he was twelve, and he was sent to grow up with an older
cousin in Hobart, who promptly bought him new clothes and insisted on
his going to Sunday School.

Several years later, riding home from school on the Glenorchy tram, a
young man asked him where he was going, and offered to take him for a
ride in his car later on that afternoon. Gerald thought about it, agreed,
and said he'd like a pound to do 'anything' the man wanted. Slightly
shocked by this precocity the man agreed, and Gerald called his aunt to
say he'd been detained at school and wouldn't be home for tea. Thus
Gerald launched himself on both a financial and sexual career.

He wasn't sure at the time what 'anything' might entail; the demand
for money arose from an instinctive sense that the approach represented
more than disinterested friendship. But from this first encounter Gerald
learnt fast; he soon discovered the area by the river, behind several
school sportsgrounds, where men loitered for the purpose of meeting
each other, and that his value to them was dramatically increased by
wearing his school uniform. 'I'd wear my summer shorts well into May,'
he reminisced once, 'so I looked younger. It was bloody cold going home
on the tram on the nights I didn't score.' On summer weekends he would
hitch out to the outer beach areas of Hobart where there were occasional
patches of naked men, some of whom could be persuaded to part with
money for the pleasure of teenage cock.

Until he turned eighteen, Gerald remained detached from his sexual
activities. 'Sex was something I thought happened with women, and I
wasn't ready for it yet. It was only when I met Ted that I decided that
what I was doing with men counted as sex.'

Gerald met Ted, as he met most of his men, on a beat. But Ted was different from the others; he was neither married nor pretending not to be homosexual—it was 1961 and 'camp' was the term we used then—and felt neither remorse nor guilt for enjoying his sexuality. This is how Gerald told me the story, late one night over too many coffees, crouched at our usual table at the Venezia.

'It was the summer after I left school, and I was working as a postman to earn money. I picked up Ted, like the others, at Cornelian Bay, but he didn't want it in the car or the change room—unlike most of the others he took me home, and he assumed I'd stay the night, which I would have except for the scene I knew the aunt would create . . . He lived in a flat in South Hobart, full of art pieces and exotic junk—he'd travelled a lot, India, Malaya, Indonesia . . . and he was into the most extraordinary sex: no more quick wanks in the car or half-hearted sucking, one eye over the shoulder in case the cops showed up. He saw sex as an art form: dim lights, music, wine, and then he'd throw himself into it for hours; he'd rub me all over with these strange scented oils, and then lick them off . . . his idea of sex was to come to the verge of climax three or four times, then calm down, and only after a few hours would we come, sometimes with him inside me—he was the first man who could fuck me easily and so that I enjoyed it and wasn't only doing it because I got a pound extra . . . I saw him for almost a year on and off, whenever he was free . . . I suppose he had others but I was so besotted that I refused to contemplate it . . . the only thing I knew was not to talk to Ted about love—he'd already said that I was too young to get serious and I knew he would piss me off if it started looking too demanding . . .'

But I have overshot myself: Gerald did not speak to me about his sexual life for almost a year, and only then because I too had met Ted. By the time I was in second year at university I admitted my homosexual desires to myself, but felt unable to go out and find partners. Despite long and elaborate fantasies centred on images of half-naked men I remained almost totally ignorant of the practicalities of sex. I drifted in and out of dreams about young men with firm chests and capacious mouths, but without much sense of how their flesh might merge with mine, nor how I might find them outside the quarters of my dreams. Looking back I am struck by the extraordinary innocence I seemed able to maintain; I cannot imagine that a nineteen-year-old today, knowing all that the media tells us, could so easily have remained willing to content himself with masturbatory fantasies.

Ted I met through his involvement in an Old Devil co-production with a local theatre group. On the first day of rehearsals I saw a short russet-haired man with golden arms and a smile that could have modelled for the cover of a Harlequin romance, hinting, as the copy editor might write, of sweetness and cruel abandon. Ted was then in his mid-thirties, and for the first time I realised the sexual attraction of maturity; he was neither conventionally good-looking nor particularly muscular, but he carried his sensuality upfront, and without fully realising it I began looking forward to rehearsals as an excuse to see Ted, began paying attention to his conversation and watching his every move in a way which would have been extremely obvious had the rest of the company not been oblivious to the reality of homosexual lust. Ted, like Gerald, had a surprisingly deep voice, and their common baritone became a part of my fantasies, so that ever since I have always been attracted to men with deep voices.

. . .

It had come as something of a shock to discover that Gerald, too, was infatuated with Ted, but a relief as well; I passed quickly from lust for Ted to eagerly listening to Gerald's stories, vicariously sharing his desire for a relationship—the word itself seemed daring, beyond our grasp—with Ted.

Fairly rapidly, whatever relationship there was between Ted and Gerald became strained, and I came to expect late night phone calls from Gerald—'He's busy tonight,' he'd say mournfully. 'He doesn't have time for me any more. Come down to the pub.'

This was in itself an act of some boldness, for I was as yet underage, and every now and then the publican, spurred by an occasional visit from the police, would mutter about checking identity cards (which we didn't possess) and not serving minors. On the whole though we were able to drink undisturbed.

The pub we went to was in one of the oldest parts of the city, in that section of narrow, crooked streets and small weatherboard and stone cottages that gives one the passing illusion that Hobart is an English town, rather than an outpost in the farthest reaches of the Antipodes. The building itself dated back to the 1920s, and was of two-storey sandstone, much of the original stucture obliterated by various additions due to the prosperity and taste of later generations. In addition to the obligatory men-only bar, with its tile floor and photos of race horses and local football players, it included a small and dark lounge—'the ladies'—where Gerald and I would sit, nursing our drinks, along with a few women in cheap, floral dresses and the occasional lonely business traveller uncomfortable with the bonhomie of the main bar.

Here, too, would come the occasional homosexual, for if The Crown and Anchor was not by any stretch of the imagination a camp bar, it was one of several pubs in Hobart where men had been known to meet each other—'Had *him*,' Gerald hissed at me, as a florid faced but still young man entered, and we giggled together as the man caught sight of Gerald, turned yet more florid, and hastily retreated to the main bar.

. . .

Meanwhile Gerald, Ted and I had the occasional meal together, usually in Ted's flat, and Gerald continued to sleep with Ted, but less and less, and never when I was around. My infatuation for Ted was long gone, and I found I had little to say to him and that it is difficult to become friends with those with whom one has imagined oneself hopelessly in love. I was alone with him only once after my initial visit, and we spoke of many things: books, his time in the army in Malaya, my future career, the camp bars of Berlin and Bangkok. But not of Gerald, nor, in any intimate way, of Ted himself.

'That'd be right,' said Gerald cynically. 'He doesn't give away very much about himself, that one.'

From Gerald I had pieced together the bare bones of Ted's life: his childhood in New Zealand and Adelaide, his half-finished pharmacy course followed by national service and a period in the army, his series of jobs and his travels across Southeast Asia, his arrival in Hobart two years earlier to work for the Department of Forests. If there had been people of significance in his life he never said; he referred remotely to a sister still in New Zealand, and a couple of photos of men in army uniform, who could have been military buddies or former lovers, hung discreetly in corners of his flat. 'No such thing as love,' Ted was fond of saying. 'It doesn't make for good sex, and you sleep better alone.'

There always seemed a slightly mysterious side to Ted, periods when he appeared to disappear; shadowy friendships, or at least acquaintances, of whom we were never aware. Ted had won entrée to the small, carefully submerged camp world of 1950s Hobart, and entertained us with stories of pretentious dinner parties and precious cocktail evenings in subdued flats. Neither Gerald nor I were invited along. But he had other social arenas, as well: he was a keen swimmer, played squash, still somewhat of a novelty in the early 1960s, belonged to an amateur dramatic society, went bushwalking and even to local chamber music concerts. People like Ted now go to cafés rather than pubs, watch home videos rather than join societies, and buy take-away food or go to restaurants, of which there were then very few. Apart from the hotel dining rooms, complete with their stiff reminders of British cuisine and convention, there existed several coffee lounges, of which Helen's was the most genteel, and two Chinese restuarants, one of them in the suburbs. Even for those who, like Ted, lived alone, eating out was something regarded as a special occasion, rather than, as is now the case, taken for granted.

Ted included Gerald in virtually none of his social activities; in retrospect, what seemed both mysterious and even cruel (to Gerald) was no more than the self-protective behaviour of a perfectly ordinary young man who could hardly afford to be seen with someone who was barely more than a teenager. Ted continued to trawl for other men—as did Gerald, though with less interest since meeting Ted. 'He's pushing me away,' said Gerald mournfully. 'And the more I want to be with him the more he rejects me.'

Once, I remember, Ted asked us both to go to a concert with him, quite an event for the local symphony orchestra was playing with the visiting wunderkind Daniel Barenboim, and for the first time in my life I consciously heard Beethoven's fourth piano concerto, and felt the shivers of revelation through my body which are supposed to come from good sex. Music, I discovered that night, carries its own epiphany: there are other pieces like that concerto—Mahler's fourth symphony, the Act One finale of *Don Giovanni*—which can still reduce me to tears. But Gerald was far more preoccupied with Ted's apparent friendship with one of the cello players—'Justin's having a small party after the concert,' said Ted as we filed from the hall, 'but I can't really bring you blokes along.' (Thus explaining why he had asked me as well as Gerald to the concert.) 'Sure,' said Gerald, all too casually and pretending to some enthusiasm, when I suggested going round to the stage door and waiting for Barenboim, with the vague fantasy that he would prefer spending a few hours with people his own age than with the violinists and flautists who were presumably readying themselves to lionise him. In the end we lost our nerve, and I doubt if he even noticed us as he left, both arms held protectively by managers, and Gerald went home on the last tram to brood that he was not socially acceptable enough to be taken to a party for a pianist little more than a year older than he.

'I finally said it,' he told me one night, his eyes sore from lack of sleep and crying. 'I told him I loved him. He said he couldn't love me, and it would be better if we stopped seeing each other.'

'Perhaps,' I said tentatively, 'he can't love anyone.'

'Well why not?' said Gerald plaintively. 'It's not that hard is it? People do it all the time.'

'Men?' I asked sceptically. 'With each other?'

'If I can love a man,' said Gerald, 'I can't believe I'm the only one.'

1993

FRANK MOORHOUSE

The Everlasting Secret Family

AN EROTIC MEMOIR IN SIX PARTS

Prepared for publication by the author from letters, monologues, conversations, diaries and other sources.

Narrator's note: This was originally to be published privately and circulated privately. I do not in any way wish to harm the conservative parties of this country. In so far as this memoir touches on political things (and caution delimited this severely) it does so simply as a fact of our lives. It may be suggested that the publication of this work is a ploy in a personal relationship—be that as it may, that also was *not* the energising motive behind my having this put down on paper. I recorded it out of joy and I dedicate it to him who gave me the highest sexual privilege.

The Bad Dog And The Angel Custodio

In that trance of black lust, like a dog, I dawdled, entranced, fixed by the shabby immigrant of uncertain nationality who had caught my submissive, available eyes in the lane and flicked back a glance, knowing and commanding, stopping me, entranced and trembling.

He moves his head for me to follow and I do at a distance, like a dog, the wordless, animal knowingness of male gutter sex.

I follow him, he taking me I suppose at first to his room, but then it becomes clear that he is looking for any place, a doorway, a porch, an alley. We come to a church. He walks into a path at the side of the church and stands there.

I follow him, the submissive dog. He does not speak but simply unzips himself. I kneel before him, burrow in with my fingers and pull out the soft, erecting penis taking it into my mouth.

I am taken down, down into that self-contained black world where there is no other thing, feeling, or sound but a moist, hot penis and my yielding mouth. There is nothing in the world for that time but his penis moving towards its explosion and my mouth moving, shaping, and pulling and wanting it. The mouth that is saying without words, yes, come, use me, fill me. No outside world existing, no other reward, no other way of being.

Holding his balls, drawing out the sperm, he grunting, his only sound, a giving grunt and then the pulsing sperm, the completed link, the joining by the highest sensation and the most brawny of fluids, two strangers in a path beside a church.

He pulls himself away, he zips himself, and he steps around me, walking away. Not a word, not a gesture, no sign.

That was right and how it should be. I was left by him on my knees, shivering with stimulation, coming out from under that black, sexual hood. The exertion and the enlivened nerves of my mouth and taste making me quietly gasp, panting there on my knees, weak from the perfection of that enactment. Our silent performance. In all its human basicness, complete. Recognition and fulfilment of need and role. The perfect rightness of it beyond morality. The weeping, honest animalism of it. I was weak with a ringing, singing gratification. I could have thanked God for permitting me to be, still, a human animal.

I stayed there for a minute as I returned to my identity, enjoying a recognition of where I'd just been and of where I was kneeling, of who I was, of my worldly connections, of my lover now waiting for me, of what I'd done—my smearing of that other life, a wilful disfigurement.

I got up, one hand against the church while my knees recovered, and then strolled back to our town house, our pied-à-terre, my penis moist in the silk of my underpants.

He was home waiting for me and I tried to be casual and not show the tired, remaining delight of my rutting.

'You look guilty,' he said.

I went and washed and showered and cleaned my teeth, sterilising myself back into our strict, shared world. Our hygienic arrangement.

'I suppose you've been prowling the lavatories again,' he said, although without menace.

He hadn't alleged that for a year or so. He had once had one of his heavies follow me and then there'd been efforts to stop me from being promiscuous, including terrifying—but unsuccessful—'therapy' in some private hospital. When I was sixteen.

'No.'

'Why all the redemptive washing, all that tired humming.'

'I just feel good.'

'Only one thing makes you *feel good.*'

'Leave me alone.'

'I have some news for you.'

'What?'

'I'm going to marry.'

I coloured. There in the lounge room I touched a Balinese carving for no reason, reaching out to it with a shaking hand, as if for balance. I stood there perilously hovering above his splintering statement.

'You can't.' That was all I could say.

He had been escorting—courting?—I don't know—this girl—woman—for a couple of years. I never thought, I had always seen it as a front for his political career, or an arrangement or *something*. I don't know about these things. She was in the Country Party or her father was something in the Country Party. I assumed they didn't do anything physically. I thought she was another sort of hostess.

'You can't.'

He smiled.

In passing I realised that I knew nothing about weddings, engagements, the etiquette of it all, another world. This thought went through my reeling mind.

'What about me, us ...' But as I said it, I knew there was no longer any leverage in 'us', or that I should not have tried to use it. Then I said, just as hopelessly, 'What about all this?' indicating the apartment.

'I'm going to leave you here—in your abnormality.'

I had never heard him say anything which disowned our life, or anything so hypocritical. The clinical word 'abnormality'. After the sexual life we'd had. After he'd inducted me into it. I was aghast.

'I've never been unfaithful to you—not since the therapy,' I said without truth or relevance.

He smiled.

'I've only been with people you wanted me to go with.'

'I know all there is to know about you.'

'It worked,' I said, desperately, 'that treatment.'

'I move out of here tonight.'

'No!!'

He laughed. 'I don't want to catch anything—wherever you've been—whatever sewer.'

'You'd better have her checked too.'

He hit me with the back of his hand, with his ring, as if he had been waiting to do it for a lifetime. It seemed so timed, so pent up. It was not like the other beatings, it was not sexual.

His college ring had split my lip wide open.

Senselessly I remembered what was different, remembered his always saying that I wasn't to be hit about the face in sexual play.

'I want,' he said deliberately, also as if rehearsed, 'a clean life, a domestic life. I intend to father a child. You have no further part to play.'

'Betrayer,' I screamed.

He hit me again and his ring cut my face and I could taste now the blood in my mouth from my lip.

'Yes,' he said, not trembling, no loss of poise at all from having struck me or from the gigantic things he was saying, 'I've arranged for someone to take my place, here. With you.'

He laughed to himself. I couldn't take in this second announcement, let alone his private laughter.

Weeping in the bathroom, dabbing my cut lip, my bleeding face, I heard him leave.

He'd taken only his clothes and toiletries, in the Vuitton luggage. He took no objet d'art nor any of the other memorabilia of our shared life.

I was left, bereft. A frantic dog. I slid within seconds from clutching on to his presence, even though he was withdrawing it, clutching to those final moments of him being there in the room, slid into that extraordinary emotional sickness known bluntly as rejection. Unexperienced by me until then.

But on top of that I was bereft of what they call 'shared pathology'. That buttressed security which came from him telling me how I had been chosen to lead a very special life. How I had no ordinary destiny. That my relationship was with the great and powerful, in a special way, to serve and belong to the elite. To what reality did I belong now? I was too young now to handle it. I belonged through him. He was gone.

I cried at my cut face. I thought, for the first time in years, of my sisters, my parents, and my blood became melting snow.

I took what Valium I had and turned my blood and nerves into a stream of sluggish, chemically polluted snow. I was visited later that night by the doctor, who injected me with some other drug, and so I remained for weeks.

I did not go to the wedding. I remember staring at the invitation which arrived and sensing, even as drugged as I was, that this was not an invitation to something but the *closure* of something. I sent them nothing, if sending something is what you are supposed to do.

I saw him once, to get him to sign something about the apartment. I came on with a drugged blankness which passed as civility, while yearning for him to put his hands on me, and he, he was buttoned up in a lawyer's suit and wore a minute lapel badge I hadn't seen before. The sort of badge which is supposed to communicate only to those who also belong. Maybe is was the League of Married Homosexual Statesmen.

I had no strength of self for months after he left me. I found it unappealing to 'play in the streets'. I worried with a drugged resignation about the 'someone' who was to take his place. No further word had been spoken about this. Still the cheques continued to arrive from his office.

Much of my time was taken with unsatisfying drinking. Never having a true desire for any particular drink, always beginning drinking by saying to myself that, although I didn't feel like it, if I drank I would feel like it. I made plans to run away. I tried to learn Spanish, became very 'Spanish'. I suppose running away to another culture. I now felt, saw, and became perplexed by 'normality', those people in the shops. It seemed so desirable to be like them now, the drab ones. After all those years of feeling privately superior. I wanted what I imagined he now had—the tidal routine of home-life, the idea of being woven into a rope of kinship and in-laws, and talkative, amusing children. In parkas.

That's how it all looked to me.

Of course, with his sexual ambiguity, and because he was who he was, and because he was controlled by ambition and by pledges and oaths and deals, he had had to pass over to this new life and he did it so lightly, passed so lightly from our bizarre homosexuality, with its rituals and peculiar mechanics, with its lubricants and locker-room maleness. My memories of it ached around the place—warm, wet semen, groins, soft body hair, silk underwear, the other specially made garments. Even its terror.

To outsiders—'special associates'—it had been good cuisine (done by a catering service—not by me), privately projected movies, and those strange evenings, lasting through until dawn, where everyone knew their part, untold, unasked, where not only were the music, the lighting, the clothing and the behaviour, satanic but the air seemed different and one's pulse and breathing changed.

And the quieter times, when I was the beautiful boy who shared this large apartment with him and was something of a mystery. A desirable young thing who obviously did what he was told. Who was directed to flirt with those important old men and sometimes more. But it had been a workable, shared ... home ... with its guest bathrooms and plenty of other space, the rambling courtyard.

I retched now, yearning for the odours of those days. I sweated in a fever of withdrawal, craving the pungency of a male intimacy.

All that remained, it seemed, was dirty laundry, unopened junk mail and a plaintive note from the cleaning person about not her job 'to pick up after occupants'. I waited for the key in the door which would tell me that the replacement, if that is the word, had arrived.

I thought I was sickening and had tests.

I was sickening, but the tests could not find the sickness. I was a sick dog with no master.

Then—suddenly, unbelievably, unexpectedly, without warning, as if in answer to a prayer, like the clouds parting, the end of a bad dream, the beginning of spring—the telephone rang.

The telephone. It lets anyone into our lives at any time, it can strike so wilfully. It can be the sword; it can be the soft wings of an angel custodio.

This time it was the soft, feathered wings of an angel custodio which folded around me.

I was just leaving. I was outside the door when I heard the ringing of the phone. I took my key out and let myself back in expecting that, as always, it would stop.

It didn't. It was he.

The first call he'd made to me since he had left for the outer world.

He began with that desultory, false conversation—how are things? living it up? Did you get those forms? And then he moved on to the shared lore of our life together, moved in that direction with a forced naturalness. How's Zonky? (the cat) and so on. Embarrassing to relate. Yes, I kept thinking, I know, I know what this is all about—but why doesn't he just come up and take me instead of behaving like some ordinary lover. I was filled with another perplexity, this behaviour of his, as if he had to 'win' me back. He kept on, about the cars in the garages of the town houses 'wetting themselves'—a reference to a joke we'd had about the oil stains on the floors of the garages. I was embarrassed by his soppiness. Say it! Say it! But no, he had to sustain this false prelude.

He suggested he might drop around and, for the first time, said, 'If it's all right.'

If it's all right.

Oh shit, I hated him like this.

As I listened, I tried on a new feeling though. Could it be the helmet of power? After all these subordinate years? I said, in my special cocksucking voice, as soon as I felt the power, 'Only if you promise to use me until I cry.'

Was my voice right? Did I say it right?

He cleared his throat. 'You know that's what I meant,' and I think I detected some disconsolation. Oh, I wasn't accustomed to this.

'What about, say—five minutes from now,' I said.

He managed to laugh and said no, it would have to be later, after a meeting.

The meetings.

Oh the time I'd spent waiting for meetings to finish. As a schoolboy dozing in his car.

But making me wait was a retaking of command.

'I'll wait,' I said, 'I want to be made to wait.'

I could have tried to make him come up now and to skip the meeting. That would have been a test of this power. But I didn't dare. And I didn't want to.

The conversation ended with me quivering and wet.

'Hah, though,' I said to myself, 'nevertheless,' prancing to the mirror, sighing, throwing myself on the bed, 'nevertheless, now who the dog and who the master?' He needed me.

I had the usual trouble filling the time until he arrived. The dreaded jigsaw. And it is unfair to a book to use it to 'fill time', I always say. Concentration is always running ahead to the time of the appointment. When he arrived I did the girlish thing of saying, 'Sit down, I won't be a minute,' and then going off to the bathroom again. Or maybe these days girls don't do that. Only hysterically dependent boy lovers.

And then to bed. I swear I have never seen so much semen. We were supposed to go out to a late dinner. But we just didn't make it. He poured out his whole self all over me. Dear Jesus, I could kiss you for bringing him back.

I didn't mention The Marriage. I felt that I shouldn't make him assert loyalty one way or the other. Yet. So I gave him joy, unconditional joy—without emotional payment. That was my tactic.

I gave him joy and he came gushing over me in a flood. And I, not too badly either. That woman must have been scaring it back inside him. It certainly rushed to greet me.

We were awash.

I brought him the instrument so that he could do his favourite number to me and I wore the nightgown he required me to wear—just to make absolutely sure that it was to be as it was before. It was, it was old times again.

As I lay there under him and he began to come, I couldn't help but register the quantity of it to myself, and I swear I rolled my eyes in pleasure. He whimpered as he let it flow out. It was nice to hear someone as important as he whimper, and to feel his involuntary clutch.

Poor man.

That wife was doing him no good.

That, though, was my last and only playing about with the idea of being Master.

I wouldn't have done it very well anyhow.

After pouring himself over me in that starved embrace, he got up with not one word of sexual gratitude, drank scotch, poked about the refrigerator and ate half a quiche.

He didn't say much, but looked relaxed almost to the point of torpor. It was then I experienced the most diminishing gesture I know. The gesture which spelled out the new contract.

He looked at his watch.

But you must realise that, because he'd said nothing, and I'd asked no questions, and because he had obviously wanted to have me so badly, I had at this point a fantasy that he had *come back to me*. Come back to live with me. Maybe he had, by using the old intimacy, moving about in it the way it had been, using the language of our domesticity, maybe he had let me have this fantasy to, say, get my total participation. Or to be able cruelly to strike it down.

But. As soon as he looked at his watch I knew where I was. I knew that a dreadful new lock had closed on me.

The looking-at-the-watch gesture said, 'I have demands on me above and beyond you.' The eating from the refrigerator said, 'I have the run of the place again.' The way he sat in the armchair now and looked at me said, 'I have reclaimed you, but in a different way.' The way he had used me, tortured me, in the bed said, 'I am still this to you.'

I felt it in my stomach as I leaned against his legs and looked up at him. I was a vassal, now to be always in some low level of need, and this would be the difference, most time I would be in need of him and having to live within the shadow of his absence.

He went then to his suit and took from its pocket a black box. I was shocked by premonition. He took out a silver bracelet. A metaphor coming true.

This was a manacle.

He said firmly, 'You are to wear this.'

He dangled it. It was a plain silver, small-link bracelet. There was no engraving on the plate.

That was right.

'Put it on,' he said.

The way he said that, it was the old days again. I had changed from sharing his daily life, I was now being kept for his pleasure.

'Yes.' My heart was hurting.

'Hold out your wrist.'

I held out my bare arm to him; liquid with submission, I could not have stood. 'Yes.'

He clicked it on.

'It has a lock to which I have the only key.'

I was breathless with feeling for him, breathless from his perfect authority, the unfaltering confidence of his command.

How hypercharged life is when it breaks out of propriety. I was sorry, as I trembled there against his legs, for those people with well-behaved love. How good it was to have one's integrity utterly infringed, to be the trembling, crushed, infringed self.

It was for me a re-experiencing of that same true feeling, the lightning-struck feeling when he had come to the school that first time and then taken me to the hotel room.

I was shaking.

'Thank you,' I said.

My eyes were crying. He ruffled my hair and said, 'I'm not passing you on. I won't pass you over to the animals,' and laughed in his private way. I was so weak I couldn't bother with the implication but allowed his words to further eliminate any false sense of self-pride, of 'integrity', and thus allowed myself still further to flow free and true in a near swoon of submission.

He then, in a business-like way, dressed back into his suit, me tying his tie, helping him with his coat, his laces. I saw him out and then fell naked back on the sheets, my anus awash with semen, my mouth still cloyed with its taste, and a silver bracelet locked on my wrist.

'I'll ring you,' he said as he left. 'The House is sitting next week.'

The new purpose of the telephone, the telephone as chain, as a chain which permitted me to go only as far as the sound of its bell.

'I'll ring you' was an instruction.

Oh, I knew who the dog and who the master now.

When I did sneak out and give myself to a drunken sailor or some migrant worker, it affirmed the meaning of the bracelet. I was restored to my sense of wholeness for all the nights I spent aching for him. I did a lot of sexual aching, harder for a virile seventeen-year-old boy. Never able to masturbate, for fear he would need me.

Always to be there for him when he wanted my body, when he was not too busy running the country. Or being a husband.

I was faithful to him, in my fashion, but I was still, too, a naughty bad dog sometimes in the early hours of morning out in the dark city.

The Letters

I'm going to get out the letters.

'I'd rather you didn't.'

And why not? I want to show you what you were once. What you were when we lived together. Before power and marriage etc made your personality into a social technique, until it hides its face behind a flashed-on smile. You've become a shimmer of courteous responses. I watch you on TV. And with me you've become a grunt. Because your personality couldn't survive your oh-so-model life.

'I said not to get out those letters.'

All those things you do at Home you've told me about to make me suffer. Do you know what they are? Elusions.

'What word is that?'

Elusions. What you do is not hobbies. They're ways of evading the eyes and faces of people. To avoid the need to truly react. I see it all now. Because I study only you. The paradox of politics. It is at the very heart of life but, for those who pursue it, it is a way of escaping life. I see it all now. It's all structured reaction. You and your coins and cannons. That's interesting. Your two prized collections of coins and cannons. Money and guns. I hadn't seen that before. When you come here, though, you drop the shimmer of courteous responses and become a grunting stasis, but at least that's real. That's animal.

'Your vocabulary is overreaching.'

Not quite a person. A grunting stasis. But that's real. I'm the last remaining person on earth who knows you. And who can sometimes find you. Your Wife doesn't know you. I can tell. The only time your muscles fall loose is when you are here. Is here, here with me! For those moments when I undress you, bring you to erection, when you lie naked, just another man, and when you moan and moan and cry out and murmur and cry and come—those noises show me that there is a writhing person in there. And my only moment of power. Oh, but then—zip—you're gone again and each piece of clothing goes back on—hey presto—the Man of Affairs. Herr Cabinet Minister.

'Don't prattle.'

I will. I will read out from the letters. Look at the letters, hundreds, now so nicely bound. Will you one day have a government person, or one of those heavies, come around and destroy them? Or destroy me. Why do you permit me to have them? I suppose because there is no way of them being linked to you. How many pages you once effused—over me. Look.

'You're becoming hysterical. Take them away. Take them away from my face.'

I will read. '. . . On that drive to Canberra you acted so impulsively, so impishly . . . did you realise that it was the first time that you didn't have to be coaxed? Or bribed or forced? Although you had always wanted to do it, once you were made to do it, it was not until that day in the car that you initiated it. You had until then, I suppose, liked the game of feeling that it was against your will, your nature, or whatever. You enjoyed playing the stubborn, sullen boy. It was from then on, from that day of that drive, that you were a different person, a special person with a special destiny and aware of it. Which I had of course known, and had of course known you would one day be made to realise . . .'

And I thought it meant at the time that I had 'fallen in love' with you. But for you it meant that I was ready for anything that you required. That I was in a new phase. But at least your letters, if they were not 'love' letters, were effusive and you were fascinated by me and you used words to me. At least there were words then, including words about yourself.

Let me recall 'the drive to Canberra'. That evocative memory. It was your election campaign. We were driving through the electorate. I was fifteen. No. I was probably fourteen. Had I even done the School Certificate? I had been released from school after one of your 'notes' had arrived at the Headmaster's office and I was told that there was a government car waiting for me. The faces of my friends staring down from the school windows. I'd pack my things knowing that I would be whisked away to some hotel, to be used until I was in a daze. And later, sometimes, to be used by your 'associates'. Made drunk. And the drugs, oh yes, the muscle relaxants. Or no—sitting around in hotel rooms while you talked to people about things I didn't understand. That is what I remember most. You talking to foreign people. I remember once hitting on the idea of filing my nails in front of them. I think I wanted to embarrass you, it seemed an outrageous thing for a schoolboy to do and you said coolly, 'Yes, your nails could do with some attention—we don't like grubby boys,' and those in the room all laughed knowingly. I went from the room flushed and confused, close to tears, but you didn't come after me. I came back later and they had gone and I cried in bed with you in the submission of utter lost confusion.

Anyhow. The drive to Canberra. We were driving fast. I moved over to sit hard against you, remember? I put my hand lovingly up to your neck and my fingers into your hair. I did it because I now felt 'in love' with you. Do you remember what you said? You said that I was too close, there'd be cars coming up behind us and you'd be recognised and lose votes. I said that you could possibly gain votes from homosexuals. You were amused by my using the word 'homosexual' and said that it was the first time you'd heard me say it. I blushed, but you made me say it again, although I didn't want to. You made me say that I was a homosexual, but I resisting saying it. And then I said it, turning weakly to you and taking your hand, putting it to my lips and saying it through your fingers and my kiss. 'Oh yes, I am, I am homosexual.'

'You have an unhealthy memory.'

And you smiled—at the time I thought you smiled because I pleased you, but I think now you smiled because of private thoughts—and you said that I was a 'special class' of homosexual. But there in the car then I undid your fly and went down on you, into that fundamental smell of urine and the lingering odour, almost imperceptible, of excreta (but it was there), down over your penis and through the imported underwear which you got for us, before you married—does she buy that dreadful underwear your wear now, or do you wear it to identify with the normal folk?—and I licked the head of your penis through the silk and it oozed its juice making the silk transparent and I worked my mouth and the silk on your penis head while we drove at 100 mph through the wheat country and the hot, dry sun. You spread your legs to give yourself. Moaning, on and on at 100 mph in that Rover car you had then. I smelled the hot leather of the upholstery. The ever-so-slight smell of petrol fumes. The slight dry-cleaning fluid smell of groin. I gobbled and stimulated you, taking your balls up into my mouth, my tongue working you around and around, playing up and down, and then a finger fully in your anus. And then you came into my mouth pulse after pulse, the semen taste overwhelming the mingle of smells, the taste of semen dominating and wiping out all the other senses, although they came back, one by one, the texture of the silk first.

'Your memory is unhealthy.'

Remember, I took from you your semen and then lay there, my face in your lap. I remember plainly, while I had my head buried down there and you were coming into me, I remember thinking—is he ever going to stop. Is he ever going to stop? Is this possible, what have I done? I was very young.

'Don't go on—stop now.'

When you finally finished, I sat up, wiped my mouth on a tissue, wiped you, and did up your fly, and we drove into town across the bridge. Within half an hour you were addressing a meeting and shaking hands with the mayor and his wife.

I remember you sending me to a newspaper office in the town to book space, or something, for your campaign advertisements, and a nosey old editor with an eye-shade asking me if I were your 'son' or a campaign worker or what. I said, 'Aide de camp.'

I thought that rather good at the time until you told me back at the motel that I had mispronounced it.

Those early campaigns were the only time, though, that you've taken me into your political life, even if I were only someone in the car, unexplained.

Excepting, of course, the Camden days, and they were hardly political. Those house parties. The old men and senators or whatever, feeling me, talking about me being 'pretty', and you saying to me after, 'Just keep smiling at them, let them do what they want.' You were so torn then— you couldn't do without my body then, but you felt that sometimes it did your career good for me to pleasure the Old Men of the Tribe. You were anxious though, the only time I could truly say you felt anxious about me, that I might become someone else's boy, but yet you had to risk it, had to prostitute me. And then you got where you wanted and put me into this, this 'town house'—is that what we call this? And it has come to this— me locked here, virtually, visited by, God what is he called? An accountant? He never lays a finger on me. More's the pity.

Why doesn't she dress you with some style? You're both rich. You used to wear such beautiful clothing, but why drip-dry shirts—why? They are for cheap travellers. And for Chinese waiters.

'You are not to mention her.'

Yes. We won't bring her into it. She's sacred. Miss Sacred Heart Country Party Whore 1955.

'Stop!'

And you came back from the meeting in town to the motel and came to my room giggling. You never giggle now. Aren't Herr Cabinet Ministers allowed to giggle? I was sitting up in the motel eating chocolates and listening to country and western music and you thanked me for washing out your underwear. But then you giggled and said that the mayor had followed our car into town and overtaken us near the bridge. You had said hastily to the mayor that I was a 'nephew'.

'Nephew?' said the mayor. 'No, you were alone in the car. There was no one else in the car when I overtook.'

'You involved me in risks.'

So you locked me away. No, we could go back to those days without the risks. I am older now. I would be a good private secretary. I've told you this so often. But, of course, I don't hold the same charm.

'You have your place.'

My head between your legs.

'I don't think, really, that you need more whisky. Put it down.'

How I wish you were always around to tell me to stop, to tell me what to do. I was reading a book by some woman and she says that's what it is all about—'extinguishing the consciousness'. Obliterating the personality. I understand my state. I relish it.

'Theoretical books are bad for you.'

Don't worry, this is not about the liberation movements. That's not my liberation. I know that. I know now that my liberation is to be found in the opposite direction. The liberation through obeisance.

'Mmmmm.'

For instance, I could cut your initials in my arm. I could do that to show you what I mean.

'Don't talk like that. I've had to stop you talking about that sort of thing before.'

What about when you had that doctor friend of yours inject me with some drug which made me helpless and warm and open and you had me, when I was fourteen, you and then those other two men. For hours. I was so dazed I couldn't work out what was happening to my body. You were training it somehow to behave in some sort of way you wanted, and you broke me so that I couldn't behave any other way.

'Oh shut up.'

All right. But I will cut your initials in my arm.

'Stop that.'

He shouted at me, but I went to the bathroom and found a razor blade and came back to him.

He sat there. I knelt before him, I was still in the tight satin underpants and satin smock that he liked me to wear, and I stretched out my bare arm.

'If you must' he said, a change of voice, he was switching now, turning on to it, participating.

You should brand me.

'It would be safer to have you tattooed.'

Yes. I'd like that too.

'Go on—cut yourself. Cut my name in your arm.'

He really wanted me to cut myself.

I cut. I did it. I cut one letter. The blood came out in a string of globules. My body went cool with the shock of it. I stopped. I baulked at the second letter. I would have done it but I was stopped, the effort required to mutilate one's skin, especially when the skin is perfect, as mine was, umblemished young skin, the effort was exhausting.

'The other letter—go on,' he said, 'cut the other letter.'

The bastard.

Bastard.

I closed my eyes, opened them, and cut the loop of the next letter and then dropped the blade. I stared at the blood on my arm and then licked it, licked both the wounds, and then I needed to sit.

I felt faint, and then his arms were about me, the world moved, unsteadily.

He pulled me to him. I had earned it.

'You stupid boy,' he said. I sunk to my knees.

He had an erection. He had an erection and I felt it through the silk of his pyjamas. I kissed his penis through the pyjamas and I was back then in the car with the hot leather, I hugged him around his thighs.

He led me over to the bedroom and pushed me down on the bed lifting the smock, pulling down the satin pants to bare my arse.

My face went down on to my bleeding arm and I tasted again my own steely blood as I felt him move himself into me, as I arched my buttocks to take him. He came, ejaculating into me, almost as soon as he entered, and the throb and the thrust of the penis were so distinctly felt that it was as if they were drawn with pen nib and ink on my nervous system, the hot sperm bursting against the sensitive lining of my anus.

When he'd had his way, he rolled off and said, 'You should put sand into the wound—to permanently scar yourself.'

I told him that I would do that. If I had been able to move, I would have done something like that. I was held to the bed by a heavy blanket of sensual pain. I was centred.

I will do that, I told him, I will.

I put my head against him and cried.

He then said something, something humorous, maybe tender, he said, 'They are the most obscene letters I have received,' and he put his fingernail on the blood-smeared initials and traced them, hurting me, tracing them with his sharp fingernail.

He then asked me to come to the bathroom, he had to go, he wanted me to wash him.

I said that I would after I had put something on the wounds.

He said that could wait.

The Little World Left Behind

Do you remember that on the day of his death, I kissed you on the mouth?

A full mouth kiss. It was at a party. You'd taken me along because of how I'd been affected. We had heard of P's death that day and everyone had been making all the right noises. We stood there on the fringe of the dancers' skirts. The dancers revolved at the centre of the party, lapping at us as we stood in the darkened room. It was a backbenchers' party. I remember water slapping along the jetty near the house. I took your head in my hands and kissed you on the lips. You went with the kiss. I had gone over the line of self-control by then with whisky and grief about P's death. Was that grief? No, it was infuriation at being denied someone I wanted, that a person was denied me who had filled my mind and days for so long—as a person—not as a lover. A person who had talked to me. I would have been interested to have felt something as classical as grief. I would have been pleased to know that I had the capacity for the grand emotion. But whatever the inadequacy of my responses, I required, looking back, intense physical solace. I used sexuality that night to push away the presence of death.

Yes, it was the gaping hole of death that I saw. The way death leaves staring, unwanted spaces in our lives. It is a penalty. It places people out of consultation or touch. They continue in your head but that is not enough, is, in fact, a reminder of the penalty.

I hadn't had much experience with death. It was a new insecurity, this realisation that the protective circle of people around us will go, one by one. And death itself, the experience of dying, must be a bad experience too, the whole self resists it, avoids it, we must sense something about the passing through to that other state.

You seemed to want the kiss. I was hungering for it. It's odd that our physical life should have gone on for years without kissing. Or maybe you kissed me when I was a boy at school, during those early days. But then the kissing must have ceased, until that night, the night of P's death. I kissed you and I wanted to do it always and not to stop.

But it was a members' party or whatever, and there were key people at the party. So it had to stop. But to your credit you did not shy. I was conscious immediately afterwards that I should not have. Although there was one person especially at the party I would have been glad to have see us. To cancel at last that sly curiosity. Of course I would have loved, too, to have declared us to them all. But there was to be no coming out for you. You knew it was the wrong historical time.

But I would have liked them to have all known and I would have liked to have declared those too who were part of our private circle from the Camden scene. It wasn't as if they were prejudiced or that they didn't know such things occurred even in their own ranks, but they did not want their category ruffled. They wanted no meddling with the well-secured boundaries of behaviour, expectation and conversation. As young A so nicely put it, no one in that crowd accepts his homosexuality when he declares it, not even his own father. They simply say he's into 'liberated chic' or that he's being deliberately 'sensational'.

But I suppose, at least, they have categories and that's one way of keeping things endurable. I prefer that in a way. I heard someone say the other day they don't believe in 'homosexuality' or 'heterosexuality', only in 'sexuality'. They want to deny the categories. Establish a broad, false harmony. They don't accept that there just might be natural hostilities, incompatibilities, inherent enmities in the human condition, in the sexual roles, in their many devious forms. They are the sort of people who hate categories because they do not wish to be excluded from *anything*. They fear exclusion as a form of rejection, I suppose.

Yes, P taught me this. Yes, P taught me lots of things. Yes, yes, and you too, you taught me too.

I felt the bristles of your growth that night and they belonged so much with the sensation. Were part of the imprint of it.

Maybe also it was my try at breaking the dumbness about us which had overtaken you after those voluble first years. Those words you wrote in letters about 'my role' and 'my reality'. Before there were so many books, so many new sexual experts. As you have said, the lessons and the knowledge hadn't been lost to the tribe, it was in the hands of those who deserved to possess the lessons and the knowledge. But then you lapsed into dumbness, a refusal to express, or connect, except physically. Was this a lesson?

But why did I think that kissing would break this dumbness? After all, kissing is another, but different, way of using the mouth, and precludes talking. Was your dumbness a way of avoiding verbal treason against your marriage? But you must have faced the disparity of your behaviour at the marriage ceremony.

You are hardly as true as steel and as straight as an arrow. You and your talk about political candour. I remember hearing you on some ABC program and getting the giggles. I suppose you say that once again it illustrates the indigestible fact—that truth is divisible. That being frank in one place and not in another is everyday human conduct. That people can be corrupt in one area of behaviour and not in another.

Yes, I know, you taught me all this a long time ago.

Did you know about P? P, nicotine-stained, decayed teeth, shingles, dirty ears. He desired me too, and I let him have me. I was very young and unsure. I knew I was supposed to go only with people you told me to go with. Maybe I knew P was not one of those. I suppose it was partly because he was famous (more famous than you at that time). I remember also him saying in a leering way that he was a 'behaviourist' and believed that he could have anything from anyone by offering the appropriate threat, or the appropriate and sufficient inducement, or the appropriate verbal formula. I remember being immobilised by revulsion when he made it clear that he wanted me. Mesmerised by it. And then actually going into his arms, saying no at the same time that I began to undress, going naked and shivering into his arms, giving him my young body. It was in chambers and I remember some files and I remember thinking that I was being 'defiled'. And it was true. I felt defiled. And it became a delicious feeling.

You have made me feel abused, ravaged and many other things. But it needed a sick, ugly and brutal old man to give me the sense of being lovingly defiled. I was young, in fettle and P was so debilitated. He knew what he wanted to do with me. Everyone you sent to me seemed to have some strange thing they wanted me to do to them, or they wanted to do to me. Their own act. Straps, pain, what-have-you. It sometimes took me days to recover and I had to go on with school as well. P had no trouble with erection, as sick as he was.

You probably fucked me later that night. Oh I forget where you were. Probably some Important Meeting. Or 'in with the PM'. Those hours that I spent dozing in your car after school while you were addressing something. All the pool drivers knew me.

You probably fucked me that night on his sperm. A fantasy you know I love, the thought of which you cannot abide. Especially the idea of P's probably infected sperm. He tried on other occasions. I said no—because of us. There, isn't that unbelievable fidelity? I was scared about saying no because he did have power in the land. Didn't he? I mean, I didn't know what would happen to me with people like him if I said no. I prayed that you could protect me. But the rotten thing was that I liked talking to him, and he taught me so much, and I hated to say no to him. I would relieve him but I wouldn't do the things he wanted. My head was full of chilling stories told to me by those boys at Camden. Probably just to scare me. I kept the act with P quite separate from our reality. I mean in my mind. Oh for all his intellect, public standing, public 'integrity', he tried to blackmail me one way or another into doing things with him again. I had to say no, too, because I knew that there were only so many times that a young body could do what he wanted me to do.

How sentimental I am deep down. Or was. But there—now the two things have joined—P now belongs to the same memory group as our 'reality', see, confession can do things to the pre-existing reality—P belongs now with our shared reality, tied with the same blue memory ribbon. Maybe you would prefer not to have had the gift of that confession?

But you were supposed to know everything. You had me followed at other times. Or was I above suspicion then? Too naïve and young to be capable of deception? Or did you know, did you engineer it?

I think that when I kissed you that night of his death, I kissed P too, goodbye, kissed the corpse with its rotting teeth.

I was only once with P, or twice or so.

My need for solace the night of his death was so crying a need because of the space he left in my life, not as a lover but as tutor. We went from the party and you had me and used me so hastily, rushing off then to meet the curfew of your marriage and you left a second space in my grasping, sad, needful consciousness, you left me doubly deserted and assailed—by death and by marriage.

After you came pumping into me and then within minutes pulled on your trousers, leaving me panting on the bed in a mess, I went looking for something more, for something that would complete the solace I sought. It was far too late. But whisky and lust—neither can tell the time.

Maybe I was trying to crowd bodies into the space left by P's death.

I found no one in the lavatories of the city and that was strange because there had on every other night, no matter what time, been someone hunting in the lavatories. But not on the night of P's death—as if by ordinance, they had been cleared.

Finally I had to telephone a woman I knew (you don't know her—and you won't) and ask her if I could come over to her place to stay for the night. She was fond and wanting to please and knew about me and felt therefore no threat from me. What I think she liked was someone unheterosexual to hold on to in the night, and she liked gossip about people in high places (I never told her *serious* gossip).

We would caress for the comfort of it and then I would go down to her anus. The absolute self-abasement of it, and the unlocked relief that self-abasement gives. By showing another person that you will do those things which the culture abhors, to behave with another person in a way that is repugnant to cultural conditioning, its hygiene, and to self-image. Bringing together those two parts of the body—mouth and anus— which are by nature so closely related in function and yet in our culture severed, separated. The organ that sings in oratorio and the organ that cannot be politely heard. By kneeling before this common woman in this act of submission, lying with my face in her anus, I lost all identity—the body who went to concerts, pottery on Thursdays, who knew so many people—those things all fell away and I went spinning, falling outside culture and outside sex into that other world. Most of all, I lost homosexual identity.

Lying there on the bed she would lift her dress, smile at me, pull down her pants, turn her arse to me and open her legs. For all I know, she probably smoked while I died there. I would put my tongue there, bury myself in her buttocks, burying myself in the smell of earth, body function and waste that had no gender.

On rare occasions, including this night, she would cause her anus to give, stimulate it to release, and I would convulse, shuddering, smeared, and die as a person and find myself, alive in another state of acute being.

It was there, in the arse of this woman who meant nothing to me, that I found release that night.

I went home and back to bed, falling asleep with sperm and excreta odours about me. I again woke, hours after, and P's death was a day or so back. I woke and tasted the night.

I was able to go calmly about sending an expensive gift to the woman, doing the other things that make my day. All this after a night of being enveloped, smudged and stained, and hurt by sexuality. I found solace in the overpowering infliction of it upon my consciousness. I had kissed your mouth and so kissed the corpse goodbye, and I still had your sperm dribbling from my anus. And I had knelt before this woman and buried myself in the excrement of her anus.

I felt an exaggerated aliveness. I had no hangover, and I had things to do. I showered, had a glass of milk, a mango, and stepped out into the world.

A friend had died and gone and I said to myself, a friend has died and gone. And I read the papers flicking through the obituaries of P, '... a key figure in the extra-parliamentary life of the fifties ... significant contribution to the constitutional history of this country ...', while at the same time I enjoyed the sore aliveness of my arse. My mind trailed in and out of the news of the day, and back and over the sensations of the night. It gave me a sharp, sunny affirmation that I was living and doing, and that I could go down the dark tunnels of sexuality with or without you, and I could forget for a while that P was dead and you were married.

A Map for the Child

This is a map for the child. I think the map is probably educationally disreputable.

'He likes those things. Brontosauruses.'

Not one word to show he understands our emotional complicity in the child. No registration of what the giving of the map to the child means.

It shows the boundaries of the world, false boundaries, it's even wrong for its time, it's an imaginative reconstruction of an old map, it is art, not navigation.

'It is unlikely that he will use it for navigation.'

Yet once, just once, but obviously from premeditation, you touched me, while we were walking the child between us—you had had it left with you unexpectedly—you touched me and said, 'The first child is ours—I think of him, I think of him as belonging to The Family.'

Take the map.

Take my heart, my blood, my sensory system—you've owned them, depraved them—give them to the child as well.

'Now stop that.'

I have never complained about that—about what you did with my body. It's my placing, my status, in your life that I can't accept now.

You have never asked me to do this, to wear her clothes. Is this a way of humiliating her and me at the same time? I don't mind that you lie back there, that you wait for me to undress you and to stimulate you, which is all too easy. But now that I have understood my role, and come to be good at it, you change everything. You want me to put on her things. It was never like this before.

'No.'

Was I gathering an identity, is that it? Do you wish to take that away? I'd rather be called a 'predilection', as you once did. I know that after all these years you say that you are not homosexual, that that is not what it is all about, you say. You live not only against yourself but against the temper of the times. You should be in the Cause. Here look — on the map — it says, 'The Course of the Great Wind Currents.'

'Fix that eyelash.'

I suppose you would simply repeat that politics and power have always been intuitive arts for those few special people who are able to use the mechanisms of power, whatever they may be, in whatever system, at whatever historical time. The trick, you would say, is always to belong to the pre-eminent elite. Did I get it right? Don't be angry with me. But use me for what I am. A male. I give you my young body. I give you imaginative love. But not this.

'Yes.'

Oh God, her clothing fits me. We must be the same size, even this corselet.

'I want you to welcome this.'

But you took me as a child — a boy — because I was male. I can't argue against you. But I could draw another map for the child, of strange routes 'outside the walled cities and cultivated lands'. Where you took me.

I was an innocent boy when you so skilfully turned me into a moaning, weeping, naked body on a hotel room floor.

'Innocent?'

All right, there is no such thing as innocence, but I was uninitiated. How did you find me? Why did you come that day to the school?

You just smile. All right, so on that day on the floor of a hotel I was given the truth about myself and I embraced it. But how did you choose me? Who were those men who pointed me out?

I wanted her to die in hospital. I would have lived with you and we could have raised the children together. Yes, I knew she had been ill. Oh the savage, regal fantasies of the subjugated.

Even hustlers get their important lovers to make commitments.

'Where do you get this nonsense?'

I sometimes hate the bizarreness of my life. Did you know that? You have made the bizarre my normality, but sometimes I try to imagine the other life. I sometimes crave in-laws, outings, and lawns. Isn't that real life? Instead I stand here in her slip and her stockings.

'Mmmmm.'

But no, I complain about the way things have changed. Me standing here dressed like this. But not only that. We were different at those lunches. I was once the sexy boy and always needed, to be fondled and so on, by your important friends, able to sit about without talking and then tell you everything that was said in your absence. It's not like that any more.

But you're not getting joy any other way, I can tell. You're not getting it from her — I can tell that. I'm the only one who can give it to you.

'The make-up is good.'

The map makes a good joke. 'Trade route,' it says, that's what my life has been. And the map says, 'Parts Yet Undiscovered.'

We'll see. Is something still to come?

'Turn around, twirl around.'

What will you tell her, for instance, about the map? That you found it in the street? That you got it from a wandering cartographer? Or that it was I who sent it as a weird present for the child. Dangerous for navigation. Does she know about me? Did she select the clothing, the underwear for me to wear?

'You're hypertense.'

I'm hysterical.

'You need the doctor.'

No. Listen to me. Please. No, listen to me. Please come away from the telephone.

'Perhaps you need to be sent away for a time.'

No. I hate it up there.

'Put on the gown now.'

I have my own friends you know. People you don't know. You claim to know everything I do and everyone I see. But you don't. I have people here. I have to put your photograph in the drawer for fear that some stickybeak will seize it and say, 'Why, you never told us ...' or 'Is he really ...?'

'Turn around. I'll do the zip.'

You are frightened that the words you might say would turn into silken ropes and bind your hands and tie you to my bed. You know that the feelings which move inside you, if once articulated, would become contracts which you'd be forced to honour.

'Now put on the shoes.'

You don't try to present yourself any more. I mean with your clothing, your appearance. You don't watch your weight. Does she really want you to dress like that? Obviously you don't care a damn. Is it because you have a safe seat? Or does it give you a Plain Man image for the public? No frills. No foppery.

'Mmmmm.'

Mmmmm.

'Fix that eyelash.'

Does she really buy those underpants for you? They're so cheap. Do you know what she's doing? She's killing you as a sensual being.

'Don't prattle.'

Why don't you take me on those trips? You have always promised. Are you frightened that I will kiss you behind the ear in public? I'm not like that now. I can converse. I read. Why don't you let me meet people now?

'You met President Johnson.'

Yes, and he let his hand rest overlong on my shoulder.

'And he wrote to you.'

Don't tease me. Yes, he wrote me a letter.

'Maybe one day we will go to live in the Greek islands.'

I don't want to go to the Greek islands to live. I don't want to go to the Greek islands. That's not what I'm saying. There is another map— that is not the only 'place to go'. I love this country. I'm more committed to this country than you, the professional patriot. I'm the one who cries at patriotic songs.

'You are a silly boy.'

I am not a 'silly boy'. I am not a silly boy. I am your male love. A male lover who does not any longer know what is happening to him or where he is. I know I can't leave you or do anything else with my life because of what I know about you and the rest. But nor do I want to. I want you. What are you now? Forty-seven? Overweight, balding. I want you to give our life emotional shape, size, status.

'You are hysterical. You have overstepped.'

Never have you thought to ask me if I was feeling well, whether I could have sex. You just come here and the next thing, without more than a grunt, you are panting, crying, holding me in desperation. But you grant me nothing.

'The doctor will be here soon.'

So the doctor will obliterate my mind, put me in a daze for weeks. Oh I know too what 'soon' means. It means that I'm wasting time and you haven't had your sex yet. All right then, I'll lift up these skirts and petticoats, and you can gaze at her stockings, her suspenders, my legs— better shaped than hers, and just as hairless too. Have your sex. Imagine whatever it is that you want. It's yours. You own it. There. I'll hold up these skirts, pull down those feminine panties—take me.

And bending over I let him take me. He stood there behind me, the skirt falling down over my head.

My beloved. I am that too. I am too a surrogate, as well as a boy, yes I am that too. And he was right, I wanted to be overlapped with someone else's identity—her identity.

And then the blinding insight. It was not only a humiliation but a victory. I could be her as well. As he entered up my body, dressed there in her clothes, I knew, it was revealed to me. I had lost another part of 'myself' and I was filled with joy. He made me feel true. He made me right with the world again.

I whimpered and tears came to my eyes.

Oh yes, and yes give the child the mariner's map. I hope it misleads him in the correct direction. I hope he realises that for some strange reason it is the wrong maps which are beautiful.

'Here is the doctor.'

He pulled out of me and, doing himself up, went to the door. He turned and said to me, 'No don't undress, stay that way.'

They stood at the door together looking at me, still bending over, anus exposed. The skirts pulled up and the woman's pants pulled down to expose my proffered self. The doctor made a gesture, a raised eyebrow, a request by gesture, and received the reply, 'Sure, go ahead.' The doctor put down his bag, took off his coat, and came towards me undoing his fly.

The Gift of a Son

It's his birthday, isn't it?

'I thought you would remember.'

He's thirteen, isn't he?

'Yes.'

We will give him a treat, and then bring him back here.

'That's correct.'

I'll make him something, his favourite dish.

'I want everything done delicately.'

Of course it will be done delicately. You said once that he was our child.

'Did I?'

And that now we would come together. The three of us.

'In the long run it has very little to do with you. But I want this thing done delicately.'

And he came. What is your favourite . . . is the school food just as . . . and which sport do . . . and when you leave?

And I prepared him a treat.

'I feel sort of good,' he said, giggling and lolling back on the meridienne after his treat.

I went with his father to the other room.

Out of sight of the boy he grabbed my wrist. 'I want this done correctly.'

It will be. And I looked at him, and I said, just as you did it to me when I was a boy.

'I'm not interested in you.'

I told him that I would pleasure the boy, and that the boy would thank me for it, for having taken him over the dreadful chasm.

He was a divided person, savouring the situation and exercising his parental responsibility at the same time.

I told him to wait, feeling my control, however slight, of this part of the situation.

I left him and went to the boy. Now to open the gate.

I was the medium for them both. It could only be me. This was my moment. My moment.

The boy was lying back blissfully on the meridienne, a lazy smile on his face.

I sat down with him, moving his body over a little, sitting against his thigh.

Feel nice?

'Yes . . . oh yes.'

I'm going to make you feel nicer.

'I know.'

How do you know?

'I just sort of know.'

You want me to do it, don't you?

'Yes, I suppose so . . .'

What am I doing to you? I asked him.

'I don't know, but . . .'

The drug was making him verbally lazy.

He smiled up at me, saying do it, do it, his boyish lips mouthing the words.

I took off his shoes and socks. I undid his belt.

This will make you comfortable.

He lifted his backside for me to take off his trousers. Has someone else done this to you? I had not considered that. Anxiety clutched my breathing.

'I feel sort of weak but nice . . . I can hardly bother to move.'

Has someone else done this to you? I tried to keep the urgency from my voice.

'No . . . just at school.'

What? What happened?

I tried not to lose him by sounding like an adult authority.

'Just sort of played around. Nothing.'

And with yourself?

'No.'

He smiled.

Was he lying?

But you know what I'm talking about and what I'm doing to you.

'Sort of,' he smiled—teasingly?

Was he already a lying virgin-pretender? A tease?

I took off his trousers and cotton underpants. All with his name sewn in.

And then his shirt.

He was languidly co-operative.

It's good for this to be done to you.

'Yes. I like you. I'm glad it's you.'

There was a genuineness in this. He was a virgin.

I knew how he felt now, tingling with the wanting. The wanting of the touch which would dissolve him. I let his body lie there, untouched for those trembling seconds or more, with him looking up at me wanting—the wanting of the touch which, if it did not come, would drive him into a craze.

His body was splendid, in the way that thirteen year olds are—an age where there can be no real defect. Physique just smoothes it away—the whole man was there, and the whole boy, and the female, all in superimposition.

The wispy hairs around his crutch were the only hairs on his body, apart from the light blond hair of childhood, so gracefully an hermaphrodite.

He took my hand then, could wait no longer, and took my hand and placed it on his penis, and gasped, quietly, with relief.

I gave it a touch of acceptance as it erected, rigid quivering, and then I took my hand away.

I bent down, pausing though, my mouth just above his penis. I looked at his face, his eyes closed, his breathing broken and reckless.

He opened his eyes pleadingly.

'Please.'

Oh, yes, I knew that 'please'. Behind that 'please' lay the offer of anything he could give.

I held his eyes, still not giving him the release for which he begged, receiving from him the begging gaze, seeing the fear that it might not happen which dances along with all tantalisation.

I closed my mouth around his penis and he murmured loudly, 'Oh yes—yes.'

My hand went under him.

His whole body, his anus, opened like a flower, as I put my finger there, an eager yielding.

'But . . . ?' Again a question he had to ask did not complete and which contained no true concern, and which drifted away.

He knows, I whispered.

'I don't care, really,' he smiled up, opening his eyes, conspiratorially, carelessly. 'I like you. I like you touching me. I knew you would—it was in your eyes. I want you to do everything.'

I know you do.

'I like your fingers in there.'

Yes, he liked everything.

He sat up, lifted my head from off his penis, taking the initiative, and, holding my head, he kissed me in that dreamily drugged way, his young saliva running to my mouth like juice from a crushed fruit.

'You get undressed too,' he murmured.

I did.

We lay there on the day bed and then tumbled off, rolling about on the carpeted floor, embracing, our mouths locked in an endless kiss. I loved him in two ways, at least—as my child, and as an object of beauty—and he probably loved me two ways, at least—as an adult with whom nothing was forbidden and everything granted, his first adult of that kind, and he probably loved me as a simple instrument of his excitement.

But I loved him another way, as the linkage, something I had not dreamed of until recently, when the dream had become a plan and I had realised that it was all part of a huge eternal program. But now it did not seem like a dream or plan, but presented itself as an inevitability. Oh yes. I sighed with the clear sudden realisation. It was an eternal inevitability.

The drug peeled him of everything and he was a physical young animal of pure feeling. The drug had put back into his blood that which a lost society had taken out. He now knew no maths, no morals, no geography, no manners, no propriety. The ultimate state of being.

I tried to slow him down but he could not wait, and I held his penis tightly as he poured himself out on me with great gasps and sighing, and I felt the outbursting too in my fingers through the lining of his anus. Thirteen solid throbs of his penis, spilling and spilling.

Opening my eyes I saw his father's face looking out from the other room. He was beyond parental apprehension now, he was the enthralled voyeur observing not only the erotic display but the loss of his own centrality in two lives—his repositioning in our lives and its endless dark possibilities. The exploding enlargement of his parenthood.

The boy was crying with the relief which comes from the only liberation.

'What happened to me?' he asked dreamily. 'I'm all wet,' and then giggled. 'Oh I think I must have fainted or something, oh I've never felt like this. This is, this is—heaven.'

You've been relaxed with something. I put something in the drink, I said, as a birthday treat.

Yes, he was right, I too felt like I had fainted. I had passed momentarily across to that special state of consciousness and back again. That orgasmic state, oblivion.

'We'll do it again? Can we do it again soon?'

Yes. I'd like you to come to visit me again. Soon.

He went to sleep in my arms. I disentangled myself, wiped him, and put a blanket over him, there on the lounge floor sleeping with a beatific smile.

I could not but help consciously acquainting myself with the fact that I had a father and a son now as lovers. I couldn't help enjoying the cheap novelty of it. But it pays to take whatever pleasures you can get your hands on, however trinkety. But there was another feeling less trinkety, a background feeling in my mind—I had a new security, a new place in the arrangement of things.

His father came into the room.

I told him that his son had loved every moment of it.

'I saw that.'

He poured himself a fresh drink.

The cheap novelty of it disappeared and I was rivetted by a realisation of yet a third implication. I was joined to a line through history which went back to the first primitive tribal person who went my way, who took a virgin boy lover, and every boy who became a man and took, in due turn, a boy lover, through to Socrates. I had played a part now in the continuation of that chain. I had played my first part as a child in becoming a man's lover. I had now played my second part. I now belonged fully in that historical line. It was a way of passing on and preserving the special reality, a way of giving new life, the birth for the boy of a new reality, a joining of him to a secret family, the other family. To belong to that chain is to belong to another life.

I went to him, promising him by words and physically that I would not use the boy against him, and thanking him. That we all belonged together now.

When the boy awoke he stretched and smiled directly at me, he looked as his father. His father told him to dress. He dressed slowly and I saw a beginning of haughtiness in the lazy way that he dressed there and the brazen acceptance of his father's presence. He showed no hint of shame.

He seemed, too, to have a consciousness of his relation to me and his father's relation to me and this I supposed relieved him of fear of his father, maybe this was his dawning in that way too, yet another new power acceded to him that day. He did something which suggested that he had realised something about his power over us. His new self. He dressed before the bedroom full-length mirror where we could watch him, and he at the same time watched himself. He touched his body with his hands, oh that body, as though feeling himself as a body for the first time, and he did so admiringly. He held his own penis for a moment, bringing it to half erection, and then, smiling at us, he tucked it into his underpants. The other thing was the way he brushed his hair, using two hand brushes, showing a new care, and he then came over to us, kissed me on the cheek and whispered, 'Thank you,' and then he kissed his father. His father looked down at his drink as he received that rare, that most preternatural kiss from his lips that would never again kiss innocently.

'We must go now,' his father said.

There was now in the boy's walk and movement a lascivious confidence and that also was in his kiss.

Again at the door he took my hand and said, 'This was the best birthday ever. May I arrange to see you again—soon?' And he leaned gently against me.

Oh yes, we'll do things together, oh yes.

'Come on now,' his father said, looking at his watch, 'I have a meeting.'

It was his son's birthday but I had received the gift.

And now we were a family of a special kind with a long, long history.

The Wand and the Cup (and the Magician)

He is fourteen now, with some soft facial hair, perhaps he would be shaving were it not for the oestrogen which he chooses to take, has long, groomed hair of the fashion now passing, which his mother and sister praise and brush.

'I dreamed of my mother, but she had no breasts.'

You are your mother—with no breasts.

'Yes, I have the female thing—my father shouts at me and makes me cry.'

But he is rugged in the Australian private-school way, although at the window of his face a dandy—and sometimes a lady—appear now and then. He is not yet dressing true to himself. He is limited to school clothing and that boring denim of the weekend.

He loves eating in good restaurants even now. He doesn't, like some of the young, repudiate all these things because of some voluntary poverty principle or food fadism.

'What is vol-au-vent?' he asked with a slightly reluctant innocence, but at least he asked. He risked his ignorance with me when the pressure is, at his age, always to pretend to knowledge. I smiled over at him, acknowledging the honour he paid me, the honour of being asked, of showing his ingenuousness.

I do not touch him there in the restaurant for fear my hands, once having touched his breathing body, would singe, burn, melt, perhaps weld to him.

I tell him what vol-au-vent is.

'Yes, I do know, I'd forgotten.'

I had so wanted someone like him in my life, so wanted to venture into my second part, and—whether by manipulating myself into liking him as a way to achieving that preternatural irony, or whether from spontaneous affection, or whether by being myself manipulated in other people's plans—it had happened.

Maybe I wanted him to break my heart and then, years hence, I could play with his heart and body when he found he needed me again and, returning to me in desperate dependency, would need that which he, now and for a couple of years, would use so lightly and thoughtlessly.

I had travelled that route. My first man, his father, I had frustrated to anger and violence in the early years. Submitted with feigned indifference. Refused to show pleasure. Forced him to use pain and narcotics. And now he used me like a goldfish in a glass tank, taken out when he wanted to hold a twisting, pulsing life, but for the most time left to swim restlessly, to look out at him, screamingly, yet unattended. To yearn for his presence over his photograph in newspapers.

I tried to introduce R, there in the restaurant, to the Sauternes experience—where the sweetness of the dessert makes the Sauternes taste dry. It didn't happen. I don't know why. The Sauternes not chilled enough?

'Doesn't taste dry,' he said, curious.

How to impress someone so impressive. The young and beautiful are so impressive within the limit of their years.

They work their enthralment with so little.

Maybe it is easier when you have so little to work with, I can't remember, it is all fresh stuff then, and they can give it such detailed attention and zest.

When older, we have much life material but have to walk the line between impressing and intimidating.

Oh, I had been in his place. Sitting youthfully, hands dangling so lithe. No matter how sloppy or unkempt, the gleam of youth turned it all to adornment.

Oh, I had known the feeling of mild, instinctively understood pleasure which comes from realising that the man is having difficulty taking his eyes from you. I saw that R realised there in the restaurant just how enthralled I was. Since that first day, his birthday, he had been swimming towards a calculation of his power over me.

I had known it all, known the fondling in the way a man had looked and talked with me.

I had known it without qualm at all, unconcerned that men were spending money on me. Buying me. And later, as the hold over men become conscious, I began demanding gifts, without shame, and exercising all privileges, exploiting by subtle test and sexual instinct the furthest limits of indulgence and demand in the entente of sexuality.

I, those years before, after uncertainly submitting to his father, after being coaxed and cajoled into a way of living about which I hadn't an inkling, had sensed after a while the beginnings of personal power, but it was power without program, exploited only in the most trivial material ways, and which resulted, later, in my being exposed to a reversal of power, when I had to accept the indignity and hurt of being kept by a man and ignored by him for long periods.

I had known the time when, stripped, my body would not be in my consciousness at all, but very much in his. There was nothing then about my body for me to consider—apart from realising that naked I was sitting on my hands, like a child, and his suggestion that I not do that, and then being self-conscious about my hands, blushing, dying.

In those days, I had only to undress and there it would be, the physical perfection, the shading of hair on my legs and buttocks, my breathing faster, my penis rising to erection—the boy homosexual.

And my moment of self-truth. That strange day when, after a sports carnival at school, I had noticed his father with two other men. I had looked across and realised they were watching me. I had met his eyes and blushed. Whatever recognition had caused the blush passed too quickly across the mind to be caught or remembered. One of the men came across, crouched down where I was flopped, and talked to me, had known my name. I kept looking over his shoulder at the person who was to become my lover, my protector. He stayed at a distance impatiently. They seemed anyhow to know something about me, and the questioning seemed, looking back, merely a formality. It was as if they had looked into my heart or my psychology while I slept and had already seen that I was ready to learn about myself. When, a week later, a note arrived excusing me from school I knew in a wild guess that it was he. It was the next step. The waiting car on that first day, as I straggled out with my things, was driven by a chauffeur. I was breathing dreadfully fast and, although my mind wouldn't let me say it, I did know why we were going to the hotel and why I had to go to that room number and who would be there.

He was not 'good looking' but I cannot ever recall thinking in those terms. Maybe I already knew that there in the rutting heat, the conformity to ideals of beauty does not matter, that beauty is a matter for admiration and aesthetics, not for sexuality. All bodies are charged with passion. I know that.

But oh, it wasn't long after the first certain detached submission of myself, with all its implicit self-pride, that I found my penis reared and ached to be touched by him and my anus went loose and pulsated ever so slightly at the thought of his penis. For a time sexual instinct told me to hide this need but there then came the time to reveal the dependency, to go down on my knees and beg for him to take me. The passing from detachment, to pretended detachment, and then to moaning submission.

He wanted to shoot the rifle when we were on the property, after his father had gone back to the city for a conference. I said all right. We put up the targets and shot for three-target, five-shot aggregate. He shot better than I—122 to 116.

I then loaded the rifle and looked at the trees. I saw a blue wren. I shot the wren out of the tree. Bright blue cap, black eyes, blue scarf, pert tail.

He gave a small wince.

There, you shoot one. I said to him, smiling.

He was perturbed but felt it was probably weak to show it.

'But why, why shoot them?' he said, as if there might be a reason.

To show you can strike against nature without reason, by pure human will, just to show yourself that you can.

He aimed and then lowered the rifle. 'No, I can't,' he said, unsettled by the feeling that perhaps this was something he should be able to do, yet obeying the call of gentleness.

I smiled, put a hand on him, and said that it didn't matter. But, I thought, it does matter as a test of personality, to see if that hardness had come yet, whether he could do the thing that had no 'sense'. Which calls and instructions did his personality still obey? I took his face in my hand and kissed him as the sun set across the eucalyptus. Never mind, I said. It marked him off, I thought, marked him off from me. Gentle boy.

When had I passed that point of hardness? Had his father forced me to? I remembered no single test.

Then, as I was getting the ammunition into the shoulder bag, picking up the spent shells, he pointed the rifle at a magpie and shot it dead.

Well, I said, you *can* do it. It was I who was now perturbed.

He walked over, picked up the dead bird, looked at its limp neck, circle-eyes, and then dropped it.

'I've never done that before.'

Every bird has its mate, you know, somewhere up there in the trees, watching you.

'Oh shut up.'

It doesn't prove anything—except that you can do the senseless thing, I said, trying to ease him, if he in fact needed his conscience eased. It doesn't mean you're cruel.

'Shut up. Don't talk about it!' he said, and pointed the rifle at me.

Oh yes. He could do that some time if not now, or even maybe now. And the afternoon chilled more than its wintery self as I looked at his wilful face and the finger around the trigger of his rifle. Knowing that, being who he was, and at his age, he could get away with it. Oh yes. And I didn't care.

I told him, anyhow, not to point firearms.

He said he would if he wanted to, and anyhow, the rules didn't apply to him any more.

Now I was sure he could pull the trigger. I didn't care much for the knowledge as we walked back across the paddocks. I resented him for having so quickly equalised our situation. Instead of me regaining through him a lost, softer self, he was becoming me. Surpassing me. I could do without another me.

There was an earlier condition, before sham indifference to sexual submission. There was the first excited curious pleasure when I did not know what was happening. He had passed from that. He had a long distance to go before he came to the fourth phase, the exquisite pleasures of the induction of a young person together with mellow appreciation of one's state.

Mellow appreciation—when did one reach that!

I told him to wash his hands. I told him that birds are filthy with vermin. Even the beautiful ones.

He asked about promiscuity. He had urgings towards 'the crumbiest people'. He said that his father wanted him to go only with me. I wanted him, I said, to go only with me. Reluctantly and with an uncharacteristic allegiance to truth above self-interest, I told him about the instinctive requirement of the special reality in which he now lived, the need to be promiscuous while with me. To give himself to the streets. To dirty men, to men who smelled, to mean men, to the lowest, in streets, trains, lavatories. It was life's compensation to them, the miserable, those denied so much of what life had. To be given, when they expected nothing from life—nothing—to be given a superb young boy, a beautiful body for their pleasure in those passing moments of the night. For the boy who was to have everything in life the obligation of nature was for him to give himself to those lost in the night streets. It was, I told him, not only an age-old equation, obligation of office, but also one of the high pleasures of depravity. He would therefore have urgings, he the angel of a boy, to go with old men in suburban railway lavatories. I told him how, when I was his age, they'd tried to stop this happening, to break the age-old urgings and duties by some crude therapy, but they couldn't tear out of me the sense that this was right. That it was part of the morality of our special condition.

He nodded. But I do not think that he yet grasped the theology of it—only the earliest visceral urgings.

I took the tarot pack there on the last evening of winter, in the room lit only by the yellow and blue of the open fire.

The glow of the open fire lifted his face, lit it from the jaw as we sat on the floor.

I took the pack and squared it, and then let it drop a few inches to the carpet. The pack divided perfectly.

Take it, I said, take that card—it must be *our* card. The pack says so.

He lifted it and turned it over. It was, of course, The Lovers.

He looked over at me and smiled out at me, beamed there in the yellow and blue glow.

Now for your card, I see you as a wand, I said. Perhaps The Page of Wands.

I did a shuffle and had him take the top card. This is your card, I said, whatever it is, whatever the pack tells us.

It was—The Page of Wands.

'Hey!' he said, grinning, 'that's spooky.'

Oh R, you are my wand. My page.

And I the receptacle.

I took the next card, saying that it would be my card. I am, I told him, his receptacle. I had him turn the card.

It was the Page of Cups.

I am the cup, the receptacle.

I didn't need to tell him the story of the cards.

He shook his head. 'I can read those cards,' he said.

He looked at the Page of Cups and said, 'He's just a little older than the Page of Wands.'

I took his hand, we are the lovers, you the wand and I the cup.

His lips jumped across the inches between us, like a spark.

We kissed, long and moist, we caressed, hands rushing to each other's body under our clothes.

Then, naked, sitting opposite each other, legs around each other, in the warmth of the fire, I told him that the cards forbade him to be anyone's boy but mine. He nodded with tears in his eyes, and a lie in his heart. I leaned down on to him, took his penis in my mouth, as I had his father's penis so many, many times, and found it, likewise, eager to give up to me. He filled my mouth. I had from it a sweeter sensation than from any other that had flowed into me. He moaned to the beat of my bursting heart.

Later, over tea, I told him that I had salted the cards and done an overhand shuffle. Old conjurers' tricks.

'You didn't!' he cried, affronted, hurt.

No, of course I didn't, I said to him quickly, touching him to reassure—frightened by how deeply cut he was by the idea of it. His tantalising gullibility. No, I said, not with the tarot pack, one must never do conjurers' tricks with a tarot pack. The tarot pack tells it as it is, I said. It was just a bad joke on our love. I'm sorry.

We kissed again, there across the table. 'There will never by anyone else but you,' he said to me.

I went to the bathroom and while I was there he called to me, 'I knew it was a trick.' A voice trying, trying to be hard. 'I knew you were tricking me.' Trying to learn the right lines. Trying to be like me.

He was on his way.

1980

Transgressing

In Australian society it is difficult to dissociate homosexual behaviour from transgression, even where it is not now illegal. It is not just a matter of 'breaking the rules'. Homosexual behaviour transgresses in much more fundamental ways, undermining the very basis of our political and economic system, which is predicated on the sharp distinction between men and women and the power that naturally grows from the distinction. Homosexuality outside the odd adolescent fumbling blurs this crucial distinction and is generally repellent to those who wish to keep the system intact. (Which is not to say that many homosexuals are not politically conservative or many politically conservative Australians are not homosexual.)

Patrick White's novel *The Twyborn Affair* is perhaps the fullest and most complex examination of transgressive sexuality in Australian literature and, as in the case of Steve J. Spears' ground-breaking play *The Elocution of Benjamin Franklin*, an extract cannot be expected to do more than hint at the work's confronting complexity. In both these works gender lines are crossed and recrossed.

Elsewhere in this selection other taboos are broken and boundaries breached. In several works (particularly Kenneth 'Seaforth' Mackenzie's extraordinarily explicit

1937 novel *The Young Desire It* and Hal Porter's baroque story 'The Dream') the sensitive boundary between schoolmaster and pupil is crossed; in Dorothy Porter's poems about the pharoah Akhenaten, from her longer work entitled *Akhenaten*, there is multiple transgression— bisexuality (Akhenaten is married to Nefertiti), incest (Smenkhare is his younger brother) and, stylistically, in Dorothy Porter's daring adoption of a homosexual male voice; while in Benedict Ciantar's first novel, *Distractions*, and Simon Payne's, *The Beat*, both set in the contemporary inner city, the revolt is against the expectations and mores of the country as a whole (not just of the middle class).

Transgression is inseparable from homosexuality in Australian society and germane to both the themes and structure of much homosexual writing. In George Steiner's words: 'The homosexual overlap[s] with the artist in being an outsider, a "grand refuser" of those standards of creativity and utilitarian relationship which define middle-class, industrial, post-Puritan civilization.' ('Eros and Idiom')

DOROTHY PORTER

The New Temple

'Are you counting my ribs?'

My brother looks over
his bare shoulder

Only sixteen.

I was watching
the new hard curve
of his bent back
as he planes the wood
for a pleasure boat

he's so good with his hands

my old hands
        dangle
like trawled octopus
good for nothing
but sex, prayers
        and scribbling

it's his back
that makes me stare
like a wall-eyed priest
at the glinting stone
        of a new temple.

1992

Just to Talk

Evening sky.

I breast-stroke
through its pink warm air.

It eddies under
the soft cotton
of my pink-white kilt.

But my breath cuts
like a red rock face.

He's coming.
Here. In a few minutes.

Just to talk.
To tell me all about his trip
to Thebes.
The night on the river.
The women in the wine shops.
The crowds on the dock.
He'd have had fun.
I'll watch his smooth hands
talk about it all
in this pink warm air.

And my own hands
will lie still and pretend
they don't long
to touch him.

1992

My Sleeping Brother

Asleep
Smenkhkare is cool.
And more fragrant
than melting scented wax.

I lean over him
and trail my hands
in his ripples.

But perhaps
I should stick to the safer lakes
    of Maru-Aten;
nothing is more dangerous
        for me
than swimming
    in the breath
of my sleeping brother.

1992

All Touch

His and my talk
is all touch.

When apart
I hallucinate
    his mouth, his eyes
and plot new ways
to touch him.

That scar on his upper lip.
I make mental notes
before I go to sleep.

I'll trace it with my thumb
ask him when it happened
take his face in my hands
bring him in close
till I feel his breath
     on my mouth

oh! the moment
when his eyes stagger!

I can't work

is my new love
my brother or my poppy juice?

1992

Lies and Tin

'Give him something to do.'

Who?
I know who.

'He needs friends of his own age.'
my wife's voice
     peevish/old

I'm his friend!

This is dangerous,
     I love talking about him.

I wait for her to say
     his name.

Her breathing
     slow, exploratory
          in the dark

'Leave him alone.'

How can she know?

I pull her into my arms
she cuddles up
     out of habit
I kiss her short fine hair
I've always liked her
     without her wig

she sighs,
    kisses my neck

'Do you love me?'

I answer
with hands, murmurs
    and nibble her ears

she pulls away
she won't play

I can't see her eyes.

'For all of our sakes
send him to Kush!'

my old snake
doesn't say please

'I can't stand it
    can't stand it.'

neither can I

I give her lies
I give her tin.

            1992

Little Brother

Smenkhkare, please,
go back to your own bed—

no,
    I'm not moralising
no,
    scales, crocodiles
    and jackals preaching in the Underworld
    don't scare me—
    priests' bullshit!

yes,
    you're more gorgeous
    than any woman in the Black Land

yes,
    I'm amazed
    your boring older brother
    makes you so randy

but
     I can't see you, my darling,
and
     I don't like fucking in the dark.

          1992

Smenkhkare's Wedding

I'm watching her
    not him

Why didn't I geld him?

Instead I gilded him
    my gold man
    my
        little king.

Marriage.
       The word puckers my mouth
       like a hen's arse.

His marriage.

Her earrings.
They wink
     like a dancing girl's.

          1992

KENNETH 'SEAFORTH' MACKENZIE

From *The Young Desire It*

Penworth walked down the aisle between the stark white beds. Laughter, cries, murmurs of familiar talk filled the dormitory. They were getting ready to go to bed. He felt restless. From the bathrooms came a sound of stamping feet bare on the concrete, and muffled echoes of some sort of horseplay. He walked slowly back, through the double doors, past the stair-head to the bathroom doors, which were closed. Someone was being put through the inevitable ordeal of going into the big linen basket that should stand by the entrance to the water-closets. When this basket was half-full of stinking socks and soiled linen, it was considered an ordeal of the higher senses for the initiate; when, as now, it was empty, all who went into it came out sore and bruised about the face and elbows and knees, from hard contact with the stiff cane sides. Penworth could hear the heavy breathing and difficult laughter of the boys who were bouncing and trundling it about on the concrete floors.

'Here, you young monkeys,' he called, and opened the doors. 'Back to your dormitories. Jameson! Drake! You—what's your name—stand that basket up, will you? All of you. Take that lid off and get out.'

Abashed, but not frightened—for it was, after all, the first night of term, an angry gala night—they straightened their backs and tried to compose their expressions to suit this expected intrusion. The shine of their eyes and lips, as they withdrew themselves from their high enterprise, was animal, provocative, brutally attractive to Penworth. He hardened himself against it, and stared coldly.

'Out you go, all of you,' he said tersely; and they went out, to loiter about the door, watchful and loth to lose any moment of sensual excitement. Their hot bodies were tense in the half-light. Over the top of the basket a boy's red, terrified face turned dully from them to the Junior Housemaster's pale, sardonic mask.

'What are you doing there?' Penworth demanded automatically. 'What's your name?'

'Charles Fox, sir.'

'Oh.' He stared. 'Well, come on—get out of that basket. Go back to your dormitory. This sort of thing isn't allowed, you know.'

'It's not my fault,' Charles said loudly, fighting back a strong urge to scream and tear the flesh of faces with his hands. 'It's not my fault at all. Why do you blame me? It's not my fault.'

This surprised Penworth greatly, both the reckless passion of the boy's eyes, and his own sudden nervousness. He was used to a deference which, even if it was only superficially respectful, at least seemed more than skin-deep. Subdued laughter hovered about the doorway behind him. He swung round, whisky-fierce, with the haughtiness of embarrassment.

'Get away from that door, and shut it.'

They went away, grumbling and laughing. His hot stomach seized on the laughter's insolence, and in a fine temper he turned upon Charles.

'Look here, young man. One of the first principles of this School is politeness to your masters ...'

Charles, shaking his head from side to side, trembling and stammering, saw the world as a nightmare that whirled a little, swayed and surrounded him.

'It's not my fault, I tell you. It's not. It's not.'

There was no insolence in this defiance, anyhow, and Penworth, becoming a little calmer, understood.

'Come on. Get out of that basket,' he said gently.

Charles's face went white; then blood reddened it; then it paled again. He stopped shaking his head.

'I ... I can't. Sir ... I can't, sir.'

'Come on,' Penworth said, roughly hiding his changed embarrassment.

He took the basket by its thick handles, and lowered it fairly gently to the floor.

'Oh,' Charles said.

He sprawled out of it, white and naked upon the concrete. Penworth stepped back not understanding his sudden agitation. To Charles, whose body was hot, marked by the hard cane of the basket, the floor felt awkwardly cool. He put himself upon his feet, still flushing and paling by turns. Until this night, since he was a very small child he had never stood naked before anyone's eyes. And certainly Penworth's eyes were on him. Certainly they were. He tried to hide his nakedness. At length he turned his back. Penworth looked at it, and felt some strange sensation of pleasure and shame course through him, dissipating all that was left of his censure, as heatless early sunlight dissipates frost on the grass.

He laughed shortly.

'Where are your clothes?'

'They took them away. They've got them, sir.'

Penworth strode to the door. The boys, of course, were still there, silent, listening, with curious smiles of pleasant anticipation. He scowled.

'You young fools. I thought you'd have had more sense. You've frightened the wits out of the boy. Haven't you any sensitiveness yourselves? Think—and do things more carefully. If you must do them. Where are Fox's clothes? Who has them?'

They saw that he had suddenly become very angry. Anyone who affronted that sort of mood in him would, as most of them knew, be fiercely punished. The pyjama suit was put into his hands, and they went away. Only in their dormitories, where they urgently told the story, did they venture again to laugh.

'Don't go into the bathrooms. Penworth's there, and he's mad.'

'Jesus, he's mad.'

'With that new kid.'

'Fox, the sissy.'

'He's not mad with Fox. Mad with us.'

'Jesus, he's mad.'

They knew it was Fox's fault.

Penworth gave Charles the pyjama suit. The boy's white skin had faint red marks upon it, round the shoulders, burning and fading. He put one hand on it, very briefly. It was as fine and as soft as a girl's skin.

'Put 'em on,' he said. 'And go along to bed. Don't you worry. You'll be all right.'

His kind, quiet tone gave Charles another shock. He began to cry, and Penworth, who became filled with a mild sentimental grief when he heard it, pretended not to notice. He picked up a towel that lay knotted in a corner. The knots were huge and thick, and loosened easily enough.

'This will be your towel,' he said at last, holding it at arm's length. 'Wash that dirty face and go along to bed.'

Then he went out hurriedly, leaving the doors wide.

. . .

Penworth said nothing to his senior in the House, nor to anyone else, of what had happened in the bathroom, but it came often to his mind. The curious pleasure he had felt when he saw that boy's white body, and when he touched the firm skin of his shoulder, would have seemed more strange than it did had he remembered it clearly; but there remained most vividly in his mind the memory of a bewilderment, of the same bewilderment with which a young man for the first time considers the revealed body of a woman—something of fear mixed sharply with the intense admiration of desire sublimated beyond material imagery. The great business of those following days and weeks would have erased even that from his mind, if he had not seen and spoken with Charles more often than he had expected. Greek and Latin classes, as well as the innumerable brevities of House routine, brought them frequently together; and, though Penworth was ready enough now to oblige the Chief, he was careful, rather for his own sake than for the sake of the boy, to prevent himself from showing any unnatural interest in him.

Charles's defiance grew as he slowly became aware of everything about himself that was different from others. He knew, without understanding why, that there was this difference; indeed, he could not have helped knowing, when in a dozen ways each day it was made very plain to him. He heard himself called names whose meaning he did not understand, but which, from the way they were mouthed, he could recognise as the shrewdest insults. Before long, he found he could face such callings; it was physical insult that he most horribly dreaded, and this he also invited by the unabating defiance with which he bore himself. Fortune had given him strong hands, and the instinct to use them in his own defence, but against a number he was, of course, soon powerless.

The dark complexity of this sort of life became increasingly dreadful as day followed day.

That February was a hot month, hotter even than an Australian February might be expected to be. Every afternoon those who were not listed for practice at the nets went down to the river which wound between its double line of trees beyond the wide scorched flats where the dairy herd was pastured. On the flats the grass was changed from gold to a bleached grey in the weeks of merciless sun. It frayed and split, seething with cicadas and insects that kept from dawn to dusk the sibilant waves of their immortal susurrus; and this sound, filling the whole world, became an unheard background to all the noises of day in the School; even at night, taken up by the crickets, the song never ceased and the air was mad with it. Sunlight was broken up like glass by the polished dry threads of stem and leaf; the grass fell flat, more than dead, and only patches of water-couch, defying the blinding heat, showed dully green about the hollow places, and spread in a scarred covering along the edges of the exhausted river.

The thick, fleshy odour of sweating mud hung in the air here. Even the river reeds, that marched like an army in the shallow water and stopped only at the sides of the platforms, and clustered by the slipways of the rowing sheds, were yellowing and breaking. When a breeze oozed warmly and fitfully down with the current, they knocked together and rattled secretly, until it seemed that the lazy ripples whispered in that swooning air. The boys came noisily down, under the care of an excellent old athletics master who sometimes made coarse army jests, and the place was shattered and outraged by their shouts and laughter. They were the blessed of the earth; they were lords of this tarnished stretch of original creation that spread flatly and wearily in the brassy light. To them, newly let out of the close afternoon heat of classrooms shuttered from the sun, it was heaven to be down here, half a mile away, with only Old Mac—lean and long like a ramrod, with silver moustaches stabbing at the pallid sky as he threw back his head to laugh—to watch them and listen delightedly, with his deafest expression, to their merry, dirty little jokes at one another's expense. On top of the distant declivity that fell down to the flats lay the School, empty now save for exhausted Masters taking some sort of ease in their shuttered studies; the red brick buildings shuddered like a long mirage in the fierce light, and through the smoke-grey tops of trees the tiled roofs pressed flat against the flat sky of the south-east. That skyline was all flatness, a poor enough backcloth against which, each afternoon, the hilarious comedy of these water-babies was played. They never looked that way. In front of them the greenish water stretched, a hundred yards to left and right of the platforms, forty yards across. Its surface was as still as a glass— something to be broken again, something to play with, to feel, to taste, something no cooler than milk cascading over shoulders and half-naked bodies as they plunged thirstily into its slow, invisible current. The soft clean odour of the water, that suggested river mud, leaves, and the secret smell of water-rotten wood, clung about their hair and bodies afterwards, reminding them of the coolness as they sat over their studies in the heavy evenings.

Charles went down. He went with the rest, running helter-skelter as madly as sheep down the ramp, down the baked clay of the slope, slowing to an eager walk in the white grass of the flats, damp with sweat already, swinging towels, singing, whistling, laughing jealously at those who, in spite of the heat, ran on before them. He had a vague idea, born of the labour of thought at night, that perhaps his one protection from further bodily shame would be to keep among them. The more people there were about him, he thought, the less likely it would be that he would seem conspicuous, a target for their eyes and their words. The first days had been busy with a confused shifting from place to place; rolls were called, scholars had given them the blank time-table forms which they filled in according to the course of their studies. Masters stood on daises, explaining, asking questions, sweeping in and out in their billowing black gowns, referring this boy and that to another classroom or another

Master. The continual cry of 'Silence, please', still echoed warmly in Charles's ears as he walked in the sun. No one had taken much notice of him; he wondered if it would last.

. . .

The mid-afternoon sunlight was still and scalding, blinding like a fire too closely peered into, yet as dull in colour as brass. He went quickly up the concrete path to the Chapel; under the shadow of the south side boys were lying about on the grass, too lax to make their usual happy noise, or to play. They sprawled on their bellies in the shade, or lay looking upwards with narrowed eyes at the white heat of the sky, chewing pieces of grass while they talked and argued as incessantly as ever. Some of them called out after him; Saunders, who lay on his back with his knees drawn up, turned his head lazily.

'There's a swim this afternoon, Foxy. Coming?'

'I might,' Charles said shortly. He was in haste to get out of the sun.

One of the half-doors was swung back, and he went in quickly, without troubling to listen to what they had to say further. Inside, in the vestry, there was a coolness; the creamy stone and the oak looked fresh in the sudden shadow. Sunlight fell in long broken blades across the dimness in the spiral stone stair that turned up from the right-hand tower base towards the organ loft. Here, to his embarrassment, he came upon his music master, sitting on the lowest choir bench with his elbows on the rail and his face smothered in his fingers.

'Oh—I'm sorry, sir,' he said.

'It's all right,' Mr Jones said, looking up and feeling for his spectacles. When he had put them on he looked again at Charles, who remained at the entrance to the loft, in hot uncertainty as to whether he should withdraw from what he knew was an intrusion.

'Oh, it's you, Fox,' Mr Jones said. 'What are you going to do here?'

'I was going to read, sir.'

'All right. What are you reading?'

Charles showed him. As he came close he saw with great confusion that the organist's hectic thin cheeks were wet in places, under the eyes.

'Ah,' Jones said. 'Well, you couldn't do better than read Shakespeare in a lovely place like this. Away from—away from interruption.'

'I'm sorry if I interrupted you, sir,' Charles said in a hurry. 'The light in the library is so bad; I thought I'd—I'd come up here.'

'Stay, stay,' Jones urged him, kindly. 'I was going, in any case. It's too hot to practise ...'

Charles believed he heard him add 'in this damnable country' under his breath; but he was smiling, although the smile was rather rueful. He had a charming quick smile with a whimsical sharpness and twist in it, suggesting a happy wit, which he had. From the low opening into the stair he said, turning back, 'I'm going home. If you care to come over to my cottage in an hour, when you'll have finished that, we could have tea together and talk about it. Mr Penworth is on duty; I'll see him on my way.' He went on down the stair without waiting for an answer; and when he had disappeared Charles heard him call out in a voice that strained at light-heartedness, 'My wife went back to England yesterday, so there'll be no one there'.

And yet again, above the clatter of his own descending heels, he said loudly from below, 'She couldn't stand the climate . . .' and in a moment there came up the fading sound of his feet going quickly away down the Chapel path.

The echo of these words died in Charles's mind when he began to read. It was hot in the loft, though the long blinds had been drawn down over the tall, narrow windows whose leaded panes, farther up the Chapel, broke into fragments of sullen gold the sunlight slanting in. Charles unbuttoned his coat and his waistcoat, and stood leaning against the northern wall. In the silence of the great vaulted roof his heart beat heavy and slow; the seductive, strangling murmur of pigeons floated down from the belfries above him. After some minutes these sounds too became the silence.

Perhaps half an hour after he had started to read *King Henry the Fifth* there was a noise of feet coming lightly but slowly up the narrow stair. Charles, however, was so concentrated upon the page that not till Penworth had spoken twice did he look up. Then, when he realised that he had heard him speak once already, the blood came quickly into his face, and he began to stammer out an apology.

'Well, and what are you doing here?' Penworth said in a friendly way, coming to stand by him. Charles let his strong broad fingers take the book out of his hands.

'H'm; you're not doing any harm reading that, anyhow.' Penworth was pleasantly decided, and Charles felt again how well he liked this cultured, easy man, who could make even Greek syntax seem a matter for smiles and small excitements.

'What do you think of it?' Penworth asked. Then he laughed and said, 'No—don't bother; schoolmasters spoil things when they start asking questions. And this is Sunday, anyhow. Read it and enjoy it alone. Nothing is nicer.'

He sat down, and Charles remained where he was standing, feeling happy that he had been surprised in such a way by such a man. Penworth was looking up at him, cocking an eye under the fine arches of his brows. From the bays of his wide temples Charles could see how the hair was already receding, as though into the bays of a coastline a tide were being sent.

His smile was weary and pleasing at first. Then, as he talked and looked at Charles, it became deeper and more lively. He confounded the heat . . . Charles listened to the colourful cadences of his voice with half-unheeding content; he was still wrapped in unfinished thoughts about the play he had been reading, and parts of it came into his mind surprisingly, and were confused with Penworth's idle words.

'. . . just between twelve and one, e'en at turning o' the tide: for after I
saw him fumble at the sheets, and play with flowers, and smile upon his
fingers' ends, I knew there was but one way; for his nose was as sharp as
a pen, and 'a babbled of green fields . . . So 'a bade me lay more clothes
on his feet . . . just between twelve and one, e'en at turning o' the tide . . .
'a babbled of green fields . . .'

Penworth ceased talking abruptly.

'You weren't listening,' he said; but his smile smoothed the abruptness
of the words.

'Yes, sir—oh, yes, I was listening,' Charles said, feeling his face
become hot. 'But that play too . . . it . . .'

'. . . kinda gets yer, eh? As your friends outside would say.'

As he said this Penworth quite carelessly put out his hand and gripped
Charles's leg firmly above the knee. His palm was warm but dry; Charles
hardly noticed it in his relief at not being thought rude. The gentle
fingers slid slowly upwards under the short trouser leg; they touched
Charles like moths, in sensitive places, for hardly a second, and then as
slowly slid down again. Penworth had not spoken; he was looking into
Charles's eyes, and smiling. His smile was in his eyes, too, as though
turned inward to deride himself. He withrew his hand and let it fall upon
his knee.

For a moment the silence was hot and intense. Then Penworth
stretched his arms up, and pulled his head back, yawning so that the skin
creased down his flat, healthy cheeks. He still looked at Charles,
sideways, and raised one eyebrow as though he would have said, 'Well,
what fools all of us are'. Charles laughed. He had already forgotten the
caressive touch, which had seemed almost as dispassionate as the touch of
his own hand upon a sheet of paper.

'It makes one wish to live like some rich Greek of centuries ago,'
Penworth said, when his yawn was ended in a gasp of breath. 'This
climate of yours, I mean. To bathe and hunt and go to the games, and in
the evening walk about in public places, and converse like men. That was
the life. But different ages, different conventions. Different moralities.'
And he added darkly, 'Intelligent men must work like any slaves, with
starved souls'.

He stood up, sighing. 'I suppose you don't trouble about what I mean.
Why should you? Anyhow, we can't put the clock back as far as that, can
we?'

'It's a pity we can't,' Charles said, in sudden enthusiasm. 'It's a pity—
yes, it is a pity. Did they have boarding schools, sir?'

Penworth laughed, a barking, Alma-Mater, wit-appreciating laugh.

'Well—not of this sort. Why, don't you like it here?'

'No. At least, not very much, sir. I do like it when you talk to me like
this, though. It makes me alive again.' He realized as he spoke that
Penworth had been speaking to him as though to an equal; and, perhaps
for that, he felt in some way an equal. In what way that was, he did not

understand. Well, he thought, it will not last. To-morrow morning I shall have to pretend that I don't know him any better than anyone else does.

But he was wonderfully heartened by such kind friendship, which was not feigned, as he knew very surely, and clearly hid no intention of doing him bodily insult.

Penworth put an arm round his shoulders and rocked him gently to and fro.

'Like it, do you?' he said quietly.

Charles felt tears suddenly burn his eyelids, and knew his face was flushing, as it did in any strong emotion.

'Yes, sir.'

Penworth looked for what seemed a long time into his eyes, with a steady, searching gaze, holding him closely with one arm round his shoulders. The pupils of his eyes were dilated darkly, as they might be in the passion of rage, or fear.

He pulled himself away miserably. A moment later Penworth had gone. There were sounds of people coming up the other stairway. He could hear the light tenor tones of the Master with the sculpted features and carven eyelids, making some small and very quaint remark. He went to the stair. Penworth was gone.

The feeling of tears was gone also. It would be good to go out through the heat of day, to have tea with Mr Jones, now, in a place that looked like a home.

. . .

Penworth himself would at that time have had great pain to explain, even to his own questing conscience, what were his objects in so cultivating the boy. He knew he wanted to touch him; he knew he felt some kind of complicated pleasure in observing the changing expressions in Charles's pale face, with its steady green-brown eyes and clear red lips; he was pleased, when one of those happy strenuous private lessons was over, to put his own white hand on the boy's touselled, ruddy crown and notice, without appearing to notice, what a fine flash of happiness and gratitude relieved the face below of its intent frown; but he would not have attempted to explain this pleasure, and he took care that the boy should not be aware of it. To this end he allowed himself moments of spoken impatience, sometimes of irritation (more genuine than he knew, and from an obscure cause), and his reward for these essays was a burning colour in Charles's face, and the hint of tears not readily to be shed.

In his own youthful self-centredness he did not at all understand the real power he was gaining over Charles. He was happy to play at an aloof intimacy expressing itself more often than not in subtly allusive quotations from one or other of the dead languages he professed, salting his conversation as young scholars down the ages, delighted at the infinite prospects of joy offered by learning, have salted it; or to enthuse tersely, by gesture and expression and with few words, over some ancient or contemporary poet; or even to discuss at length, as though to himself, in a word-imagery much above the intellectual height of Charles (but not beyond his affectionate admiration) the beauties and associations of certain musical compositions.

All this was as disturbing and as sublimely serious to Charles as the passions of religion or the pangs of love would be. Its evident danger was, in some sort, pardoned by the tremendous ardour it fired in him to learn what he desperately needed to learn—the cold, unsuggestive truths of earlier Latin syntax and accidence, and certain textbook rules of English study and composition. Penworth's sensual, smiling lips driving creases into the flat pallor of the cheeks, his bold, white brow already straightly seamed, and above all his grey eyes in their arched and beautiful setting of brow, lid and nose, all became associated for Charles with irregular Latin verbs and the obstinate eccentricities of the fourth and fifth declensions. They gave particular urgency to the understanding of the prologue to the *Canterbury Tales*, and to the elucidation of obscure word-usages in *Hamlet*, which Penworth joyfully insisted on reading with him out of class, in addition to conducting the whole form through it soberly in the classroom. He was a young man who loved his work. Charles began to have some understanding of the joys and travails of studying Shakespeare and Chaucer with an enthusiast whose Master's degree entitled him to expound richly and with force.

Charles became suddenly happier, during those weeks. He did not notice that Penworth's hand more often touched his, or was liable to caress his head or his knee in moments when the air in the little white study was fierce and tense and attentive. He knew only that he was learning, as he had never learned before, the beauties of his own language and of that from which so much of it had grown. He had the ideal experience of being in harmony with the close brotherhood of Latin and English learned at the same time and in the same way; his heart was full and overflowing, at such times, with the passionless ecstasy of knowing.

Only the memory of [Margaret's] comely face, and the incommunicable secret harboured in her breasts, in the sighing shadow of the grove, came from the outside world to surprise into a surrender his moments of straying thought. The harder his mind spent itself in toiling, seizing, claiming and assimilating the facts that contained fluid essences of knowledge, the more vividly, afterwards, it turned away to receive those thoughts of her. Reacting from the labour of days he made in his mind a wild but innocent life of actions and contacts, as remote from probability as a dream, in its perfect carelessness of experience. Vaguely she took her part in the fantasy of his real night dreams, when his body lay sprawled and still in that double row of sprawled, still bodies, doing its work of sober recuperation for his brain and his mind winging so gladly away in darkness that was light. He had never seen the secret bloom of a woman's breasts before; but, as though schooled by poets and others through all time, he perceived in them nourishment for the mind and foundations on which to build dreams. And the line of brow and cheek, of smooth hair and neck and shoulder, of obstinate knees and straight legs—these in memory took on a large significance of which life must certainly soon try to rob him. With such knowledge of her, the smallest yet, perhaps, the choicest he could have known, his mind in sleep or day dreaming, during a noisy morning recess or under the meaningless glory of a service in Chapel, composed ecstasies whose frailty and unworldliness were mercifully kept from him. In a rare and lonely way he was learning, as those others were learning, with surprise and happiness, to live.

. . .

It was that rainy Friday that began for Mawley a conscious friendship with Charles. There were several—individualists all, no doubt—who had gathered together to monopolise the springboard and vaulting horse; they had the horse broad-on, and were, with that sober self-examination and approval so good to indulge in in youth, going from short-arm bend to long-arm. The responsive thrust and clatter of the board gave great animation to these serious proceedings, and it was the general excitement, as well as an habitual excess of confidence and blind zeal, that made Mawley forget his feet in the first long-arm, and left him laid out on the mattress with a tendon torn out of the right ankle, in such overwhelming perfection of pain as few are allowed to know while remaining conscious. Lying there, hidden from the others by the varnished broadside of the horse, it was possible to observe with one of those receptive abettors of consciousness, how the great hall had suddenly deserted him, its merry activity unabated but his own place in it closed up and gone. Its white walls became intensely more white; faces and all vanished, but the shouting and the laughter went on, the clatter of the springboard sent invisible bodies thudding over onto that mattress, and suddenly there were Charles's eyes, horrified. Speech at that moment was not in Mawley's power; it was for Charles. Suddenly again, as though consciousness were being released in abrupt jerks, there was his body dancing frantically and his mouth open, shouting, and his hands waving. Something seemed to have frightened him properly, for his face was greenish with pallor; it must have been Mawley's foot doubled unnaturally outwards, lying flat and out of line with leg and body, looking, as he said a long time later, 'worse than murder'. He said, 'I'd rather see a chap dead than lying like that and being alive enough to laugh'. His antics must have been worth laughter.

The next gift of consciousness to Mawley was a dawning sight of the lower bathroom in Chatterton materializing swiftly out of a white blankness, and a foreshortened vista of his own leg and foot extended into a flooding wash-basin. If only there had been blood, Charles thought, it would not have looked so horrible. You could not mistake

Old Mac's dry, flat fingers, with the small one on the left hand gripped by a heavy signet ring. Charles's white face, drawn down in a ghastly tension of colour from the slowly turning eyes, was peering; Penworth, terse before animal suffering, let out monosyllables abruptly. Pain, so immediate in its need for exclamation, does not aid coherent speech when it grasps body and heart like a great hand, and stirs the guts with an icy, inquisitive forefinger. But hearing seems to have become minutely acute. Every tremble in Charles's breath, as his heart stamped the action of his lungs, throbbed on the air. Something had greatly shocked him. It must have been that gold and purple royalty which was, ten minutes ago, a happy and obedient joint. Penworth observed its effect on Charles, also.

'Better have a drink of water, Fox,' he snapped. 'Glass in my . . . Oh, the young idiot. Damn.'

Charles slid comfortably down the wall, moving his hands in blind groping as he went over sideways. Penworth cupped a double handful of water from the flooded basin and flung it into the shrunken whiteness of his face.

'Leave it,' said Old Mac impatiently. 'Upstairs with this one.'

From the bed in Dormitory C it was a surprise to Mawley to hear the turmoil in the gymnasium going on as before, with a crash and clatter still from the springboard and a chinking rattle of rings. Old Mac's hands were neat and orderly, resting on his chest to hold him still, while his voice said, 'Hold still, sir. A nasty fall, by gad,' calmly, as though to himself. The pain located itself at last, withdrawing its false rumour downwards. Steps and words rose on the stairs; the School's nursing sister smiled and murmured like a brown dove over his shivering:

'What have *you* done with yourself? Let's have a look.'

Penworth, with drops of water still falling from fingers and wrists, lifted Charles half-conscious from that foolish tumble between wall and floor, and bore him off to his room.

Charles was struggling, saying: 'It's all right, sir, really it is,' but Penworth as abruptly as before bade him shut up. He closed the door by kicking it with his heel, and laid Charles on the bed.

'Now,' he said, and suddenly was smiling. Charles sat up, and at once lay back again; waves of light and darkness still swept steadily into his brain, but that tide was going out.

'Lie still,' Penworth said, and busied himself with a glass and a bottle.

'If this makes you drunk,' he muttered, 'it'll be the open road for me, my lad. What on earth made you go off like that?'

Charles turned his face to the wall, as though to read reason on its white page.

'I don't know,' he began, and then, with tears in his eyes, said sharply, 'It was so horrible, wasn't it? All torn sideways like that.' He hovered uncertainly between tears and a relaxed force of laughter. Penworth handed him the tumbler.

'Whisky,' he said. 'It's a waste giving it to you, but still, you'd better drink it. There's not much.'

Charles swallowed it, and as it fumed in his nose and throat his teeth began to chatter again on the thin edge of the glass. A memory of his mother's face hanging like a calm mask above the light of a candle by his bed, as she said almost those words—'You'd better drink this, son. There's not much'—grew up vividly in his mind. There was her head's great shadow doubled in the angle of wall and ceiling like a torn piece of paper; and her hands coming out of the brown darkness to comfort him after the unwieldy horror of a nightmare. The reek of whisky was something very real, to which from the anguish of the mind it was good to turn.

He told Penworth shyly of this memory, and of others.

'Nightmares, eh? Do you still have them?'

'Sometimes,' Charles said, looking away to think. 'Not often, sir.'

'What sort of dreams now?' Penworth seated himself at the foot of the bed, and took Charles's feet in his two hands firmly, as though without seeing he did it. Charles looked at him suddenly from the pillow.

'I dream a lot,' he explained, 'but in a sort of muddled way. I don't often remember.'

'Your dreams now,' Penworth said thoughtfully, his eyes upon the boy's pale face, 'should be interesting. I wonder . . .'

Charles felt some relief in his confidence. He told him, in a new assurance of sympathy, of some of his dreams. His unwitting frankness shocked Penworth into looking away, and then attracted him so that he turned his face to Charles again, his deep pupils dilated, his sensual lips full of passionate seriousness.

'I know,' he said. 'Of course, one doesn't . . .'

'What worried me,' Charles said gravely, 'was just at first—you know, sir. There is no one to explain. I suppose everyone's the same.'

'Yes, yes,' Penworth murmured, his eyes looking back into his own initiations and experiments. 'All of us, sometime or other.'

'You see, I don't know anything—about that,' Charles explained.

'The shock of discovering your own body,' Penworth began; but he stopped himself. Looking upwards to the grey face of the window he could see the ghost of rain against the sky, as mysterious and vanishing as marks made on still water. Looking upwards, he seemed to be having some inward debate with himself; Charles could see how blind were his eyes beneath the white curve of the forehead above its deeply arched brows. His full lips were moving and trembling with every turn of his thought. He still gripped Charles's feet with his broad hands. Through the near silence of the room floated a sustained echo of tumult from the gymnasium.

At last Charles struggled to ask, 'What are you thinking of now, Mr Penworth?'

He turned his head sideways and down, looking into the boy's serious eyes.

'Of myself,' he said quietly. 'As usual. And of you. Has no one ever told you anything?—anything about physical development and your own body?'

'No, sir.'

'What about living here? Surely you can't live among these—these boys and not have learned a lot?'

Charles considered his own mind, frowning unconsciously.

'I hear what they say, you know,' he said at length, after Penworth had stared into his face unwaveringly for a minute or more. 'But I don't think I understand ... I mean, I sort of know what it's about and yet I—I sort of don't know. That sounds muddled ...'

'I understand,' Penworth said shortly, as though he had come to the end of a train of thought which he had been following even while he listened to the boy's difficulties in speaking of his own mind. He was surprised to find that Charles was speaking the truth, and speaking it simply. He neither dramatized his innocence and half-knowledge, nor attempted, as others would have done, to make it seem, without actually saying, that he knew more and was willing enough to talk about it. Penworth, while he was puzzled, and confused also in certain depths of which he was only just now discovering the nature, was turned a little compassionate in his own belief and admiration.

'Well,' he said, 'I'd find it rather hard to tell you everything face to face like this ...'

'I'd probably find it hard, too,' Charles said with a smile.

'Anyhow,' Penworth went on unheeding, 'there are things you'll learn; and it's probably just as fair to you to let you find them out for yourself. As the gods see fit. But,' he said, 'don't get into the habit of talking as the other boys talk until you know what you're speaking of and what it all means. You'll only do yourself harm—in your own opinion, later.'

His charity just then surprised and flattered him. He felt driven to it, at first, because he had finally discovered and admitted to himself why he liked the boy as he did. He was, despite his youngness, honest enough and lonely enough to admit that this was a physical attraction, of exactly the same sort as he would have felt in the untutored presence of a girl of the same age. Had he been rather older, separated from his own deeply impressionable boyhood by darker, longer years, he might have regarded with jealous hatred the idea of himself desiring the unknowable body of this boy ten years his junior and a lifetime apart in ignorance; but he was at that time still subjectively familiar with the rules of philosophy and domesticity of the ancients he studied, and, because also desire can reason against itself without for one instant quitting its intention or questioning its present emotion, he considered himself calmly, and, had he been alone, would have shrugged his shoulders, as though to say, 'Well, let it be so, then.'

'Action can wait,' he heard himself murmur; and to the urgent question in Charles's eyes he could not reply for a moment. At last, when the silence between them had calmed to a quietened current of thought, he spoke again.

'You don't need to worry about yourself, nor about those dreams. You are made to grow like that so that one day you can have a wife and children. One day ...'

Deserted as suddenly as he had been possessed by that charitable restraint, he took his hands from the boy's feet, reached forward impulsively and took his cold fingers into his own, pulling him up to a sitting position, feeling with a heart-beat of fear the weight of the body communicated to his own back and shoulders, and imagining with rage its warmth and deathly whiteness. When their faces were close together he looked desperately into Charles's eyes, striving with the stubbornness of despair to find in their far depths some response to his own will.

Charles went stiff with the alarm of this. When he turned his eyes sideways, startled beyond thought by what was happening to him, seeing only the stillness and finality of the closed door, Penworth kissed him clumsily and hard on the lips.

The silence of the room roared like a surf in their ears. It was as big as the dreadful silence of his own nightmares to Charles. He could not move; he could not even turn his head more to avoid further contact with the dry eager lips of another man. Slowly his eyes came round. At the uncomprehending alarm in them Penworth laughed shortly, and let his hands slide free; that clipped, low laugh exploded like a long-awaited thunderclap in the still room.

'It's all right, dear lad,' he said. 'Don't be frightened—I shan't hurt you.'

Charles stood up; and he too rose; so they faced each other.

'Were you frightened of—something that might have happened?' Penworth asked, lightness lifting his voice out of the mire of emotional extravagance. 'There's nothing to be frightened of now. Is there?'

Charles shook his head several times, without being able to speak. He did not clearly know what he felt. It seemed somehow like happiness, but there was a black colour of doubt and regret hanging undefined about it. The goodness of having such a friend, so quickly in sympathy, so spontaneous in showing sympathy, was a warm glow in his heart; but he knew without being told that men do not kiss one another so. It was such an impossible thing that he had never even imagined it; and now ... He shook his head. That was the origin of the enormous doubt and the shamed regret he felt; he understood that something had been done which should not have been done, though he did not understand why there was argument against it. Instinct warned him uncertainly that from this moment he would never talk of it, and his own shyness made it impossible that he should turn to Penworth there by the window and ask, Why? For he had been made most conscious, in the last fifteen minutes, of the vastness and danger of his ignorance. The coil of life was about him, and as yet he could not follow it with his eyes, nor sink back in the empowered calm of understanding; he must remain poised, keeping balance deliberately and with effort.

'Here's the damned winter,' Penworth said at length, without turning round; and immediately he asked, 'Do you by any chance know what it is to be as lonely as hell?'

Charles nodded; and then, remembering with confusion that he was not being observed, he said, 'I do now, sir,' struggling to reach the high and windy level of the other's thought. 'Since I've been here, at school,' he said slowly.

'Exactly.' Penworth swung round upon him as sharply as though he had been angered by the words. 'Here,' he said, 'in a place like this—to be lonely; to want some sort of peace; to want love. To be lonely among so many. A microcosm that mirrors the worldly macrocosm—this place. An analogy with life in all the world—so many, and each one alone. If we try to touch each other's heart, it's misunderstood. And, worst of all, we don't understand it ourselves. We're lost; in a crowd it's as though we're ... I can't tell you.'

'I do know; I feel it,' Charles said as calmly as he might.

'Well, don't say it so smugly,' Penworth said bitterly; but his stare softened and became warmer, and he said, 'I forgot that you're so young. Why do I talk to you like this? Why should I? I haven't the right; I haven't the right to do it. There it is again: every action and inclination blasted by life's discreet irony. We're always at the mercy of that.'

He came close and took Charles's face between his palms, looking down not now with desire but with something clearer and more assured.

'I can't expect you to understand,' he murmured coldly. 'You're a child. What can you know? For all your pretty looks you're as masculine as any of us—and more than some. What can you know?'

He stared unwaveringly into his eyes.

'And yet—perhaps you're not. If you're not, it's not for me to know—not now.' And he muttered to himself between his clenched teeth, 'I haven't the courage.'

With a gesture as of one dropping something into space he let Charles's face slip from between his hot palms, and stood back from him. To Charles there was nothing deliberately dramatic in this; but to Penworth there was, and he watched its effect reflected in the boy's face, in the unhappy striving to understand and to keep pace with the thought spoken.

Charles made an effort and answered him.

'I may not know it all, but even if I am so young I do know you're unhappy; and if I could help I would. If I can.'

Penworth smiled, but his eyes were steadily watchful.

'Nobly spoken. Nobly said. However'—and once again he changed in that sudden way that so bemused Charles—'I believe you mean it.'

'I do, sir,' Charles said, and felt once more uncertain of his ground.

'But I don't know what I can do—except talk to you. I do like that. I like it awfully. No one else talks like you.'

He hesitated, and found he could say no more.

'I should not have upset you like this,' Penworth said. 'I should have remembered that you are working hard, and that you can't be normal when you're doing that. I try to solve a physical problem with intellectual co-equivalents and get an answer in spiritual terms; and it can't be done. Anyone could tell you that. It can't be done.'

His smile shone at last in his eyes. He put one arm round Charles's shoulders, rocking him from side to side, gently, as he had done once before, in the heat of afternoon up there in the choir loft. He looked down affectionately into his face.

'You're doing well, too. Now—let's forget about this afternoon altogether. Is that a bargain?'

'Oh, yes, sir,' Charles said earnestly, not thinking whom the bargain might profit because of the full return of happiness and assurance that leapt up within him.

'Right. Now go upstairs and see how Mawley is getting on.'

Steps paused at the door and a fist pounded softly on the panels.

'Come in,' Penworth snapped; and, when Waters put his mild pink face round the dark edge of the door, he turned to Charles from the other side of the room, and said coldly, 'All right, Fox, you can go now. And don't be a fool and faint next time you see a sprained ankle.'

When he had gone Waters came into the room and shut the door with care.

'What happened? Faint?'

Penworth flung away an impatient gesture.

'Young Mawley hurt himself in the gym—pretty badly, I think—and that young idiot fainted in the bathroom. I gave him some perfectly good whisky; wasted it, in fact. You'd better sample it yourself.'

'He's a pretty child,' Waters mumbled amiably, seating himself on the bed.

'He is,' Penworth said, his back still turned. 'That's his misfortune. This is our good luck.'

Waters took the tumbler from his hand, and asked about news from Home.

. . .

At the brief knock on the panel, Penworth, who had been staring darkly through the open window and feeling at odds with the cheer of sunlight slanting into the pooled lawn outside, called to come in without turning round. Charles saw his head and shoulders cut out against the trees and the sky; the shoulders sloping dispiritedly, pulled down by the deep thrust of hands into trousers pockets.

'Sir, it's me,' he said.

Penworth brought himself slowly round; his frown remained dark, and the full melancholy of his lips reflected in his eyes.

'It's not "me",' he remarked coldly. 'It's "I".'

'Yes, sir,' said Charles, on guard before this mood.

'Well,' he said. 'What do you want? Did I send for you? Oh, I know — this morning, yes.'

He seated himself in his chair, so that the light from the windows behind him fell thinly on his brown, wide head. Charles once more measured with his eyes the width and height of that forehead, and its deep downward arc of whiteness from temple to temple. His admiration for the sensual beauty of the face would not change, no matter how darkly he was considered. The bold nose with fine nostrils, the wonderful setting of the eyes that could look so cold, and the sensitive, full mouth reminded him of kind words and friendship. Only the chin was small, round and womanish; but he did not see that, for the man's eyes drew his look always.

'So you're going to run races, eh?' Penworth said, after regarding him for some time as though he were a stranger. 'Will that leave you enough time for working with me, or can you dispense with me now?'

Charles stared, and his lips trembled when he spoke.

'No, sir — please don't think that. I only gave my name because — I only gave my name so as not to seem to want to dis — dissociate myself too much — so as not to seem out of it too much, sir.'

Penworth raised his eyebrows, without smiling.

'I see you remember my words,' he said. 'Come here. No, right round the table, this side. There. Now look at me.'

He took Charles's face between his cool palms, and stared into his eyes.

'What the matter with you? You're trembling.'

Charles said nothing, concentrating his mind on returning that deep look.

'Well,' said Penworth quietly, 'what have you got to say for yourself?'

Charles said: 'Nothing, sir. I just came. You told me to.'

Again Penworth raised his eyebrows.

'I see. You came because I told you to. I see. If I hadn't sent for you, told you to come, you wouldn't have come. Am I right to assume that?'

'Oh, sir! Of course I'd have come, anyway. Of course I would.'

Penworth looked from his eyes to his lips, and back again to his eyes. The glance was bold and quick, as sudden as the fall of a hawk from its hover. Charles instinctively moved his head, and the blood flung across his cheeks.

'Come here,' Penworth said deliberately. 'You silly young ninny.' His regard was big with anger. 'I sometimes think,' he said, 'that you're a danger to this School, Fox.'

He let Charles go out of his hands, and laughed.

'You have the vanity, too, to talk about love — and girls — you do, you! With a face ...'

He stopped himself. Charles stood helplessly, while tears of rage filled his eyes, and became tears of misery; they fell and he was unable to move to conceal them. His breath choked in his throat.

'I don't talk about it,' he cried, with shame and misery and ebbing anger tearing at him.

'Oh, yes you do,' Penworth remarked lightly. 'Kindly don't contradict me like that.' A voice was asking clearly and curiously in his mind why he was doing what he did. He shook it aside as he would at that moment have shaken aside the hand of any mendicant. It came again; it was Charles's voice.

'Why do you say this to me? Is this why I was to come and see you? You were my great friend, and now you say this to me, and you don't even know what it means. I wish I had never come here. I wish I had never been born.'

Penworth swallowed, determined to look unconcerned before such childish hysterics; but he could not see the anguish he had brought into the boy's face without seeing also that it was as true as his own pretended coldness was false and cruel. Yet the pain he watched gave him a great surge of—was that pleasure, then, that overpowering sense of elation, and self-pity? Was that pleasure?

He regarded Charles for some minutes, saying nothing, noticing the curve from his averted head to his neck and shoulders, and the way those shoulders shook, almost as though he were being whipped. Then he stood up and turned once more to the window, enjoying the curious sensations of his secret shame and elation, and above all enjoying now that supreme and most godly power, the power to comfort when his dramatic sense admitted comfort.

It was some time before the silence in the white room was broken. When Charles spoke, his voice came steadily.

'Mr Penworth, I'm sorry. I'm sorry if I've made you angry. I didn't mean to, sir. It was just that I felt so unhappy coming back here, and looked forward to seeing you; that was all I did look forward to. I didn't know you'd be feeling wretched. Even in form this morning—I thought it was just—just you, and I thought it was just a sort of pretence and that you didn't really mean what you said, sir.'

Penworth followed his dramatic sense, and turned round. Charles was confused to see him smiling. He had expected further reprimand, spoken to make his difficult apology seem only right and apposite, spoken rather stiffly as though to any boy, and to be followed by a brief dismissal. To see, instead, the old smile of friendship and interest made him wonder what would happen next. His attention was so concentrated that he could not smile himself.

'They call me the Bad Penny, don't they? Well—It's all right, you needn't give them away—perhaps I am. Always turning up. He that turneth up—a stone ... He that turneth up the stone of my heavy humour finds a worm beneath.'

He laughed pleasantly at his thought.

'It's all right,' he said again. 'You needn't frown like that over what I mean. Or do you see it? Perhaps you do—you of all people, Charles Fox. The long and the short of it is, Charles, that nothing in the School's prospectus, or curriculum, gives me the right to treat you as I like to, and do. Mr Jolly will tell you that it's a bad policy for a Master to make a boy an especial friend, just as it's bad policy to be everlastingly hard on a particular boy in class. Mr Jolly will tell you, if you care to ask him, that especial friendships are bad for the Master's disciplinary powers, and not fair to the boy; they hamper him in his efforts to assume his rightful social status as an ordinary member of our happy community. So, Charles, I do wrong to you, and I do wrong to make you the slave of my humours—or to be willing to make you. Now you shall choose: whether do I continue for the next eight or nine weeks to coach you in here, or whether do I inform Mr Jolly that my time is too much occupied, and ask him to free me from the arrangement. Now choose.'

He leaned against the window-frame, put into a gentle humour again by the pleasing sound of his own words, and by his certainty of how the boy's choice would fall. Self-confidence had returned to him with the affirmation, during these last minutes, of his own singular personality; and when he was assured in self-confidence his desire was always to be kind. He watched Charles.

'Well, sir,' Charles said hesitantly. 'If you would—would you mind, just until the exams are over, going on as we were?'

'I should be glad,' Penworth replied with amiable frankness. 'You are doing particularly well. Come here, old thing.'

He put his arm round his shoulders in the old way of friendship, and rocked him gently from side to side.

'You look tired,' he said, and he closed his fingers in the ruddy curls and tilted his face far back. 'Yes, you do look tired. You've worked too hard. And,' he said slowly, as though piecing together the thought as he spoke it, 'I believe you feel too hard, too. I believe you do. Your hair, now, is said to be the colour that indicates an excitable nature. Let me have a good look at you. There.'

He held him away, gripping his shoulders with his broad, strong hands.

'An excitable nature. A good nose, though; a nose suggesting will-power, or determination. Same thing. Same thing? I wonder. Anyhow ... Eyebrows rather thick—concentration. But eyes too dreamy even for a youth, and a mouth too soft, altogether too soft and generous, not sharp-cut. Eyes and lips like yours are a nice combination in a boy, I must say! You might have been an artist; but I don't think you will: you're not hard enough. So, if you feel too deeply, I don't know what you'll do. And God help you, anyhow.'

He let him go, watching him.

'Now—am I not nice to you? What do you think of my summing-up? The temperament of an excitable girl combined with a very masculine strength of will and a masculine mind ... It's no good, Charles; you'll get into awful messes. But I expect you'll get out of them too. What do you think?'

'I suppose you're right, sir,' Charles said. 'I don't know; is it—is it always possible to tell from a person's face what he's like?'

'Ah, now that depends upon the teller. Just as if you were a small depositor. And you needn't laugh at me like that. You see—an excitable nature, as I said. You're laughing from nervousness.'

He taunted him affably; and as he did so he was startled by a thought that irritated him suddenly in spite of himself and made him wonder whether something in their relationship had not been resolved that afternoon, so that now certain desires of his, stale desires once warm, begotten of a loneliness of which he must make himself master, were assuredly hopeless. He cursed himself for having shown his feelings as he had done earlier, and made a determination.

'You've worked too hard this year, Charles,' he said. 'I shall have to keep an eye on you when the examinations are finished. Life will be easier for you then, and for me and all of us. You can come and read poetry to me in your spare time. There'll be lots of that.'

'Oh, I should love to, sir.' Charles's expression was dubious, yet flattered. 'You've been so very kind to me; if it hadn't been for you I don't know what I'd have done. Honestly I don't, sir.'

'You talk as though it were all over and done with,' Penworth said abruptly. 'Anyhow, that remains to be seen.'

He sat down, lost in thought for a minute.

'Now, let's get things clear. When do you have to go and run races; what afternoons?

. . .

So in those last weeks, strict against himself in keeping silence, he came to find once more a sort of consolation in his hours of work in Penworth's room. Penworth himself was beginning to show in his face and voice the strain of the year's endeavour. His eyes were tired, and more unwilling to be kind, and in his classes he talked little, sitting silently bowed over his book above the room where a feverish murmur of application echoed the sound of bees outside in the sun. But to Charles he now remained the same always and made no gesture; his friendliness did not turn sour, and whatever went on in his own mind was concealed there, beneath an aloof gravity of manner which was what the boy most needed to lubricate the hot working of his brain. He spoke of little now but the work in hand; only at times, when perhaps his day had been calmer and the signs in his forms reassuring, he would lean back in his chair, look out through the window into the paling, late sky, and discourse in the old way upon learning, or poetry, or the obscurer delights of whatever music he happened to have in his mind. Then, in the energy of a chosen enthusiasm, his voice lost its accent of tiredness, and took colour into it from what he discussed.

'The year,' he remarked once, 'is a parabola. We are on the downward swing now. It sometimes reminds me of the best works of art. You can feel it in the air, at this time; we speed down the curve. Perhaps if it weren't for the life here, I wouldn't notice it so much; but it fits in with what I'm used to—down, down, October, November, December— Christmas and winter and the dead end of the year. In England that's how it is.'

He thought about it, and it confused him subtly.

'Here, after all, you're on an upward swing really, outside these walls of artificiality. Spring, with summer close behind; outside that's what it's like. But in here we move towards a close—you know, you get that in the middle of the third movement; a sudden restatement of a theme ... "Remember what I said at first" sort of thing. You know what I mean?'

'You talk,' Charles said, 'as though you were dying—no, no, not dying; but something. As though you were going away.'

Penworth looked at him in a quiet speculation, without speaking, for a minute or more, observing the question in the steady hazel-coloured eyes that regarded him, the frown between their dark brows. Then he reached forward for his pipe and tobacco, and began to fill, rolling the tobacco to a wad in the palm of his left hand with the outer edge of the right hand; and still looking at Charles. Then, as he glanced down to adjust the bowl so that it would receive the fill easily, he replied:

'I am going away—that's right.'

They looked at each other.

'Why?' Charles began. 'Why—oh?'

For the first time, with a sharp and conscious emotion, he strove to imagine his next year at the School, and saw, not himself but Penworth's absence, as though it were a positive phenomenon. Somebody else would sit in this room, behind this orderly table; some other man's books and prints would replace these. No more was he to be gladdened and amused by the arrogant fullness of Penworth's gown as the young man strode into a classroom, still with that elasticity of knee and shoulder which he salvaged from a life now past; no more to see that pleasant, condescending smile, as, having reached the dais, he swung round suddenly, smoothly, to confront a class alert with the expectancy his entry had aroused. No more would he see such small, important dramas as that measuring out the days; and no more might he look forward with pleasure to hours like this hour, secure in this small white room with its immaculate bed and its soft odour of tobacco smoke well enjoyed, of books, ink, paper, and wood, seeing opposite him the familiar beauty of the eyes that knew him so well, hearing the quiet voice, full of praise or scorn or mild laughter, to which he had so willingly paid respect.

'Oh,' he said, 'I am so sorry. I don't know—it won't be the same here, without you, sir. I'll feel quite different.'

Penworth, lighting his pipe, glanced up secretly under his brows and laughed with pleasure, but shook his head in half-mechanical denial.

'Nonsense. You'll make plenty of other friends. I've told you, next year won't be like this. You'll have far more time, and you'll be able to live some sort of a life of your own, and get to know what the other fellow is thinking. That's more important than anything I can teach you.'

'It won't be the same.' Charles put his own meaning into the words. He looked up, smiling. 'I don't know how I shall manage to work without your help, sir, now. You've helped me very much.'

'That's what I'm paid for. And anyhow, it's been great fun. And furthermore you can have too much of help; you must be able to stand by yourself. Don't imagine that the work is beyond you; you happen to have more intelligence than the average, that's your trouble. And in the end it's the very opposite to a cause for doubting yourself.'

Charles said nothing, rubbing his hand backwards and forwards along the edge of the table whose corner separated them.

'Don't, of course, tell the rest of them yet,' Penworth said after a while. 'You have a right to know. I'm going—for the sake of other people as well as for my own. I want a change, that's chiefly why. What I shall do I don't know; but at any rate I shan't be here. If I stayed too long I'd simply get—stale.'

Charles nodded.

'Even a schoolmaster,' Penworth said, 'leads a life of his own at odd moments, you know. You do know ...'

'Oh, I know, sir,' Charles said nervously. 'I know—it must be pretty terrible here. I used to think how nice it must be to be a Master—free, and all that.'

'I may be mistaken,' Penworth said slowly. 'One never knows. I may be trying to escape from my own self, from something I never shall escape by running away. To go may be a coward's way out—leading simply to other cowardices. But I must go, before I can find that out for certain. For each one of us life's chiefly a matter of trial-and-error proof, you see.'

He talked easily on, and Charles, as he listened and watched his pale, expressive face, thought of the coming year, and of the year after it. It was not himself he saw, for he was still visualising only Penworth's absence from the familiar scene, and feeling as one feels when a picture has been secretly taken down from a wall, leaving a characterless wide space behind which looms, a memory of the eye itself, the shadow of what was once there, affronting the gaze with the faint melancholy of so much strangeness ...

Penworth had moved suddenly, and was standing beside the chair where he sat. It was a swift movement, calculated, not clumsy, and it took Charles by surprise. He looked up as the other's pale face came down above his own. Trying to move and unable, being walled by the side of the table and by Penworth, he felt almost like laughing. He was held by the shoulders, and did not know what to do.

'Now,' Penworth said in a low voice, urgently. 'Now, Charles. Before we say good-bye for good.'

The pupils of his eyes were dilated, as though by anger, or fear. Charles stared into them, afraid, and unable to rise under the hands resting on his shoulders. The way those words were spoken had frightened him; the beseeching tone of a voice used always in command, in careful, interested but dispassionate explanation, alarmed him more than any anger would have done. He felt the blood drain from his head and face, and with an effort restrained himself from crying out. Penworth made another sudden movement, and had him strongly, gently by the wrists. Automatically he stood up and drew back.

'Let go,' he said, and the surprising steadiness of his voice gave him courage. He heard the other's breath, coming and going quickly. Outside that room the afternoon was placid and still.

'Let go, please,' he said again firmly. 'Please don't do this. It spoils everything.'

What he meant by that he did not afterwards know; but it caused Penworth to laugh shakily.

'You talk like a damned schoolgirl being seduced.'

'I'm not a girl,' Charles said slowly, 'even if I do look like one.'

That was difficult to say, but it had the effect of making Penworth release his wrists. He stepped suddenly back as his weight came free, and the chair fell noisily. They heard the sound of steps approaching through the changing room.

'Don't make such a row, you little fool,' Penworth said.

He spoke with a bitter scorn; but he said nothing more, sitting down on the bed and putting his white face into his hands, breathing unevenly. He looked like one who had escaped a vicious, uncontrollable danger, without knowing by what means he had escaped it.

The whole thing had taken no more than two minutes. The steps crossed the hall outside, faded, vanished, while they listened. Charles, trembling now with the release of tension, stooped blindly down and set the chair upright, by the table where it had been before, where he himself had sat, listening to that cultured voice talk easily to him of life and beauty. He stood staring at the chair, not knowing what to do or how to break the spell of what was a perfect conclusion for them both.

'Better go,' Penworth said at last with difficulty, still pressing his hands to his face, his elbows on his knees. That position was so strange, so dramatically out of character, that Charles felt tears come into his eyes. He went to the door, and did not hesitate to open it and go out. On the way up the stairs he thought he was going to be sick, and hastened his steps; but in the upper bathroom, a place of sure solitude at that hour of the afternoon, nausea gave way to the misery of reaction, and tears blinded him. He leaned against the wall at the end of a row of basins, and, as Penworth had done, hid his face in his hands.

But even in the sharpness of that misery he felt, surprisingly, a great coolness of relief, as though a decision had been made for him, and as though at last he were in an open place here, with a free wind blowing in his face, and his vision clear before him.

1937

DON MAYNARD

Athlete

Adam is a pupil of mine
apple of teacher's eye
is not a carpenter
or a thinker
still something of each
and is singularly attracted to
sprinting & hurdling

Squatter's son Adam likes
the land when it is fresh & green
oranges with navels
and to be seen
in the lithe grass (would surely pass
any old lovemaking test you like)

Poised set to sprint the 100
he feels the future pause with him
then break into the wide skin
as he strides the wind

His early experience the songs of birds
every season of the year
and me yelling at him
I say 'Poise Adam is to be
desired' (say to him drawn back
like an arrow on a bow)

1962

HAL PORTER

The Dream

After two years of it—hospital, convalescence, refining of body (pain departed like a soul)—here I am, purified, in a city of rosemary and apricot-coloured stone. So clearly seen—mansions, garden walls, bridges, a cathedral, all apricot. Light surges along streets, along furlongs of rosemary hedges enough to air linen of a surfeit of Holy Infants; wall-tops bristle with barbaric jewellery of broken bottles. Here I am, pain certainly aside, penetrating an unknown. In the taxi are nickelled vase-holders, slender vases, apricot gerberas. This last corner: now, St Bardolph's Terrace, sir. A tinge richer—left: unhaunted houses, poinsettias and Moreton Bay figs with shadows of many qualities. Right: a parkland awash with ponds of heat; heat of most fragrant kind suspiring from blond hairy earth and pine boles. The taxi stops. There's a brass plate, *Duke's College Boarding House*, on the inert, shabby gate. I have arrived.

Hot! I feel that my shadow is that of glass; the pavement crackles like pastry.

So, without foreboding, elated, I reach the gate in the ruffled pittosporum hedge high with age and filmed by powder. Opposite, the parkland is breathing ... ah ... a-a-a-a-ah! ... olive-trees, cannas, kurrajongs, the arrangement sliding away and down and into and through lakes of tiny pretty slums, fellmongers' tiled with scales of iridescence, minute spires pricking up, sixpence-sized gasometers, factory chimneys dreaming out flossy threads ... on and on miles until, there, at last, the gulf, the sea vibrates up brilliants into a sky blue but almost white. A-a-a-a-ah!

Without foreboding, I push the gate. After effort against me it moves. Here—almost—the dream begins. But not quite yet. There is a clotting.

I am under the cowl of arbutus overhanging the gate now resigned into its feet-made trough. There is rankness. There are weeds, rococo leaves blistered and measled, too pale, too dark, stems furred like crayfish legs, corkscrew tendrils, seed-cases sifting dust. In them a swathe has been cut; it lies suppurating like charnel-house rags. Who?—that is the peculiar thought—who killed, who scythed? There is inkling of sophisticated ache somewhere, something mendacious. Path to verandah is gravelled—no, not gravelled; is sprinkled with chips of stone, apricot. The verandah fence is of iron ferns, the iron chocolate. Black roses—tortures of branches of chocolate-black roses, prickles like steel teeth of sharks—climb, claw, reject burnt-paper petals at the very door. A china bell-knob. If I pull the knob ...? Why pause? What is happening? What is to be aroused by one of the verdigrised voices on helices of wire? *Some*-thing happening; clot twitches, nausea. The brilliants bleed together; all melts, blurs, slithers; thoughts boil up an ectoplasm of omens, or future squirts inkily into present; the shadow falls; a sooty rose falls. Quick, quick, the glittering bits, the healed fissures again, the surge and exaltation ... sanity at least. Here then—speckless day; I am fit as a fiddle; over the border I have come to the place appointed. My trunks must be inside; suits, handkerchiefs, shirts, shoe-trees and so on. I am to teach English and Latin, Upper and Middle School. Resident master; widower; C. of E.; B.A., Dip. Ed.; experience so much. Name ...

All clear; pull the bell thousands have pulled before me.

It is as though I touch a sort of mind. The interior of *Duke's College Boarding House* knows I am here. Or am I someone else? A new housemaid? An aunt with a fruit cake? A crank touting anti-anti-Semitic pamphlets? Decidedly not. There's no doubt it knows and's ready. The tumour bursts; I lip the desecrated tumbler. The I with the shadow of glass is past, mute, under the ether. Door opens. The dream begins.

Poised on bone legs stuck with spider-black hairs, grimy feet bare, it seems about thirteen; its junket face peeps coquettishly and flat eyes shine. It is a schoolboy, its clothes skimpy — twisted toenails, unclean forelock. That's the glimpse, the surface. It speaks.

'You're the new mastah . . . ?'

Do I say anything? Or is the thickening or withdrawal of the colour of my startled eyes a word?

'How d'y'do, sir?' Sticky claw extended, gripped. What forgery my gesture is. (So soon, so soon.) This is a being fed on exhalations from — what? The Black Death of weeds? Guile? The institution linoleum which glares with a swabbed-on slime of kidney-coloured oil?

'Entah, sir. Mai name is Darke — with an *e*. Slut's in the bawth. She said Ai was to entertain you if you arraived before she'd tubbed herself. *She* says "tubbed". The Head won't be heah till aftah luncheon.' Its voice has a sham perfection behind which minces the shade of its model — *luncheon*.

Next, under a succession of plaster arches.

And 'This is Slut's room' (the English *oo*). Uneasy wicker chair. Cretonne cushions — the colours rhubarb, cineraria, concrete grey — floral. Clothes-horse saddled by a grey deformity of pink stays. Cretonne curtains — the colours tracing-paper, brick, tomato sauce — floral. (The curtains drench the burnished outside, the elation and expectation: too late for them, no hope at all, no clotting, the dream is out to sea, into the tunnel, over the cliff.) Calendars there are with thatched cottages, hollyhocks, delphiniums; a card table with blotched baize; doilies jumbled with unironed celanese bloomers in the drawers, I think; two bottles: 'Care for a sherreh, sir? There's drai and sweet. Slut said to offah you one.'

I refuse. Have I asked — quizzically (already at that stage, you see) — 'Who is Slut?' I'm certain not.

Yet: 'Slut is Matron.' It has with aplomb lifted a bottle and poured. 'She's not a bad sort, reahlly; but she's pretteh base, sir. Ai'm her pet.' Pet — pasty hairy pet — eyes glossed as they peek from the undergrowth of foxed leaves and liver-coloured peonies. 'Between you and Ai — that is, you and *me*, sir — ' . . . the lips roll back: a smile silky and complicating . . . 'she doesn't get much lucre, but she does what she laikes, she gets what she wants.' A pause. I return no token, merely bogus negation. I am unsatisfactory yet I am part of the situation so, fractionally, it shrugs. The subject, however, must be changed. 'Ai'm going to quaff this sherreh. Ai *laike* sweet.' It gulps sweet. Fastidiously, it moves again and, tenderly, hooks toes over a cotton reel on the matting. 'Excuse me, sir, Ai've fallen arches. This is *supposed* to improve them.' Griffin's toenails scratch; hands balance on each side; the mild hump so much older than the rest meantime retracts sleeves farther from wrists. The voice, more precise for so difficult a guest, accuses, but with reticence. 'Ai don't know whether you'll laike it heah. The last English mastah said he was appalled.' Sorrow next, a polite fragment: 'We've had masses of new mastahs in mai day. Ai'm resaigned to it, sir. A boardah for faive years. Ai spend mai hols heah too. Mothah's divorced but she makes a packet out of beauteh salons in Melbourne. She doesn't worreh about me. But Ai get masses of gelt, shekels, moola, doubloons, oof ...' Then, trans-formed, dying to watch the effect on me. 'She approacheth, sir!'

Mothah? No. Slut.

Slut, naturally, is easier. Curtains, cushions, calendars have revealed her. Remember it's a dream, and that I could waken, turn about, slam doors, re-enter sunlight, take a taxi, a train, escape over the border. I don't. Put it thus: the sherry I didn't have needed not to be sipped to have its effect. It is a philtre that Darke's tossing off, even familiarity with, I have allowed poison me. Away clarity! That one sherry is the opiate Tolerance, the decoy Tolerance, Tolerance the most insidious of charities. One is to nullify oneself and accept all—the grotesque, spurious, shoddy, unsanctified, the melodrama and masquerade, omissions and passions, animal impurity, laxities of mind and spirit, subterfuge, all the intricate ritual of adulterated living. No need to describe Slut. But her entrance is, as Darke knows I find it, interesting. It is taken with lumbering gaiety. The dressing-gown, floral step-sister to curtains and cushions, distorts by beetroot, lime and sienna her distortions. She is arch. She laikes laife bright and naice. She *adores* an itsy-bitsy of the unconventional, but she never forgets that she's *et cetera, et cetera*. She's a soda. *She* tolerates. She is lenient with herself, sybil of numberless derelictions. At the moment her hair or wig, of which one sees ever only the dyed slice like cheap wool below the nurse's veil, brews in a turban of old towel. Beneath this considered negligence are triangular dabs of rouge, china ear-rings, hoodwinking, porcelain teeth with tangerine gums. Decorated thus the apparatus progresses: gestures picked up as stewardess on a South American coastal steamer, intonations acquired in mothering aborigines or the bachelor beyond Alice Springs whose house-keeper she was, some suburban flourish filched from her slavery with arthritic women known as leedies—coarse fingers curled out from sherry glass or teacup. Superstitions, fallacies, self-pity, mawkishness, maternal brutality, stu-pidity, devotion—all hers. There puffs the broken-down adventuress come to haven in fraudulent white shoes. She lugs the bucket that is the sick-room commode, agitates bottles of purges, binds mumps in red flannel, compounds kerosene gargles, raises her telephone voice—'Juke's Coll-edge heah. Matron speaking'—and, sometimes, is encountered groping toothless and drunken to the lavatory she shares with the resident masters who have found sitting there this bewildered beast with dribbling eyes ... But that's enough. She (or is it Darke?) parlourmaids me to my room.

It's deeper than a grave and as wide, a vault with spinach-green walls.

There's almost always on the walls the sweat in which one writes with apathy, with cold fingertip, at some nerveless hour, *O God*. At the bottom is the iron bed two inches short, the horse-hair mattress in which is the impression of a curled-up boy, the one shape of countless boys now old men or bones; the chest of drawers filthed by enamel, cedar speckling through in a rash; the teetering triangular wardrobe with its poplin askew to half-reveal one coat-hanger. The ceiling is far up and stained by seepings under the slab. When light's out and I lie, effigy, upon dead boys' depression, what more could one want? *That* is the drug drunk carelessly, that's detachment, that's forebearance, that's my sin. I am, then, unpacking. It's to be done with muzzled face. People are like Darke and Slut, crooked roots, stingy subsoil. Who are you to expect better anywhere, anyway?—that sort of immoral collusion. I see in the looking-glass—shaking out here the academic gown preposterous as roué's cloak (1902)—that the face is not really that at all. There's, for instance, the line, the cut returned (so soon) to the left cheek; the end of the mouth tilts up a little ... affectedly? sardonically? The eyes question. The imaged question answers. There's a shrug behind the question. Blandness! Acceptance! That wasn't there forty minutes ago, outside in the glorious undisclosed city.

Now sounds a swindling tap on the door. Headmaster? No, it's Ah Ket. Or is his visit later, in second term, after the swimming carnival and the three-cornered Jacks and thread-bare cricket matches and sunburned necks; after musty breakfast egg, bitter mutton, grease-poxed soup in school-crested hotel-ware? If so, summer's gone and the wickets are broken, the roller rusted and the matting rotten; Mr Krantz's cane has lashed across Rossiter's freckles, Mr Robson has fawned a hundred times at the Head's elbow, Wilkins *Secundus* has had boils, the lavatory has been blocked with sandshoes, French dictionaries, football socks ... and ...

And clear-eyed Callanin has said, '... and the *coup de grâce* was ...'

If so, in autumn, leaves have been rotating in the wind, in my mind. Rotating down, many at first, later twos or ones, the ultimate, leaving the air clear. Nevertheless it's certain that it has been cut by the leaf edges—the mind, the air. The mind, the air heals, is clean again; but below, even after the rustling is finished and the corruption to fine powder, there remain some skeletons, there remains powder. So, perhaps, it's later. There's indubitably the glitter of gold through the vault door. Come in, Ah Ket, come in; make stage.

It's well done. Always is. Has he heard the expression *bland Oriental countenance*? That is what he carries vigilantly in, seventeen years old, behind spectacles with gold rims. Gold—gold fountain pen, gold Eversharp, gold ring, gold wrist-watch on band of gold, gold-stuffed teeth. The scent is strong. It comes from polished nails, brilliantined hair, talced armpits, silk pyjamas, dressing-gown weighted by golden dragons, from sharkskin coats, shirts like stacks of envelopes, gold-topped tooth-powder bottles, stud-cases of gold, gold-backed brushes, from the

recesses of wardrobe trunks with brass-gold locks. There is even a ribbon
of scent, of effeminacy, in the plaited voice with its other ribbons (Leys
School, Cambridge, whence eldest son of Number One Wife is evacuated
to Duke's College), the American ribbon ('... my parp's yarts, sir-r-r,
and a swall set-up in Singapor-r-re, sir-r-r ...'), the ribbon that whips
the other ribbons into unoccidental keys ... Mandarin? It's Ah Ket with
Oriental countenance, ten pound notes, cables, gossip, horsehair hair and
'weak bladder'.

Ah, the bladder! In the youngish night while a wagtail sings in the
frozen next-door almond-tree there's the plaited voice imploring in the
moonlit dormitory, 'For the last time I'd like to know who has hidden
my jerry.' Only the bird singing, otherwise delighted silence listening at
blanket edges. 'I demand to know who has hidden my jerry.' Already
he's beaten. Silence. (But the bird shrills on.) 'Do you realise that I am a
House Prefect? You ought to feel honour and respect. The Headmaster
has given me this position from the first day of my arrival. He'd a reason
for it, and you should respect.' Giggles. (The bird still sings.) Despair
unplaits the voice a little, 'You're a lot of filthy cads. You know I have a
weak bladder and that I'd a special permission from the Head to have my
jerry. You're a lot of rotters.' Silence still.

Now something else, little and telling. The Chinese throat opens like a
freesia salted with gold: 'Garner, do you know where it is?' That's the
something—Garner.

'No, Ket,' whispers Garner. Everyone in shadow hisses.

'Certain?'

'Yes, Ket,' says Garner. Everyone hisses.

Who says, 'Ket's pet! Bum boy!'?

'Filthy cads!'

Who says, 'Aw, pipe down, Oriental bastard.'?

Now they chant from their blanket edges, 'Or-i-*ent*-al bastard! Or-i-
ent-al bastard!'

Who does not chant? Silence is Garner's speech.

Who says, '*Tais-toi*, you Dodswell; you smell like a white mouse
anyway.'? That—that is clear-eyed Callanin.

Who, eavesdropping, yawns and goes to his tomb?

In my chairless tomb now is scented Ah Ket.

'Sit down,' I say, 'and—ah—' (this is the kind of thing that lengthens
deepens the line on the left cheek) 'and—ah—make yourself comfortable.' Ah Ket, of course, doesn't get it. Here's his pose: 'I'd rather not sit
down, sir.' Murmured, this, very seriously, petals straight. I keep mine in
order too. 'I hardly know how to begin, sir.'

Very well. Chinese gossip, I'll ping-pong along. I'll be liberal: ball
springing to you, to me, so Old-School-Tie-ishly, no fancy shots. Here's
an easy one:

'You sound very—ah—serious, Ah Ket.'

'It's a serious matter, sir.' Pinchbeck suavity.

Fifteen all. My head begins to ache.

'School matter? House matter? Or is it—ah—personal?' That's
somewhat tricky of me. The skull behind the brown face perhaps makes
it grimace, something leaps between us, but the coating of flesh shows
nothing.

'A school matter, sir.'

Thirty all. O God, it's only just after tea—fritz and bread and stale
rainbow cake. This could go on far into night, after the Headmaster has
forced himself to pass the light from my sepulchre, has gone miserably to
his house, chewed his nails, agonized, trotted back, tapped at my door,
hissing like taffeta, 'Oh ... so sorry ... struck me you were asleep with it
still on ... bills much bigger, yes-s-s ... stay up as long as you wish,
yes-s-s ...' This last an almost killing effort.

Therefore I say to Ah Ket, 'Well,' the scar surely twitching deeper,
'tell me *quickly* in your own way.' That's more sudden than he expected.
Still, like Darke and Slut and the others, he knows what he's after. He
arranges his emotions, he's suaver, he's off. 'Well, sir, on behalf of the
House Prefects and the senior boarders, sir ...'

On behalf, that is, of *graffiti*-artist Richards, of Hore-Smith the
scholarship boy who lies of his parents' riches, of Nathan the arrogant
and cringing Jew, of Tannet who steals and sells costly text-books, of
Grimwade who scavenges to hoard anything—toothpaste, shoe polish,
hair-oil, singlets, of ... well, on behalf of this cabal tracking excitement,
whispering in the bicycle shed, spying from behind doors: 'We've
suspected this person from last year, sir. One night, just after prep., this
person took Miller to the Music Room ... One Saturday *exeat* Tannet
saw this person behind the big tree with Russel *Secundus* ... Garner told
me that when he was in the bathroom this person ... Higgins was in the
infirmary when ... Garner was cleaning the Fourth Form cupboard ...'
Denunciation mounts like a dung-heap. Garner's name, how many
times? The defiling bits always float to the top; try to keep them down;
poke them down; up they come—Garner, Garner, Garner.

'And, Ah Ket, who is—ah—This Person?' I ask the question but my
mind yawns, my headache is worse.

'Sir, it's Mr Steb. He's had—*affaires* with lots of boys. Garner—and—
and ...' There: he can't think of any more. Why should he, rich
Chinaman's poor golden worldling? Here is jealousy the deputy of
spurious indignations; whispering in the dormitory, fever in the bicycle
shed, teeth glimmering behind panels. Here is the quest to make
knowledge into salacious mystery, here is the plea for dirty glamour.
What do I say? What can I say? So much already accepted; the bottle
opened, the potion downed. I say, 'I had suspected so.' From the first
night, in fact.

First night; the music dwindles; the footlights wake; curtain up! Darke
with shoes on is squealing as though he, too, had had authentic holiday;
his face surges on the creek of faces of the sons of cow-cocky snobs, the
gullible, child-sellers, petty social climbers riding their school-uniformed
sons like jockeys. Suitcases, tennis racquets, straw boaters, Sunday suits

on hangers, stamp albums, bags of fruit, shrieks and growls of artificial
joy, adolescent eyes netted in veins and dilated with evanescent
madness—tide-race bearing on its surface the shoulders in tatty gowns
and the marred faces of masters useless as wreckage. Here's Slut afloat,
buoyant with sherry, refinement and power: 'Ovah theah, Rossitah! Put
it ovah theah, you wick-ed boy. Callanin! *Callanin*! You'll be in Big
Dorm. this term. Ovah heah, Wilkins! Wilkins! *Wilkins Secundus*!'

Meantime, shut away in the Masters' Common Room, Mr Steb and
me. Masters' Common Room: bookcase of ragged books, inkstained
table, pewter inkwell without lid, inky rulers, empty red-ink bottles,
megaphone in grate. Nothing else except the brown electric light bulb,
one that pulleys up or down balanced by a shot-weighted porcelain egg.
Oh, and the gowns behind the door. These reveal something, indeed
much, by neatness or tatters or spots. They are suspended as differently—dry-cleaned on hanger, rakish on nail, limp and filthy—as
their wearers are suspended from ...? The rack shoved into the
background? The 'strings of fate'? Rafters of rag-shop? Ach! not worth it
to translate these gowns into owners; Duke's door is damning enough.
Earning less as years befoul them more, they exhibit their flaws, cheap
labour in this last booth, as does Cook who had toured when young with
Annette Kellerman, and used to eat a banana under water in a glass tank
on vaudeville stages.

Outside and strung across the window of the Masters' Common Room
is the grapeless vine, weighted by black-and-white caterpillars which eat
more riddled the riddled leaves, nibbling like thought to the veins ...
disguising vine, filter, fruitless, ah, fruitless. Shut away, then, I and Mr
Steb who monologues hoarsely while caterpillars fretwork in the
mosquito-thridded twilight. I'm not caterpillar; I don't have to chew
away the green of his words; the green is shaped by the veins. Dead easy!

Mr Steb resembles mature Queen Victoria: Pekinese eyes immodest as
a mother's, tight eyelids, neat double chin, rum-coloured pout, small
plump hands—these tremble incessantly with their 'nice' fingernails.
And here's green, some of the transparent stuff that makes caterpillar
nibble to veins.

With intemperate subtlety Mr Steb has reached Masturbation in the
Boarding House, example A, example B, example C. Now the Steb's
Treatment. Mr Steb suspects a boy. Mr Steb bides time. Night so
inevitably, so inducingly falls. Mr Steb wears slippers, or goes sock-
footed, creeps. I see, within sour-breathed him, the flourishing weed,
foliage pallid and stale, roots deep, nodding seedless blooms in a
treacherous shame. He creeps, listens outside the dormitory. He hears
what he wishes to. Ah, that *wishes*! little and telling, the grout come to
the surface. And so Mr Steb gets what he wishes. Mr Steb flings aside a
sinner's bedclothes; Mr Steb takes him to Mr Steb's room and canes bare
buttocks. But naturally, bare. That's the green.

The veins? There are the ever-trembling hands half-afraid and all-
desiring by the youth in the cinema or somehow near by in the public

urinal, there are the ... oh, it's a joke for back bar and revue. And it floats to the top; the letter torn to confetti has the slogan of fire on the scrap left. Are you afraid, Mr Steb, that the sun will see your weed nid-nodding? Afraid you'll be found out? You are found out.

Time passes. Time passes. Quadrangle, changing-room, corridor, song of the cane, hours of night like a Ganges of lascivious melancholy. Time passes. Mr Krantz and I are playing chess badly when, through the vine, we see you stumbling, uncouth and flushed, between obvious detectives. You are found out.

Time passes, passes. Eyes around the oval, eyes above Bibles, eyes in tongues behind the stirring lips. Time passes. I am on duty; time to ring the bell for evening prep. At assembly the Headmaster has hissed, to cheat no one at all, 'Mr Steb will be absent for some days. He is sick, yes-s-s.' I am about to ring the bell when there is a noise. It is, at first, low, succulent, and merely odious, but it races to a jubilant scream enriched by malice. The evening paper is in the paws of the pack. You are found out.

Safe, gammoning virtue, they give in chorus their howl of perjury.

I ring the bell.

Within minutes, radiant and pious, your animals, Mr Steb, who have taken the bribe of chocolate frogs, cigarettes, foreign stamps and balsa aeroplane models, are writing—like schoolboys of fiction—within their dream. You are forgotten. You are awake.

'Yes, Ah Ket, I had suspected so.' My headache and I stand in the vault.

Well, damn him, what else does he want? I hold the ball and do not tip it back. Ah Ket does not move, but a mist rises from the puddle of his mind, his flesh fades less bland, he slow-motion takes out the revolver, wipes it with Chowish calm, and fires: 'Young, Callanin, too, sir!'

Shrewd bullet! It flies straight to ... to what? The heart? Decidedly to somewhere that startles. Or am I startled afresh at the perception, the cupidity of these tough minor men, acres of them in school halls or chapels, scalps inclined with trumped-up chastity before the giant slabs of wet toffee: those honour rolls in the depths of which, beneath the flotsam of gilt, glow rich entrails and blood, the muck of exploding flame. Their voices like seraphim's rise to tarnished shields, to electro-plated cups won by forgotten boys on forgotten afternoons and now urns for blowflies and pellets of chewed paper. Am I startled afresh that these charlatans reeking of football mud, these diddling masks in a rind of pimples, these flannelled attitudes at their cruelties, are the disguise of even one instinct not factitious? Yes, it startles. It does not confound; the adult must protect himself; neither bullet-hole nor blood must show.

'Young Callanin, sir. He's going to the Music Room with Mr Steb, and we thought that you might sneak—that you might go along and see if ... if everything is all right.'

I eye him colourlessly. He fronts me with muffled impertinence.

'Don't you mean, Ah Ket, that you and your—ah—ah—earnestly

desire me to sneak down and—ah—satisfy you that everything is all—ah—wrong?'

His mind says something bold and flashing, his lips blink.

'Why me?' I continue. Disinterest, done obliquely, is not another bullet but the best I can do. 'Why not Mr Krantz, Mr Alain, even—ah—Mr Robson? Why me?' Indeed, why me? They know what they want. Can't they leave me the indifference I want, poor tatters? To hell with 'em. However, my headache is gone.

Leave Ah Ket, then, returning to the others with empty creel, without news of a bite, unless, of course, he knows the pranks of the line on the left cheek. Leave them delirious. And I?

Outside, a wind swoops like an avalanche of birds to ravage the grasses, streaks up to empty cages of plane-trees, up to the swannery of clouds. My thoughts, mere reeds, are beaten down to writhe and lash. I walk the storm of almond blossom petals, under the brummy Tudor arch; I am near the Music Room. No music, no talking. Whispering? Sunset's wind harping through fretted ventilators?

Two are so intent and impudent that they are easy to examine: Mr Steb and his drugged smile, and clever clever Callanin. At the moment Callanin is a . . . a chalice, transparent and empty: intelligent eyes. First, in the depths of the chalice, a faint smoke-wreath; and then the fondled chalice, the body, glows with desire which rises inexorably, transforming as wine transforms a shell of glass. It rises to the brink of the lips whence escapes a flat syllable of approbation. It rises to the eyes, quenched now. The weed in Mr Steb and the phantom weed in his little lover arch, horse-like, their foliages at each other; the chalice brimmed with lust uplifts itself to the mouth of lust.

The wind still swings and chutes; almond petals map the outlines of air; rosemary is as high as my heart; the savage flicks of Mr Alain's passing gown, of all gowns, whip behind tree-guards. I wade the eternity of hacked desks; examination foolscap hurricanes down the sky and scatters over the glimmering slums and factories to the gulf. I am hunted through the sour-sobs; I hunt myself, snarling pack, hoaxed deer. 'Callanin too, even he!' keens wind in ink-blotted branches. For a silly moment knock with fist on that locked door of a pine. Darke, Slut, the Cook, Ah Ket, Mr Steb, Callanin, they get what they want. What do I want? Some perfection not there, never to be found in the vegetation of life? Idiot, rub your knuckles; knuckles are all you've hurt. It's always anywhere the same: remember! . . . one runs down the stairs of the pub at Port Elliott, out. It is night. It rains. Wormwood hedges are saturated, coprosma flashes. At the church corner, where through spring days the flowers of the broom deliciously breathe, all is drenched; the spirit within the shrub dark and wet as a witch. Down the slope to the cove . . . the waters roar . . . the spray never leaves the air . . . the blue-bush is lost . . . one is seeking in rain and the foam of the sea to find . . . nothing. Nothing . . . Stop, fool! Where am I now?

This is the Headmaster. Once more it's the face, you know, that seems to tell: hyphenated eyes, the twitchings. The squab body in a natty suit (gourd on meretricious vine), the white band of the wristwatch, the well-ironed gown with glazed ribbons, all tell nothing.

I, with the Headmaster, echo Ah Ket with me. There's a difference though: years of playing the celluloid ball, rules regretfully and evilly learnt—*too* smooth. The Headmaster's twitches harden to a wire mesh as ultimatum succeeds ping-pong: 'I am pleased you have spoken, yes-s-s. We must, nevertheless-s-s, be discreet, yes-s-s. We may be scandalizing a schoolmaster who is of inestimable value to the school, yes-s-s.' Value: the piece that floats. Value: cheap labour. But Steb gets his animal rake-off—yes? 'He's a single man, a solitary man, and merely, I think, very affectionate, yes-s-s.' All this, I'm certain, has happened before. The Headmaster's speech is too well done, comes pat. He knows what he wants. He sways sedately on his vine, ripe but not to fall, pitted with seeds of iron. I? Don't care. Don't care? Why am I here? Ah Ket? The Music Room? Good versus Evil? Knight on white charger? Busybody? '... am pleased you have seen me. I shall discreetly question those possibly concerned, yes-s-s ...' And thus he hisses me sweetly out.

He sends for me at last: my gown austere and distinterested, my elbowful of exercises and *Macbeth* just so. I face precise table, precise tie, precise face, the hissing more seductive than ever: 'I instituted inquiries, questioned seniors, spoke to Steb, yes-s-s. He is absolutely, unmistakably innocent, unmistakably, yes-s-s.' He will perform a smile and purposefully rise, dismissing. Of course. But, rising, doesn't he see ahead, doesn't he hear the cries floating back from the future and that one jeering howl? Of course not: he knows what he wants to see and hear.

Heigho! The bell rings, rings again and again, morning, noon, evening, night; mouths open and dolorously sing; pens sigh a million errors along the blue lines; Boy Scouts scrabble in dust like aborigines; cold showers stream on bodies; the cane rises and falls—that's Mr Krantz hysterical with hate; cores fly through geometry lessons—Mr Robson; the Bishop elocutes on; the kitchen stinks drift into the Common Room; Smedhurst breaks his arm; Cook's drunk again; the cricket pitch is rolled, rolled, rolled; the scales stumble along and back along the sallow keys; the leaves slip from the vine; its knobbed wires are glued across the unopenable window while webs of dried nerves are revealed sucking into the stone of the wall.

What else? Prayers and lies; split cricket balls, unstrung racquets; muddy towels squashed in lockers; fissured egg-cups with crest; chilblains and dirty yarns; rages and measles and broken fountain pens; pawns lost from the chess set; burnt meals and lies and lies; *benedictus benedicat*; lies and lies. Who shrieks out late, some sickly one or oaf tortured in a dream within the dream? Awake in my pit; worth bothering? No. Put on the light, nevertheless; look towards the looking-glass. There there's some hurt. Or perhaps merely the glass smitten with cold. Turn out the light and let horror infest who make horror, let lust tiptoe where it will to who lust. After all, what's the payment? The body's trite self? And the cost? Not worth considering. How deep the tide of night, how drowned hushed its booty! Yet listen! One walks the seabed of dark. Turn on the light again, open the door: 'Who's that?' Drifting in the tides, alight, soiled and . . . and intelligent: 'It is I, sir—Callanin.' Watch him. Watch. See, he cannot move. Now, *now*, speak. Don't say, 'Where have you been, Callanin, at three o'clock in the morning?' That's too simple and wonted for a dream such as this. Say, 'I trust you'll not be chewing the fruits of your—ah—(the so deliberate *ah*) *amour* in my English class tomorrow.'

'No, I shan't, sir.' Thus might a young angel have looked, wisely and purely, thus modestly and holily have uttered.

And that, really, is all. Good morning, good morning. Straw boaters now, summer's on us, sandy bathers, the smoke from mosquito smoke-tablets scribbling on fevered air, rotten grapes in desks, figs, languors and affectations.

Here's Callanin again, but it doesn't matter, under the Moreton Bay figs, in nearly night giddy with mosquitoes. He wears—God knows why, but it gives him some sort of pathos—his straw boater. It's outside the stucco library with mullioned windows—smashed naturally. Plumed weeds everywhere, rosemary somewhere, a tap dripping time away.

'What are you doing here, Callanin? Oughtn't you to be in prep.?'

'Yes, sir. But Mr Alain gave me permission to get a book.'

'You have it?'

'Yes, sir.'

'Well, why are you—ah—loitering here?'

'I was waiting for you, sir.'

Beware! I shut off my thought's engine. Silence; silence the bait for revelation.

'I've wanted to tell you, sir, right from first term, how much I enjoy the English lessons.'

'Thank you.' Dryly, is it? 'One usually likes what one condescends to be interested in.'

'It's not only that, sir.' He moves, lava towards Pompeii, becomes clearer, begins to blaze beneath his boater. He tries to will the touch— mental? spiritual? physical? *He* knows what he wants. I don't. Does he feel as I stand there shrouded in the rubbish of my indifference that only one extra effort is needed to strip me? 'Not only that, sir; I admire the way you teach.' Still shrouded. Therefore, finally, the irresistible: 'I like you, sir. Very much.' He is more transparent than he'll ever be again— the chalice of the Music Room, the angel of the early morning, the vessel of the phantom weed. I have but to . . .

I take my pipe from between my teeth. I expel smoke into the indigo air. I say, 'One is flattered—ah—Callanin. You'd better scamper back to prep. Why—ah—Callanin, are you wearing your boater at twilight?'

That smashes him. He's nothing. Surely, here, at this moment, I know what I want, get an answer from myself. Not quite. The dream still lasts and drugs. But one is tossing and turning, the mists are thinning.

It is the last day. I am not coming back: it's that sort of school. They, the rest of them, have gone into the rain. Coathangers everywhere, names on them: *Max Garner, David Nathan, Stephen K. Blake, Philip Callanin* ... so they had cute, fashionable names and—ah—*Christian* names! Mattresses are rolled back, there are mothers' letters on the floors and screwed-up papers like bleached hearts, brilliantine bottles, ice-cream spoons, peppermint cartons bought by the imprisoned Mr Steb. With silent bells the red and yellow costume of the jester in the school play lies sick. Everything of mine is gone; the tomb is as it was when I came. Halt! That photograph of the Taj Mahal—have I seen it before, stuck by cobwebs to the sweating wall? Last look in the glass: shut face, shell over emptiness eroded within by tolerance, self-revilement, disillusion, indifference, and ... and frustration of some sort. I have said good-byes to secondhand masters in gowns like old umbrellas, to Slut, Cook, the Headmaster, the little actors dazzled by the flashiness of their own performances. Isn't there someone I haven't said good-bye to, or is it someone to whom I have? Out, out. Snuff the face from the glass. The taxi waits.

Darke stands in the rain, hump wet. A year older only? Ageing or ageless? It is not going away for the hols. But mothah has sent it oodles of kanga, and Slut will look aftah it. It's quaite resaigned. The arbutus piddles on the sickly face. It reahlly didn't think I'd laike Duke's; the last English mastah was appalled. Good-bai.

Into the taxi. Good-bye, good-bai. One is tossing and turning, almost awake. The slums and factories are behind rain; so is the sea.

Who is it runs away in the straw boater under the olives? Who zigzags among the wet, dark crowds, that boy in the boater? Now the saturated city of rosemary and apricot-coloured stone lies at the bases of the darkening hills. Who flees by the train, away from it, under the darkening trees in the wet hills? Among the umbrellas and the platform hydrangeas at Aldgate, who dodges in a boater? Who sidles off through the maples of Ambleside? It is darker, wetter. Shall I lean from the window and shout out, relenting, to the rumbling hills, into the forests of rain, calling the name, hearing the voice answer from the dark, darkly from under the boater, '... a-a-a-and the *cou-ou-ou-oup de grâ-â-â-âce* wa-a-a-as ...'?

I don't. But that wakes me fully. I shudder.

'Have a whisky?' says the blunt-nosed airman—one of those faces to a pattern, a railway carriage face. And so, on and on, over the border. Night, night, night ... awake all night ... intolerably, firmly ... knowing what one wants and escaping to it ... awake.

1942

Finola Moorhead

From *Remember the Tarantella*

Frances and Sophie were lovers at school. Between the nightmare which began their affair and the scandal which ended it, perhaps Frances lived some of the happiest days of her life.

To relieve loneliness in a large family, and with precocious intelligence, Frances taught herself remember-games to go to sleep by. In the third form she earned a scholarship to an expensive Catholic boarding school in a large country town. Nightly after lights out, she would recall every detail of the day: French verbs, geography, biology, chemistry, a look exchanged in the corridor, a smell coming from another girl in the ranks they had to form along the walls, the taste of a vegetable, a new way of balancing for a backhand, everything that happened, then carefully she would sift and evaluate. All while she gently caressed her clitoris. Her mind so stuffed with compartments like filing cabinets, the small orgasm of masturbation would explode it all into a kaleidoscope of fractured knowledge and she would sleep. Sheer exhaustion tossed her on her right side and she slept like a log with hard-earned and short-lived peace.

Then the uncontrolled subconscious, having broken the chains of the trained mind, sped off into primitive regions of violent action and ferocious honesty, making catastrophes and hideous monsters come at her. Frances was at the mercies of her pitiless fears. This night a searing pain in her uterus woke her. The bed was damp. She got up and leaned against the window.

The moon was a scimitar and the stars and planets the bits and pieces of the pure white body it had disembowelled in a passionate rage, laid out on the navy forensic blanket of the sky. Shivering there at the window she tried to know more, but her body felt like splinters of ice. She couldn't move. It seemed to her that one must always be a victim. Unless one could be both sexes at once.

She contemplated suicide as she thought of the dampness in her bed.

Unlike Frances, Sophie was a light sleeper, but a generally untroubled one. She was woken by Frances' stifled grunts of sleep-bound terror. She watched her fluorescent watch for five minutes, anticipating the moment she would go to offer comfort. Frances, the scholarship student, brainy, serious and withdrawn, topping the class in music theory, the only one to really like Bartok and Shostakovich, was not popular. She, Sophie, was big and played the saxophone, preferably by ear, listened exclusively to New Orleans jazz and did, where possible, the easiest subjects. Even if she was to be disappointed, for Frances might throw her off, abuse her, the waiting time was delicious. She would put her ample arms about that long intelligent head and press it into her breasts. When she heard the scrape on the windowpane and the sniffle, she could contain her friendliness no longer.

Nothing else could have saved Frances that night. The girls made love until dawn.

By Mass, at seven thirty, they were in love. As they filed up to Communion, all Frances' suspicions about Sophie's wealth and popularity melted before the glorious beauty she had discovered in this lazy, spoilt brat who was sneakily touching her hand. What she loathed before now made her giggle.

Sophie had taken many girls into her bed in her long boarding-school career, with gentle affection and innocent animal warmth, their ignorance of sexual finesse saving them from the horrors of sin. No such innocence was possible with Frances. She had discovered her nervy pleasure centres long ago, and was born with a respect for the body and the amazing intelligence of matter.

Six months of bliss. Sophie's wonderful voice rang out in the chapel with lusty holiness. Her comfortably large head of hair carried the blue veil of the Children of Mary as her right. She cheerfully deceived as they pursued their secret passion and remained popular with both nuns and pupils. She exuded an impression of overall goodness. Her great lungs gave praise to the godhead in the finest way devised by Christianity, through the hymn, and her love of singing compounded with her being in love. Whatever faith was, she had it, obviously. Theological analysis didn't bother her.

Frances began to understand truths she would never disprove. Real, palpable beauty was only experienced through matter. The pinnacle was a merging of mind and body and the sum was a whole beyond the parts. She hated the authority of boarding school even more, because they were wrong. Unjust. They said the finest thing in life was a sin, a vice. She did not fritter away her new knowledge in useless daydreaming and senti- mental fantasies; she thought about love as she loved. The quality of Sophie's voice she sought to find in her body through sexual experiment in an environment of horrid hostility and hypocrisy. In defiance she thought of the devil as equal to god. He was the definer, the separator, the real father of humanity. The fall was a fall away from androgyny, a fall into two or multiple parts, as a single bucket of water falls into many drops and remains water. There was both male and female sexuality within herself. The real difference was between making love with someone and masturbating.

The scandal began six months after the nightmare. The moon was round but incomplete. A fresh-faced postulant was nervously checking the dormitories after lights out. The young woman brought from her sheltered home a noctophobia of near pathological proportions, so the spooky rounds, a part of her training, were a very real penance for her sins. She gathered in her insecurity and determined to shoo the girls off into their own beds if they were breaking house rules.

Her habit having no rosary beads, she crept along soundlessly. She heard movement. She flicked open the nearest curtain to see a neatly made, unoccupied bed, altogether an eerie experience in the moonlight. She shuddered, then flicked open the next curtain, and gasped. The passion of it was disgusting. There could be no mistaking what Frances and Sophia were doing. Sheets and blankets had been thrown off by thrashing legs. Frances' thighs were clinging around Sophie's long, damp hair. Frances' page-boy haircut was bobbing up and down on top of Sophie's belly not two feet from the postulant's eyes. The two girls evidently did not hear the rasping of the rings on the curtain-rod or the nervous cough of the young woman in her grey serge outfit. She, for a moment, was paralysed by such close iniquity. She watched horrified before she let out a scream and went running off to fetch a more senior nun.

Frances did not scuttle back to her own bed after the disturbance. Coldly conscious of the situation, she made the bed and placed herself in it beside Sophie, who had retrieved her nightgown and had its virginal flannel all over her Venutian flesh. Sophie could have lied, in fact the ecclesiastical authorities would have liked her to point the finger so that they could have a single scapegoat. Frances would have been expelled. But she was dismayed, caught on the horns of two self-sacrifices and unable to choose. Frances had decided. She was defiant and articulate.

The senior nun was not shaken to the core. It was the postulant who had seen it and her inadequacy in the language necessary, combined with the older nun's limited imagination in the field, gave an inadequate description of the crime.

The Reverend Mother called a special assembly the following day to shout hellfire and damnation and let off some steam.

—From now on, she bellowed, no touching. No seeking warmth in the beds of other. This sacred chore is saved for married couples who do it for God. Lesbian practices will not be tolerated in this school. They shall not cast their satanic shadows in these halls again, nor shall they degrade the grounds. Never, especially if you are wearing your school uniform, are you to so much as hold hands.

Et cetera, for an hour.

While the scandal shook the whole school, no expulsions were carried out. Frances' parents begged the Mother Superior to mend Fanny's dreadful ways with her severest penalties. From thence until the end of her school days, Frances was blamed and punished for all the misdemeanours done by others. In revenge she never denied, she never even deigned to answer. Ironically, her results in Matric were brilliant, the best in the school in her subjects. Sophie's well-off parents took it all in their easy-going stride. They happened to calm the Principal with a timely gift of sporting equipment.

Nevertheless, the scandal and the entire experience seared an indelible scar into Frances' soul. She would not forget a single detail of her treatment, ever.

1987

BENEDICT CIANTAR

From *Distractions*

The Ecstasy

There are these things called friends.
There are these things called boyfriends.
There is a difference.
Who decides the difference, of course, is altogether
      another question.

I live in a big house in a big street.
There are lots of people everywhere.
Some male, some female, some big, some small, some
      loud, some soft, some bright, some dull, some
      homosexual, some heterosexual.
There are lots of people everywhere.
There are lots of people, everywhere.

•   •   •

I'm sitting by myself in the corner of the room. There are thousands of people everywhere and I've had an ecy so I'm really out of it. I'm just sitting there, watching and observing everybody. My body is buzzing. I feel as though I am the most gorgeous man in the room. People strut by with similar notions. There is a boy in front of me wearing thin black footy shorts and no underpants, black boots. His crotch is huge and as he dances flops from side to side. He knows I am watching. The show is for me. A friend of a friend dances by, arms around his flatmate, a wink, I almost see light reflect from his teeth. The boy in front seems to be getting an erection. I move my chair, adjust position as if uncomfortable, spreading my legs. He is directly in front now. Beneath the constant thud I hear a familiar bassline. Adeva's *Respect?* No ... Over my friend's shoulder I notice two men I am obsessed with. Both are in their early thirties. They are Sydney's Tom of Finland. The shorter one is cutest. He is wearing his usual attire: running shoes, footy shorts, old sweaty t-shirt. His boyfriend in blue jeans, shirtless. I fantasize of living with them in their apartment, the three of us happy ... I glare at them hoping they will notice me. Nothing. My friend with the erection seems to have found someone else to play with. That bassline again. I rush down onto the dance floor. My pelvis is loose, it swings and thrusts with ease. My little friend appears from nowhere. Don't be too obvious. I turn my back on him and casually move closer. I can almost feel his crotch against my arse. I am horny as hell. I pull out my bottle and take a huge sniff through each nostril. A tap on the shoulder. It is amazing how many friends you discover when in possession of a bottle of amyl. Both of us are spinning. We dance hard and long, crotches rubbing to the music. I am so horny that I could almost take him on the dance floor this very second. Slowly I become aware of the surroundings. Not wanting to be too tacky I move slightly away.

Arms around my waist, 'We've been lookin' for you everywhere!' My flatmate and friends. 'Wanna go outside for a while?'

Now!?

I contemplate the thought for a second as if unsure. I also notice that my friend in the black shorts has found someone else.

'Yeah. Why not.'

We weave our way through the crowd, hand in hand, to the edge of the dance floor. There are lots of people standing around. There is a man sitting over against the wall by himself. Boots and blue jeans, bare chest, huge and hairless. He is beautiful. My stomach churns. I cannot feel my feet. My legs are numb. I am floating.

It is a hot night. I look for a patch of grass to sit on. There are lots of people everywhere. Lots of semi-naked bodies, bulging crotches, bare shaven chests . . . I tell Emma about the guy in the shorts.

'Do you want to go back in hon?'

'No, no. Didn't like that song much anyway.'

My feelings have changed. No longer am I sexy. There is too much competition. No longer do I love everyone. There is too much pretentiousness. I start to feel contemplative. The two Tom of Finland clones are over by the bar. I watch them for a while. Who are they? What are they doing? But it is still early and I cannot afford to get depressed.

'I need to move.'

'Oh . . .' She does not want to.

Regardless, we return inside, back to the crowds and the sweaty bodies. Back to distraction.

It is dawn. My body refuses to give in. I have been dancing for a good eight hours. Endlessly moving and thrashing about. Constantly perving and searching. There are still at least three thousand people here. What on earth is everybody doing? While the rest of the world sleeps these few thousand people insist on defying all sense of logic, all sensibility. Most of my friends have gone home but I cannot commit myself to leave, I may miss something. The music has slowed to a funky seventies beat. Only the hard core party animals remain. (Me?) We scream and hoot for another hour or so.

Slowly I find boredom. Slowly I discover reality.

It is a strange thing strolling home at eight in the morning. The air is misty and fresh, grass wet and green. Signs of life become apparent. Newspapers strewn across sparkling lawns, a lone jogger blindly obsessed, the occasional push-bike rider glides silently down the street, the distant growl of a garbage truck collecting its last load. It is an effort to walk, a struggle to move. Emma and I discuss highlights. Like the couple we saw fucking high up in the stands, and the man I danced with clad in only his

y-front jockeys, of snorting amyl and spinning out in a haze of smoke . . .
'Wasn't it great the way they mixed Adeva's *Respect* with Aretha
Franklin's?' 'Yeah, I just went wild.'

We arrive back at the house. Our flatmates are all in bed but the
kitchen is full with people. A friend and a friend and their friends . . . We
drink coffee and smoke cigarettes for hours. Story after story of the
night and what it held. The music, the lights, the decorations, the stupid
drag shows . . . By midday I feel myself tiring. I wish these people would
leave, I need to sleep. The party is over. Go home! Nobody seems to be
aware, or even care that they are in somebody else's home. Hints are
dropped. As the hours drag I become less subtle. The chatter continues.
Eventually I go to bed leaving Emma to cope with it all.

It is almost 1.30 p.m. and the sun attacks my bed with viciousness and
contempt. I pull the blinds, strip and crawl under the sheet. No music
today. Silence is bliss.

As I wake I am confronted with a confusing image. Complete
darkness. I look to my clock for clarity, 6.25 p.m. Then I remember . . .
There is a faint but constant thud rising from below. My bedroom
bounces and shakes. Surely they are not playing dance music! I become
increasingly confused and immediately angered. The lounge room
contains at least ten people. I enter, turn and leave, their laughter
echoing in my head. The kitchen, as usual, is a complete mess. I try to
ignore the overflowing ashtrays and garbage bins. I cannot bring myself
to return to the lounge room. Do they not have a home to go to? Have
they not slept? I am boiling the kettle as Emma finds her way into the
kitchen.

In disbelief, 'I came downstairs and they were all just sitting there.'

'Haven't they been home yet?' I ask, realising it's the same crowd I
left here five and a half hours prior.

'No. They've just been sitting in our lounge room all day.'

'Fucking hell!' I am ropable. 'These people amaze me.'

But don't be angry, I tell myself. This is Darlinghurst after all.

•   •   •

> One day I was in a bar with a friend.
> My friend met a boy.
> I met his friend.

•   •   •

Black Doc Martins (steel capped), black Levis 501's, black t-shirt (old
and torn), and black leather jacket. I check myself out in the mirror and
adjust the collar to a happy medium somewhere between trendy and
tough. Hair, few regular poses . . . Tonight is a special night. Tonight he
is with us. I must make my mark. The doorbell signals their arrival.
Within minutes a flatmate will tap on my door. Footsteps on the stairs,
along the corridor . . .

'Matt, they're here.'

'Oh, okay,' unconcerned.

Descending the stairs I begin my transformation.

Attitude. Unemotional, verging on arrogance.

Secondly, physique. It should reflect the attitude. Relax the pelvis enabling the hips to sway. This will cause a sort of strut. You'll find that your shoulders swing only slightly more than usual but the subtle change will make all the difference.

Thirdly, and most importantly, state of mind. Get into party mode (any way will do). Prepare yourself for a rage. Set your sights on picking up the most beautiful person and whatever you do, if taking drugs:

    (i) Don't take too many, and
    (ii) If you do, don't make a scene.

Remember, your main aim is to look like you're having fun.

He is the first person I see. He looks me over with speculation. Immediately I turn away. Introductions are made and I try my hardest to greet him with the same level of interest I would anyone else. Emma pops in and out, host that she is, saying all the right things.

'So, where's the party?'

'Pyrmont. In some film studio I think.'

'Well you have a good time won't you,' patting me on the back.

He is staring. I feel my face begin to redden.

'Shall we go then?'

Travelling to a dance party is as important as what to wear. There are two options:

    (i) Car (models pre '69 are preferable), and
    (ii) Taxi.

The latter is best as you don't need to worry about keys or alcohol.

Time of arrival is fairly important:

    (i) Don't be too early. It's boring as all hell if there's no one to perve at, and
    (ii) If taking drugs, you'll find by mid-morning they'll wear off and you'll want to go home.

So, we arrive way before midnight and leave at 4.00 a.m.

'Come and dance,' physically pulling me off the chair.

We bop away for a few numbers. I watch him dance with curiosity and lust. He moves like no one I have ever seen. This is good. It indicates individuality and radical tendencies. One off-putting feature is the eyes: they remain permanently closed. This is not good. Not for any aesthetic reason, I just want some attention. I glance across the floor to discover Trent and Brian, quite off the planet by this stage, with their heads inside a speaker. They motion me over.

'This is wild! Try it.'

I try it. It was wild.

Going to the toilet is an experience and a half.

General rule: never go by yourself. There are two reasons for this:

(i) You may never see your friends again, and

(ii) You may find that being on your own under the influence of chemical stimulants too much to handle.

Chances are you'll cope, but it's better not to take the risk.

There is a row of only five or six Port-a-loos. Thing about some warehouse parties that is a real *in*convenience are the toilets. If you happen to fluke a Port-a-loo then expect to wait, and wait ... This is another good reason not to go alone.

So I'm waiting and waiting, alone, and all of a sudden I realise, 'Fuck, I'm really out of it!' I quickly glance around to see if anyone is looking at me. Whilst pissing I break out into stream of consciousness, gabbling and raving on about I don't know what. When I step out a girl wearing platform shoes, black hotpants and lace bra gives me a really strange look. Did she hear my inner dialogue? I am gliding towards a doorway. There are people all around me. They cannot touch me, only I, them. I step through the arch into a den of eccentrics and bores. A guy strolls past clad only in cycling shorts and boots. A shivery wave undulates down my body. The others sit on some chairs. No sooner have I joined them than one of my favourite songs comes on.

He is in front of me.

Again we groove and again the eyes are shut. I begin to wonder about the purpose of my presence. I dance hard, squeezing every ounce of pleasure from the movements. Maybe if I shut my eyes he will sneak a look. In my own little world now I become one with the music. It dances me. All inhibitions to the wind I move with funk and rhythm. I am determined to get his attention. I know I am being watched, I can feel it. A new track is mixed and the mood of the crowd rises in obvious fever. I open my eyes.

There is a definite flair to buying a drink. One simple rule applies: snap out of your drug-fucked state for a moment, and push. It's the only way.

We're all sitting around a table, feeding our thirst and watching the people. There is a guy on the edge of the dance floor doing the most amazing things with a hat. I can't stop wondering where he learnt to move like that. Absolutely amazing. We all clap and cheer when he finally stops but he pretends not to notice and disappears into the crowd. I look around at him, he looks away. My second favourite song comes on.

He is in front of me.

Brian and Trent smile at me with knowing grins. What it is they know I haven't quite worked out? Sweat pours off me but I push through all barriers of endurance and keep on moving. 'Don't stop,' I tell myself. 'I've no intention of it,' I reply. The music has slowed to a cruisy beat. I'm really into it now.

'Relax.'

I turn and discover Trent. He smiles with wisdom and understanding. 'Is it that obvious?'

'Yes.'

Immediately I find myself moving away. He is right. What's the urgency? Let the boy come to you.

It is close to 4.00 a.m. and the drugs have made a rather fast retreat. There is another rule here, it is my own personal rule: when you find yourself wandering around at a dance party with nothing to do, go home. Don't worry about missing anything, you can plan it better next weekend.

●　　●　　●

One day I met a boy in a bar.
He offered me a cigarette,
So I took up smoking.

●　　●　　●

Never Let Me Down Again. Depeche Mode.

'I love this song.'

'So do I,' he agrees.

'I don't know anyone who's got it. Never heard it played at a party, have you?'

'No.' He reaches for a cigarette and offers me one.

'Yeah, thanks.' And lights it for me. 'Ta.' I stretch out on the lounge and enjoy the music. I close my eyes. The after-effects of drugs linger and stimulate my body inspiring another wave of serenity. I begin to drift off but muffled giggling from the kitchen snaps me back. Brian, no doubt, is molesting Trent. I focus on the eyes. 'Oh ... I can't keep awake.'

He smiles.

I notice a photograph in an ornate frame on the bookcase.

'Who's that? The one with you,' I ask, pointing to it.

'My boyfriend back in London.'

'Oh, right.' I look away.

He makes no attempt to initiate any discussion. I am being tested.

'So, how long have you been here?'

'Three months.'

'Oh, really. Like it?'

'Mmm. I want to stay.'

'Can you? Legally, I mean.'

'Don't know.'

'We may have to find you a wife.'

A polite chuckle and a drag on the cigarette. The song has finished, leaving us deserted and desolate. I cannot think of anything else to say. I feel like walking over, looking him straight in the eye and demanding some sort of input.

'How long have you known Trent?'

'About fifteen years. We went to school together.'

This seems to shock him. 'Long time.'

'Yeah, too long,' I jest.

'It's nice.' He looks at me and smiles warmly. The eyes are intense and incredibly blue. There is thought behind them.

'Err ... Get her!' Brian bellows.

'What?' A cryptic smirk triggers a touch of paranoia. 'What did you say?' I demand.

'Sprawled out on that couch like a bitch on heat.'

Brian is one of those people who ease their own insecurities by increasing someone else's. Trent almost drops both mugs of coffee on my lap. I don't know where to turn.

'It's nearly five in the morning! I'm tired,' I justify, getting up ...

Of course, there is no reaction at all from the other end of the room.

The four of us sit sipping our respective coffees. Lack of conversation isn't usually a major trauma for me but I cannot stay in this room with him staring at me the way he is.

'What are you doing today?' I ask Trent.

'Sleeping!' But I notice Brian giving him the eye.

'We should have a coffee or something before you leave for Perth.'

'Mmm ... Why don't you two come? Do you want to?'

'That'd be nice.'

Yes, wouldn't it.

So I'm running around my room like a headless chook.

'Why don't you wear those jeans I bought you in the States?'

'They're too big.'

'Oh ...' wounded and hurt.

'I want to feel—'

'Your blue ones look good. Show your butt off.'

'The ripped ones?'

'Yeah.'

'Oh please!'

'Well *I* like them.'

'But it ain't you I'm trying to impress.'

Slightly offended, 'They look good on you.'

'My arse hangs out of 'em.'

'I know.'

I throw her my hairy eyeball. 'Emma, this may come as a shock to you, but it's nineteen *eighty* nine.'

'Bastard! I'm not that old.'

'White t-shirt or stylish blouse?'

'Blouse?' She asks, confused at my poor humour.

'Which one?'

'Oh, t-shirt.'

'Right. Clone it is.' I put it on and cautiously approach the mirror. 'Fuck I hate these dreadlocks.'

'Why? They're great.'

'Make me look like a queen.'

'I think you're sexy.'

'Think I'll chop 'em off. What did you say?'

'I'd fuck you.'

'Bitch.' She giggles mischievously. 'Got any gel?'

'What for?'

I turn from the mirror to show her the one lone dread jutting out from the side of my skull.

'Oh, no. Only wax. You want me to get it for you?'

'No, it wouldn't work.'

'Matt, Trent's here,' Stephen yells up the stairs.

'Okay,' I yell. 'Shit!'

'Money?' Emma asks.

'Yep.'

'Key?'

'Yep.'

'Fags?'

'Always.'

'Have a nice time on your date hon,' kissing me on the cheek.

'Date? We're just going out for coffee for christsake!'

Emma, in her room now, sniggers at my manic insecurities. Stephen, in the kitchen, I'm sure is just waiting on my rejection to make his move. Trent, Brian and him are in the lounge room anticipating the evening's events.

There is pressure from every angle.

I, of course, hold no limits when it comes to inflicting huge amounts of pain upon my person.

'You look good,' Trent comments.

'Thanks. We going?'

The four of us huddle around a table.

There are lots of people everywhere.

Brian: 'Ooh! He's looking for it tonight.'

Me: 'Who?'

Trent: 'Him.'

Gigglegigglegiggle . . .

Now Mathew's mind is a funny thing. It contains this unique ability to overpower the body's verbal functions when they are most required. Say, for example, a situation arises where he is put on the spot. Nine times out of ten a reply of reasonable insight and humour is quite effortlessly flung back into the lap of the so called blackmailer and he stays relaxed and unaffected by the attempted embarrassment.

BUT

when we're talking sex, fear, for some obscure motivation, leaps eagerly to the forefront of his being and not only prevents any aural interchange, but also quite successfully manages to sabotage any secondary attempt to gloss over his sudden and rather bewildering lack of retort. What this means in real terms is that Brian's absence of tact left me, to put it mildly, speechless. And to humiliate further,

'He's been wanting it all day.'

'Brian!' Trent interjects.

'Want to share a chocolate cake?'

'Love to,' I reply.

It's your classic scene. We eat our cake and cream, drink our coffee and compare musical tastes for the remainder of the evening. Trent and Brian are completely ignored, which under the circumstances, suits me fine.

One night I sat in a bar watching Him look for someone to fuck.
There were lots of people everywhere ...

'So, what're we doing?' I ask, not wanting to go home just yet.

'Well, Brian and I are going back to my place,' Trent replies.

Good.

'Feel like doing something?'

'Wouldn't mind going somewhere for a drink.'

Not good.

When you're out on the town with God, one place you do not take Him is a gay bar.

'Do you want to?'

'Yeah, why not.'

So, the disciples are hovering ... These men are amazing! They have this strange notion that they can act as crass and blatant as they like but not actually be classified as a yobbo. They're out on the footpath drinking and gawking, hanging over the bar rating the barmen, they're yelling and screaming and spilling their beer, or pinching your arse. Everything, basically, that the great Australian yobbo is renowned for, but they seem to think they have an excuse.

'He's cute.'

'Which one?' I ask, not really that interested.

'Over by the door. Blond hair, Levis.'

I spot the offender. A bulging carcass of biceps and pecs. Muscle Mary is the term my boss frequently uses.

'You're kidding.'

'He's alright,' he adds, backing down a touch.

'Oh yeah, s'pose.'

I glance around the bar in search of something remotely interesting.

'I'm really horny tonight,' he informs me.

'What about the dark haired guy over by the cigarette machine?' I suggest, why I suggest I'm not too sure.

'No. I like blonds.'

And to think only a few months ago I was blond.

'You want a beer or something?' he offers.

'Yeah, why not.' Why bloody not.

Now, getting service in this establishment is not an easy feat for the average individual, but if you're fortunate enough to score above average you will soon find yourself bombarded with an abundance of offers. There are three bare chested barmen standing in front of us. He chooses the blond.

'What would you like?'

'Just a beer and a mineral water.'

'Not drinking?' I inquire.

'Don't drink,' he replies, eyes directly ahead.

I follow their line and find destiny amongst the cheeks of our blond Muscle Mary.

'Like him do you?'

'He's alright.'

He found no one.

On the street, on a journey to nowhere.

'I really feel like sex tonight.'

'Oh well ...'

Every man that passes by is potential bait.

'I'm really horny.'

'Is it that important to you?' I ask, beginning to comprehend the magnitude of his dilemma.

'I haven't had it for weeks!' he moans.

(Weeks?) 'Well, I don't know ...'

And I didn't. If we ended up in the cot now, somehow I feel it wouldn't be the earth shattering experience that I had in mind. I didn't want him to go home though.

So He came home with me.

'Well,' gulp, 'you could always come back to my place, listen to music. I've got that Kate Bush and Peter Gabriel song you like.'

He ponders on this one for a while.

Then, 'Alright. I just ... don't want you to think, like ... you're my last resort or anything.'

I am thrust into the twilight zone. Nerve endings sparkle and pulsate, throwing me off balance. The pavement begins to shudder and for a moment I completely forget where and who I am. Lights flash and alarm bells sound with resounding immediacy. Now if my interpretation of the situation is *in*correct then I may risk possible, in fact almost certain death for my reputation. On the other hand, if I am right then I *am* the last resort in which case he can get fucked.

'Hang on,' I am almost muffled, 'do you mean, like, um ... you and I, umm ...'

He scratches his head, trying to place the words. A nervous laugh escapes from the corner of his mouth. He takes a very long pause and then at the crucial moment, just when the initial words begin to form, right at the dawn of judgement day, a really loud semi-trailer roars ferociously down the street and I miss the whole damned thing. True. I couldn't believe it! And to add to this outrageous and tragic string of events I was too shy to find out what he had said.

We talked about our lives and listened to music until 3.00 a.m.

'So, you were in the Navy?'

'Yeah,' eyes avoiding, not wanting to discuss it.

'Why did you join?'

'Had nothing better to do. What about you?' he asks.

'Me? I wasn't in the Navy.'

He laughs at my silly joke. 'No, I meant . . .' and stops short, realizing he didn't actually know what he meant. Then, 'It wasn't that bad. The first two years were okay.'

'Yeah . . .?'

'Yeah . . .'

'And the rest?'

'Awful!'

'I can imagine.'

Then he snaps, 'Everyone says that! You have no idea how much I hated it.'

'You're right, I don't,' I apologize. 'How old were you when you joined?'

'Sixteen.'

'That's very young.'

'I was in charge. I didn't know what I was doing.'

'In charge of what?'

'Everything!' He exclaims. 'I had to make sure everyone was up in the morning, make sure they were on deck on time. I was in charge of this whole group of guys. Most of them were older than me.'

'Did they do what you said?'

'Mostly. Sometimes they'd fart arse around, just to piss me off. I'd get abused by the captain or something. Once this guy wouldn't get out of bed . . .' and he stops, deep in thought.

'And . . .'

'What?' he asks.

'What happened?' He looks confused. 'This guy wouldn't get out of bed . . .' I prompt.

'Oh. He was just being an arsehole. I kept screaming at him to get up and he just kept shouting at me, telling me to fuck off.'

'What did you do?'

'I told him if he didn't get up I'd beat the shit out of him.'

'Did it work?'

'No.' Then suddenly, 'What do you want to hear?'

'Oh I don't mind,' I reply. He gets up and puts on *The Funeral* from *Cry Freedom*. 'Did you know you were gay?'

'No, not at first.'

'So what happened to make you realise?' I ask, raising an eyebrow, pushing for a dirty story.

'No, you're wrong,' he objects, 'Nothing like that ever happened.'

'Ever?'

'It's not like everyone thinks ... There was one other guy I knew was gay. He worked in another section of the boat and sometimes I had to take over papers and stuff. I always used to look at him.'

'How did you find out?'

'When we were in Port I used to go to the bars and—'

'You're kidding!'

'No ... Anyway, there was this little section where I'd sort of hang—'

'You bumped into him!' I interrupt.

'Who's telling this story?'

'Sorry. Go on.'

'And, well, yeah ... I bumped into him.'

'Did you talk to each other?'

'No. We just walked straight past.'

'Why? You should've spoken to him.'

'Don't know really.'

'He could've been a really nice guy.'

'Suppose ...'

'What happened when you saw him on the boat?'

'Oh we never said anything. Sometimes he'd sort of smile when no one was around.'

'What a great story.' I am completely captivated. 'You know, all that is so alien to me. I've got no comprehension of what it would be like.'

'You're lucky. It's awful. Hey, you know what I'd really like to hear?' he asks, moving toward the CD player.

'What?' But there is no reply. 'What?' I repeat.

'Never you mind ...'

I am so relaxed. I watch him search through my CD's and tapes. I wonder who he is and what is going on in his mind. And then the familiar introduction, and:

'OOH! Whatchoo want ... baby I got ...' He's bopping around the lounge room now. I smile and laugh at his silliness. I can't help but wonder what motivates someone, a stranger to carry on like this. 'Come on,' he coaxes. 'Whatchoo need ... you know I got it. All I'm askin' ... is for a little Respect.'

I do the 'just a little bit's' and he does the 'OO!'s' ...

Who is this guy? I find myself thinking. He tells me his life story, sings and dances for me in my own lounge room. He doesn't know me. I begin to feel awkward and silly when I remember the time.

'We better turn it down,' pointing upstairs to the sleeping flatmates. 'Oh dear!' I exclaim, for no apparent reason.

'What?' he asks, falling onto the couch beside me.

'You dancing around ...'

He pauses momentarily. Then, 'What about it?'

'Well, just that it's funny, you know. We hardly know each other.'

'So?' he asks, with an inquisitive grin. Then repeats, harder this time, 'So?'

'I didn't know you had a tattoo.'

'Oh yuk!' and he quickly covers it up. 'I really hate it.'

'Why?'

'It's just awful.'

'Can I have a look?'

'No.'

I look him in the eye. Stirring now, 'Why?'

'I try to keep it covered.'

'But why?' I press.

'I just really hate it okay?' slightly edgy now.

'Why, 'cause it's so cliché?'

'Yes, 'cause it's so cliché. I went out one night, got pissed and got a tattoo, alright?'

'Alright,' I reply. There is nearly an uncomfortable silence but I am determined to prevent it. 'What do you feel like listening to?'

'What?' He is lost.

'Never mind. I'll put on—'

'Put on—Oh, sorry. Go ahead.'

'What?' I ask.

'No you go first.'

'Okay.'

Soul To Soul. *Keep On Moving*.

He looks at me with confusion and amazement.

'Don't you like this?' I ask.

'This is what I was going to ask you to put on.'

It felt like a scene out of a trashy B-grade.

'You're kidding!' I exclaim, sitting down next to him. 'It's a great song.'

'Yeah,' he says, stretching. 'Makes me feel like fucking.'

> He said He was glad He hadn't found a fuck as He enjoyed the evening much better with me.

'It's getting late.'

'What time is it?' I ask.

'Nearly three.'

'Shit!' But I don't really care.

We walk to the door.

'Oh well . . .' He is tense.

'Nice night,' I state.

'Yes, it was.'

We hesitate for a second, both waiting for the other to speak. I start.

'Well, umm . . .'

'I'll give you a call.'

'Okay. That'd be good.' Then, from nowhere, 'Wonder what Trent and Brian are doing now?' Freud would've had a field day. My face begins to redden as I realize the implications of my thoughtless outburst. I am almost at the point of obviousness when he leans over and pecks me on the cheek.

'I'm glad I came over. I had a much better time than if I'd gone home with a complete stranger.'

'I *am* a complete stranger,' I point out.

'You know what I mean.'

But did he know what *he* meant?

There are people I know.

Trent, with his endless array of men, his constant short-lived obessions.

I see him.

I know him.

There is familiarity and understanding.

We have met before.

> One day I met a boy in a bar
> And I thought,
> I want to know Him

•   •   •

One day I was in a cafe with a friend and a friend and a
    friend.

After a while, a friend came over to talk to a friend about
    another friend's friend's friend who had been sleeping
    around with this friend's friend's friend's friend even
    though she shouldn't have been.

My friend couldn't understand why.

One day my doctor asked me how many people I had
    slept with.

There are lots of people everywhere.

1991

STEVE J. SPEARS

From *The Elocution of Benjamin Franklin*

Author's note: The word '*BLINK*' which is used in the stage directions indicates a lighting change to represent the passing of time. The length of these passages varies from a few seconds to several days.

ACT ONE

A living room cum studio in a small house in Toorak. A door at Prompt leads to the hall, the front door and the bedroom. A door at OP leads to the bathroom and, farther on, to the kitchen. Furniture includes a piano, a telephone table with an ornate lamp, a rolltop desk, a bust of Shakespeare prominently displayed, some comfortable chairs, a coffee table, a cuckoo clock on a wall. A shotgun is mounted over the fireplace. An electric heater is on in the fireplace. There is a bay window at the back with the words 'SHAKESPEARE SPEECH AND DRAMA' lettered on it. The Venetian blinds on this window are open and the morning sun streams through.

MONDAY 1ST

The MAN enters, naked, a bath towel over his shoulder, whistling. He is jovial, fat and fiftyish. He rolls up the rolltop desk, takes out a make-up case and mirror and begins quickly and expertly to apply rouge and other make-up. During this, he turns on the record player: the music is Skyhooks' 'Ego is not a Dirty Word'. He finishes making up, takes out a large battered poster of Mick Jagger and sticks it on the wall. He wraps towel around him, turns off the record player, takes a pair of black leather gloves from the rolltop, puts them on and stands in front of the poster. He begins to caress himself, then stops, turns the bust of Shakespeare away, and stands in front of the poster again.

MAN: (*in a girlish voice*) Yes, Mick. I . . . I thought so too. Oooooo, it's such an honour to meet you, Mick. Yes, I was at the show. I thought you were fabulous. Keith too. I think you're both dreamy. Oooooo. Yes. You like my gloves, Mick? They're very sensuous, don't you think? Hmmmmm. They feel smooth. Yes. Smooth. Hmmmmm.

(*He starts crooning and getting all bothered. The telephone rings.*)

Shit!

(*He strides purposefully to the telephone, calling to it as he moves.*)

Shut up! (*To poster*) Excuse me. (*Picking up the telephone*) Good morning. Shakespeare Speech and Drama Academy . . . Yes. This is he. Yes, Mrs Franklin?

(*Pause.*)

Yes . . . I dare say. Oh. Yes, stuttering can be painful (*glancing at the poster*), absolutely painful. Especially for a twelve year old . . . Oh, that's so unnecessary for the little man, Mrs Franklin. Aren't children cruel? . . . Well, I'd certainly like to try to help him, Mrs Franklin. Unless it's something physical, these problems can be overcome. You see, good speech is as much an art as music or painting. Correct speech is not accidental . . . Yes. Yes. Certainly, today would be fine. (*Making a 'shit' face*) This morning? (*Making another 'shit' face*) Well, um . . . (*Looking through his notebook*) Shall we say eleven? (*Jotting it down*) Fine. Fine. Don't worry, Mrs Franklin, we'll have that stutter licked before you can say Susan stole thirty-three thistle sticks. Hahahahaha . . . Well, my fee is eight dollars per half hour lesson. Very well. Yes, we'll see you and little Benjamin at eleven. Yes. Bye bye, Mrs. Franklin.

(*He hangs up and speaks to poster.*)

Well, Michael, I'm sorry, but we've got another stutterer. (*Taking poster from wall*) Anyway, don't you think you're getting a bit old for this sort of thing? (*Putting make-up, gloves and mirror away*) Benjamin Franklin. Ugghhh. (*Turning bust around*) Tell me, William, if your last name happened to be Franklin, what sort of person would you have to be to name your son Benjamin? Hmmm? A fuckwit, that's what. God, there's some weird people in the world. Well, I don't know about you, but I'm going to put some clothes on. (*Fingering the rouge*) And I suppose I'd better get this stuff off too . . . Why thank you. (*Pinching the bust's cheek*) You too.

(MAN *exits, OP.*)

. . .

(MAN *springs into room, singing 'How's your love life?', and prepares to exit P. Telephone rings. He does a military about face.*)

Shakespeare Speech and Drama. Bruce! How nice. Why, you filthy animal . . . Listen, I can't talk, I've got someone coming . . . No, stupid, a new pupil. Listen, pet, you take them when you can get them at eight bucks a pop. Didn't bat a vocal organ. They never do. Not in Toorak, pet . . . It's a young boy who stutters. They're my speciality. No, Bruce. Stutterers! Oh, you'll like this. The mother's name is Franklin. Guess what they named the poor kid . . . (*Bitterly*) God, you're a bore, Bruce. Yes. Top marks. Uh huh. Eleven o'clock. *What's* the time? Shit! I must go. They probably won't come. If you knew how many stutterers and stammerers and mumblers and toneless monotonous nasal voices ring up and solemnly assure me, yes, they really want to improve their diction and, yes, I'll be there, and then disappear into that inarticulate void at the other end of this phone without showing their tonsils . . . Bruce, I'm going. Goodbye. I'm half naked and . . . No, I don't plan to greet them naked. And I don't plan to greet them in my lounging outfit. No, come eleven, they'll be greeted by *the* most masculine Aussie since Bob (*spit!*) Hawke ... Oh Bruce, he is not. Fuck you. Goodbye. What? No. Not tonight, love. I've got classes till (*consulting his notebook*) ten. Hmmm. Then I thought I'd just go to bed with Mick Jagger. Never mind. I'll ring you. (*Looking at watch*) Shit! Bye bye.

(MAN *exits hurriedly, P. We hear him grunting and getting dressed. The doorbell rings. He calls from offstage.*)

Just a minute.

(MAN *enters, wearing checked trousers and maroon shirt, clambering into shoes. The doorbell rings.*)

Just a minute.

BLINK

MAN: (*sitting in spot*) Yes, Mrs Franklin. Feel free to smoke if you wish. You'll find the ashtray there. No smoking for you, though, Benjamin. Hahaha. Just a joke, Mrs, er, Franklin. I must congratulate you on your choice of a name for your son. Very imaginative and a fine name too. Well, Benjamin. Not many people know this, but when I was your age, I used to stutter too. Yes. And oh dear, it was much worse than yours. And the other kids used to make fun of me. They do the same to you, do they? It's not very nice, is it? They used to call me Tommy-gun. But, believe me, it's not worth worrying about what other kids say. You should just tell them to get ... lost. Anyway, do you know what we're going to do? Hmmmmm? We're going to stop you stuttering once and for all. I could do it in ten minutes but I want your Mum's money. Hahaha. Just a joke, Mrs, er, Franklin. So we'll take a bit longer than that. How old are you? ... (*Smiling*) That's all right. I know how tough those Ts are, and the Ps. Hmmmmm? (*Winking reassuringly*) Well, Ben, would you wait outside, I'd like to talk to Mum. (*Watching him leave*) Beautiful boy. Mrs Franklin, you're to be congratulated again. For bringing your son here, or to any speech therapy school for that matter. People go through life crippled by (*tapping throat and face*) just six inches of their body, by an inability to communicate and then refusing, stupidly refusing to seek help. Help is what I offer. We won't consider today's little get-together a lesson. I think, er, tomorrow? Right. (*Jotting it down in his notebook*) We'll start him off tomorrow then with a ten week course every Tuesday at four? Fine. Certainly in advance, if you'd care to. I think I might throw in a few drama lessons, too. Who knows? Once the stutter's gone, we might have a budding Frank Thring on our hands. No. On second thoughts, Frank's rather poor on his Ss. Hahahaha. Oh, and the lessons are private of course, and I do prefer if parents aren't in the room, it makes them shy, you understand. And I'm afraid I don't have a waiting room, so if you do drive him here, you will have to wait in your car. Most uncivilised, I know, but I hope you'll forgive me. (*Taking the cheque*) Thanks so much. We'll see young Benjamin at four sharp tomorrow. Fine. (*Getting up*) I'll see you to the door.

BLINK

. . .

TUESDAY 2ND

MAN: (*sitting in spot*) Well, Benjamin. Is your Mum waiting outside? Fine. We'll be having lessons for the next ten weeks. Don't tell your Mum, but we'll piss that stutter off in three weeks, then we'll get onto something really interesting. (*Taking out a cigar*) You move well, Benjamin, and there's something in your voice I like. I've got a feeling there's an actor inside you. (*Lighting the cigar*) I guess you never go into school plays or whatnot? Huh?

(*He makes an explosive P that blows out match.*)

Here. (*Tossing 'Ben' the matches*) Light one of those up and go Puh! That's right. That's good. Do it again. Sure. Do it again. (*Wryly*) Fun, isn't it? Hmmmm? Menthol or plain? There's a packet on the piano. Don't you tell your Mum or I'll put you over my knee. (*Mumbling*) Come to think of it, don't tell your Mum *if* I put you over my knee. Nothing. Sit down. Breathe. Just breathe. Nice big one. Bigger. Bigger. Did you notice then, when you took a deep breath you filled up here? (*Tapping his chest*) This time try it differently, feel around—Come here. Feel around the bottom of my rib cage just here.

(*He puts 'Ben's' hands around his ribs with a look of ecstasy.*)

Yes, that's right. Um, well. When I breathe you notice that I fill up down there. That's the diaphragm. That's where you have to fill up. Can you feel that? Okay. Now squiggle your hands down round your hips and feel around for your diaphragm. Think your breath down there. Let me feel. (*Putting out his hands with a look of concentration*) Hmmmm. Again. Again. Great. Okay. Good. This time really take it down there and say: (*Singing*) Bell, bell, bell, bell, bell.

(*Pause.*)

Try it. Come on. Don't be shy with me. Bell, bell, bell, bell, bell. Come on, Benjamin. You are shy, aren't you? Listen, if I can sit here making a fool of myself, then you can too. All right? I'll let you keep the packet. Okay? Okay. Off you go.

(*Pause.*)

Good, Ben. Good. Now relax, unwind, breathe down in your diaphragm and do it again. Beautiful. I'll give you two packets. Now. (*Shaking himself*) Relax. Sit down. Have a smoke. Let me tell you about speech. Breath is the basis of all speech. Breath. Fill your diaphragm with enough breath and you can shake the window and rattle the walls. You can count to a hundred without pausing. Watch.

(MAN *starts counting slowly and distinctly. He reaches sixty or seventy and grins shyly.*)

See? You'll be doing that soon. Anyway, breath. Breath. Breath passes up to the voice box, which has two vocal chords, a big one and a little one, and the breath causes them to vibrate, just like a guitar string. This sound is then made into speech by teeth, nasal cavities, tongue and all sorts of stuff in your mouth. So that instead of going, 'woof, woof', we can go, 'Benjamin, if you must smoke, use an ashtray.' Now your problem is that you aren't breathing correctly and your speech muscles aren't performing properly. It's a bit complicated, but it's certainly nothing to worry about and it's nothing to be ashamed of. It's just ... there. Like ... pimples. Okay. Now, next week when you come back, I want to hear you saying the bells with a nice rich forward tone. There's a rainbow from your mouth to mine and you're going to send it out, up and over. Bell, bell, bell. *And* I want to hear you counting slowly and distinctly up to thirty. And I bet you won't be able to. Okay? That's all. You're doing well, Benjamin. See, it doesn't hurt much, does it? Now, what do you normally do after school?

(*Slow fade. Cuckoo clock strikes six. Lights fade up. Night time.*)

. . .

(MAN *enters, tense. He is wearing women's knickers and a stuffed bra.*)

Hit the deck, boys. (*Falling to the ground, impersonating a marine*) Okay, youse guys, lizzen. See dat winda over there? De Luxaflex's open, see? It's supposed to be shut, see? We got orders. Ain't no one supposed to see me, get it? Ain't no one supposed to look through de winda, see? And see me knickers, see? Okay. Let's go.

(*Dramatic war music. MAN inches way across room, past the piano. Finally, dramatically, he closes the blind and draws the curtain. He stands, exhausted but victorious, and looks proudly at his men.*)

You did all right, boys.

(MAN *staggers off, P, then re-enters, putting on fluffy dressing gown.*)

BLINK

MAN: (*in spot, sipping tea daintily*) Let me bore you for a minute, Bruce. Remember I was telling you about this boy who stutters? Benjamin Franklin? Oh, I told you about him. Jesus, Bruce, you never listen. Anyway, he's this beautiful, beautiful twelve year old boy who moves like a prince with this long, dark, curly hair ... stop drooling. I'm being serious. Anyway, he's a great kid. Well, Benjamin has this mother. (*Pulling a face*) The most rigid, humourless, clinging, tight-arsed bitch I've ever seen ... apart from my ex-wife. And Benjamin is literally terrified of her. He had his first lesson today and good old Mum was waiting outside in her P76 like this (*miming a chain-smoker*), and Ben kept glancing back through the window (*miming a paranoid glance*) every thirty seconds on the second. I swear to Christ he had me doing it. I thought the old lady was going to come crashing through my window, waving a tyre jack, beat my brains out and effect a rescue. And she wonders why he stutters. Christ, I'm amazed he can talk!

(*He pauses to light his cigar.*)

Hmmmm? What do you mean it (*the cigar*) spoils the atmosphere? Look, I got lace doilies, real china tea-cups. (*Grabbing tea-pot*) Look! I even knitted this tea-cosy. (*Dramatic*) What do you want from me? (*Grabbing bosom*) Milk? Yes, Bruce.

(*Pause.*)

Yes, Bruce. (*Stubbing out cigar*) Better? Where was I? (*Enthusiastic*) Ah, Benjamin. Anyway, I carefully pointed out the miracle of Luxaflex blinds and gave him a cigarette — Oh, give me a cigarette will you, darling? — and just talked with him for a while.

(*Pause.*)

This kid's fucked more women than I have. He's going around with an older lady now. She's sixteen and works at Mum's hairdressing salon. And just for one minute ... he didn't stutter. There was this twelve year old man of the world quietly sitting back, fag in mouth, telling me about what a great gobbler his Mum's hairdresser is. Hahaha. Isn't that superb? And for that one minute ... he didn't stutter.

(*Reflective pause.*)

Huh? Oh, knock it off, Bruce. You know I'm strictly a fantasy man. Okay. Bore me. How are your kids?

(MAN *pours tea, then listens for a time. Clock strikes eleven. He yawns.*)

Shit, I hate that clock. Can't think why I keep it. Come on, Bruce, time to turn back into a pumpkin. I'm for bed and you're for home, wife and kiddies.

(*Pause.*)

Bruce. I think your outfit's lovely and to get terribly maudlin ...
I'm glad you're my friend. (*Defiantly*) Okay? Anyway, you're the
best transvestite stockbroker I know. Get changed. I'll see you to
the door.

BLINK

WEDNESDAY 3RD

. . .

(*We hear front door, OP, being opened. Lights gradually come up.*)

[MAN]: Bye bye, Mrs Clifton. (*Waving*) Hello, Mrs Broad! (*Muttering*)
Nosy bitch.

(MAN *closes door. Clock strikes six. There is still some light outside
window. MAN idles to piano, is about to play it, when he changes his mind
and reaches behind piano, takes out bottle of whisky and swigs. He walks with
bottle to door OP and exits, swigging. He re-enters, swigging, with globe, and
replaces globe in the lamp beside the telephone. He tries it a couple of times
and swigs. He dials and swigs.*)

Oh, hello, Edith. How are you? Yes, I saw it last night. I think it
suits him to a tee. No Edith, I thought the hem-line was just right.
Oh, you raised it yourself, did you? Why that rotten bit—bastard
told me he did it. Can, ooops, may I speak to him? Thanks. Oh,
how are the kids? Great.

(*Pause.*)

Bruce, my pet, do you realise what a fine woman your wife is?
Why don't you bring her over for one of our evenings? I've got
some great recipes she'd love. Listen, I'm sorry to call you at
home, but I wanted you to congratulate me. Because I thought that
today was definitely the day that I wouldn't make it through and I
did, that's why. Well (*looking at bottle*), a bit. (*Swigging*) Come over,
can you? You're taking her where? The (*current state theatre company
production*)? Ah Bruce! I want to celebrate! Making it through
today! Jesus, you never listen to me. All right. Take the bitch to see
it. It's lousy! Yes, yes. *Dominus vobiscum*, creep. (*Slamming down
telephone*) Christ, it's hard being the other woman.

(MAN *takes a swig, then strides to darkening window.*)

That's right, sun! Phoebus, you coward! Go on, desert me too, you
cunt! Go and set! See if I care. But remember, Phoebus, when you
come tomorrow, I'll still be here! You want to know why? (*Giving
sky the finger*) Because, Phoeb, I got staying power! I got balls. And
you can fucking set and—

(*Telephone rings.* MAN *strides to it, picks it up.*)

What? Oh Mrs Broad. You could hear me all the way over there? Heh. That's diaphragm breathing for you, does it every time. Tell me, have you ever thought of taking speech lessons, dear? Look, I'd love to talk some more, Mrs Broad, but I think I can smell my cake burning. Bye bye.

(*He puts telephone down and turns to bust.*)

That was Mrs Broad. She thinks I'm a pervert. You know what I think. I think she does it with dogs. 'Sright. (*Reaching behind piano, bringing out portable TV*) 'Sright. I think she's got a dalmation for a lover.

(MAN *exits OP door. We hear things rattling in kitchen. He enters with bread rolls, tins of food, cheese, fritz, can-openers, biscuits, etc. and heaps them on tray with TV.*)

And I think she's got her eye on that cute little dachshund down the road. And what's more she's nosey.

(MAN *strides to window and shouts.*)

How's the bulldogs these days? Huh! Up the mighty Saints! Go, you big men! Come on! Go Jezza, you little beauty! Wahoooooooooooooo. Get 'em in the nuts, Ron! Wahoooooooooooo.

(MAN *moves to telephone. It rings. He picks it up, puts it down on table and exits to P door with tray of food and TV set. We hear squabbling from the telephone.* MAN *switches off main light, switches on bedroom light. Telephone lamp is left on. Bust looks unimpressed. We hear* MAN *rustling around in room, and sounds of TV.*)

END ACT ONE

ACT TWO

TUESDAY 9TH

It is raining outside the window. Alarm clock sounds in bedroom and is shut off with a curse. MAN *eventually emerges from P wrapped in his fluffy dressing gown, irritable. He exits, OP. We hear the shower running.* MAN *enters, trips, puts 'Living in the 70s' on the record player and exits, OP.* MAN *sings with record. It gets stuck on 'It's a horror movie right there . . . It's a horror movie right there . . .' (from 'Horror Movie').* MAN *enters, irritable, dripping, and smashes record. He puts on another (Side One: 'Let It Bleed' by Rolling Stones). He exits OP.* MAN *sings with record. Shower noises finish.* MAN *enters with towel wrapped around him. As he passes the record player, the needle slips and jumps.* MAN, *scarcely pausing, picks up record and smashes it, then exits P door. We hear towel-rubbing and grunting.* MAN *enters in undies and singlet, towelling his hair, and exits OP to kitchen. We hear dishes rattling. One breaks.* MAN *enters with bowl of cornflakes, irritable. He moves to window, shovelling the cornflakes down.*

MAN: Good morning, Melbourne. I see you've got another great day planned for me. (*Spilling some cornflakes on his singlet*) Yes.

(*He patiently pulls singlet up and sucks them off. He turns to face room, irritable, and looks ruefully around.*)

Huh.

(MAN *exits to kitchen. We hear many dishes breaking. Slowly* MAN *enters, dignified.*)

BLINK

MAN: (*in spot*) In England, plays were first performed in the churches in front of the altar. People, you see, weren't attending Mass because they weren't educated and couldn't read and write, so they didn't understand Latin or anything. So, to get full houses, the priests would dress up and act out Nativity and Easter plays and make up morality tales where the goodies always win in the end. Well, that got rave reviews, so other people thought, 'Well, if the Mick priests . . .' Um, you're not Catholic, are you, Tony? Good. 'Well, if the Mick priests can do it, so can I.' So these secular actors used to roam around in carts, which they used as stages and went to all the market towns and acted out tales and legends and people would toss them the odd penny or two. Yes, sort of like Hare Krishnas except they make a lot more. Anyway, actors were not well thought of at all, so theatres weren't allowed to be built in town. Even Shakespeare had to build his theatres on the outskirts of London. They were called the Globe, the Swan and the Blackfriars. Of course women weren't allowed on stage till the reign of Charles the Second, so they used young men dressed up as women for all the ladies' roles. Hmmm. Yes, it is a bit silly, isn't it?

. . .

BLINK

MAN: (*in spot, pirate voice*) You see that shotgun over the fireplace? There's an awful lot of dead little girls buried in my cellar who didn't practise Naughty Nancy ate nine nice new cakes. Pow! Straight through the eyes. (*Normal voice*) I, er, hope it won't be necessary to take that gun down, Maura, I sincerely hope it won't be necessary. Let's hear you.

(*Pause as he listens.*)

Not bad. You won't have to join (*pointing to the floor*) the others. In fact, just between you and me, oops, I, ooops, me, I'll tell you something. You say those things better than I do. I think you've done a good job. You're ready for . . . the big one, pet. You're ready for: Rolling river roaring rushing rafters rocks in your ruthless rapture crushing. How about *that*?

BLINK

MAN: (*in spot*) Tong tong tong a tong tong
That is the rhythm of the elephant's song.

BLINK

MAN: (*in spot*) Hark to the echo of London's old bells.

BLINK

MAN: (*in spot*) Tip a tap tap. Tip a tap tap.

BLINK

MAN: (*in spot*) *But* soft. *What* light, er, what *light* through yonder window breaks? It is ...

BLINK

MAN: (*in spot*) Get it up your nose, Mrs Clifton.

BLINK

MAN: (*in spot*) How many can you count up to? Forty-two? Bullshit. All right. Let's hear you.

(*Long pause as 'Ben' counts. MAN starts mouthing the numbers with him. Pause.*)

That's, um, that's great, Benjamin. (*Tossing him packet of cigarettes*) It's good that you're doing your exercises. (*Eagerly*) How's the hairdresser?

(*Slow fade to black. Laughter. Lights fade up. MAN is at telephone. It is darkening outside window.*)

Anyway, apparently, the hairdresser had the clap! Yes! And Benjamin had to sneak down to the VD Clinic after cricket on Saturday. Hahahaha. Then ... then ... he found out he ... had crabs too! Hahahahaha. And his Mum can't understand why he doesn't want her to get his hair cut there any more! Hahahahaha. See you tonight. Right, Bruce. Bye bye.

(*MAN puts down telephone and starts laughing. Hooting, he exits P door. More laughter. Lights fade into spot. MAN enters in fluffy dressing gown, sipping tea, and sits down in spot.*)

I tell you, Bruce, this kid's a born actor. You should have been there when he was telling the story. You would have died, honestly. Everything. The gestures, the faces. And his stutter: it's barely noticeable when he's really ... giving out. His Ps are still (*so-so gesture*) but he's coming along. After one week! I'm making history with this kid. I should get a write up in the Speech Therapy Gazette. See, I think all he needs is a father figure. (*Sipping daintily*) His Dad's always off somewhere, Singapore, America, you know. Hither and thither. And ... oh ... he counted up to forty-nine in one breath. That's incredible for anyone, let alone a twelve year old. Natural breath control. So, I want to crack that stutter and move on to drama. Honestly, with his looks and my talent, he could be great.

(*Pause.*)

I sound like a proud parent, don't I? As soon as I think he's ready, I'm going to get onto Healy at the ABC. They've got a series coming up that Benjamin would be ideal for. Yes. I might get into management. Fuck this elocution crap. Christ, I might even get back into the business. There's plenty of nice juicy roles for fat fifty year olds.

(*Pause.*)

In five years, Benjamin Franklin ... (*Distasteful face*) Benjamin Franklin. Benjamin Nicholas Franklin. Nicholas Franklin. Nicholas B. Franklin. Nick Franklin. Frank Nicholas. Ben Franklin. What do you think?

(*Pause.*)

Oh come off it, Bruce. If you can talk about that fucking Stock Exchange and your saintly martyred wife and those cretinous medical students with pimples you sired, then I can talk about my boy. Bruce. Listen. This kid is more than adequate. For the first time I feel like I can be more than adequate. I was an adequate actor, I'm an adequate teacher and an adequate man. I'm even just an adequate transvestite. Jesus, I can't even fantasise further than Mick Jagger. This kid can save me.

(*Pause.*)

Listen, you, (*sternly*) I want a bit of empathy and understanding from you or I'll bite your balls off, *capisce*? Okay. And if you're good, I'll wear that wig you bought me. (*Coaxing*) Come on, stop pouting. I'll buy your kids some Clearasil. All right. My final offer. I'll go to the Art Gallery with you next Sunday all dressed up, how's that? Yes. Thought that would perk you up. Next Sunday. *But* you pay for a hotel room for us to change in. And since you're so rich, I want a room at the Old Melbourne. Them's me conditions.

(*Pause.*)

And I'll never smoke cigars again and I'll call you Belinda when you're dressed up. You drive a hard bargain . . . Belinda.

(*Doorbell rings.* MAN *ignores it. Doorbell rings.* MAN *ignores it. Doorbell rings. He whispers.*)

I hate not answering the door.

(*We hear footsteps outside window.*)

Shit! They're trying to peek in! I hope those Luxaflex . . . It might be a burglar!

(MAN *takes off high-heeled shoe. We hear footsteps and window rattling.* MAN *whispers.*)

He's trying to get in! The window's not locked!

(*Silence. Clock strikes nine very loudly.* MAN *is startled. Silence.*)

He's gone. (*Picking up tea-cup, rattlingly*) How about a real drink?

(*Pause.*)

We might have been raped!

BLACKOUT

SUNDAY 14TH

Daylight in room. Clock strikes four. The door OP opens.

MAN: (*off, at door*) Well, let's keep our fingers crossed. Bye bye.

(MAN *enters, tosses down an overnight bag and a plastic suit-carrier. He is thoughtful, agitated, pacing nervously. He lights candles on piano, falls dramatically to his knees and makes the sign of the cross.*)

Dear God. You know I haven't been to Mass in a long time and that I've done a lot of things that Pope Paul wouldn't approve of. I know I'm in mortal sin and without grace and all that but listen. I used to be an altar boy and I was a bloody good one, wasn't I? And all those questions on the Assumption and the Resurrection and Transubstantiation, Papal Infallibility, the Trinity, Virgin Birth and all that stuff, I knew it all with footnotes, right? So please, if it's within your power, please don't let it be that Benjamin and Mrs Franklin saw through my drag at the Art Gallery. Please let them think it was just another fat grannie out with her sister. I know, we both know they were giving us funny looks, but don't let them make the connection. It's extremely important. So please, if they had any suspicion, please dispel it from their minds. (*Starting to stand, then kneeling again*) And I'll start going to Mass again. (*Starting to stand, then kneeling*) Amen.

(MAN *makes sign of the cross. Telephone rings.*)

Shakespeare Speech and Drama. Good ... Mrs Franklin!

BLINK

TUESDAY 16TH

Several flashes from camera flashbulb. Lights up. MAN *is in spot. He takes one final snap.*

MAN: Hmmmmm. Very good, Ben. I should be able to get something from these photos. I don't think it's physical or, um, but well, we'll see. They, er, probably won't be much use but ... Okay. Talk to me. What are your other interests besides hairdressers? Have you seen the exhibition at the Art Gallery? What did you think of it? No, I haven't seen it.

(*Pause.*)

Um, do you like sports? Yes, it is pretty boring, isn't it?

(*Pause.*)

How's your clap?

BLINK

WEDNESDAY 17TH

Mid morning. Telephone rings. MAN *answers it.*

MAN: Bruce? Hi.

(*Pause.*)

I *couldn't* ring last night. After Ben came I got smashed. We're in the clear. In fact, Mrs Franklin thinks I'm a genius. She's most effusive about the change I've wrought in Benjamin's speech. How's that, eh? *And* she's got a girlfriend who can't pronounce her Ws and she's going to highly recommend me to her. That's the beauty of Toorak: everyone knows everyone and everyone wants to speak gooder than the next. It's like a big fat rich interwoven network of speech defects.

(*Pause.*)

I'm not sure. I think Benjamin knows. It was weird. Like he knew and he knew I knew or knew that I thought he knew or knew I knew he thought it was me, oops I, but he wasn't going to say anything. As it's our little secret. Anyway, it's all right.

(*Pause.*)

Bruce, he wouldn't. I know it. He's a good boy. It doesn't matter. He wouldn't say anything. Look, you're being silly. I don't even know if he knows, so why worry?

(*Pause.*)

Look Bruce, I don't give a fuck what the Stock Exchange thinks ... *Bruce!* What do you want me to do? Shoot him! He doesn't know. Relax. (*Soothing*) Come over now. Right away. Okay? Bye.

(MAN *slumps, tired. The sun is setting. Telephone rings.*)

Shakespeare Speech and Drama. Bruce. Don't tell me, let me guess. You're taking Edith and the kids to the circus. You can't come over and you're dreadfully sorry. You wish to offer your apologies, which I accept. You're a creep. Goodbye.

(*He slams the receiver down. Telephone rings again immediately.*)

Listen, shithead—Ah, Mrs Franklin? I'm dreadfully sorry, I thought it was someone else. Pardon? ... No, um, I don't think so. As far as I'm aware there are no neurotic side effects to speech therapy. He keeps nagging at you to what? To stop going to your hairdresser? Oh, he wants you to change hairdressers? Hahaha. Um, no. I can't really explain that, Mrs Franklin. But as a matter of fact, he did tell me that you take him there to get his hair cut. Is that right? Well, he mentioned something about the assistant, the apprentice. I gather she cuts both your hairs, I mean she gives both your heads—ah, pardon? She's a he? You mean the apprentice is a man? (*Shocked*) Oh, um. No I, er, can't explain why he doesn't want you to go there, Mrs, er, Franklin but well, if he's that insistent, perhaps you should change hairdressers. Um, you see, stuttering is a funny sort of thing. No one can really explain why we stutter. It's a peculiarly Western phenomenon, and, um, he should be under as little pressure as possible. See, there are two schools of thought. If you give in and change hairdressers, you might be spoiling him, thus aggravating his desire for attention, thus prolonging his stutter. *Or* if you don't back down, then you might be putting more pressure on him and reinforcing his stutter. Do you understand? Look, for the present, Mrs Franklin, take him to a different barber, perhaps a men's barber, and I'll have a chat with him next Tuesday and see what I can find out. All right? Bye bye.

(MAN *puts down telephone. Silence. He turns to bust.*)

I'm going to have a serious talk to that boy.

(*Silence.* MAN *puts on overcoat, muttering, exits front door OP. Light changes slightly.* MAN *enters with bag of groceries, still muttering, exits to kitchen. He enters with paper bag full of pharmaceutical things and takes them out. He selects a pack of photographic prints and slowly leafs through them. He moves to window, shuts the blinds, moves to rolltop desk and gets out leather gloves. He exits P door with gloves and photos, then re-enters and dials on the telephone.*)

Service-phone? Oh hello, pet. Don't you ever stop working? Listen, take my calls tonight and I'll get them in the morning.

(*Pause.*)

Yes, I'm in love again. We've got a date tonight. (*Looking at photos*) Yep. She's as pretty as a picture.

(*Pause.*)

Who? Benjamin Franklin? Don't you mean Mrs Franklin? Oh. What was the message? He's what? Would you repeat that? He's got some *better* photos for me? Are you sure that's what he said? Jesus. Um, is that all? Thanks.

(MAN *puts down telephone and looks at bust.*)

Jesus, William. The little bastard's trying to seduce me.

BLINK

THURSDAY 18TH

MAN: (*in spot, after a long pause*) Um. Listen, Benjamin. Did you ring me Wednesday? Uh huh. You, er, knew it was me, oooops I, at the Art Gallery, didn't you? Your Mum didn't . . . thank Christ. Um, and it was you outside my window the other night when . . . I was with my friend? Um. And your hairdresser friend who's such a great gobbler is . . . a man? A boy? Freddy? Listen Ben, kids of your age often . . . well they often . . . fool around with, um, with kids of their own . . . sex. It's normal. It's a phase we all go through. But you have to be careful, especially when you do things with older men. Even sixteen year old men. Because when you're twelve, well, sixteen is bloody old. Do you understand what I'm saying? I mean that hairdresser could get into all sorts of shit for . . . interfering with you. And he's only sixteen. But . . . when you get to fifty-six like I am, and when you are a teacher with lots of young kiddies under you, like I am, well, you wouldn't believe what sort of shit they can throw at you. Pederasty, sodomy, corrupting minors, indecent assault on children, homosexual rape, statutory rape. I mean, the things they can *do* to dirty old men . . . well it's frightening. I think they can *whip* me. And, Jesus, if your Mum found out, well, they have ways of telling if a little boy isn't . . . isn't a virgin where they should be virgins (*pause*) all their lives. So all the cops have to do is take one look at my rack of dresses and one look up your arse and they'll just throw away the key.

(*Pause.*)

Stop preening, Benjamin, this is serious! Listen, I'm flattered that you should want to interfere with me and if you were old enough to know what you were doing or, more importantly, old enough for the cops and lawyers and judges and parliamentarians to say you were old enough to know what you were doing, then it would be different. I'd probably make like the proverbial rat. But you're not. You're a kid. You're the sort of kid they have on TV to sell Crazy Maze and Kellogg's Cornflakes. You're the sort of kid that judges and juries want to protect from perverts. *Capisce*?

(*Pause.*)

Stop preening! Look, I've been teaching kids long enough to know things have changed. When I was your age, I thought my cock was something you pissed out of then rushed to Confession with at the first sign of tumescence. Huh? Um, stiffening. When I was twelve years old, you see, twelve years old meant twelve years old. It meant you were (*indicating small height*) that tall and you had a bicycle and a dog. I know things are different. Kids are different. It seems like you're all rushing from diapers to dope without stopping to be cute. See. I know. There's something . . . something weird going on with your generation like . . . there's been a nuclear explosion that no one noticed and we're breeding a race of mutants. But, the point is this. Out there, *Father Knows Best* and *Leave It To Beaver* is the *law*. If I laid a hand on you, if you told your Mum what you know, then I'm fucked. Besides, in spite of that nuclear explosion and the ten year old gang-bangers and the primary school skinheads and all your big talk and bullshit, you are twelve years old. And I am your teacher. Did you bring any photos? Let me have them. (*Glancing at one*) Jesus! (*Going through the rest of them in astonishment*) You ought to be ashamed of yourself.

(*Long pause as he thinks.*)

Okay, listen to me. (*Pocketing the photos*) If you've got any more photos, or love-letters, get rid of them. Because, sooner or later, Mum will find them then you're headed for Childrens' Court or, worse, a psychiatrist and I'm headed for gaol. Understand? Two. Don't tell *anyone* who's straight what you're doing, because . . . straights hate. And if anyone talks then we're both in trouble and so's your poxy hairdresser. Three. There is no way that I am going to touch you. I'm too old and I have, believe it or not, a code of ethics. In any case (*waving photos*) these are plenty. So you can stop preening like a princess. Four. Think seriously about whether you want to come here. Because if you're not serious about acting, piss off. I can teach you a lot, Benjamin, and I can open doors for you, but it's on my terms. Hmmmm? Five. Try women. I was married to one. They're fun. They've got tits. They feel nice. Try it, you might find you like it.

(*We hear a car horn outside.*)

That's your Mum. Don't forget, that bum of yours is a time bomb. Huh? See you next week. (*As we hear front door opening*) And do your bells!

(*Door closes. Lights slowly come up to reveal room. MAN looks at photos fondly, then looks at his watch.*)

Shit. The party!

(*MAN hurries off, then re-enters with wig, slip, stuffed bra, high heels. He puts on the wig and high heels, then lights a cigar. He takes his trousers off to reveal pink knickers. He puts on the bra and slip and exits, P. He re-enters with dress on and starts to put on make-up in front of small mirror. We hear a rock breaking the bay window, loudly. MAN looks up, startled. The Venetian blinds are open. Another rock.*)

VOICE: (*off*) Get out of Toorak, poofter!
SEVERAL VOICES: Yeah. Get out of here. (*Etc, ad lib.*)

(*Another rock. MAN walks quickly to window, closes Venetian blind. Noises continue outside during remainder of scene. MAN walks to telephone, dials and waits nervously.*)

MAN: Bruce. It's me. Listen, for once in your life. *Listen.* I want you to take care of Benjamin for me. Take him to David. I haven't got time. There's going to be some nasty things happening. The party's off, pet. Oh ... and come visit me, will you? Goodbye.

(*Another rock comes through the window. MAN hangs up. We hear a police siren. MAN makes a pile out of the photos, exits P door, comes back with letters and a notebook which he shreds into pile. He lights it. Knock on door.*)

VOICE: (*off*) Open up, please. It's the police.

(*MAN picks up shotgun.*)

MAN: (*sweetly*) Just a minute.

VOICE: (*off*) Open up, please. It's the police.
MAN: Just a minute.
VOICE: (*off*) All right, you people, shut up and stop throwing those rocks.

(*Long silence. Cuckoo clock strikes loudly. MAN fires at it. It explodes.*)

VOICES: (*off*) He's got a gun. Jesus, he fired a gun. (*Etc, ad lib.*)
VOICE: (*off*) Listen, friend, that won't do you any good.
MAN: (*sweetly*) Just a minute.

(*MAN seats himself comfortably with cigar in mouth, watching the pile burn.*)

END ACT TWO

1976

PATRICK WHITE

From *The Twyborn Affair*

Seated beside the fire, irritably agitating an ankle beneath her broad sable hem, she bent and picked up her sleeping Maltese dog, to comfort one who was in no need of comforting.

. . .

As the only conscious male present, perhaps he should put on another log, for Greg had let out the faint sizzle of a snore, followed by a short, querulous fart.

Marcia immediately raised her voice. 'Don't you think you ought to go to bed, darling? We know you're tired. Eddie will forgive you.'

The old boy rose, tottering like an enormous cherubic baby, and said after sliding his hand down one of his protégé's shoulder blades, 'Anyway I think I'll—take a little nap. See you later, everyone.'

After that there was an opening and closing of doors, a lavatory flushed, and a final closing.

Marcia said, 'He's taken a great fancy to you. Greg badly wanted a son. I failed him. But he doesn't hold it against me. He's a good man in all his instincts. That's what makes it more dreadful.'

'Why should it?' His teeth were chattering.

'If a man is truly good, he rises above hurt. We're the ones who are hurt.'

She sat watching her own tossed ankle. 'What do you think of Prowse?' she asked.

'I haven't thought about him enough.' He wondered whether she would know he was lying.

'No,' she said. 'Prowse is a human animal. No more. But the poor brute has suffered.'

Marcia too, was shivering, hugging herself more closely inside her Oriental coat.

He bent down and began clumsily stacking logs on the fire.

'Rather extravagant!' she twittered.

The fresh logs spat and crackled.

Marcia was leaning forward in the direction of the renewed flames. 'Do you know about the bogong moth?'

He did of course, but was not allowed to resist the reprise she was launching into, '. . . up into the mountains at a certain time of year, to eat this moth. It's said to taste rich and nutty . . .'

Hunched above the crumpled poppy in her beige cleavage, she had parted her lips on the strong teeth, in the gaps between which the downy sacs of moths might have been disgorging their nutty cream.

Marcia herself at that moment was not unlike a great downy moth irrationally involved in an obscene but delicious cannibalistic rite; in which she must involve some other being for his initiation or destruction.

She said, in a very intimate voice, for they were both crouched over the fire, 'No one has been able to explain to me why you came here. There's something too fine about you for this kind of life.'

He was balanced again on the razor-edge of motives, between truth and lies. 'I wanted to live simply for a while. To think things out. Yes, to think.'

She said sourly, 'You've come to the very worst place! It numbs thought, or pinches it out. We've hardly one between us.'

'There's the country.'

'Oh, yes, there's the country!' She threw back her thick, creamy throat, and closed her eyes, and smiled with the expression of fulfilment which explained what Prowse had said of her. 'The country itself is what makes it possible—even at its worst, its bitterest. But one needs more than that, surely?' She opened her eyes and looked at him. 'Wouldn't you agree, Eddie Twyborn?'

How false was Marcia Lushington of the grand piano for standing things on, the Spode tureen, the French Burgundy, and mock-Tudor dining room? He couldn't very well decide for being something of a fake himself.

'I think,' she said, and now she was probably dead-level honest, 'you may have something I've always wanted. That fineness I mentioned.'

'What about your husband? A good man. Isn't that something better than whatever this "fineness" may be?'

She bared her wide-spaced teeth in what was a mirthless smile, and he found himself responding to it, while repelled. 'Oh yes, we know all that! The good—the virtuous—they're what we admire—depend on to shore us up against our own shortcomings—with loving affection.'

She feel silent after that, and looked down along his wrist, his thigh.

'The other,' she said, 'needn't be lust, need it?'

Half burnt half chilled beside the leaping fire, he discovered himself, to his amazement and only transitory repugnance, lusting after Marcia's female forms.

They stood up simultaneously. If they had hoped to escape by withdrawing from the heat of the fire, the diminishing circles of warmth inside the room brought them closer together.

Her body was a revelation of strength in softness.

'What about Greg?' It was his conscience letting out a last gasp.

'He won't wake this side of daylight.' She sounded ominously certain.

She led him through a frozen house from which the servants had already dispersed, either to its fringes or its outhouses. They bumped against each other, slightly and at first silently, then in more vigorous, noisy collusion, the little Maltese terrier staggering sleepily behind them, trailing the plume of his tail.

When the sky had started greening she switched on the lamp to verify the time. They were by then a shambles of sheet and flesh, the Maltese dog exposing in his sleep a pink belly and tufted pizzle.

Switching back to green darkness she said, 'I was right, Eddie.'

'About what?' Considering his own respect for the old man her husband, he was not too willing to allow Marcia Lushington the benefit of knowing her own mind.

'The fineness.'

'Oh, *stuff*!'

He started extricating himself from what he had begun to see as a trap, a sticky one at that.

'Perhaps I'm wrong after all,' she murmured and heaved. 'Perhaps all men are the same. The same crudeness. Blaming you for what they've had.'

'It isn't that,' he said. 'You wouldn't understand. Or would be too shocked if I tried to explain.'

She was hesitating in the dark.

'Why? We didn't do anything perverse, did we? I can't bear perversion of any kind.'

Bumping and shivering, he started putting on his clothes. Once the Maltese terrier whimpered.

'Eddie?' Again she switched on the light. 'Men can be so brutal. And you are not. That's why I'm attracted to you. I don't believe you'd ever hurt me by refusing what I have to offer.'

Heaped amongst the blankets, the crisscrossed sheets, and punch-drunk pillows, her mound of quaking female flesh appeared on the verge of sculpturing itself into the classic monument to woman's betrayal by callous man. What he looked like, half-dressed in underpants, shirt-tails, and socks with holes in the heels, it gave him gooseflesh to imagine.

'Even if you haven't quite the delicacy I'd hoped for, perhaps we could comfort each other,' she blurted through naked lips, 'in lots of un-demanding ways.'

He buckled his belt, which to some extent increased his masculine assurance, but it was not to his masculine self that Marcia was making her appeal. He was won over by a voice wooing him back into childhood, the pervasive warmth of a no longer sexual, but protective body, cajoling him into morning embraces in a bed disarrayed by a male, reviving memories of toast, chilblains, rising bread, scented plums, cats curled on sheets of mountain violets, hibiscus trumpets furling into sticky phalluses in Sydney gardens, his mother whom he should have loved but didn't, the girl Marian he should have married but from whom he had escaped, from the ivied prison of a tennis-court, leaving her to bear the children who were her right and fate, the seed of some socially acceptable, decent, boring man.

He was drawn back to Marcia by the bright colours of retrospect, the more sombre tones of remorse. He lowered his face into the tumult of her breasts.

'There,' she murmured, comforting, 'I knew! My darling! My darling!'

She was ready to accept him back into her body; she would have liked to imprison him in her womb, and he might have been prepared to go along with it if they hadn't heard the rushing of a cistern in the distance.

'I better go,' he mumbled.

'Oh, no! It's only his bladder. I know his form. Poor old darling! You don't live with someone half a lifetime without getting wise to every movement of the clockwork.'

The little dog whinged, and dug a deeper nest in the blankets in which to finish his normal sleep.

'Eddie?'

He resisted her warmth reaching out through the dark to repossess him. He withdrew into the outer cold, not through any access of virtue, rather from disgust for his use of Lushington's wife in an attempt to establish his own masculine identity. Marcia apart, or even Marcia considered, women were probably honester than men, unless the latter were sustained by an innocent strength such as Greg Lushington and Judge Twyborn enjoyed.

As Eddie let himself out into the night the images of Eadie his mother and Joan Golson joined forces with that of Marcia Lushington, who had, incredibly, become his *mistress*! [. . .]

Eddie went stumbling down the hill through the increasing green of the false dawn, the light from an outhouse window, and the scented breath of ruminating cows. In his own experience, in whichever sexual role he had been playing, self-searching had never led more than briefly to self-acceptance. He suspected that salvation most likely lay in the natural phenomena surrounding those unable to rise to the spiritual heights of a religious faith: in his present situation the shabby hills, their contours practically breathing as the light embraced them, stars fulfilled by their logical dowsing, the river never so supple as at daybreak, as dappled as the trout it camouflaged, the whole ambience finally united by the harsh but healing epiphany of cockcrow.

Scattering a convocation of rabbits, he went in through the hedge of winter-blasted hawthorns, into the mean cottage in which physical exhaustion persuaded him it was his good fortune to be living. He lay down smiling, and slept, under the dusty army blankets, in the grey room.

That noon, while enjoying the luxury of a solitary Sunday frowst, after the minimum of cold mutton with mustard pickle, and the dwindling warmth of a brew of tea, he heard a sound of hooves and the metal of a horse's bridle. He looked out and saw, not his mistress of last night, but Mrs Lushington his employer's wife tethering her hack to the rail outside the feed room.

It was startling in these circumstances and at this hour of day. He heard himself muttering. He took up the pot to pour another cup of tea, by now tepid and repulsive, but found himself instead draining the pot to its dregs through the spout.

Fortified, if ashamed, he went out to the encounter with this stranger already knocking at the door.

'I hope I'm not intruding,' she began what sounded a prepared speech. 'Usually on Sunday, after lunch, I go for a ride, otherwise Ham gets out of hand. As I was passing this way I thought I'd look in—see how they're treating you—whether they've made you comfortable.'

She smiled out of unadorned lips, unnatural only in dealing with a rehearsed recitative.

He brought her in, or rather, she brought herself.

She said, 'It's a horrid little house if you look at it squarely.'

'I've grown attached to it.' He might begin resenting Marcia.

'At least in your case it's only temporary.'

Her conscience salved, she started stalking through the house as though she didn't own it and hadn't been there before; perhaps she hadn't. For Sunday afternoon and the land which was hers, she was shabbily dressed, in the old dead-green velour and stretched cardigan in natural wool, with riding pants which, in spite of exclusive tailoring, did not show her at her best. As she went she peered into rooms, dilating and contracting her nostrils in the manager's doorway while glancing with a frown at the photographs of Kath and Kim, murmuring on reaching the cook's bedroom, 'Poor Peggy Tyrrell—rough as bags, but such a dear,' turning her back on Eddie Twyborn's unmade bed.

When they reached the dining-kitchen she started rapping on the oilcloth, which made the crumbs on its surface tremble and her engagement finger flash.

'I ought to apologize,' she said, teeth champing on the words the other side of those bland lips, 'for anything that happened. It was my fault. Oh, I know you'd think it was, Eddie, even if I didn't admit it. Because you're a man.'

She paused as though giving him a chance to exonerate her.

'I shouldn't have thought of blaming you,' he said. 'It was a moment of shared lust. It surprised me that I enjoyed it. But I did.'

Marcia looked most surprised. She suppressed a little gasp. Her eyes were glowing. 'Well,' she said, 'it isn't the sort of thing a man usually says to his mistress. I knew I was right. You're different, Eddie. You have a quality I've always hoped for—and never found—in a man.'

'To me it's only conscience—for having fucked the wife of a man I respect.'

'Oh, darling,' she breathed, all the masculinity gone out of the tailored riding breeches, the imperiousness out of her engagement finger, 'don't put it like that! I adore my husband. That's something else.'

She was reduced to cajoling sighs, and whimpers she might have learnt from her Maltese terrier, and whiffs of the perfume she had been wearing the night before, which he now realized was predominantly hyacinth, and that hyacinth is haunted by the ghosts of wood-smoke and warm ash.

She might, they might both have wanted it again, wood-smoke and ash and all, on the army blankets of his unmade bed. She had brushed against him, the full breasts, the fleshy lips. He was about to respond when repugnance took over.

She said, 'You're right, darling,' and re-settled the green velour.

Then they were walking back along the passage, from which rooms opened in accordance with the accepted pattern, from suburbia to the Dead Heart. Their feet went *trott trott* over the linoleum lozenges.

Her voice cut in. 'Have you noticed how the exceptional person almost never turns up in the beginning?'

'But Greg—the husband you love—the man I'm fond of?'

'Yes,' she moaned, 'I love him.'

They had reached the fly-proof door. He must let her out before they established whose dishonesty was the greater.

'What about this Sunday ride you were on about—to work the oats out of your horse?'

'Well,' she said, 'yes. Do you want to come for a breath of air? You look pale—Eddie. Then we'll go back to tea with Greg.'

She gave him a rather wan smile. The flesh seemed to have slipped from her cheekbones, the eyes more enormous and liquid than ever: she had assumed that invalid expression he had noticed in those who suffer from guilt, or who hope to effect a complete conversion.

Again he felt physically drawn to her. He could have fucked her on the fallen hawthorn leaves amongst the rabbit pellets.

She must have felt they were preparing a desecration, for she coughed and said, 'Mrs Quimby makes the loveliest pikelets. We always have them for Sunday tea. Greg insists on them.'

While he went to saddle his horse, she was fiddling with hers, stroking his neck, adjusting the girth, generally seducing Hamlet her overfed bay.

'Why,' she called when he re-appeared, 'the *Blue Mule!*'

He laughed back. 'I've become attached to him too.'

'Oh, but that's typical! We must find you something—something more appropriate.'

'How "typical"?' he asked.

'Of Prowse.'

'But why?'

She had lapsed into a mystery of silence and the wood-smoke of stale hyacinth perfume, which a brash wind set about exorcizing.

They were heading in the direction she had chosen, or which, perhaps, had been chosen for them. His dislocated nag had difficulty in keeping up with her splendidly paced bay gelding. Hamlet gave the impression of responding to his rider's wishes without surrendering his independence. Ears pricked, neck arched, his eyes surveyed the landscape from under sculptured lids. From time to time he snorted through veined nostrils, either in surprise, or out of contempt.

The Blue Mule galumphed slightly to the rear or, if his rider succeeded in coaxing him level with their companions by dint of heel-kicks, bumped Hamlet's flank. Occasionally there was a clash of stirrup-irons and grazing of boot against boot. Some of their progress was humiliating for Eddie Twyborn, some of it comforting: like keeping up with Mummy.

It made him laugh at one point, breaking in on Marcia's thoughtfulness. She had fallen silent as though brooding over the acres which, seemingly, she loved, or perhaps dissecting her questionable adultery of the night before.

'What is it?' She laughed back less in mirth than from sociability.

'I believe you know my mother,' he said.

She began by a series of little murmurs implying denial. 'Yes and no,' she admitted at last. 'We've met. I'm *acquainted* with Eadie Twyborn, but you couldn't say we *know* each other.'

'Where,' he asked, 'does acquaintanceship end and knowing begin?'

Their horses carried them forward as Marcia considered in silence and frowns how she might answer that great social question.

'Do we know each other?' he asked.

She bit an unpainted lip. 'You have a streak of cruelty!' But had to laugh finally. 'I hope we know each other—and shall deepen our friendship.' She reached out and stroked the back of his hand. 'I need you.'

But he persisted; it must have been the 'cruel streak', 'You don't answer my question: where acquaintanceship ends and friendship begins, and why my mother remained the wrong side of the barrier.'

Marcia frowned one of those frowns which blackened the skin between her eyebrows. She must have dug her spurs into Hamlet, for he started cavorting and she had to rein him back. Only when she had brought him round on a curve, almost nose to nose with that abnormality the Blue Mule, was she prepared or forced to answer.

'Well,' she said, 'as you've asked for it, I'll tell you what I think of Eadie Twyborn. She's a frowzy old drunken Lesbian—who once made a pass at me,' she said.

'Shouldn't you feel flattered? Any pass is better than none.'

'Ugh!' she regurgitated. 'Not between women. And that nice man—the Judge.'

She rode ahead aloof and virtuous, until the Blue Mule chugged abreast again.

'Of course there are some women,' she said. 'Take Joan Golson—Eadie's friend—everybody knows about that. You couldn't hold it against Joan—not altogether—because she's in most ways—so—so *normal*. You must have met the Boyd Golsons although you were away so many years.'

Eddie muttered that he was acquainted, but did not know them. Marcia may not have heard; she had fallen into a trance, from which she issued in the tone of voice they adopt for money and pedigrees.

'. . . frightfully rich in all directions . . . Joan was Joanie Sewell of Sewell's Felt. Ghastly if you come to think, but substantial. And Curly—Golson's Emporium. Curly's the bore of bores, but another substantial investment. So there you are.'

'A normal conjunction.'

'But darling,' she screamed against the wind while seizing his wrist, 'leaving Joan Golson aside—and Eadie—it was you who brought your mother up—I just don't care to associate with abnormality.' After a little pause she continued, 'Some women are *inveterate*.' He wondered where she had learnt it. 'They adore to have queer men around. They find it amusing. A sort of court fool. I couldn't bear to touch one.'

'You must have touched a few,' he suggested, 'a few of your women friends' fools—if only in shaking hands.'

She said, 'Oh well—as a social formality one has to—don't you understand? Fortunately,' she added, 'most of them go away to Europe. They're too ashamed.'

The riders rode.

The winter sun was forcibly withdrawn behind a sliver of nacreous cloud. The hills undulated in time with the horses' gait, or at least with Hamlet's. Eddie's disastrous mount only created a tumult, as though they were stumbling over molehills or excavated rabbit warrens.

Marcia remarked, 'Nobody understands or loves this part of the world as I do. Not even Greg who was born here. None of them.'

He saw no reason for questioning the sincerity of what she had said.

'I believe Don understands how you feel,' he told her.

'*Don!*' She bared her wide-spaced teeth as she had at the moment when telling about the bogong moths and he had visualized her devouring them. 'What has Prowse been saying? That crude and repulsive man.'

'Only that you love the country.'

'Oh.'

She subsided after that.

They had completed a circuit, he realized, and were returning towards the homestead and the clutter of cottages and sheds which comprised the heart of the Lushington property of 'Bogong'. The paddocks were a grey-green like Marcia Lushington's old velour. They rode past eruptions of wiry briar, graced by notes of tingling scarlet and a flickering of wings or incipient leaves. Invisible birds were calling through the cold air along the river, the wraiths of curlew or plover; he could not have told; Marcia would have.

Suddenly she began chanting, at no one so much as the landscape spread out before them, 'A foreigner came here once—one of those complacent Hunter Valley squatters—and said—behind my back of course—that "Bogong" is sterile country. Would you dismiss it as that having lived here?'

'Hardly barren. You'd be out of business if you were,' he tried to console.

'Oh,' she coughed, or spat, 'you're talking like a man now! *Business—*super-phosphate—*cross*breeding!'

She turned in her saddle and wrenched his hand from the pommel where it was resting.

She said, 'Darling, you know what I mean.'

He did, but he couldn't do anything for her.

They rode on hand in hand till they reached the outskirts of the Lushington garden and the walled graveyard he had found on the occasion of a walk.

They drew in their horses outside the elaborate gate, or perhaps Hamlet knew where to halt.

'Did somebody—did *Prowse*,' Marcia asked, 'tell you about this too?'

'He told me only that Greg had wanted a son.'

'All men do, I expect,' she said, 'to vindicate themselves.'

'I think I'd prefer a daughter.'

'But you're more sensitive, Eddie,' she blurted, 'whatever you may do or say to destroy my opinion of you.'

Briskets pressed to the wall, the resting horses forced him to read the inscriptions on the headstones inside:

GREGORY LUSHINGTON
born 28 May 1912
died 5 August 1912

GREGORY LUSHINGTON
born 5 May 1914
died 6 January 1915

GREGORY DONALD PROWSE LUSHINGTON
born 17 May 1917
died 19 November 1918

The riders did not linger.

'Why "Donald Prowse" if you despise him?' he asked as they rode away.

'Oh—it was after Kath walked out. Greg wanted to do something for him. I did too, for that matter. We thought it might help to make him our child's godfather. The child died,' she ended. 'He died.'

They rode on, the horses bowing their heads, so it seemed, though of course they were returning to home, fodder, and idleness.

After unsaddling their horses at the stables, they walked towards the house, where they saw Mr Lushington had come out and was waiting for them, the lenses of his spectacles discs of gold.

Adopting a tone of jovial annoyance, he told them, 'I'd begun to worry.'

'Why? That I'd fallen off?' asked his wife chidingly.

'No. That the pikelets would go soggy, and Mrs Quimby give notice.'

'We'll eat them soggy or not,' Mrs Lushington declared. 'As far as I'm concerned, pikelets are a means of conveying melted butter to the mouth.'

She gave her companion a melting smile at the same time as her husband brushed up against his son *manqué*.

'Did you have a good ride?' Mr Lushington asked Eddie.

'Yes,' she answered for him. 'And talk. So much better than stewing in the house over old stud books and agricultural pamphlets.'

'Oh,' said Mr Lushington, 'what did you talk about?'

'Things,' Mrs Lushington replied. 'Life, I suppose. But not in any intellectual way. So you needn't worry.'

He hiccuped once or twice and stumbled on the steps they were mounting.

'If you'd like to know, I didn't stew over old stud books or agricultural stuff.'

'What did you do then?' his wife asked with an aloofness which suggested she was listening intently as she took off her stretchy cardigan and faded velour.

'I wrote a poem,' Mr Lushington confessed.

'Those!' she sighed, tizzing up her hair, and when they had emerged into stronger light, 'You've got it over?'

He said he had—'more or less.'

They were all three staggering slightly.

'What was it about?' Mrs Lushington asked, now that it was out in front of one who was, in most essentials, a stranger.

Thus cornered, Greg Lushington bleated, not unlike one of his own stud rams, 'I expect it's about love—that's where everything seems to lead—in some form or other. Unfulfilled love.'

His wife hurried the party as quickly as she could towards a room referred to as the Library, where she knew the deliquescent pikelets would be found, and which housed the encyclopaedia, the dictionary, and her ration of novels from a lending library in Sydney. Anything else in the way of books, anything suggestive of Greg's vice, must have been hidden from neighbourhood eyes in some unfrequented attic.

The Lushingtons brightened at the prospect of pikelets and tea, and Beppi joined them from the kitchen regions where he must have scoured a pan already.

They distributed themselves in what was another neo-Tudor room: dark panels, stone fireplace, with a suite of leather furniture straining at its buttons where it wasn't sagging on its springs.

Marcia poured tea into Staffordshire cups skating uneasily in their saucers. Some of the service had been riveted. She heaped their plates with pikelets. Little embroidered napkins had been provided, which was just as well, for the Lushingtons were soon in a somewhat buttery condition.

He too, in their company, was transported back to nurseryland, to Mummy and 'your father', which was what the Lushingtons wanted, except that for a moment Marcia's pikelet must have turned to flesh, and Greg's mouthful to a difficult word in one of the disgraceful poems.

Greg wiped his fingers on one of the embroidered napkins; as fingers they were rather too delicate, and in their efforts to demonstrate their practical worth, one of them had gone missing; a thumb wore its purple nail like a medal; yet the palms, showing pink, were those of a rich and idle man, who mumbled through the last of his mouthful of pikelet, 'The word should have been "placebo"'' before dabbing at a trickle of butter.

'Oh God,' Marcia complained, 'I wonder what you'll come out with next.'

Wiping his fingers and turning to Eddie, Greg Lushington began telling, '. . . when I was a boy foxes used to kill the turkeys. We never heard a sound. But sometimes a terrier—we always kept a pack of them—would bring in a dead fox. All done most silently. Once, I remember, an old dog—Patch—almost blind with cataract—brought in a turkey gobbler's head instead. I had a governess, Miss Delbridge, who fancied herself at the piano. She was playing a Chopin mazurka at the time. As she was pedalling her soul away, Patch laid the turkey's head at her feet. A kind of love offering—or that's how I saw it.'

'A love offering!' Marcia exclaimed. 'How could a little boy have known?'

'By instinct of course—like dogs. I bet Eddie would have known.' Mr Lushington paused, thoughtfully exploring the corners of his mouth. 'Old men know more perhaps, but never grow as wise as they hope.'

The fire leaped in the stone hearth, then relapsed into a drowsier tempo; it should have been a comfort to those seated round it.

'Oh dear, all this is horrid—morbid. I wasn't expecting anything like it—with my pikelets—after our ride.'

Beppi must have interpreted her disapproval as an invitation. He started barking, and from lying on the sofa, jumped upon his mistress's lap, put his front paws on her bosom and started licking her glossy lips.

Mrs Lushington laughed. 'Disgusting little dog!' she shrieked, and pushed him down, but immediately snatched him back, and gave him a kiss on his wet blackberry of a nose.

'Hydatids, Marcia . . .' her husband warned.

Which she ignored. 'I adore you,' she told her dog, 'as you ought to know.'

Greg started groaning up out of his chair, not without a faint fart or two. 'I'm going to leave you,' he announced. 'There's something, I realize, I ought to alter in the last line.'

He was obviously obsessed by words, when Eddie had thought his obsessions lay almost anywhere else: sheep, worms, the sons he hadn't got.

He reproached Marcia for not having told him about the poems.

'Why should I have told?' She pouted. 'If you tell too much in the beginning there's nothing left for later on. That's why so many marriages break up.'

'Why are you against poetry?' he asked.

'I'm not. Everyone else is. So I don't make a point of flaunting it in their faces. It might put them off us. Actually, I always leave a book of verse on the stool in the visitors' lav. Nothing too long. Narrative poems,' she turned appealing eyes on him, 'are no go in a cold climate.'

Contrary to reason, his mistress was warming him again. He went and propped a knee on the sofa beside her, where a whiff of last night's perfume and a smell of cleanly dog rose up around him. At the moment he was perhaps drawn to Greg's unexpected dedication to poetry as much as to his wife's voluptuous charms. He was even disturbed by a ripple of grudging affection for his own mother. For it occurred to him that the unexpected in Eadie Twyborn was similar to that which linked the Lushingtons. He would have liked to share his discovery of their common trait, but remembering Marcia's antipathy, he confined himself to fingering her cleavage where a blob of butter, fallen from a pikelet, had hardened into what could have passed for one of Eadie's antique brooches.

'Darling,' Marcia sighed, looking up, 'not on Sunday, and while Greg is tidying a poem.'

So he realised that he was dismissed, and had better lump it, together with the Mule, down to the cottage. What surprised him more than anything was his desire to possess Marcia again, and in spite of the dangers inherent in the act.

With this thought, he pressed a kiss into her mouth, and was received into some buttery depths before firm rejection.

. . .

His horse had carried him perhaps a mile when he was overcome by drowsiness. He dismounted, and after tethering the mare to one of her front fetlocks, lay down beneath a tree, on the pricking grass, amongst the lengthening shadows. He did not sleep, but fell into that state between waking and sleeping in which he usually came closest to being his actual self.

This evening he started remembering or re-living an occasion, it was a Sunday afternoon, when he had felt the urge to see his fortuitous mistress. Never in his life had he felt so aggressive, so masculine, or so impelled by the desire to fuck this coarsely feminine woman. He deliberately thought of it as *fucking*, and spoke the word on his way up the hill between the cottage and the homestead. As he walked he was looking down at his coarse, labourer's boots which he was in the habit of treating with rendered-down mutton fat. The boots matched his intention, just as no other word would have fitted the acts he performed with Marcia, nothing of love, in spite of her protestations. Except on another, more accidental occasion when they had ridden together through the paddocks, sidestepping the imperfect expressions of perfection.

Each incident had taken place so long ago, if not in time, in experience, Eddie Twyborn could only watch them in detachment as he lay dozing or re-living beneath his tree, the face of Greg Lushington, that amiable absentee, re-forming amongst the branches. However intangible, Greg's presence made his own behaviour the coarser, the more shocking.

The house when he reached it on this Sunday afternoon had about it an air of desertion. A cat raised its head from where it was lying in a patch of winter sunlight. A wiry strand of climbing rose was rubbing deeper the scar it had worn on a corner of painted brickwork.

As he wandered round, considering his plan of attack, chains rattled against kennels, mingling with abortive barks and faint moans of affection for one who had ceased to be a total stranger. He entered by the kitchen door. The servants were gone, either to town or their own quarters. The only life in the living rooms was a stirring of almost extinct coals (on tables, copies of the London *Tatler* and library books from Sydney which amounted to Marcia's intellectual life).

He looked inside her bedroom more cautiously, for fear of disturbing a migraine or a monthly.

Silence and the absence of its owner played on the frustration growing in him.

He flung himself on the bed, of the same oyster- or scallop-tones as those of Marcia his mistress (incredible word). There was Marcia's familiar scent, not so much a synthetic perfume as that of her body. He lay punching at the down pillows, prising out of crumpled satin handfuls of opulent flesh, until present impotence and an undertow of memory forced him off the bed to rummage through the clothes hanging in the wardrobes.

Starting in frustration and anger, he was cajoled, pricked, and finally seduced by the empty garments, the soft and slithery, the harsh and grainy, the almost live-animal, which he held in his arms. He fumbled with his own crude moleskins, the bargain shirt from the Chinaman's store. The laces of his wrinkled boots, stinking of rancid mutton fat, lashed at him as he got them off. He stood shivering in what now passed for his actual body, muscular instead of sinuous, hairier than formerly, less subtle but more experienced.

He needed no guidance in entering the labyrinth of gold thread and sable, the sombre, yet glowing, brocaded tribute to one of Marcia's less neutral selves. And still was not satisfied by the image Marcia's glass presented.

He stormed at the dressing-table, roughing up his hair, dabbling with the beige puff in armpits from which the heavy brocaded sleeves fell back, outstaring himself feverishly, then working on the mouth till it glistened like the pale, coral trap of some great tremulous sea anemone.

He fell back on Marcia's bed.

And the foorsteps began advancing with a male assurance which had been his own till recently. Eudoxia Vatatzes lay palpitating, if contradictorily erect, awaiting the ravishment of male thighs.

The movement of her heart had taken over from all other manifestations as the door was pushed farther ajar, and the head intruded. It was Greg Lushington, sightless behind his spectacles. Neither the glare from Norwegian glaciers, nor the heady air of Himalayas or Andes could have blinded him, for he was still rooted in his own country of pale, nut-flavoured moths.

'I just wanted to tell you, Marce, that the word was wrong—in the poem, I mean. What I thought of as "placebo", you remember? ought to have been "purulence".'

Then he smiled, and immediately withdrew, not wanting to disturb his wife's rest.

And Eudoxia Vatatzes threw off her borrowed clothes, as Eddie Twyborn broke up the scene he was re-living in the gathering shadows, returning from the boundary paddock after a day's crutching.

He untethered his mare from her own fetlock and returned to the settlement known as 'Bogong', where Peggy Tyrrell, inside the illuminated kitchen, was engaged in the evening ritual of maltreating food into the semblance of a meal. Tonight there was a smell of onions — and was it beef on the boil instead of mutton? Some days earlier Jim Allen had destroyed a cow, her leg broken by a fall down a gully.

This luxury of cooking smells united with the stench of his own body, greasy wool, and tar from the anointing of sheeps' wounds and fly-blown wrinkles, while inside the shed, as he mixed his horse a feed, the sweet scents of chaff and oats mingled with the no less intoxicating, if baser stenches he had brought with him.

In the darkness beyond the feed-room proper, in the depths of the shed where a soft mountain of chaff was stored, a landslide had been started by a cat pursuing a rat. There was a deathly squeal as the cat pounced and worried its prey, growling at the human intruder.

From her stall the mare was whinnying at him impatiently. She glared and snorted, stamping on the brickwork with small, elegant, shod hooves. Her greed as he poured the oats and chaff whetted his own appetite for sodden onions and stringy cow passing as beef. (He would have liked to believe his own disguises more convincing. Well, it had been proved that they were.)

Leaving his ravenous horse to her feed he heard the iron door pushed farther open on grudging hinges. Against a sky paling into darkness it could only have been Prowse's bulk advancing unsteadily into the sweet must of the shed's enveloping gloom.

'What is it, Don? What've I done wrong this time?'

The form came shambling on. 'Wrong?' A familiar blast of whiskied breath was introduced into the gentler scents of the stable and the dusty draught from chaff set in motion by the huntress cat.

'Yes. I'd like to know. I never seem to do the right thing by you.' It wasn't quite honest.

'Nothing wrong, I suppose — Eddie — in being true to yerself.'

Prowse's bulk had reached the point where they were bumping against each other in the darkness.

Eddie realised that, up against this laborious drunk, he was simulating drunkeness.

'And what's myself?' he dared.

There was a pause, and the sounds of overheated, crackling iron and slithering chaff.

Till Prowse was prepared to come out with it. 'I reckon I recognised you, Eddie, the day you jumped in—into the river—and started flashing yer tail at us. I reckon I recognised a fuckun queen.'

All the while Don Prowse was pushing his bulk up against Eddie Twyborn's more slender offering.

'See?'

'If that's what you saw ...' Eddie knew that his voice, like his body, was trembling.

Prowse suddenly grew enraged. He, too, had started trembling in a massive way, smelling of sodden red hair almost stronger than the whiskey breath, shouting, pushing his opponent around and about with chest and thighs, spinning him face down in the chaff.

'A queen! A queen! A fuckun queen!' Sobbing as though it was his wife Kath walking out on him.

Prowse was tearing at all that had ever offended him in life, at the same time exposing all that he had never confessed, unless in the snapshot album.

His victim's face was buried always deeper, breathless, in the loose chaff as Don Prowse entered the past through the present.

Eddie Twyborn was breathing chaff, sobbing back, not for the indignity to which he was being subjected, but finally for his acceptance of it.

When Prowse had had his way they lay coupled, breathing in some kind of harmony.

Till the male animal withdrew, muttering what could have been, 'You asked for it—you fuckun asked ...'

And got himself out of the shed.

The victim lay awhile, wholly exhausted by the switch to this other role. Then stood up, chaff trickling down skin wherever it did not stick inside rucked-up shirt and torn pants—the disguise which didn't disguise.

Complete darkness had fallen outside, except where Peggy Tyrrell's sibyl, in the illuminated window across the yard, was rising through the steam from the suet pudding she was easing out of its cloth. She glanced up once into the outer darkness, her sibyl's eyes contracting, before resuming the ritual of her suet pud.

. . .

The following day was a Saturday, and Prowse had driven into town, to pubs and other less salubrious pastures, taking with him Mrs Tyrrell, who was looking forward to a scene with her mother and a funeral scheduled for the afternoon.

Towards four o'clock, after shaving and bathing, Eddie went up the hill to the house. He found Marcia alone on the verandah, reclining on an old bleached cane chaise. On her outstretched thighs, one of her library books, which more than likely she hadn't been reading, was lying spine upward. She was dressed in a worn grey flannel skirt and a blouse unbuttoned to the opulent cleavage, sleeves turned back to expose the elbows and the blue veins on the reverse side. Her arms were hanging listlessly for the brief but intense Monaro heat. Her face expressed a disenchantment, whether real or cultivated, radiating from a nose made thicker, soggier, by the heavy cold Mrs Tyrrell had reported.

'Can I be dreaming?' she said at last, cutting into the remark with a grudging smile, and coughing thickly to enlist her cold.

'No,' he said, 'I think we're real enough,' and laughed.

He sat down on an upright chair, another member of the suite in dilapidated, bleached cane.

Whereas he had planned to be cruel, biting, dramatic, he felt sympathetic towards her: it must have been those red, swollen eyelids, or else his bath had cooled him off. His clothes sat so lightly on him, he might in other circumstances have felt the urge to take them off, to stretch alongside her, no longer a lover, but some lean and ingratiating breed of hairless dog, licking her wrists, expecting an exchange of caresses.

'Why did you treat me like that? And as far as I can see, all because of the poor Golsons. Now, why?' She hectored mildly.

'I'm not prepared to go into that.' He sounded tense; his light mood was leaving him.

'You've made me very unhappy,' she told him, 'Eddie, dearest—for no good reason that I can imagine. When I most need your—company— your confidence, you treat me as though I'm in some way diseased.'

'They tell me Greg is expected back at any moment. That will be fine for you, Marcia.'

She almost suppressed a frown. 'Dear Old Greg! Not everyone appreciates him, but I think, Eddie, you do—you and your father.'

There was a silence in which the cane furniture showed signs of disintegrating.

Marcia said, 'I must go and make us some tea.'

'Don't bother.'

'But it's what we do at four o'clock. Don't expect a lot of food, though. Mrs Quimby's mumping over something or other, probably preparing to give notice.'

The fact that he, too, was more than probably going to leave made him melancholy, sitting on the Lushington's verandah with the river flat spread before him, the brown river meandering through bleached tussock, the sensuous forms of naked hills on either side: a landscape which had engaged his feelings in a brief and unlikely love affair he was about to end.

If all love affairs are not, perhaps, unlikely. Only the meat of marriage convinces, if you are made for it, and open to conviction.

A hornet was somewhere ceaselessly working on its citadel, and under the eaves hung a swallow's nest temporarily abandoned by its tenant, in each case evidence of the continuity which convinces animals better than it does human beings, unless they are human vegetables.

Marcia returned carrying a tray as though it were the sort of act she wasn't used to performing. Her shoulders drooped, her bare arms looked defenceless, even pathetic. Perhaps she expected him, as a lover, or simply as a man, to jump up and help her with the tray.

But he didn't: he was too distant, and at the same time too absorbed in everything happening around him, the fidgeting sound of the hornet, on the faded plain the brown river, static now, swift in memory, over the verandah tiles Marcia's shuffle in a pair of scuffed, once elegant, crocodile shoes.

She arranged the tray on a table, yet another member of the weathered cane family.

A generous wedge was missing from the jam sandwich, its pink icing buttoned down and slightly stained by a wreath of crystallised violets. Though a cake for a country occasion, the recalcitrant Mrs Quimbly had failed to pipe a message on it.

Marcia let off a misplaced giggle. 'There we are, darling!' She would have liked to appear girlish, but suspected at once that he would not allow her.

He sat, chin lowered, staring ahead. He saw himself, alas, as a farouche schoolboy refusing to let Mum have him on. Poor Marce didn't know about it, while he had the unfair advantage, at any rate since last night, of knowing almost everything.

She poured the tea, of a delicacy which must have been wasted on the district, and which they would have discussed afterwards: that hogwash of Marcia Lushington's.

Along with the barbarians, Eddie was not appreciative enough. The pink festive cake was stale. The cruel scene he had rehearsed would have to be enacted eventually.

'There you are,' she said very humbly as she tried a fragment of the cake, 'I warned you.'

'But did you?' His cup slithered like stone on the saucer, his chair grated on the tiled verandah.

While Marcia Lushington sat holding her teacup in both hands, to prevent a trembling from showing, and to let the steam take the blame for her watering eyes.

She protested, 'I don't understand. I thought you loved me.'

In his case, it was the crumbs of the stale cake which were trembling; he brushed them off with a disapproving, and as he saw it, suddenly old-maidish hand.

'I was fond of you,' he admitted; and then not too honestly, 'because affection was what I thought you wanted;' less honest still, 'I couldn't love you for respecting poor old Greg.'

She sat up jerkily on the edge of the grating chaise.

'There you've caught me out, Eddie. You've caught us both. Because,' and now it was her turn to look out along the bleached plain, 'I find I'm pregnant.'

The hornet was worrying the silence worse that ever, a fiery copper wire piercing but never aborting a situation the enormity of which could only be human.

Eddie began to laugh. It made Marcia look more becolded.

'However cynical you may like to be thought, I'm glad the child will be yours. Greg is fond of you,' she said, 'and it may be the son he and I have failed to get.'

'It might be another failure—like the one you had with Prowse.'

He thought the silence would never end: a balloon swelling and swelling, but never bursting, in spite of the hornet's efforts, in the late light of a summer afternoon.

When Marcia said, 'I don't know what you mean'.

'I was going by the names on the graves—as well as more positive evidence.'

She leaned forward, her chin broader for being propped on the heel of a hand. 'It could be Greg's—just—from before he went away. But you were what I wanted.'

'Or Prowse?'

She ignored it. He got up soon after. She was still staring at the breached cake, its yellow more unnatural, its pink more lurid in the evening light.

'I think you're cruel by nature,' she said.

He didn't answer: he was arranging his belt, because his manly shirt was coming out.

'Now I believe you're what I was told you are.'

He didn't bother to expose any of them worse than they were already exposed.

. . .

He awoke to hear the car manoeuvred under cover, the crackle of paper as parcels were undone in the kitchen, a man's curse when a wing was grazed on a corner of corrugated iron, a woman's sighs and invocations as the depths of her body, and even more, her spiritual tatters, caused her pain.

The walls of his normally putty-coloured room were spattered with light from the manoeuvred car, translucent patches, with iridescent threads superimposed as he rubbed his eyeballs to rid them of an itch and hurry them into awareness of what was happening. He reached down to cover up his nakedness, but fell back upon the stretcher where he had been dozing: it was too hot, it was too hot. He couldn't bother. The blanket too hairy. Since coming to 'Bogong' he had dispensed with sheets, out of masochism or delusions of masculinity.

The petals of light flowering on the walls were suddenly wiped out by darkness.

Silence was broken by the creaking of a fly-proof door, a renewed outburst of female sighs, male boots hurled against the wall of a fragile weatherboard house.

Any frail male could only cower and try to assemble an acceptable identity, any female, because tougher, more fibrous, consolidate her position inside the cloak of darkness.

Though Peggy did creep along the passage to hiss, 'I oughter warn yer, love, 'e's 'ad a fair few. Don't let yerself get drawn in. 'E's cantankerous ternight.'

After Prowse had martyrised the skirting-board with his boots, and let out a round fart or two, and the housekeeper had shut her door, silence again descended where the rats hadn't taken over, the rabbits and the hawthorns—night in fact, but not yet dreams.

'Eddie?'

It was Don Prowse in the doorway: a heavy body bungling, stomping, chafing, a voice reaching out after what it hoped might be conciliation. If the thought hadn't been so grotesque, Prowse was less cantankerous than what he probably considered seductive.

'Ed.' No query, it was pure statement in search of a solid presence.

The body continued advancing, stubbing its toes here and there, groaning, gasping. A rite of sorts had started taking place in the shuddering dark of this dry-rotted room.

'. . . you got me worried, boy. I never did anything like it before. Don't know what came over me. I been thinkin' about it—what you must think . . .'

The penitent must have had a fair idea of his bearings, either from instinct or from a glimmer of light the hawthorns allowed through their locked branches, for he reached a point where he crashed on the stretcher alongside its occupant.

Prowse was crying, expostulating, and apparently stark naked. Eddie's own fastidious nakedness became aware of prickling hair, tingling with moisture like a rain forest, at the same time the smell exuded by sodden human fur. He was surrounded by, almost dunked in, these practically liquid exhalations.

What was both alarming and gratifying, he knew that he was being won over, not by the orange brute so much as poor old Prowse of the snapshots with meticulous white-ink captions, the husband of Kath, and by the spirit of Angelos Vatatzes, whose cold eyelids and rigid feet still haunted memory.

It was too much for Eddie Twyborn to endure. He was rocking this hairy body in his arms, to envelop suffering in some semblance of love, to resuscitate two human beings from drowning.

Prowse managed to extricate himself. He rolled over.

'Go on,' he moaned, 'Ed!' and bit the pillow.

Eddie Twyborn's feminine compassion which had moved him to tenderness for a pitiable man was shocked into what was less lust than a desire for male revenge. He plunged deep into this passive yet quaking carcase offered up as a sacrifice. He bit into the damp nape of a taut neck. Hair sprouting from the shoulders, he twisted by merciless handfuls as he dragged his body back and forth, lacerated by his own vengeance.

Prowse was crying, 'Oh God! Oh Christ!' before a final whimper which was also his ravisher's sigh.

They fell apart finally.

Eddie said, 'Go on, Don. That's what it's about, that's what you wanted.'

He couldn't deny it, except, 'I hope you won't hold it against me, Eddie.'

'Go on, get out!'

Prowse heaved, protested, curled himself into the shape of a prawn against a form which, having vindicated itself, refused to respond. Prowse's sighs of entreaty, his redundancies of love, were surprisingly like Marcia's.

'If that's what you say—and feel.'

'All I want to say is, I'll catch the train tomorrow evening at Fossickers, and would like you to run me over, Don. Otherwise, if you'd rather, I'll hire a car from town.'

After a short whimpering silence, 'If that's what you've decided, I'll run yer there.'

A damp paw put out on a renewed voyage of exploration. Eddie Twyborn rejected it, in spite of the scabs on the obverse side, the dry cracks, and the freckles he remembered.

'Go on, Don—get!' It sounded unconvincingly male.

The manager heaved, the stretcher creaked. Prowse was diving in the direction of the doorway. He must have bumped his head or some other part of his anatomy on something more solid than darkness.

He cried out, 'Oh Jesus! Oh fuck!' before slewing round the corner into the passage, slithering several yards on the lino, and falling into his own room.

•   •   •

Mrs Tyrrell was tearful. 'I dunno wot's took you, Eddie. I thought you was more dependable. Most men aren't dependable. Rowley weren't— though 'e was me husband, an' dead since. The boys aren't—they got their wives. Only the girls. Well, that's 'ow it is. I thought you was different—like me daughters, but different.'

Eddie was at first embarrassed, then moved to feel her weather-cured face, together with a smear of tears, ground against his cheek. At the same time he became enveloped in the bobbled shawl, in whiffs of kero, eaudy Cologne, and the overall stench of mutton fat.

A brown-paper parcel was thrust at him. 'A few bloody sandwiches fer the journey. There's mustard in 'em ter make 'em more tasty.'

In the corrugated shed the manager was revving up the Ford, the afternoon light as remorseless as the fossicking hens.

Eddie Twyborn could only say, 'We'll write, Peggy,' regretting that it sounded so upper class.

''Oo'll write? You, if I'm lucky. But 'oo's gunner read it to me? 'Oo that I can trust—at "Bogong"—or anywheres—fer that matter?'

He got himself out, together with the greasy parcel, the suitcase and valise with which he had arrived, lighter for his boots and work clothes which he was leaving for Denny. The too ostentatious cabin trunk was already strapped to the rack.

The manager drove doggedly, his heavy hands bumped by the wheel. Eddie dared not look at the hands, let alone the face, which smelled overpoweringly of shaving soap.

In a paddock through which they were passing, sulphur-crested cockatoos were screeching as they tore down stooks of oats.

'Bloody cockies! You can't win,' Prowse mumbled; he sounded fairly acceptant for the moment.

'Greg'll be back,' he announced farther on, as though pleased to think his responsibility for marauding cockatoos, and anything else, might be ended by the owner's return. 'Nothing lasts for ever, eh?'

He glanced sideways, no doubt hoping for his passenger to corroborate, or even suggest that past events are expungeable if you put your will to it.

Eddie did not return the glance for fear of finding a mirror to his own thoughts. Instead, he glanced down and encountered the wristwatch. A utilitarian affair, sitting rather high on the hairy wrist, the watch was attached to a sweat-eaten strap, narrow to the point of daintiness. He had barely noticed this watch before. Now it wrung him. Had he been a child instead of this pseudo-man-cum-crypto-woman, he might have put out a finger and touched it, to the consolation of both of them.

In the light of shared desire, it was some consolation to himself to remember a moment in which he had embraced, not so much a lustful male, as a human being exposed in its frailty and tenderness.

This, of course, was no consolation to Don Prowse. Who knew. But only the half of it.

They drove bumping through the paddocks, and as on arrival, so on departure, brumby horses wheeled and approached, eyeing them through wild forelocks, sheep milled and halted and stamped, wooden masks conveying that expression of disbelief for the same two intruders, who had got to know each other in the meantime, so much better, or so much worse.

They drove, and arrived at Fossickers Flat.

Prowse looked at the wristwatch and grumbled, 'Don't know why you got us here so early.'

And Eddie replied, 'I arrive everywhere too early, or too late. It's my worst vice.' He laughed, but Prowse's expression could have been taken for thoughtful.

After unloading the luggage they stood about together on the siding.

'Look, Don, you don't have to hang about.'

But Don did: mouthing, swallowing words to which the thick lips failed to give birth.

'Should 'uv rung to reserve a sleeper. But you caught me on the hop, Ed.'

'Probably no sleepers left. Not at the last moment. Anyhow, I don't expect I'll sleep.'

Was it too perilous an admission? They crunched up and down the siding, beneath the painted sign FOSSICKERS FLAT. A rudimentary shelter might have offered asylum to a parcel, never to escaping prisoners or queered lovers. In the scrub across the track, the zither notes of small birds seemed to be conveying bird facts which evaded expression in human terms.

'We'll all miss you, Eddie.'

'Oh, go on, Don! Don't be a cunt—for God's sake go!'

GO!

Legs apart, shoulders hunched, the bare hills behind him, the man looked every bit a puzzled, panting, red ox.

But as time ticked away on the crude wristwatch, it was Eddie Twyborn awaiting the pole-axe.

'All right, Ed. All *right*!' Again the manager, Mr Prowse had matters in hand. 'You got yer bags. You'll get yer ticket on the train. I'll shove off.'

As he did.

Eddie turned his back on the diminishing trail of dust, and the Mail arrived eventually, the guard descending to jolly the ascending passenger.

'Not offn we get one at Fossickers, sir.'

After the two had heaved up the baggage, he flagged the engine.

Eddie Twyborn sat in the corner of his empty compartment and was rushed away, past the skeleton trees, the hill with its cairn of lichened rocks, faces hungry for events outside a shack at a level crossing. A bronzed, exhausted, country evening gave way to night, which had the smell of soot.

The brown-paper parcel had fallen off the seat on to the floor. He ought to pick it up.

He was too passive, it seemed. Jolted onward, through Bungendore and the rest, he closed his eyes. But did not sleep. Sleep might always be denied him, except in the form of dreams, or nightmares.

1979

SIMON PAYNE

From *The Beat*

Friday Night

It wasn't the first time Kevin had been poofter-bashing. They went quite often on a Friday night after drinking at the pub. If they didn't write themselves off and obliterate the week-end to come, they would go on a hunt of all the dunnies for a bit of sport. Poofters were pretty easy game and never squealed to the police after. They'd never done any real harm, it was just sport. One queer had got a pretty busted jaw the other week. It wobbled funny when he tried to speak and blood oozed from it. More like a fanny than a mouth by the time they had finished. A fanny needing rags.

Heads and balls usually got most of the punishment. Taught the queer bastards a lesson. That was what they used most, heads and balls, so that was what you went for. Stopped them practising their perverted ways for quite a while. Doing them a favour, and society too, keeping them out of the dunnies. You can't molest small boys if you have a pain in your gut because your stomach's been kicked in. They learn. They learn slow but they learn. Trouble is that there's always lots more to take their place.

There was this one guy they'd chased in the car one night. Spotlighting. Shit, you should have seen him run. He was so fast, dodging in and out of the headlights as they'd got him halfway across the park. They would have got him too, if it hadn't been for a tree that caused them to swerve and lose him. He went to ground so fast they lost him just like that. Cunning bastards, some of these poofters. Disappeared 'poof' into the air, that's what Kevin would say.

They should have chased him on foot but some of these queers are fast. All jogging around with their cocks trailing out of their shorts, as they run from dunnie to dunnie. It's getting harder to pick some of them these days. You can tell when they stand around limp-like, or when they speak, but it's hard to pick them on the run. Best way is to speak to them first, get their confidence; then when they speak back—whammo!

Kevin and his mate had got one the other day. He was walking along the footpath—must have been as blind as a bat. Broad daylight, there he was coming towards them, not looking at anyone. You could tell he was one of them by the way he walked, sort of like he had his knees tied together. Anyway, when he was about ten feet away, Kevin and his mate could see he was trying to stick to the fence, thinking he would get past them on that side. Kevin's mate moved over right up to the fence, so the poof had to pass between them. Just as he was going through, not looking at anyone, they closed in and knocked into him real hard. He reeled. For a second it looked as if he would lose his balance, but on he stumbled along the street. Didn't even look back at them.

'Ah,' Kevin yelled.

He took no notice. So Kevin yells again. The silly bastard turns and looks.

'Yes?' he says, polite as he could.

'Don't you look where you're going?' Kevin yelled.

The guy shrugged and turned. Kevin steps towards him.

'You bumped my mate,' he says. 'What you got to say?'

'Sorry,' says the poof, as if it doesn't matter, but you can see it does.

'You better be careful, uh?' says Kevin.

'OK,' says the poof.

Again he turns and starts to walk away.

'You going to let him get away with that?' says Kevin's mate.

'Watch out, you fucking cunt,' yells Kevin.

And the poof starts to walk real fast.

'I'll be after you,' shouts Kevin. Then he starts making these funny poofter whooping noises.

The poof just hightailed and ran. That was the last they saw of that cunt.

It was usually good for a laugh. Kevin used to call it getting his exercise. He knew more about doing the dunnies than most of the queers did. It was no good starting too early, and you had to look out for police cars. Sometimes they would come interfering and you wouldn't see any queers again for weeks. They would all move on to somewhere new and you'd have to cruise around until you spotted them.

Kevin used to say he could smell them from the Aramis in the air. Maybe he could. For sure he could spot them even in the dark. He would see them under the trees strolling around. Out like possums at night. Avoided all the lights and just hung around in the shadows. Sometimes you could spot them having it off up against one of the trees, or some guy down sucking another's tool while the second guy went lookout. Funny they looked, peering round with some guy slobbering over their meat. They would get carried away and that was when they wouldn't notice you coming.

Up through the trees and whammo. Or you would see them tearing off with their tools still out, swinging before them like 'roos running backwards.

They'd tried mugging poofters for the bread at one stage, but it was useless. They all left their wallets in their cars. You could thump into them—but steal their bread, no way. Seemed strange the way they were so careful about that and careless about themselves—not smart at all really. No such thing as a smart poofter, it stood to reason. If you were smart you wouldn't be a poofter.

It was Friday night and they were pissed. Kevin had been at the pub since six. They had stopped drinking to have a counter meal. One of the guys had thrown it almost straight up, shit food that it was. He'd only just made it to the dunnie. Then he had sat there and moaned a bit. Kevin had reckoned he'd found a mate in there, he was gone so long. He was looking pretty bad now, just sitting quiet in the corner.

The rest of them weren't that bad. Until the last hour there had been some chicks there and the guys had kept sober enough to try and con onto them. But then they had gone off and now only the drinkers were left.

Kevin wanted to kick on a bit and have some fun. One of the guys was making noises about going home to his wife. Said he wanted to screw her senseless. He probably just wanted to rest, collapse at home. He had to keep his wits about him because he was getting the train. You couldn't let yourself doze off on those things, not with the way they were these days. In the past he had fallen asleep and been woken up in time for his stop, but these days drunks got mugged courtesy of Vic Rail as they slept their way home. He had to go soon.

There was no one much to kick on. Kevin's best mate was still standing up but the one that had spewed was a write-off and so was this married guy. Just the two of them wanted to go on.

'Me car's up near the market,' Kevin said. 'Reckon you can make it?'

They half carried their corpse friend out into the street where the cold air hit him. For a moment he looked like he'd collapse.

The married one left them. He was a bit quiet too. A bit scared he would have to get off at each stop. The vibration of the train sometimes made you chuck after a few drinks. He'd known it before. You could feel alright till the thing started to move — whoops, and away you would go, redecorate the carriage in a steam of spew.

They got the corpse as far as the traffic lights. He hung onto the pole and wouldn't cross. Then he sort of folded up into a heap at the base, still clinging on. He reckoned the ground was nice and cool and he needed to cool off. They got him to his feet and across the lights. He could walk when he concentrated.

'I'll be no good for footie on Sunday,' he moaned. The thought sobered him a little and he staggered forward.

'Did aerobics on the oval on Thursday,' he mused. 'Did this guy's back in,' and he stumbled. 'Shit, help us one of you bastards.'

'Aerobics is for poofs.' Kevin spat.

It hit the ground in front of him and sat in a wet globule on the cold surface.

'Not the way we do it,' the drunk persisted. 'No poofs at footie.'

'Bunch of fairies.'

It was Kevin's last word on the subject and he flicked his mate in the crotch to make his point.

'Watch it,' the drunk retorted, bending over in supposed pain. By now he could feel practically nothing. 'You nearly ruined me.' He lurched on up the street in the wake of his mates. 'Where the fuck's this car?'

The third one had been fairly quiet until now. 'Fucked if I know', came the reply, and they looked around bewildered.

'Oh yeah, I know,' said Kevin and they were off again lurching up the street.

Their mate's mother wasn't too pleased when they dropped him off. They had to stay and hold him under the shower, she wasn't touching him in that state. He wouldn't let them take his jocks off, said they were a bunch of poofters, but had just crouched under the jets of water in his own vomit. When they got him out most of it had washed down the plughole. His old lady could clean up the rest.

She had made them sit and drink black coffee while she bullied him to bed. Kevin felt great by now and still wanted some action. The walk to the car, the concentration on driving and the coffee had revived him. While the old girl was out of the kitchen, he suggested they go poofter-bashing for a bit of sport. And it was on for the night. As soon as they could get away from the old girl they would head straight for the park. Kevin downed his coffee in a single swallow. He didn't want to waste any more time.

They cruised down the side of the park and past the bog the first time. It didn't look too promising but it was worth a second try. Kevin thought he saw a figure moving between the trees, but it was on its own and miles from the dunnies. You couldn't tell if the cars there were parked for the bog or not. They were too drunk to count them to see if there were any new arrivals the second time around.

The car lurched onto the main road to do another circuit. In the mirror Kevin could see a set of lights crawling slowly behind them past the bog. He thought they were drawing to a stop. It was hard to tell for sure as he'd only seen them just as he'd swung out into the main road. The lights seemed to fade.

'Got one,' yelled his mate, pointing back.

'Don't know,' mumbled Kevin.

'Give it another try?'

Back round the block. This time they crawled along the edge of the park. It was pretty dark; the trees were quite a way in, the toilets only a dozen yards or so in from the road. The lights inside had been broken. That, or some poof collected them.

Ahead they could see a figure walking along on the same side of the road.

'Cut the lights. Pull over,' his mate urged.

The lights dimmed and the car pulled over. They sat staring ahead at the lone pedestrian. He looked back over his shoulder. He must have been aware of the car and that it had stopped somewhere behind him. His look questioned the driver's motives. Friend or foe? it asked in a glance.

'Get down,' Kevin ordered. 'Better chance if he thinks it's just one of us.'

The figure continued to walk but glanced back again. It was hard to see him in the dark but he looked fairly young—tight jeans and a short jacket. The poof looked back again and decided it was alright. He walked slowly across the road at a diagonal, using it as an excuse to look back at the darkened car in an assessing stare. You could see him fairly well for a few seconds as he crossed under one of the lights. He could have avoided it, so he obviously wanted to be seen. They got their look at him. He was young, sure enough, and a little uneasy—just what they were after. Twitchy, you might say, but not going to give up.

'Yep, we've got one.'

Kevin was sure this time. He leered back out of the window. 'Thinks he's got it made.'

His mate was laughing by now.

'Yep, I really fancy this one,' Kevin smart-talked.

'Jeez, shut up will you or I'll piss myself down here.'

'Stay put,' Kevin ordered.

He switched on the parking lights and started the engine. Their quarry turned at the soft noise but kept walking towards the dunnies. The car cruised slowly up trailing him, then pulled over again in the shadows between the sparse street lighting. It was pretty dark. You couldn't tell if there was anyone else around. It looked safe enough.

'I'll get him when he comes out. You stay put.'

It was unfair on his mate that Kevin should be having all the say. Usually they acted together; tonight Kevin was hogging it.

'Next one's mine, mate,' reckoned his friend.

'Yeah, next one.'

The young guy turned into the toilet block, disappearing from sight. He didn't bother to look back one last time.

'Ripper.'

And Kevin was out of the car and across the road in a flash. It was a bit of a fucking letdown for his mate. He got up off the floor and stared over the dashboard. He was dying for a piss but it would have to wait now. He could use the bog after Kevin had finished. He could see him in the dark bushes that screened the toilets from the park.

Any minute now he'll get the cunt. But Kevin seemed a bit far off for his mate's liking. Shit, he would probably blow it and they would have to wait to set up the next.

'Next one's mine,' he grumbled to himself.

Kevin was standing out clearly, he wasn't trying to hide. He was waiting for the figure to re-emerge. He'd call the poof over to him for sure. They'd done it before. Kevin would stand there looking at them and just unzip his fly, resting his hand on his tool. They always came running after a fat prick and Kevin always reckoned he had that to show.

In the dim light from the street he could see the figure come out of the bog and look around. He must have been looking for Kevin. No one else inside to pull off.

Kevin strode out of the bushes and beckoned the guy over. He went towards him.

'He's got him,' Kevin's mate chortled to himself, and leant over behind the steering wheel for a better look.

The two figures were almost together and he could see that Kevin was bracing himself ready for the big whammo. Nothing unfair, no iron bars or tyre levers, just bare fists. Kevin's mate was still pretty pissed but he didn't want to miss much. He moved across the seat just a little more to see through the side window, and his elbow caught the horn. It was only a short muffled blast but they all heard it.

Like lightning the poof saw the figure in the car and knew what was up. Kevin slugged but only winged the bastard. There was a shout and the guy scrabbled off back towards the bog. Stupid bastard, Kevin would get him in there easy. Lay him out in the dark.

As the young man stumbled back into the toilet block, obscure figures jumped apart, retreating defensively into darker corners and cubicles. The young man scrabbled towards the wall opposite the doorway and groaned. Figures moved in the shadows. Then there was Kevin charging through the door. He was still yelling:

'Come and get it, you bastard.'

He skidded to a halt, blinded by the dark. He stared into blackness, his eyes unable to focus. A figure moved behind him. He swung round.

'There you are, you cunt.'

The young man clung to the damp wall of the urinal and said nothing.

Figures moved in the shadows. Kevin could hear them breathing, watching. He stood stock still. Vague shapes began to loom up around him, timid and inquiring, like jungle apes investigating a strange object suddenly in their midst.

'Shit, how many of you bastards are there?' And he lashed out towards the amorphous shapes. There was a thud. He had made contact. A figure stumbled back in the darkness. Then new figures moved in.

He felt hands reach out to touch him. It was eerie, like the blind identifying an object by touch alone. They didn't seem to fear him at all. He was an alien and must be known. Then he felt the figures drawing back. No word had been spoken. He waited.

There was a sharp crack behind him. He swung around. A solid figure blocked the door.

'You fucking poofter!' he screamed.

Another quick movement behind him and still he couldn't see properly.

A cigarette lighter flashed its fire for a moment. It was held high. For a second faces were illuminated around him, then darkness. In the flash of light it was like a witches' coven. Faces illuminated against dank walls . . . male heads, eyes staring, like ancient cave paintings. Then darkness again. The unity was primeval.

Stillness, blackness; he waited.

Suddenly the silence was broken by the crack of an arm across his face. It was a crashing blow, throwing his head sideways. He caught the dark smell of leather. He lurched backwards. Nothing. He waited.

He heard an intake of breath and something crashed down on his skull. He reeled forward to meet a knee butting into his groin. There were sounds of movement everywhere. He lost his nerve. He screamed. A blow smashed into the side of his face and another into his groin. He was sinking fast. He was on his knees, his arms cradling his head. The warm smell of semen greeted him from the ground.

A boot slammed into his back. He jerked out involuntarily. A boot slammed into his groin and he doubled forward again, his hands flung out above his head. Sounds stopped around him. He tried to move, preparing in the dark for the next blow. If he could only get to the protection of one of the corners. He dragged his way along the floor. His hand reached up the dampness of a wall. He felt someone's leg still and quiet. He let go and waited. The blow came. His head crashed to the cement. The smell of deodorant balls and urine; the taste of blood in his mouth.

His mate was getting bored in the car. He'd heard the poof scream once or twice. Kevin must be doing a good job this time. He was still dying for a piss. What the fuck was Kevin up to? He couldn't hold on any longer.

Swinging open the car door, he hauled himself out to piss in the gutter. He was still pretty drunk because he pissed uphill. It ran back on his boots. He swung round to face downhill, spraying the side of the car as he did so.

He was still fumbling with his zip when he saw the first figure coming out of the bog. He expected it to be Kevin. It wasn't. Something was wrong. Then out comes another figure and another. One could have been the poof Kevin chased in; they all looked alike in the dark.

Groping for the open door, he bundled back into the car and pushed down the locks, watching. If something was wrong he wasn't going to be in on it. Kevin would be alright—just a bunch of poofs. Jeez, but how many of them had there been? All these dark shapes just pissing off into the trees.

A figure got into one of the cars parked ahead. He heard a motor bike starting up and he dropped down onto the seat of the car. Another car started up and pulled away. He hid from the lights. He didn't want to be part of it. It was Kevin's idea.

The keys were still in the ignition. Carefully he slid over to the driver's seat. He would just idle the car down to the end of the street in the darkness and then get the hell out of it. But what if the bastards heard him? Better stay there. He cringed back onto the floor and waited. Minutes passed—perhaps five, he couldn't tell.

Kevin would be alright. He could look after himself. He'd scared all the poofs out like rabbits bolting the warren. But he was sure taking his time.

He sat up a little and peered round. No one about. He started the car up and cruised a few yards closer to the bog. The engine running, he gave a few blasts on the horn and waited. What the fuck? Kevin was trying to give him the creeps. What could a bunch of poofs do? Another blast on the horn. Nothing. He switched off the engine and got out of the car. He stood there on the road, then headed for the bog.

Sometimes Kevin could give you the shits when he put the wind up you like this.

No point in waiting any longer. He strode over. Get Kevin at his own game. He crunched over the gravel, then growled in an assumed voice: 'Police here, stay where you are.'

He sprang through the door.

'Got you, you bastard,' he yelled.

Shit, it was so dark, he couldn't see a thing. It was quiet too. He edged carefully forward. There was no one there. His foot hit something. He bent down and felt it. It was a fucking corpse.

1985

Loving

The English word 'loving' has almost too many meanings to mean anything at all. It can denote, after all, anything from an obsessive desire to copulate with someone to a gentle feeling of admiration and gratitude, free of the slightest carnal thought. It can refer to the feelings a wife has for her husband as well as the feelings she has for her garden or the new blinds. While the poems, extracts from longer works and one performance piece in this selection hardly cover the full range, they do give a sense of the possibilities for loving open to those with a homosexual sensibility.

Historically, the homosexual narrative tends to end badly—in frustration, self-loathing and, frequently, death. Even homosexual writers have had difficulty imagining other kinds of narrative, especially since the early 1980s when AIDS took on the role tuberculosis once played in literature, engendering storylines of despair, noble suffering, unfulfilled hopes and, it must be said, at times quite clichéd sentimentality. The extract from Nigel Krauth's brilliant post-colonial novel *JF Was Here* is the only work represented here in which AIDS has a large presence, but for Krauth, unlike many gay writers, AIDS works as a powerful political metaphor, not just a medical reality.

Interestingly enough, it is the women writers in this selection (Helen Garner, Sandra Shotlander, Bev Roberts) who seem least cynical about loving and its many possibilities. Indeed, in this anthology as a whole, with the notable exception of Beverley Farmer in her first novel *Alone*, women writers seem to feel freer than their male peers to depart from traditional forms and storylines to experiment energetically with un-expected, hopeful solutions.

What this selection demonstrates is that loving for the homosexual can, with imagination, cover much the same gamut of emotions and responses as it does for the heterosexual. It can, apparently, be romantic, self-sacrificing, faithful, silly, lustful, despairing, comic, tragic, ephemeral, neurotic, serene, perverse—almost anything, in fact, except, perhaps, to date, epic. That may come.

HELEN GARNER

La Chance Existe

I am the kind of person who always gets stopped at Customs. Julie says it's because I can't keep my eyes still. 'You look as if you're constantly checking the whereabouts of the exits,' she said. She'll never really trust me again, I suppose. It shits me but I can't blame her. I love her, that's all, and I feel like serving her.

When we got to Boulogne we had to hang around for three hours waiting for the ferry because of a strike on the other side. I would have sat in a café and read *Le Monde*, but Julie wanted to walk round and look at things, seeing she'd only been in France a couple of days. Her French was hopeless and she was too proud to try. When I met her plane at Orly she was already agitated about not being able to understand. We went straight to a bar in the airport and she insisted on ordering. The waiter, tricked by her good accent, made a friendly remark which seemed to require an answer: her face went rigid with panic and she turned away. The waiter shrugged and went back behind the counter. She hit the table with her fist and groaned between clenched teeth. 'It's pathetic! I should be able to! I'm not stupid!'

'For Christ's sake, woman,' I said. 'You've only been in the country fifteen minutes. What do you *want* from yourself?'

Boulogne was dismal, as I had predicted. I kept telling her we should go south, down to Italy where she'd never been, but she had to go to London, she said, to meet this bloke she'd fallen in love with just before she left Australia. He was coming after her, she was dying to see him again. She fell in love with this guy, who was a musician, because at a gig she found him between sets sitting by himself in a sort of booth thing reading a book called *The Meaning of Meaning*. She told me he was extremely thin. It sounded like a disaster to me. Love will not survive a channel crossing, I pointed out, let alone the thirty-six hours from Melbourne to London. But I was so glad to be with her again, and she wasn't listening.

We walked, in our Paris boulevard shoes, over the lumpy cobbles of Boulogne. We found a huge archway which led on to a beaten dirt track that curved round the outside of the old city, at the foot of its high walls. Julie was excited. 'It's old! It must have been trying to be impregnable!' The track was narrow. 'Single file, Indian style,' she chanted, charging ahead of me.

It was eleven o'clock on a weekday morning in July, and there was no one about. A nippy breeze came up off the channel. The water was grey and disturbed, a sea of shivers.

We tramped along merrily for twenty minutes, round the shoulder of the hill the old city stood on, turning back now and then to look at the view. The track became narrower.

'Let's go back,' I said. 'You can't see the sea round this side. It stinks.'

'Not yet. Look. What are those caravans down there?'

'I dunno. Gypsies or something. Come on, Julie.'

She pressed on. The track was hardly a track at all: it was brambly, and was obviously about to run out against a wing of a castle about a hundred yards ahead. I was ten steps behind her when she gave a sharp cry of disgust and stopped dead. I caught up with her. There was a terrible smell, of shit and things rotting. At her feet was the mangled corpse of a large bird: it looked as if it had been torn to bits. Its head was a yard away from its neck, half its beak had been wrenched off, and there were dirty feathers everywhere, stuck in the spiky bushes, fluttering in the seawind. The shit was human. Its shapes were man-made; it was meat-eater's shit, foul.

We looked at each other. The murder was fresh. In the crisp breeze the feathers of the creature's breast riffled and subsided like an expensive haircut. It was very quiet up there.

'Someone's looking at us from one of those caravans,' said Julie without moving her lips. 'This is their shitting place. It's their fucking dunny. They must be laughing at us.' She gave a high-pitched giggle, pushed past me, and ploughed away through the prickly bushes, back the way we'd come.

Back amongst the houses, we stood at the top of an alley in the depths of which two little boys were engaged in a complicated, urgent game with a ball and a piece of rope. One dropped his end in annoyance and walked away. The other, who had glasses and a fringe and a white face, sang out after him, in a voice clear enough for even Julie to understand.

'*La chance exis—te!*'

'What a sophisticated remark,' said Julie.

On the boat, when it finally turned up, we didn't even have the money for a drink. The sky and the sea were grey. The line between them tilted this way and that.

'Will it be rough?' said Julie. 'What if I spew?'

'You won't spew. We'll walk around and talk to each other. I'll keep your mind off your stomach.'

My glasses are the kind that are supposed to adapt automatically to the intensity of the light, but they failed to go clear again when we went down into the inside part of the ship. Cheap rubbish. The downstairs part was badly lit. I hate going back to England. I hate being able to understand everything that's going on around me. I miss that feeling of your senses having to strain an inch beyond your skin that you get in places where people aren't speaking your language.

Julie darted down the stairs and grabbed a couple of seats. We got out books and kicked our bags under the little table. On the wall near us was the multi-lingual sign warning passengers about the danger of rabies and the fines you get. Julie knelt up on her seat and read it with interest.

'Rabies. What's that in French. *La rage.* Ha. You don't have to be a dog to die of *that.*'

Julie is suspicious, and full of disgust. When she laughs you see that one of her back teeth is missing on the left side. If she chooses you she loves you fiercely, lashes you if you fail yourself. A faint air of contempt hangs about her even when she's in good spirits. She says she's never going home. Everyone always says that when they first get here.

She flung herself round into the seat. 'I saw Lou just before I left Melbourne,' she said. 'I told him I'd be seeing you. He laughed. He said, "*That* fuckin' little poofter!"' She glanced sideways.

'News travels fast.' I knew that's what Lou would have said. It made me tired. He could do the dope and the bum cheques on his own now. I took a breath and went in at the deep end.

'When I first got here,' I said, 'I knew I was going to have to do something. That's what I came for. I used to walk around Paris all night, looking for men and running away from them. For example. One night I was in the metro. It was packed and I was standing up holding on to one of those vertical chrome poles. A boy got on at Clignancourt. He squeezed through the crowd to the pole.

'He wasn't looking at me, but I could feel him—I might've been imagining it, but warmth passed between us. I was burning all down one side. My heart was thumping. His hand on the pole was so close to my mouth I could have kissed it. The train was swaying, all the people were swaying, and I edged my hand up the pole till it was almost touching his. I felt sick, I wanted to touch him so much. I could smell his skin. I thought I was going to pass out. Then at the next stop he calmly let go of the pole and pushed through the crowd and got off.'

Julie put her feet up on the low table between us and folded her arms round her legs and laid her head sideways on her knees. She was having trouble controlling her mouth. 'What's your favourite name of a metro station?' she said.

'What? I don't know. Trocadéro.'

'Mine's Château d'Eau.'

'Ever been up on top of that station? You'd hate it. It's not safe for women.'

'Remember that time you shat on my green Lois Lane jacket?'

'It was an accident! I had diarrhoea!'

'You were so busy looking at yourself in the mirror you didn't know you were standing on my clothes.'

'The dry cleaner got it off! Why do you have to remind me?'

'"It's dog mess," you said to the lady at the dry cleaner. Dog *mess*.' She gave a snort of laughter.

'It came off, anyway.' I opened the newspaper and rattled it.

'Being homosexual must mean something,' she said. 'What happens? Is everything possible?'

'How do you mean?' Was she going to ask me what we did? I'd tell her. I'd tell her anything.

'I mean, if both of you have the same equipment does that mean it's more equal? Do people fall into habits of fucking or being fucked? Or does everyone do everything?'

'It's not really all that different,' I said, feeling shy but trying to be helpful. 'Not when you're in a relationship, anyway.'

'Oh.' She looked disappointed, and stared out the porthole at the grey sky and the grey water. Her cardigan sleeves were pushed up to her elbows and I could see the mist of blond hairs that fogged her skin. Her legs were downy like that, too. We can wear each other's clothes. She's the same height as me, with slightly more cowboy-like hips: light passes between the tops of her thighs.

'I never want to fuck with anyone unless it puts me in danger,' she said suddenly. 'I don't mean physical. I mean unless there's a chance they'll make me sad.'

'Break your heart.'

'I'll never get married. Or even live with anyone again, probably.'

'What about shithead? The bass player? Isn't that why we're making this fucking trip?'

'Are you afraid of getting old?' she said in a peculiar voice.

'My hair's starting to recede.' I pulled it back off my forehead to show her.

'Oh, bullshit. What are you, twenty-five? Look at your little round forehead. A pretty little globe.'

'And I'm getting hairs on my back,' I said, 'like my father.' I didn't mention that I twist round in front of the bathroom mirror with the tweezers in my hand.

'Can't we afford one drink and share it?' she said.

'No. We have to get the bus to Rowena's.'

'Last week,' she said, her head still on her knees, 'I was in the Louvre. I was upstairs, heading along one of the main galleries. I saw this young bloke sitting on a bench with a little pack on his back. He was about your age, English I'd say. He looked tired, and lonely, and he gave me a look. I wanted to go and sit next to him and say, "Will we go and have a cup of coffee? Or talk to each other?" But I was too ... I kept walking and went down the steps to the room where all those Rubens paintings are, of Louis Whichever-it-was and Marie de Medici. I stayed in there for ten minutes walking round, and I hated the paintings, they made me feel like spewing—all those pursed-up little mouths smirking. I went back up the steps and the boy was gone.'

The boat heaved on towards Folkestone.

'Why is it so hard to talk about sex?' she said, almost in tears. 'Every time you think you're close to saying what you mean, your mind just veers away from it, and you say something that's not quite the point.'

What would they know here about summer? The wind was sharp. People in the queue had blue lips. I was stopped before we got anywhere near Customs, this time by a smart bastard in plain clothes who was cruising up and down the bedraggled line of tourists with passports in their hands.

'His *jacket*,' muttered Julie. It was orange and black houndstooth. 'My God. What's happened to this country?'

'Don't get me started on that subject.' I stood still and proffered my bag. Some look must appear on my face in their presence, or maybe it's the smell of fear they say dogs can pick up. He was nasty in that bored way; idle malice. No point getting hot under the collar. While he rooted through our bags, and Julie stood with her arms folded and her chin up and her eyes far away over his garish shoulder, he asked her an impertinent question.

'How long've you known this feller?'

'I beg your pardon?'

'I said, how long've you known this feller you're travelling with?'

You can't take that tone to a woman these days. 'What's that got to do with you?' said Julie.

He stopped rummaging and looked up at her, with one of her shirts in his hand. God, she still had that old pink thing with the mended collar. He narrowed his eyes and let his slot of a mouth drop open half an inch. Here's a go, he was thinking. I kicked her ankle. She reached out, took the pink shirt and said, folding it as skilfully as a salesgirl in Georges, 'Six years or so. Nice jacket. Is that Harris?'

He wasn't quite stupid enough to answer. He shoved the pink shirt back in among the other garments and walked away. Our bags stood unzipped, sprouting private objects.

On the train to London I read and she stared at people. At Leicester Square we ran down the stairs into the tube. I caught the eye of a good-looking boy who was coming up. I turned to look back at him as he passed and she slashed me across the face with her raincoat. The zip got me near the eye.

'What did you—' I yelled.

She was laughing furiously. 'You should have seen the look on your face.'

'What look?'

'Like *this*.' She pulled a face: mouth half-open, eyes rolling up and to one side, like a dim-witted whore.

In the basement room we were supposed to keep the wooden shutters closed because Rowena said there was a prowler who stood up on the windowsill. But the room was dim and stuffy. I took off my clothes, then slid the window up and shoved open the top half of the slatted shutter. Julie whipped off her dress and stared at me.

'You still look like a little goat,' she said. 'Pan, up on his hind legs.'

I got under the sheet. 'Come on. Let's go to sleep.'

'I'm all speeded up. I'm looking for something to read.'

'Well, don't rustle the pages all night.' I turned on my side and closed my eyes. When she got into the bed she hardly weighed it down at all.

'Talk to me,' she said behind me.

I flipped over onto my back and saw she was lying there with her hands under her head. 'What'll I say?'

'Do you get just as miserable as you used to when you were straight?'

'Are you kidding?'

She shifted so that the sides of our legs touched lightly, all the way down. 'Come on. Talk.'

'Maybe more miserable,' I said. 'It's all real now. Before, I was in a dream for years, even when I was with you. Everything was blurred and messy. Now I know exactly what I want, and I also know I'll never get it.'

'Oh hell.'

'What?'

'What *do* you want?'

'Everything. I want to love some man forever and at the same time I want to fuck everyone I see. Some days I could fuck trees. Lamp posts! Dogs! The air!'

She whistled a little tune, and laughed.

'In the Tuileries,' I said, 'there is a powdery white dust.'

'What else?'

'It's a cruising place at night. Not that part with the rows of trees, they lock that. The part between the gates and the Maillol statues. I love it.'

'Why?'

'It's like a dance. It's mysterious. People move together and apart, no one speaks, everyone's faceless. It's terrifically exciting, and graceful. The point of it is nothing to do with who.'

Her face was quite calm, her eyes raised to the ceiling. Turning my head I could see pale freckles, a gold sleeper, a series of tiny parallel cracks in her lower lip. The skin of her leg felt very much alive to me, almost humming with life.

'Once,' she said, 'I was coming down that narrow winding stair-case in one of the towers of Notre-Dame. Two American blokes were coming down behind me, and I heard one of them say, "Hey! This is *steep*! My depth perception is shot already!"'

We rolled towards each other and into each other's arms. I pushed myself against her belly, pushed my face into her neck and she took me in her arms, in her legs. I cooled myself on her. Her limbs were as strong as mine. Her face hung over me and blurred in the dim room. I could smell her open flesh, she smelled like metal, salty. I swam into her and we fucked, so slow I could have fainted. She turned over and lay on her back on me; I was in her from behind and had my hand on her cunt from above as if it were my own, my arm holding her.

And then under the hum and murmur of breathing I heard the soft thump of the man's foot against the closed lower half of the shutter. Fingers gripped the edge and a head floated in silhouette, fuzzy against the glimmer of the garden. My skin opened to welcome him.

1985

SASHA SOLDATOW

Requiem

My eyelids I have closed to phantoms
But distant hopes
Disturb my heart at times.

Aleksandr Pushkin
Evgeniy Onegin 1831

I am trying to remember what my father's cock looked like. It is a dim memory, coloured by fantasy and masturbation. And an aura of loss. He's dead. Decayed most completely by now. It makes we wonder what I should do with my body when I'm dead. Or, to be more precise, what I now direct should be done, for I will not be around to witness anything. There is no post death, only dust by burning or dirt by decay. I prefer the dirt. I always have preferred processes that lead to filth in comparison to efficient disposal. To my ears, there is no music to cremation. Burning of a body should end in a fantastic explosion, the bitterest end.

Summoned to return home urgently and acting against my better judgement, I travel back and forth from Sydney to Melbourne. It is always Andrew I ring to pick me up from Tullamarine airport. In these moods of comparative loneliness he makes me feel less neglected. I try not to abuse his generosity. On the few occasions that I do, he snaps at me, quite correctly, too. Though I have to add that he too is sometimes moody.

It is May in Melbourne. Andrew drives me along the freeway to stay in his one bedroom flat in South Yarra. He is wearing his dirty boots and gardening work clothes, having taken time off work to pick me up. The city looms in the distance. I take small loving looks at him when he's not watching me. I am in such a state that I cannot tell if these loving looks are returned, though we laugh as we tell each other stories about our respective mothers.

It is May both here and in Vitebsk. That's where my grandmother was born. My grandmother is now in Box Hill Hospital, in intensive care, a catheter in her urethra, a drip in her arm and an oxygen mask over her face. She is dying. It is her time.

She has prepared herself for this. Privately, eight years ago, she told me that she has prayed for thirty years for this death. Her spiritual crisis is well and truly over. This, now, is the physical crisis. Falling on her knees in my mother's spare bedroom for the past thirty mornings and thirty nights before her ancient silver icon, she has begged The Holy Virgin to help her die. Unfortunately, her body has never obeyed her religious beliefs. It is a separation of needs.

After a marriage at thirteen in the 1920s in Soviet Russia, she birthed four children in eight years. Only the first child died, her only boy, of meningitis. He was two years old. Then, after a secret silence of sixteen years which no-one will tell me about, her husband died. This is all I know of him. Not a soldier, he was incarcerated in a prison camp by the German invaders for three months. The cause of his death was *Schwindsucht*, a form of consumption, as it was called then, but the dictionary also defines it as 'a wasting disease that eats away at you'.

You'd think by now, now that she wishes to die so badly, so desperately, that my grandmother would be granted this ultimate favour. But her body won't listen. Through a heart attack and the insistent deterioration of old age, her body keeps on working, beating, breathing, shitting, her hapless lips telling her three dark daughters off in the most degrading, vulgar language, words that bubble out from somewhere in her past.

'You wouldn't believe how nasty she can be,' says one of her daughters, the one who wiped up her shit and piss the first time anyone was aware that this disgrace would be her permanent final state.

'Why won't He let me die?' my grandmother says, secretly, to me, of God. Her religion helps her. It is God that has let her down. But her faith will never let her confront such insolence.

When I arrive at the hospital, I sit at her bedside. Her lungs are packed tight with fluid. My mother tells me that this is all natural, that this is a process that has to happen. I don't know who she is talking to, me or herself.

My family has warned me that my grandmother recognises no-one, that she is in a semi-lucid coma and going quickly. Yet, when she sees me, she attempts a smile, repeats my diminutive name, Sashenka, over and over through her oxygen mask, tries to talk of something loving for a couple of minutes. It is difficult for her to say anything through her missing dentures and the mask that keeps her breathing. After a while she moves her head to one side and falls into a half-dream sleep. It is both tiredness and dignity. I stroke her beautiful hair. Throughout her whole life, her hair has always been as soft as down. While I tender her, she turns to me and softly says, 'That is the caress of my angel.' Then closes her eyes and falls into a deep calm sleep.

'You always die alone,' I said to her, the last time she was in hospital.

'Yes,' she replied, her eyes looking past her soul. 'That is as it should be.'

There is no ambivalence about my memories or the way I use them. That's why I can never call them correct. They're not historically accurate. But that does not impede their vividness, their colour. This is the knowledge that I carry, the truth I have learned which has taught me to recognise when people have to be left alone.

As I leave the hospital, never to return to see her alive again, I am reminded of my father. I see him naked in a bathroom, but it is a green tiled bathroom in Sydney where he has never stood, never been. He never went to Sydney. So the cock I see, the cock I witness at this edge of memory, is something else. However, I have to note the fact that it is definitely still my father's cock, not someone else's. I have taken it upon myself to reconstruct the shape, the colour, the object, the desire. The place is of no importance. This cock is his and no-one else's.

I was never fucked by my father. I tell you this quickly in case temptation brings these thoughts to your mind. I'm also not interested in religion, in the subconscious or the archetype. Nor am I interested in psychoanalysis or shrinks, something a local unknown doctor tries to suggest to me when I go to him for a simple script for Valium, for a drug which I know and, at this moment, need badly. To blot out the present, some would say, but which actually acts to blot out old beginnings.

I have to break this writing here. A bit of light relief, a pull of my own cock on the bed. Not only one pull as it turns out, but many, each one a quickly fantasised rebellion to rid the body of anxiety which even the Valium cannot allay.

Let me tell you what happens when I write about sex, even in a time of grief. Thinking these thoughts and writing them down, I get sexed up. I stroke myself, touch my nipples as I tap the keys of my word processor. To not get stiff would be unnatural, to my male mind anyway. Though, when I write of murder I do not feel a similar need.

Men find masturbation simple. The spurt of sperm like phlegm. Easy to cough up. The penis is mightier than the sword. Laugh with me as I ejaculate.

I was never touched up by my father, never raped. Love and respect. No sin. That was dad when he was clothed. Naked, I have made him something else. Something more beautiful, like a soft caress, the touch, in retrospect, of a lover.

This last statement is spoken as a joke, but be warned. This writing is also sacred. I am burying my grandmother and, through her, particles of myself, though some pieces, like viruses, stay hidden, ready to re-infect.

A traditional Russian Orthodox funeral is exhausting. An open casket is frighteningly final. I enter the church bearing my gift of two wild roses which I place with her body. They are white. Everything is white except for her lips, the brightest red lipstick I've ever seen, applied as if by a crazed surrealist. The morticians have done an excellent job, made her look fifty-five whereas she was almost eighty-seven. Without realising it, the gash they have created across her mouth makes her look angry, makes her look like she has proudly taken on all of the dislocation of this century.

At her funeral, wearing an inappropriately old-fashioned tie (Ben's), a fancy jacket (borrowed from Bruce) and proper shoes (borrowed from Nelson), suddenly I am transformed. I am now the male elder-head of the family. It is a role I slip into easily, almost naturally. It is a role I do not want and do not respect, but I perform it magically, not showing the regression in my mind.

I am twelve again. My father is shaving. He is naked. Looking at my reflection in the mirror, he speaks to me of science, of mathematics and the universe.

We talk, I look. I can remember nothing in his face, his arms, shoulders, back or legs. That is not surprising since, as I am twelve, he is already dead. What I do remember is a description of a dick in a pre-teens sex education booklet. 'A penis is like a short hose that hangs between your father's legs.' The next book, for the adolescent boy, tells you of erections, even pictures a man with one, in black silhouette. The picture is silly. It is a boy's erection, not a man's. My father's cock was thicker. I know, I sucked it later, alone in my bed.

There is a lot of residual bullshit when you try to reconstruct the past, but fantasy surprisingly provides a certain and necessary corrective. Like a fever, it is calm, sincere and undemanding, but it can also take its toll.

A friend tells me, recalling when he was a child, of having a bath after gardening, him sitting in the bath, his father standing under the shower. He remembers his father's cock level with his face. My friend is not sure—he thinks he is ten, maybe twelve. Every man I have asked tells of their father's cock in that moment just before puberty. When a cock becomes something to look out for. When a cock becomes something different to, say, your nose.

I have a thesis. Boys remember their father's cocks only when they realise the importance that their own cocks assume as the primary experience and focus of their own changing bodies. I do not use the word importance loosely. Previous to this interest, and even after, I am certain that all of us boys have seen our father nude, but very few of us remember the dangling hose till then, and afterwards we look and see it with a knowing, calculated disinterest. We invent a distance.

Boys' first thoughts are of their mother. Is this true? I do not know. It is a speculation. Except that my younger brother cannot bring himself to kiss the corpse of his mother's mother and stands behind all the mourners, lost in his own grief at this next repetition of a series of further mortalities.

I touched my grandmother's cunt once. She was lying in the dark in her bedroom in the family home in Victoria Street, Camberwell, weeping inconsolably after a screaming and unfair, vicious family fight. The actual facts of the argument will always remain forgotten, but her burning tears, alone in her room, were for herself and the status she was losing on the announcement that my mother was to remarry. Her favourite son-in-law, my father, was truly and finally never to return. In the darkness I came to comfort her.

Orientating myself badly in the dark, I walked blindly to her bed and touched her soft hair gently till I realised I was touching her between her legs and that she was naked. Her bitterness was so great that she did not respond.

This is in no way written to explain the reasons why I am gay. I was already thinking of men well before then. It is simply a statement of fact.

I am grateful that in Melbourne I have a man I love, a man I can stay with so that I can escape the destructive intimacy of my family. My love for all of them is deep, but the depth is harrowing.

Imagine me in Melbourne, staying with Andrew and Nelson, his new lover. Imagine me masturbating my anxiety away over and over in the spare bed that Andrew always makes up for me. Imagine having adolescent feelings about my father at the age of forty-three in this death crisis. Imagine these two men whom I love, putting up with my undignified, brooding boring presence. Then flying home from Melbourne and having crying eyes, dead eyes. And that wrenched-out feeling of having just lost a father thirty years ago. And soon another death.

At home in Sydney I sleep on drugs for fifteen hours.

A friend the next day says I look rested, says I look wonderfully well. I smile with her and understand that she too is aging. It's not that the years start to rush by more quickly — it's more that the last years of my life, be they five or forty, demand more intensity, less wasting of time, more companions, more intimacy, less people. More me and you and your lover and maybe a few other friends. You see, the youthful cry for help has evaporated, but the infant cry still persists.

After the death, when I return to Melbourne, I look at my mother at her own mother's funeral, standing by the casket with her two sisters, each one holding fast to a sensible black handbag. Later, after the event, the burial in the hole, I half-dream in Andrew's spare bed in the morning as Nelson kisses me as he leaves for work, and again later, in full daylight, as Andrew kisses me and leaves. I dream of my mother lying dead in her casket, and the only image is of some future memory, of her lying lifeless and of me passionately kissing her breasts.

I have not forgotten how much I need to talk with people about life. About its vicissitudes. How much I need to stay up late and chatter. Cry sometimes when I'm alone and, if I can't help myself, listen to the recordings which sing of agony. It is a variant on sleeping with a man, you and you, and another you, though you might all turn into images of my father if I let you, because I am older than all of you.

There is a sexuality to death which is never discussed. I mention this in passing and won't elaborate because I am tired now from writing. My eyes hurt at the edges. They've got grit in them. Bits of shell. The sands of time.

It was nine years ago that I immediately fell in love with Andrew when I saw him at a party. One look, one conversation, one laugh. Obviously at first it was sexual, the feeling in my cock for a fuck. But our bodies did not connect correctly — you know these responses immediately though your ego will never let you acknowledge this, especially not in bed after trying. Even though we went to sleep tightly together after both coming off, we woke up apart. I do not know which of us has allowed our relationship to expand for this extent of time. For me it is a mutual love but I can only speak of myself. Then I arrive in Melbourne and he introduces me to his lover and I fall hopelessly in love again.

The love of another look, too quick, too fast, caused this while I was sitting next to you in your car. Nelson, my fast new friend, the lights changed to green too quickly to kiss you. And I suddenly knew I had to leave this city immediately because if I stayed any longer I would ask you for a fuck and you would say no and the question and the answer would ruin everything for everyone.

I am not taking any risk in writing this. I have told this to both Andrew and Nelson. They will make of it as they will while I sit in Sydney and churn my heart out into a hundred drunken nights.

All my writing is an act of love. Some of it is specific, some less generous. Nelson, I once wrote my love out on paper for Andrew. I have also written it out for others. Never for my father. This is the first mention of him.

Writing about life is writing out a series of loving frustrations punctured through with heart-breaking longings. We attempt to delay these crises by eating and drinking with our friends. Making our talk an abandonment, an infinite enjoyment, which is ultimately the secret decay of hurt.

With some friends we also talk about life, try to unravel the conundrum, discover the obvious. Sometimes, while laughing heartily, I also hear myself hesitantly whispering as well. I listen to other's experiences, enjoin in a communion of deep conclusions about ourselves. But more often we unabatedly chatter, enjoy the arguments, the consolations. Then suddenly, usually when drunk, when the shark has mauled us and dragged us to the depths, we stagger into a battered silence about the things we cannot tell, about people we love and their deaths, things that are not proper talk.

With some few friends, though, and you have become one of these, we leave nothing to the imagination, no thought to chance. Then, after we have talked these life talks, searched and wrung out our souls, we part with each other to a taxi somewhere or, staying with you, to a bed in the next room, the room away from where both of you sleep and fuck. Hardly ever do true friends remain together afterwards. We always recognise when the time has come for the last embrace of the night.

There's a cute guy I remember while doing the beat in a toilet in Marrickville probably twelve years ago. I remember because he couldn't get his cock stiff.

'Fuck.' he says. I play with his dick but nothing happens. It's the hose from my youth but I'm older now and insane for action.

'Sorry,' he says, as another man enters. I suck this new man's cock. It's a nondescript engagement. Finally he pulls his cock out of my mouth and lifts me up, turns me around to fuck me. Anything, I'll do anything. I spread my legs, offer my bum, bend my legs a bit to make his entry easier.

There are three of us. Me, the man behind me fucking my arse, and the guy I like. He stands there hoping the sight and smell of buggery will turn him on. The guy behind me is doing his job—it's pleasant enough, but it's more like a wank than a fuck. I'm a hole, that's enough for him. I don't mind. For a moment I am a compliant partner.

The man with the limp dick, my no-action friend, as I decide to think of him, watches me being fucked, not knowing whether to go or stay.

'Play with my nipples,' I say quietly to this lost soul, as I arch my back so that the man behind can finish his business.

After the cock shoving is all over and the man has come and gone, as it were, zipping his pants up, I kiss my half-neglected friend gently on the lips.

'Do you live with anyone?' he asks.

'No-one,' I reply, his tongue kissing me.

I cannot remember any detail of the night we spent together. Nothing. My diary entry for that day reads, 'Ring Phillip re tape.' Then enigmatically in pencil, 'I'll wipe your tears.'

It doesn't puzzle me, but it intrigues me a little, these boy-friends that I have accumulated that I can ring up after midnight. Friends I can talk to about my father's cock. Friends who will pick me up at the airport in a moment of crisis. Friends who will open a bottle of wine for me when I arrive and who will wipe away my tears with harsh but accurate words of truth that make us both laugh.

As my tears well in my eyes and I wipe them quickly away because I do not really want to cry, you pour me another drink and tell me I'm drinking far too much. Then you make me a sandwich because I am not hungry any more. Eat it, you say. I obey.

Alone in my single bed, after you have both left me, I have a recurring fantasy. I am walking somewhere in the snow. It is getting dark and I am lost. I am also running a fever. There is a solitary house in the distance. Lights shine through the windows like bright stars on a moonless night. I approach, knock on the door. It is opened by a man and I am hit from all directions by warmth and coldness at the same time. Without a word, he takes me in. Feels my brow. Then carefully puts me to bed.

When I wake, I do not know how many centuries have passed, but I am over the worst. Looking around, I see him by my side. He smiles and makes me some tea, sits with me as I drink it. The tea has lemon and sugar, just as I like it.

'You should get up. I'll help you have a shower,' he says, tentatively touching me. 'It'll help you feel better.' Then adds, 'Don't be embarrassed about being naked. After all, I did have to undress you, so there's nothing I haven't seen.'

As I get out of bed, he hands me a towel and touches me again. It is the touch of kindness. After I have washed, I stand before him like an unprotected newborn child. He hugs me, like a lover, then wipes my body dry of the tears of generations.

This piece of writing is for the many of you, my new and aging boys, one of whom I call my dad.

1991

TIM HERBERT

Pumpkin Max

Guttersnipes and starbursts were often on Benny's mind. An aversion to any kind of middle ground. Meantime, his lover Joseph had his own routine to perform; one that kept him ribbing and hissing for much of the morning and getting Benny in a fluster.

'We are all of us lying in the gutter; but some of us are looking at the stars.'

'Such a tired old cliché, Benny,' said Joseph, goading him further with a moonstruck stare.

Benny knew he was innocent. That he had only just discovered the glittering quotation.

'Do you know whose lines you're pilfering?' asked Joseph.

Lingering by the window, copper sunbeams glowed in warm silhouettes through the eucalypts. Benny was ready to try and answer — Poe maybe, then changed his mind to Oscar Wilde. No, it didn't matter. The glow was so enticing.

'Think I'll go out for a while.'

Joseph said nothing. Slippery and smug, thought Benny, for the disdain followed him right out the door.

'And so easy to intimidate.' That was the snarl from Joseph. Certain enough.

At times Benny was clumsy and vulnerable. Overreacting like a snail in close company, he had been brushed with salt and was smarting.

Benny followed the glistening sandstone wall of the Barracks. The soldier in the drab khaki grinned under his slouch hat. On the bus Benny skipped frames between Joseph and the soldier. There was no mistaking it. Life with Joseph was constricting. The Paddo python queen who valued relationships for the crush of intellectual advantage. Benny figured if he stayed there much longer his lover might swallow him whole.

Benny Morrison had not always lived in Sydney. Dad and his Illawarra milking Shorthorns still relished lush pastures at Jamberoo, while Old Dan Morrison coped much better with his bulls than with a son who reckoned he was gay. No, he could not believe it, and neither could teenage Benny when he first encountered the golden mile. Here on Oxford Street he quickly aligned himself to the body sensuous. The granite handshakes of home gave way to timorous fingers of curiosity. Penetration. Those farmers' mouths were parched and hollow. Sydney proffered him love — sultry breath, tongues of fire and the celebration of 'coming out'.

The traders down at Paddy's Market were finishing up. Loading onto the fruit trucks made almost combustible in the afternoon heat, Benny focussed on a swarthy pair of colossi. They were hauling up sacks of pumpkins. Sweat erupted on vexed biceps. A pulse under worn blue overalls. The desire for an exotic fruit: a papaya, custard apple, maybe a sweet yellow babaco had been forgotten. Benny's mind was in reverie to the rhythms of male action.

Dreams bristled when the truck's horn glared and Benny caught the driver's eyes in the rear-vision mirror. 'Perhaps he's been watching me just as long,' he mused, but fantasy revived, evaporated soon when the man tossed himself from the cabin and strode towards him.

Benny was usually shy and always paranoid. The wide grimace on the driver's face seemed a portent of some grim irony. He cantered off, side-stepping broken crates and a path festooned with rotten cabbages.

Through a crack in the warehouse wall Benny re-emerged into the dusty sunlight. It was isolated on this side of the market. Big stacks of rusted storage bins and a wizened Chinese woman fossicking in the gutter. He turned the other way. The taut arms of the driver found him and pushed his body against the wall.

Tropical fruit was unappetising. It seemed almost passé. Benny thought of massy, tubered leeks and pumpkins. Max had a body like that. Smooth, hard buttocks like the perfect sections of a Queensland blue, its firm ribbing unyielding of the dark orange heart. But his own heart had complied. Behind the drums where he lay bare-chested, imperious fingers running over his tan belly and whispering pleasure when Max squeezed him, Benny's joy was maintained, as deep in his pocket he fingered the slip of his new love's address. He would call him Pumpkin Max.

Joseph found out on Wednesday. There really wasn't much to go on. The slip bearing Max's identity had remained in Benny's trousers, but something else escaped. Obsession makes one careless and it hung out like a lurid diorama. Joseph offered his soft, damp hands: a gesture of empathy, perhaps of remorse, for he wanted to communicate without patronising his youthful companion.

Once again the dial on the telephone was spinning into oblivion. Behind the door, Joseph listened to the stale chords of frustration. Max's telephone was impregnable. Benny's fingers cracked the receiver down.

It was Joseph's moment to appear. To be debonair and scathing like at the dinner party when Benny shrivelled up amongst his straight friends: 'Oh we are both homosexual. Didn't you know?' And then he reconsidered. Benny was traumatised. That was enough satisfaction. Joseph wanted his lover to absorb the echoes of himself; to face the consequences of an affirmative sexuality and not to be hounded by the iron shadows of a spurious straightness. To resist the ghouls he needed a thicker skin. Even a vacant obsession would lead to fortitude eventually.

On another day Benny stood outside a terrace. An impeccable blend of sky blue and lemon in an Ultimo lane. A peeling of door chimes rivalled the distant roar of juggernauts along Harris Street, while in the postbox a *Reader's Digest* brochure for Max Slotwinsky confirmed that Benny's passionate letters had found their mark. But while his efforts may have been fruitless, he had not yet despaired. A palpable ideal is its own

preservation, as within Benny's mind another existence could be defined—
a robust and electric presence, beyond the fluff of the Paddington ghetto.
This love was raw and unfathomable. He sat beside Max's door.

At two in the morning his eyes were turgid with grit from the
intermittent gusts of a hot westerly wind. Benny had few vivid memoirs
of a long and banal evening; the stolid citizen from Neighbourhood
Watch, a drunkard's caterwaul at a 'slope-head' intimidator, and some
blood-sporting skinheads: 'Beat 'em on the raps, beat 'em on the raps
with baseball bats, Oi Oi.' At last it was Saturday. Market day. He
caught a taxi home.

Benny figured Joseph would harass him. He stole into the downstairs
bedroom. At ten a.m. and with a tentative 'Hello,' Benny faced a bare-
bottomed man in his kitchen. His smile agitated Benny: 'Who are you?'
The wanton look faded, replaced with the square grin and hard grip of a
Messianic fundamentalist.

'My name's Ti, that's T-I. Joseph's upstairs and you're Benny?'

Benny allowed his hand to slip. 'Are they all the details you have on
me?'

Ti laughed and reached for a tea towel. 'Sorry about the strip-tease.'

Benny had brightened up. This blond boy was handsome, winsome,
yet Benny felt no jealousy. He also seemed a lot smarter than he looked,
with the extra bonus of being refreshingly indiscreet, Benny was given a
spontaneous account of the night's events. Joseph had broken taboo:
entered the forbidden zone of the Midnight Shift, charging his nostrils
with half a phial of amyl and thrusting his frame with Ti in a five hour
marathon of techno-funk. Benny was incredulous. It was hilarious. He
wanted to wake Joseph and interrogate him, but it was like rescuing an
ant from a honey jar.

Had Joseph wanted Benny to follow his lead and perform the un-
expected, he would have been disappointed. Then again, there was only
pessimism in Benny's anticipation of his encounter at the market. He
could depend on Max to ignore him until closing time.

After a month, his antics had become pedestrian. Every time Max had
responded almost identically to his first feverish pursuit. Benny felt he
had become a kind of degraded barrel girl. The nook among the storage
bins being Max's personal boudoir; the only acceptable outlet for a
sexuality removed from love. Benny had figured this all out in logical
progression, logic that is dull and unashamedly predictable and which
Benny had spurned up to now. Two days later he was tossing it off yet
again, shocked by Max phoning for the very first time. His sensuous
voice gave lustre to Benny's dry stone offerings. Benny asked him over.

Benny found Joseph strangely good humoured. Ti even offered to fix
dinner, though Benny knew they were trying to placate him. After all,
Ti's moving into the spare room the day before was just a ruse. They
were fucking each other when he was not at home. There was no anger.
Pumpkin Max was still the priority.

He arrived in cerise singlet, glossy arm muscles locked around a carton of beer. Joseph could win a few points on style, but Max won out on athleticism. Conversation shuffled from terrace renovation, through politics and onto vegetables. Max could be docile and often missed Joseph's innuendo.

'Yes, we do do a good trade in cucumbers,' Max replied.

At other times Max defied expectations. Approving of multiculturalism, land rights, feminism, it did not fit into a working class sensibility. Ti bamboozled Joseph for his 'bourgeois insularity', while Benny felt a great release to spot Joseph in such a demeanour—all coiled up and deflated at meeting an intellectual match in Ti.

Ti's enthusiasm for Max might have also sparked some latent jealousy in Joseph, bringing on a fiery reaction. But though words failed him, his self-control did not and Benny was impressed that the plates of vindaloo had stayed on the table.

Benny's opinion of Joseph had certainly turned around since Ti's arrival. There was now more substance in his ardour, while that customary cynicism had been well diluted. Or perhaps Benny's love of Max had redeemed the now sometime boyfriend. Certainly Joseph was happy with Ti and even acted as his benefactor, for though the new boy may have been bright, he was also unemployed and needed Joseph's money to augment his stained glass dabblings. And Joseph had faith. He liked his bedroom radiating like the Folies Bergères, decked out as it was in rainbow panels of lead-light. Benny liked it as well. They were a flashy trio instead of a dull couple.

'You settled your head athwart my hips and gently turned over upon me. And parted the shirt from my bosom-bone, and plunged your tongue to my barestript heart.'

'That's nice. I like that.'

'It's Walt Whitman.'

'Australian?' . . . 'No, American.'

'Gay?' . . . 'Uh huh.'

They embraced in a dark doorway. Having slipped out to buy more beer, Max carried Benny along. Benny did not approve of the detour (there were garbage bins in the lane), but he stood in the rubbish overspill to hear Max's confession: 'You know that I love you Benny.' He undid his belt.

Benny bought beer in the saloon as Max wandered to the men's room. Benny was glad he had resisted. There was euphoria in his desire for Max and the power from resistance was some ego compensation. Benny had fine-tuned their reception. Instant gratification had been removed, with a rich promise of lovemaking on Max's bed.

Benny waited ten minutes with the brown bagged bottles of beer.

'The bastard's slinked off!'

Benny did not understand, though he understood his perversity in following. In the taxi he observed Max folding into the shadows on Darlinghurst Road. The city's most notorious beat loomed. Benny stood in the doorway, enticed and then terrified at entering. Someone groaned in a cubicle. He moved away. Leaning behind a Moreton Bay fig, inhaling the wet musk of bark and diverting his mind from a screaming heart.

'Max was a liar. Max did the beats. Max loved him.' It was hard to focus.

Five minutes in an Oxford Street bar and Max's arms were draped around a pimply, red-headed teenager. Benny felt even more humiliated, until Max noticed him. Sex was facile, love is pain. It was not profound. Just an insight into Max's gesture, prompting him to go all the way. It was only a glance but enough to transmit the joy of the chase. Benny could have heard him say: 'Be my fanatic and I'll love you.' He found another taxi and soon was back in Ultimo.

There was a hose curled up on the landing of Max's house. He would turn on the tap and thrust the high pressure nozzle under the door. It was madness and he grinned. The front bedroom awash as he fondled the hard red cap and foresaw the spurting jets of water. He saw an irony too. His sex denied as everything about Max was sexual. His logic surprised him.

Max entered the lane with the red-headed boy. Benny squatted in the gutter at the darkest end. He viewed the cerise singlet and green pants as part of the disguise: the man was half lorikeet, half taipan. They breezed inside.

Benny had finally remembered. 'Lying. All of us lying in the gutter.' It was Oscar Wilde. Caught on love's dunghill. If he had matches Benny would purge himself with fire. There was still the hose.

He listened to Max, screeching and hissing lust. Behind the muslin curtains the two men danced in passionate silhouettes. He knocked hard, called his name and tapped on the glass. The shadows stayed. Benny had always hated being ignored. The nozzle cracked the glass easily. Benny felt like a riot squad breaking up an unruly demonstration.

There was no enjoyment in having Max's big arms around him. To be held up by a body slimy with sweat and water was more repellent, he told himself. Max was explaining, but Benny saw himself as a player in a crazy burlesque. Out on the street, the neighbours watched the wet man Max, his hard cock feebly disguised under a hand towel. Then there was the red-headed boy sprinting down the lane, hugging clothes to his nakedness. And now Pumpkin Max was trying to explain.

'You know that I love you.'

Benny was looking at the stars and laughing.

1986

DAVID MALOUF

Unholding Here

Unread, the book you asked for
lies open on the sill,
its pages in the sunlight
curling as the wave
curls on its dark, your brown
fingers in half-sleep
involuntary curl:

and waking at your side,
I watch, unholding here,
fingers, pages, waves—
an evocation of
related absences:
the dream, the poem unread,
the sea's perfected arc.

1962

Dark Destroyer

Coils of wind and water in their wake
leave ruin we can measure, flat suburban
gardens in whose havoc
of root and flower the cyclone
has spent itself; we track it to the breeze
that softly lifts our hair; we see it snared
in a curtain-net—shadow of a destroyer's
anger on a chart, its grim ghost laid.

But you are such a subtle
destroyer, no powder-keg
whose fury is uncoiled in a blaze of words;
in you dark ruin breeds
from silence; your calm, indifferent smile
poisons the air, fills seven rooms with plague.

1962

Stars

The stars have so far to go
alone or in harness
across a window pane.

Hour after hour tonight
I've journeyed with them, steady
the waves of your breath.

Dark space between our beds;
on the table a full tumbler
splits the lights of stars

to stars, or floats
a column of dead water,
dead sky. From centuries

off, out of the reign
of one of nineteen pharaohs,
a planet's dust, metallic,

alive, is sifted down,
hovers in a bright
arc upon your cheek.

Miraculous! I lean
across the dark and touch it,
you smile in your sleep.

How far, how far we've come
together, tumbling like stars
in harness or alone.

1970

Hearing you read the poems

Hearing you read the poems   hearing you breathe
      through them   feeling your breath
   rub the world of objects
      I move in   today
they glow with peculiar power   a frictional excitement as
            high up two continents
of air slide past each other and the event
            for us down here
      is chain lightning   It ripples
through us to the earth   We are conductors
            of an absolute music
      It plays at our fingertips   illuminating
the plainest household facts   so that plunging
            tonic into gin is suddenly given
      (as the room lights up
a scene in some further room) another meaning
      than the one our hands intended   or as headlamps
            cut we find ourselves

at a place darker than this
    has ever been   your breath
that rises   falls   rises between the lines
        is not yours only   The earth
breathes   the dancers sink towards breathlessness
    in the heavy grass   lovers
        falling through the dark net of their bodies
    breathe into each other
        light   life   another ceremony
takes them than the one their hands intended   I bend
    an ear toward the pauses   where air
        is drawn back to your lungs
and changed   recharged   I'm carried
    forward as it swells into the place of
        your other reading   past
where dancers catch their second breath and lovers
    the one breath like a wave   We are conductors
        of heaven's fire   its current
music striking through us to the earth

1976

Poem

    You move by contradictions:
    out of a moment
    of silence far off
    in Poland or January
    you smile and your body
    returns to my touch.

    Entering a winter
    room I find myself
    dazzled: all summer
    in the throats of vases, windows
    ablaze with air, our pear-tree
    brimming with wasps.

    My dull hands follow
    at night your unseasonable
    kindling and cooling
    through twelve dreams and the twelve
    colours of darkness
    between midnight and dawn.

1970

ROBERT ADAMSON AND
BRUCE HANFORD

From *Zimmer's Essay*

The night range screw was a man who had slipped most of his threads. On the cell allocation list he found seven cells with a third bunk. He must have looked at Glaister and considered the possibilities.

'Walk ahead.'

It's hard to say how much Glaister apprehended. Range 2 might have reminded him of the prison sets of Hollywood movies, only a bit smaller. On either side over and against him were long sandstone walls, and in these were set two levels of cell doors, grey, with red numbers. Catwalks ran along the level of the upper cells. Between the catwalks a shark-net of six-inch mesh was stretched. Above that, far overhead, the lights: bulbs in white industrial fittings. What would Glaister have thought of the net? He wouldn't have realised it had been placed to prevent bankers from plummeting their creditors, or demented inmates from taking a dive.

Glaister's concentration in those moments would have been tactile rather than visual. Psychodrama teaches that human beings have a 'body space', a corona of sensitivity that extends beyond the flesh; the tenderest extension is to the rear, and the margin of Glaister's nerves would have been reaching for seven feet behind him—the screw was in them, a writhing vortex only four blind feet behind: Glaister's pain centre was poised for hurt.

The screw moved along the catwalk in an easy audible scuffle. His eyes ran along the level of the red stencilled numbers 120, 121, 122, then 124. The screw made a sharp sound Glaister didn't understand, though he knew to stop and turn.

The screw stopped in front of 124, and he drew a key from his hip. Without supporting the padlock, which was at thigh level, the screw drove the key into its hole with an uppercut motion. Worn tumblers rolled with his wrist and let go the shackle and the padlock came away impaled on the key—this is the screw's equivalent of the cop's knock—and with his left hand he slapped the free locking-bar clear of the solid staple in the sandstone wall ... shooting, so to speak, The Bolt, and swinging the door out.

'In here.'

About thirty feet down the range, past the night range screw, standing in the shadow of the net, Glaister saw another screw, hands high on his hips, elbows out. In the door past him, there was a third screw, also standing. He felt a hand on his arm.

That year there were no toilets or radios in the peters of The Bay, and the most entertaining fitting was the unfrosted 100 watt bulb fixed just inside above the door, on a stalk of pipe, like an incandescent crab's eye.

There's a way of shorting that to light cigarettes, and another technique for converting it to a water heater.

Say the peter was fourteen feet deep, seven wide, ten high. Red pavement paint on the floor. At the far end of the peter, near the ceiling, was the window, a yard wide and not quite a foot deep, barred horizontally by two pipes. Inside the pipes are tool-proof rods, unfixed, so if you saw through the pipes the hackblade slides without cutting the rod rolling around inside it.

At this time of day, the lights outside were glaring through the window chamfer onto the glossy paint of the ceiling. The air was salt wet and blood warm. A couple of Christmas beetles had come to visit the bulb. Halfway into the peter, on the right, was a Brownbuilt steel locker, with hooks on the side for towels, and three shelves. In the shelves were some felt shovel-slippers, a Gideon Bible, a copy of The Regulations, and a few books from the library. At the left was a double deck bunk. At the end of the peter in the left corner was a small diagonal shelf of marble holding a galvanised iron jug. Under the shelf was the shit tub, with a number on its lid, 124. At the back was a single bed.

Glaister saw only the two shirtless crims sitting on that single bed, playing cards. They were both about 20 years old.

-57 was thick-lipped and well-built, with shiny black hair. -16 was skinny, blond, and leaning forward. They were smart enough numbers to have worked the clip on the peephole, and they had seen Glaister coming: they had just picked up their hands for the look of it, and as if inviting Glaister to sit in, -16 asked him, 'You fuck?'

The screw looked at -16.

Glaister stood still holding his towel, his half-loaf, and his dixie and spoon. His spine was stiff, and his hips turned under as a dog with tail between legs.

The screw turned and moved and shut and locked the door with the same economy with which he had opened it. Glaister wondered if he stayed and observed through the peep. He turned and put his blind nerves to the door, and faced his new friends.

'Drop your gear,' suggested -57.

Glaister complied by putting his towel, half-loaf, dixie and spoon neatly on the locker. He stood there and said, 'I'm Larry Glaister.'

'Good on you,' said -57. He rose and took two steps, so his face was five inches from Glaister's. 'I'm -57.'

'I'm -16,' came the other voice.

'Shuddup,' said -57. 'Sit down.'

Glaister supposed that the second instruction was meant for him. He moved to sit on the locker, but -57's body said that was wrong. He then moved to the double bunk, and sat hunched under on a lower corner. -57 faced him and told him, 'You're on my bed.'

Glaister understood that both the bed above him and the single bed would be -16's bed. He understood that the joke was on him. He smiled, and said, 'I'm sorry.'

'Got any grouse?'

'How's that?'

'You got any grouse?'

Glaister wasn't certain.

'Aw, -57, you're confusing the lad. He is obviously not with you. Perhaps he . . .'

'You bring any smokes in with you?'

'I don't smoke.'

'Well now,' said -57, 'how are you going to make it up to me if you don't got any tobacco?'

-16 moved across to the locker, tapped the dixie lid to see how hot it was, threw the lid on the floor, sniffed the stew, and tore hunks off the half-loaf.

'Do you want the stew?' said -16.

'No,' said Glaister.

'How would you like some bread with some of our jam on it?' asked -57.

'Sure,' Glaister agreed.

-57 performed a ceremony. He went to a post of the single bed, removed the rubber cap in the pipe, and pulled up a string. He made much of it by pulling from hand to hand, as though it were a fishing line. At the end of the string was a shiv made from a spoon. The spoon's bill had been stomped flat, and wrapped with shoelaces, to form an oval grip. The spoon's handle had been rubbed against the sandstone until it was pointed and sharp on both sides. 'See this,' said -57, 'this is contraband. I taking a risk incurring grave penalties to cut you a neat slice of bread.'

'You're probably a pretty neat person,' said -16.

Glaister did not say anything.

-57 sliced some bread, not too neatly—the shiv wasn't much good for the job. He used Glaister's spoon to spread some jam on the bread, not too lavishly. He licked the spoon clean, put it between two of the shovel slippers, and handed the bread slice to Glaister. Glaister bit a corner off. -57 stood like a chef with the shiv in his hand, and asked: 'You like that?'

'Very much.'

-16 laughed.

-57 said, 'That'll cost ya two smokes.'

-16 remarked: 'He reckons he got no grouse.'

'We could search him.'

Glaister saw sparks as the back of his head hit the frame of the upper bunk. A hand was pressed hard on his upper chest, there were two fingers digging into the notch above his clavicle. He lay on the bed on his back and -57 stood over him and cracked a fat, and said, 'Suck this.'

'No.' said Glaister. He turned his head away towards the wall. The hand came away from his chest. And hit him, hard, in the hollow in the side of his neck, behind the ear, just below the skull. His mouth gaped. They took off his clothes, his shoes got in the way of his trousers, and they hit him a few more times while they were getting his shirt off, to tenderize him.

There were three belts in the peter. They strapped both of Glaister's wrists to the headposts of the single bed, so he was belly down. They gagged him by putting a sock in his mouth and tying the pillow slip tight around his head. They strapped the ankle of his right leg down—this leg was the one nearest to the outside of the bed. They threw a blanket over him. They sat there and talked about him until nine p.m., when the crab's eye shut for the night, and then they took off their clothes.

'Wanna go first Barry?'

'Go ahead Ray.'

'Naw, I like it sloppy.'

'Right oh.'

Ray, the blond kid, pulled the blanket. Glaister hadn't moved for a long time. 'Think he's hard up for air?' Ray said. 'Larry, hey baby, you feel this? Ooo don't be upset Larry-baby, ain't me cock, this is old -57's spoon,' that Glaister felt in the skin above the spine in the small of the back. He choked trying to shout around the sock.

Barry and Ray looked at each other. Both of them had hold of themselves. Barry sat in the top bunk, the light from the window on his shiny hair, stroking himself up. Ray said, 'Larry, you bawl I gonna cut your cord, you hear me Larry.'

Glaister lay still and quiet.

Ray said, 'I gonna take that off and talk to you Larry. You mind you don't bawl.'

Ray took off the pillow slip. Glaister choked up the sock, retched, lay still taking deep breaths, and crying, he cried silently. Ray said, 'Larry, hey listen, sweetie, hey.'

Barry laughed.

Ray took a harder line. 'Hey, we're gonna fuck you. One way or another. Want the straps off Larry? You might, you know, not want to be tied down Larry.'

Glaister was thinking about morning. He supposed something else happened in the mornings. He wanted morning to come. 'What time is it?' he asked, in a cracked voice.

Half-wittily Ray said, 'It's later than you think, Larry.'

But Barry understood Glaister perfectly. He had heard the same tone, the same words, in Salvation Army night shelters in mid-winter, when the ceiling was flaring from chats lighting cigarettes, and morning was relief. Barry replied with a bit of anger in his voice, anger out of the realisation that this bitch was so silly she might try to get the screws into the peter, or lag in the morning.

'Larry, you little bitch, you little bitch, there's time to root you four hundred times before the bell. You want the bloody straps off, say so.

'But I'm telling you, you make trouble, you make noise, you lag now or later, I kill you, I cut your nuts off with my spoon, you hear me? You little bitch, you get it straight.'

Glaister's voice came up from the bed even thinner and higher, and he promised, 'I'll give you the tobacco. I'll pay you back. I promise.'

'Fucking oath you will,' says Ray, a little jealous of Barry, who has got a rise. He sticks his limp stump in Larry's ear and tries to piss, but can't. He asks Larry how he likes that. Glaister retches again, but he doesn't have much in his stomach. Barry gets the margarine jar from the locker, gouges out a lump, and rolls it until it is broken down into grease in his palm. He takes a wodge of the margarine, and shoves it up Glaister's arse. He opens the hole up with the old index. He wipes the margarine-juice on his fingers off upon his prong, and shoves his finger in Glaister again. Glaister starts gagging, loud. -16 puts the shiv behind Glaister's ear, and digs the tip in a bit, but it doesn't affect the noise level very much, only makes him turn the leg closest the wall under his strapped leg, and tighten up, so they get the gag back on him. He still makes noise. -16 kicks Glaister's left leg out from under, and Barry fucks him, or her — actually, just ersatz, doesn't turn -57 on the way real pussy would, takes him about half an hour, it seems, to drop his rocks, takes a long time and work with the hands, and -16 is laughing at him a bit, which makes it harder, or rather, softer, he keeps slipping through the image he is working on back into this peter . . .

While -16 is in, Glaister's arse begins to bleed a lot, onto the blankets, and he says: 'No worries about jack in this one. A virgin, no worries Barry old boy. Bleeding, Barry. Bleeding.'

'Bleeding, eh.'

'Too right.'

. . .

The exercise yard is much larger and dirtier than the yards yard sweepers sweep. It is bounded by two fences of spiked bars ten feet high running between, say, range 1 and range 2. The crims of range 2 loiter there waiting for the shit tub soldiers to return. There are more than a hundred men in blue denim in a space a little smaller than a basketball court. They maybe wash at one of the four washbasins. They maybe sit on one of the six white porcelain seatless toilets, under the bus shelter arrangement at the back fence. Or pace, or smoke, or talk about things of interest like who they fucked last night.

'I believe I heard some singing.'

'Bloody oath mate, she sang so good, me and Barry named her Carol. Pity she wasn't with us for Christmas.'

'Better late than never.'

. . .

O Carol

'What's your lagging?'

The woman of mystery moved away, without a word.

Glaister was scatty. The last time he had been spoken to as a friend was months past, that time had been in the North Sydney lockup, where a kindly old cop had extracted a prolix confession from him. When the confession had been shown to him in writing, when he had seen the editorial treatment, where his friend had bent his words ... Glaister's suspicions had grown from whens and wheres and he was withdrawn ... he swept his yard meticulously, and hoped the wind would blow something interesting into his life, a stalk of grass, a swirl of sand. He would not answer to my kind words, but he began to see me as I passed by. [. . .]

I travelled between groups in the exercise yard, getting easy laughs, receiving cigarettes. I was free, I walked all around the prison, and I stopped at each gate to converse with our guards. Even yard sweeps have library privileges, and I was helpful with Glaister's choice of reading. [. . .]

The yard Glaister swept was five short strides by ten short strides and enclosed by inch-thick steel bars that went to spear points high above his head. In the centre of one of the narrow sides was a padlocked bar gate. That was the front of the yard. Behind and over the yard was a dark stone wall, and a screw patrolled the catwalk along this wall from the corner tower. His job was to agitate the yard sweepers, and to prevent them from sitting, smoking, talking or whistling while they swept. As the screw passed by above, I came to the front of her yard. She ignored me, from fear. The screw shouted, 'Don't drop anything -7, ya might have to bend over.' I smiled and waved in appreciation. Glaister kept his head bent, sweeping slowly.

'Hey 14-.'

Glaister looked up. The screw was moving away.

'Don't bother, he'll give us a minute,' I promised.

Glaister came to the gate, his broom in both hands, and vertical, the end moving. I asked him how he was going. He said all right. I told him there were better jobs, but he didn't say anything. I told him I didn't like to see him doing it so hard. He flushed. I asked him if he would like another job. He nodded.

'Look, Carol, I been in your shoes.'

'What?' The rumour name was a spider bite.

'I been in your shoes. I did three months in the yards at Bathurst once, in July, it was fifteen below, or fifteen, anyway.'

She stood there.

'You want me to get you another job?'

'What do you ...' Glaister stopped, flushed again, rocked.

'I told you. I've been your way. I see me in you. Now I could get you a job in the laundry, a good job. I know the screw there. He's a good screw. Okay?' I watched. It was hanging. I asked: 'Look, be straight—do you like this, here?'

'I hate this here. I hate this here.'

'Okay, I'll see what I can do. Maybe it'll take a few days. Just keep cool, okay?'

'Okay.'

'I'm called Robin. Now don't do anything stupid, and it'll be okay.'

. . .

Lobey was the laundry screw. The legend was that Cloe had bitten off his earlobe, whilst doing him a favour. Lobey was fat, about 50, and he combed the fringe of his hair across a bald spot. His forehead bulged, like his abdomen. His forehead hung over his nose and eyes ripely, and the skin of his face was covered with hundreds of hair-thin wrinkles, so that any expression looked like a movement of crushed pink silk. He clicked his false teeth when he was annoyed, but the queens in the laundry had a special truce with him, and he did time easier than anyone else I've met. He spoke softly, asked people to do things instead of ordering them, and in conversation dropped the odd camp phrase. [. . .]

We had a special shared interest. Fishing. My father's side of the family was estuary fishermen. I didn't talk about this to other crims—it clashed with my swinging queen role—but Lobey was so rapt about my views on fishing that he gave me copies of *Angler's Digest* to smuggle back to my peter for a sly read, and then asked me for my critical opinion on various articles. When I was running for Brunswick, I sometimes dropped by the laundry, and Lobey would lead me behind the dryer, so that his seven servants could not hear, and we would have a scholarly talk about the Jew and the tailor and the properties of German Damyl monofilament, or the challenge the Americans were offering to the dynasty of French baitcasters. Our conversations, like many in prison, were serial, beginning again where they had left off, even if interrupted by weeks or months.

I went there several times and waited for his mood. There came a moment when Lobey was talking about the young people, about the things that were possible for them through technology that he had not dreamed of, like game reels with seven gears. When he left an opening for me, I asked him to give a mate of mine a job. 'Blankets are coming up, you'll need another hand.'

'I will, that's true,' Lobey allowed.

'You'll be seeing the overseer about it pretty soon?'

'All right, all right, who is it?'

'The little queen down in the yards. She's doing it hard down there, sir, she's just fading away.'

'Who?'

'14-. She's beaut. Haven't you noticed her?'

'The skinny one? The one with red hair and freckles?'

'She's slim.'

'Something said at mess about that one.' Lobey looked at me, and thought, and shook his head. 'No,' he said. 'No, jesus, Robin, she's got a bitch of a report. Not me, mate.'

'She's all right now. She had a tough run in The Bay, and went bad after some screw slammed her with the hoons. She'll come good, she deserves a break.'

'Robin, I'm not running a shrink shop no matter what they say. I like an easy life.'

'I'll see she behaves herself, Lobey. I will.'

'I don't want a stir.'

'I promise she'll behave.'

'Look, what's your angle?'

'I think she's sweet, that's all.'

'You're pretty sweet yourself. Don't you have some time to do yourself?'

'She's doing it awful hard, and I feel sorry for her.'

'Look, Robin, I'll think about it. I'm not promising anything.'

Lobey saw the overseer, who decided that the Governor had forgotten about 14-. Glaister was allocated to the laundry, and somebody in solitary cellular was moved into the vacant yard, which was handy, because the visiting magistrate was due.

Lobey looked Glaister over, and decided she was an okay kid. He gave her a pressing job, which is the easiest in the laundry. The queens were nice to Glaister, in their way. Glaister was sullen at first, because everybody seemed to treat him like a little girl, but within a week he came into an open place in his mind that almost seemed like happiness. His responses to things became sharper, and everything in the laundry except the people seemed real. He counted the garments he received. He estimated their weight—about two hundred pounds a day, clothes, towels, socks, calico bed sheets and pillow cases; he heard that blankets would come soon. He heard the queens talking about stains. He starched the linen from the screws' mess, and loved the surface as it cooled to a glaze behind his old-fashioned iron.

In the big yard for segregated prisoners, there are five nonconformists. One is the banker who handles a tobacco book. He is stationed under the verandah near the front fence, listening to the screw's radio through an open door, sweating over his book as each result comes over the air. Two crims are pacing together, mates, talking of their release and their life together and the job to do. And Zimmer sits under the verandah with his Carol at the back of the yard, explaining how it was.

'... it really mucked me up for a few weeks, but think about it, now, won't you—it only lasts for about four hours, the pain only lasted while they were on top of me, and that was because they were clumsy. And look at it this way: *I* hadn't changed. And how had it affected *them*?'

Two pigeons flapped over the verandah guttering, and landed to strut on the gritty bitumen. Grunting. Drumming. And ruffling when they turned their backs to the wind. Glaister looked as though he had sealed his lips by locking the insides between his incisors.

'I'll tell you. I'll tell you how. You think they were really something, don't you? Really tough, really animal. And you haven't got a clue, because they were more screwed up than you feel now, they were trying to be big tough men and prove something to themselves and the yahoos in the yards, but they're nothing and they know it and so does everybody else. They're *hollow* men. Think about them, they're probably gonna get married, what happens when somebody says the word "queer"—*not me, not me* he'll be screaming, but not out loud, you can bet. He'll have his own wiggy prosecutor and a greasy defence counsel inside his head—and your face and your bloody arse for exhibits . . .'

Zimmer shot his half-finished fag out into the yard, where it curved and rolled under the wind. The checker pigeons flew a few yards ahead of it, and resumed their business with exaggerated dignity. Glaister's lips went loose. He said, 'I've got something too.'

Zimmer looked at him, replied softly: 'Of course you do. I know.'

'I don't want it.'

'You got the name: Carol.'

Carol shuddered. Zimmer saw she wouldn't look at him so didn't bother smiling. He put his effort into a voice like a shawl. 'Okay baby, you really think so, aye? Aye. You put your head down and your bum up and really work on feeling sorry for yourself. You're a real martyr, a real victim of the system, aren't you? You are a real stupid cunt is what you are. *Don't press me anybody, I might self-destruct*—what kind of threat do you think that is in here? Nobody is going to pay on that act, Carol, baby, and if you had an ounce of guts you'd fucking come up with a better one. You don't think you're defending your masculinity by going around weepy, do you? Is that what you think you've got to defend? Oh sweet jesus Carol you're playing the bloody *foolish virgin*,' and Zimmer could see that Glaister was crying and trying not to make any noise. 'Learn to use the guilt, Carol. Learn to use the things you can use.'

Time passes outside. Inside the days circle. A few turns and the cell next to Zimmer's became vacant. Its occupant had been a neurotically tidy queen, and Zimmer had been promised the peter by the wing screw. Instead of claiming it, he installed Carol there.

This was the time of the shit bowl sermons. The one-out peters of Maitland Gaol are plumbed. At the back wall of each cell is a white porcelain toilet. Robin's and Carol's cells were on the second tier of the cellblock, and their toilets were connected to the same standpipe. All they needed to do to communicate was to splash the water standing in the traps of their toilets down the standpipe, and they had an intercom tube with a *cor anglais* resonance.

Zimmer prescribed readings. The first important one was old Sam's *Lives of the Poets*. Then biographies, the most important of these, *Ariel*, being a romantic Victorian's life of Shelley.

'You look like Shelley,' Zimmer spoke into the shit bowl and Glaister identified with Shelley.

Zimmer explained about *persona*—through imagination, a poet could become another personality. Glaister began to hope he had an imagination; it was, according to Zimmer, the only way one could be saved.

Shelley, the suffering effeminate, voyaging, searching for great causes. Shelley the doomed, finding only hypocrisy, pains, and meanness, the petty bitcheries and the tightening days of Maitland Gaol. Shelley as Carol. Zimmer gave her poetry, edited from context to save her any irrelevant responses. There were lines in *Epipsychidion* which might have been precisely about the coronation of Carol . . .

> . . . remain a vestal sister still;
> To the intense, the deep, the imperishable,
> Not mine, but me, henceforth be thou united
> Even as a bride, delighting and delighted,
> The hour is come:—the destined Star has risen
> Which shall descend upon a vacant prison.
> The walls are high, the gates are strong, thick set
> The sentinels—but true *free* Love never yet
> Was thus constrained: it overleaps all fence:
> Like lightning, with invisible violence
> Piercing its continents . . .

Zimmer had never been more than a cute queen. He was a strong boy, with hair, black hair on his limbs. He had a botched navel, only a scar. His back was covered with huge freckles, and his teeth were going bad. He was getting old and there was no future for him outside. But Carol was beautiful. Carol could work for Sammy Lee's all-male revue, she was that beautiful. And he would make her a gift of his mind, for her to carry in the temple of her body, through wide years of being loved.

Zimmer discovered he knew things. He took comfort from poetry as a sybarite. He took a teacher's pleasure; he was evolving a theory of personification not taught in schools. He watched Glaister realise a person could be anything he needed to be, anything he wanted to be. This was a powerful magic he gave his Carol, the magic of changes. A man survives as best he can. Zimmer was a magician in a hard place, a place of stone. How could he have known tenderness was so dangerous? Through his Carol Zimmer was Sappho. Zimmer was eagle. Zimmer was fish sounding in the deep Sulu sea. The earth is raddled with burrows of burrowing things, and Zimmer was marmot. Zimmer swung from tree to tree. Glaister identified with Shelley and felt better. Zimmer made a mistake and thought Glaister had become stronger. Zimmer gave her a copy of *The Poor Wedding Guest.*

The book reads easily. Set in Paris about the time of the Franco—Prussian War, the story concerns some literary gents. Verlaine is an established poet who has made a good marriage. He gets some poems from a fan, a provincial schoolboy. Verlaine sees that this unpublished kid is a genius, and sends him an invitation to drop by if he ever gets to town. Arthur Rimbaud, 17, leaves school and family and lobs at Verlaine's town house, where he becomes the most ungracious guest since Penelope's suitors.

Verlaine's wife and in-laws are *nouveau riche* and angst-ridden and even the servants are snobs, and he expresses his disapproval by visiting the

master bedroom during the day and depositing several Rimbaudian turds
on the nuptial cot. Madam Verlaine says it's either this freak or me, Paul,
and Verlaine opts for Arthur. Rimbaud comes up as the butch partner,
and they are off on a famous binge, fuelling on absinthe and hashish.
After a while, Verlaine sees he has blown his chances for a peaceful life.
Rimbaud attempts to desert him. Verlaine shoots his butch in the leg on a
railway platform.

Glaister said through the shitcan intercom, 'I think Rimbaud was a
perfect bastard.'

Zimmer asked, 'How do you read Verlaine?'

'He wasn't a bad bloke. He was generous, he did everything for
Rimbaud, got him printed and fed him and gave him money and then
sacrificed everything for him because of the way he felt. He was conned,
that's what I think.'

'You don't understand.'

'I suppose you take Rimbaud's side.'

'I don't take Rimbaud's side at all. I mean, there are no sides to it,
Carol, get that through your head. Rimbaud just did what he had to do.'

'Which was act like a *hoon*.'

'Look, Carol, Verlaine wrecked the best part of Rimbaud's writing.
Verlaine was just a weak, silly bitch, a fucking cat who was jealous of
Rimbaud. You haven't learned a fucking thing, have you? Not in your
whole bloody life. Rimbaud never asked for nothing. He just paid out.
He just took what he needed, he needed grist for his mill, people were
just something he could use, and if he couldn't use them in what he had to
do he got out of their way. Verlaine *used* Rimbaud. Rimbaud pissed him
off. Verlaine was a lame cunt, Carol, he pretended to be something he
wasn't, and what he was, a snobby nowhere queen, didn't impress
Rimbaud either.'

Glaister thought about that, and said, 'That'd be right. You think
Rimbaud's the hero. I know why, I think I know why, all right. You're
just a manipulator, Robin. You're like him, you hope. He gives you a . . .
justification for your way of living. You think you're some kind of
precious person. You're trying to be a god, or a screw, or something that
can steamroller people into whatever shape you like. Is that what you're
getting at—I think it is, it sure seems like it.'

It was dangerous to talk at night through that apparatus, and Glaister's
prepared accusation had been delivered in a whisper so that it almost
denied itself. There was a theatrical pause, and Zimmer exploded as
though he didn't care if the world was ended by a midnight ramp of the
whole cellblock: 'You silly fucking little shit-ass queer! You silly fucker!
You got a lot of gall to put down fucking Rimbaud! It's so fucking easy
for you, isn't it? I got you the best fucking peter in the place, and try to
teach you something, and you can't get over being a silly cunt! You got a
one-out peter and you're safe under lock and key and you don't have to

come across for anyone for anything—how would you fucking live on the street, like Rimbaud had to? You couldn't fucking do a bloody spring to make candy money, let alone make rent—you know what you're good for? You know what you are bloody good for? A finger-fuck! That's all!' and Glaister heard the booming flush at the other end of the intercom.

Zimmer apologised the next morning in the yard, with a face set as though still hurt. Glaister was impressed at Zimmer's obvious emotion. Zimmer was too. After paying out on Carol, he had gone to his bunk, laughed, then plunged into a vertiginous feeling which he could not understand or control.

Zimmer was in love. Zimmer couldn't keep his hands off Carol in the yard. Zimmer couldn't wait to talk to Carol at night. Zimmer ached for Carol. The argument over Rimbaud had sunk the barb. He had been insulated from his growing need to love by making an object, a vessel out of Carol. But her perversity on that night had hit him with the fact of her separateness—she was not an extension of his will, but an *other* who meant something to him, who was part of his very idea of self. To give up completeness, to sacrifice the things one has made.

Zimmer had in fact blown it. From the comfort of poetry and the self-assurance of pedagoguery, he had blown through to a need for meaning, and Carol was it. Because he had this thing, and because Carol reciprocated in a mysterious way, not physically, but by knowing Zimmer's weaknesses without wanting to hurt, Zimmer's world began to disintegrate. Zimmer's world was not built on love and Zimmer's love failed that world. His relationships with other crims and the screws, which had received his full lucid attention for years, began to suffer from neglect. He failed to please the screws at the gates with repartee. He was not available when bankers wanted news. He noticed that fewer people offered smokes in the yards. He found it amusing that crims were ambivalent towards Robin and Carol, two queens, getting it together. Only Dick Brunswick, who considered the possibilities, seemed to encourage them.

Love's periods and uncertainties masked the cause of disorder in Zimmer's existence. Once again, he found a clue in the library. Human nature was to blame. 'It is to be asserted in general of men that they are ungrateful, fickle, false, cowards, covetous and as long as you succeed they are yours entirely.' Thus spoke an unemployed Italian pubic servant named Niccolo Machiavelli, who suffered from the 1512 replacement of the Florentine administration. The critics of his memorandum rightly assert that he identified expediency with right conduct; his defenders rightly assert that his work was not innovative, but descriptive of the established practice of state power. This memo, called *The Prince*, was intended for limited circulation. It came to be considered one of the Great Books of the Western World and as such was bound in leather and donated to the prisoners of Maitland Gaol for the purpose of their rehabilitation.

That late autumn 'Twinkletoes' by Roy Orbison was a big radio hit. Your modern prison cells have three-inch speakers and your modern prisoners heard 'Twinkletoes' twice an hour. 'Twinkletoes' was Larry Glaister's favourite song.

Larry Glaister through the shitcan intercom told Robert Zimmer: 'I really dig "Twinkletoes".'

'Listen Carol,' said Zimmer, 'I'm reading a book that gets across perfectly what I've been trying to tell you for months. Believe me, sweety, the Big O has got nothing on the Big M.'

Nobody feels any pain . . .

Zimmer almost said the Big D, standing for Dylan, who had a big radio hit then called 'Just Like a Woman.' However, it was hard to allude to that knowing the fruitful parodies the queens in the laundry had devised.

'I don't want to read any more of this book, Robin. It gives me the *creeps*.'

'What gives you the creeps?'

'This Prince is just too *cynical*, Robin.'

'If you're so hurt,' said Zimmer, 'why then don't you show it?' And flushed. Carol was so *stupid*.

> Love seeketh not itself to please,
> Nor for itself hath any care,
> But for another gives its ease,
> And builds a Heaven in Hell's despair.
>
> So sung a little Clod of Clay,
> Trodden with the cattle's feet,
> But a Pebble of the brook
> Warbled out these metres meet:
>
> Love seeketh only Self to please,
> To bind another to its delight,
> Joy in another's loss of ease,
> And builds a Hell in Heaven's despite.

Zimmer carefully wrote the note in longhand, and then typed it several times so that there wasn't a single error in it.

Dearest Carol,

You know I love you and you would not treat me this way unless you wanted to stir me up inside. I have just been trying to help you and that is why I have insisted on you reading the big M. It is easy to do and you would learn a lot but you will not make the effort. The risks I have taken for you are amazing. I got you a good job, and a good cell. I have got you to read good books for yourself. I have got unpopular because you are my constant devotion. Then I think my efforts are failed. You never do anything for me. I got terrible headaches and you made them worse. I need pills from the infirmary and I nearly got sprung yesterday. You realise I could be transferred to another gaol for that. I just want you to talk about things intelligently and not be so stupid. That is not much to ask. I spend a lot of time on you you know.

Your closest friend
& Lover

Zimmer bopped out of the library and into the laundry, and gave the note to Carol, and turned straight away and went back outside. A new screw, a fuckwit, thought he saw something pass between the two prisoners from across the yard, through the laundry door. He went into the laundry and spoke to Lobey. Lobey just shook his head, as though he couldn't hear over the machines. The fuckwitted screw ramped Carol and sprang the note. His eyes lit up as he read it. He had discovered a queer prison drug ring.

The machinery caught the note like a rotary printing press catches a wedding ring, and ran on swiftly. Larry Glaister was charged with possession of contraband, and slammed in the black peter to await the Visiting Justice. Zimmer was hauled before the Governor's big desk.

It was an old-fashioned desk with elaborate relief. One of the Governor's tricks was to stare a standing man in the eye for thirty seconds or so, and then start reading from a file or charge sheet. Zimmer adopted a fixed stare at an imaginary point two inches above and two feet behind the Governor's head. He hadn't been charged. The evidence was technically inadequate. The fuckwitted screw could claim to have seen the note pass hands, but he needed some corroboration. The note had been found on Glaister, not Zimmer. Lobey wouldn't say anything. Carol had not lagged, nor would any other prisoner in the laundry. But ... only four crims had access to the machine which had typed the note. Was the class large enough? It was dicey. The Governor accepted no score on the staring game, and began speaking. Zimmer did not move his eyes, even though he had to blink. He followed the sound carefully as a critic confronting a new concerto by an old composer.

'-7, did you write this note?'

'No, sir.'

'You have knowledge of its existence, then.'

'I may have heard from your runner, sir.'

'I'll ask him.'

'It could have been from someone else.'

'I suppose it's the talk of the gaol.'

'Yes sir.'

'Well it damn well shall be, -7. What does this reference to em in the note mean?'

'What em sir?'

'The big em.'

'I beg your pardon sir?'

'Would you like me to read you the note, -7?'

'No sir. If you wish, sir.' Zimmer waited through the pause, knowing that the way it ended would be a signal of how the game would end. When the Governor began to read the note deliberately, he knew the game would end badly.

'Do you find that ambiguous, -7?'

'Yes sir.'

'You realise there are only what?—four prisoners? five prisoners? How many, -7? How many prisoners had access to that machine?'

'I'm not sure, sir.'

'You know which machine.'

'If I knew which machine, sir, I would be certain, yes.'

'Well, then we both know that four prisoners had access to the machine on which this note was written. This note, besides being contraband, raises some disturbing questions about security here, and it will have to be tendered to the Visiting Justice.

'-7, I'm no Leavisite but there are certain internal indications in this note which point to an author. Now would it be fair if I lock up the four prisoners who have access to this machine, -7?'

He answered reasonably, 'Yes sir. That seems quite fair.'

A paper folder drifted across the desk. The chair moved forward on its swivel-base. 'I don't think it's fair, -7.' There was a pause. Zimmer felt queasy. He felt he had won the point, but he knew who scored the game. The Governor's face swam up into view, and the deep, affected voice continued. 'I don't think it's fair to lock up all four of them.' Of course, he couldn't *legally*, could he? 'I don't think I'll lock anybody up. But offences of this nature threaten prison security and discipline, and I am going to see that you are safely removed from access to a typewriter, and then I'm going to wait, -7, and see if offences of this nature cease. Does that sound fair?'

Zimmer felt like his femoral artery had been cut and he was shrinking with each pulse.

'Fair enough -7?'

'Yes sir.'

The swivel chair swung out. The Governor moved over the carpet on foot, and out of the room by his private door.

The prison overseer handles the allocation of jobs. There was a vacancy in the laundry. There were no typewriters in the laundry. 'Jesus -7, that was a passionate little letter. You know, there were things in that letter that never should of been writ.' Zimmer almost laughed. Ordinarily the overseer was a very laconic screw, but his composition had *affected* people. 'You know, we all thought you were pretty smart.' In Lobey's warm aviary, Zimmer felt like a magnificent bird with clipped pinions.

Before the Visiting Justice, Lawrence R. Glaister pleaded guilty as the Governor had asked him to do. The Governor looked grim when the Justice asked Glaister where he had got the note referred to in the charge. Glaister said he had found it in clothing passing through the laundry. The Governor looked relieved when the Visiting Justice did not ask any questions about the text of the note, and said that in his opinion Glaister had been a good prisoner except for this one episode of withholding a contraband article. The Governor said it was impossible to detect the real offenders under the circumstances, but that Glaister had not been uncooperative if his story of finding the note was true. The Justice gave Glaister 24 hours in the black peter. Glaister had already done four days in the black peter waiting for his charge to be heard. Life in the black peter is terrible punishment, but in prison you are guilty until proven innocent. When Glaister came out of the black peter, the overseer did not slam him in the yards. Glaister was given a job straight away, at the woodpile.

. . .

Of all the jobs they call hard labour, only the woodpile is hard work.

Glaister was weak. The woodpile screw was terrified of his own homosexual fantasies and showed Glaister no favours. He made the boy swing a fourteen pound hammer which he could hardly lift, and the cheap handle pulled skin away on each stroke. Only when Glaister's hands wept did the screw give him a different job. Sweeping and bagging. This meant Glaister spent all day with his back bent, collecting splinters in his hands and forearms. Ironbark splinters contain a toxic resin which causes local inflammation and suppuration. After a while, the woodpile screw put Glaister back on the hammer.

'Would you like to hold the wedge while someone else swings your hammer?'

'No sir.'

'Then swing that fucking hammer.'

Glaister swung that hammer, hanging onto the rough handle like a man hangs onto the edge of a cliff in some political cartoon. Beneath him were the yards and the black peter, a void. He was unhappy. He asked to go to the toilet.

'Tell me if you piss standing up,' ordered the woodpile screw.

'Yes sir.'

'Yes sir, you'll tell me, or yes sir, you piss standing up?'

'I do sir.'

'I know you do. I want to know if you piss standing up.'

'I piss standing up sir.'

'Well, you can piss where you're standing then.'

Maitland Gaol is covered and recovered in paint by the maintenance crew. They have ladders and brushes and buckets and scrapers and gallons of murky pastel hi-gloss paints and bright red pavement paint and strippers and thinners and they rather like their job. The fumes leave you slightly dissociated and you get to see different parts of the gaol, and a change is as good as a holiday. They operate from a sheet-iron shed by the woodpile, which is a joke to them, and when Carol the Gorgeous

Queen approached them for some materials for a little interior decorating, they were happy to donate her the stripper she requested. She got quite a bit from them over a week. She put it in plastic bags and wrapped the bags in her towel, and carried it off with her when she left the woodpile for her shower. She would smile boyishly at them as she went by, and the maintenance crew were all secretly feeling romantic and hardly ever made smart remarks.

Sometimes the stripper seemed to eat the plastic bag and drench her towel before she could get it back to her peter and pour it into her water jug.

Zimmer was too impotent to even write an epigram about how he felt. His world had shrunk, and the smaller world was more hostile. He had made several screws angry, and even Lobey was diffident. The bankers were vexed by the ramps that followed the note incident. The infirmary had become an unfriendly place, and everyone suspected that Zimmer was a loser and a spoiler. Zimmer was disappointed, frustrated, a field for freshets of anger, and he even felt a little guilty. He could do nothing for Carol, because the woodpile screw was terrified of Zimmer, who personified trouble, and would begin screeching if Zimmer so much as appeared near his caddywompus pyramids.

'How are you feeling, Carol? How are your hands?' The shitcan conversations had grown mechanical, and Zimmer felt like a motor lugging in front of a sprung machine.

'They don't hurt anymore.' Her voice was tired and flat.

'You'll probably develop muscles any day,' joked Robin.

'I suppose.'

'You haven't got much to release, you know.'

'No, that's true, only two months.'

Zimmer couldn't read Glaister's voice. On some days it sounded tired and tense, and he tried to loosen and boost the kid. But over a week or so Glaister's voice had become just tired, or tired and flat. Zimmer thought maybe Glaister was learning to do it easy, but he couldn't really believe that. 'You're okay, aren't you?'

'I'm beat, Robin.' There was a pause. 'I think I'll clean up and turn in.'

Zimmer said, 'Cool, Carol, I understand.' He didn't even launch into one of the future movies he had been playing. Glaister had stopped responding to the future movies. Zimmer thought maybe Glaister didn't want to think about this love continuing outside, but he couldn't really believe that.

'I think I'd just rather listen to the radio. I'm not really feeling like talk,' she said, almost dreamily.

'All right,' said he, 'leave the tube open ... if you want to talk later, after lights-out, all right ... I really do ... love you Carol—I just feel so down myself ...' and Zimmer changed the discomfort of squatting over the empty bowl to the ease of the bunk and listening vacantly to the radio.

The lights went out, and afterwards he smelled smoke. His imagination led him through annoyance (it seemed like Carol had smuggled a blowtorch into her cell and was burning off the paint and this was silly and she would be charged and go back to the black peter ...) to wakefulness. Awake in the cell, he decided there definitely was a fire. He went to the toilet bowl and whispered, 'Hey, Carol.' He smelled it through the toilet, and shouted, 'Hey Carol! Hey!'

Glaister may have heard the voice because that was when the scream started—it wasn't a loud scream, and it tapered quickly away into odd noises. Zimmer began shouting and kicking the door of his cell. A few other people did too—the smoke must have gone all through the cell-block, Zimmer thought. Everybody can smell it.

Five or six minutes later a screw came marching deliberately up the iron stairs to the second tier. He went along the tier deliberately until he came to the number that Zimmer was yelling, and looked in the peephole. Of course he couldn't see anything, and of course regulations state that cells are not to be entered unless two officers are present. The wing screw was probably still in his office reading a novel or finishing a cup of tea, because the junior screw took a couple of quick steps and began shouting.

'Hey Jack, we got to go in, Jack. C'mon up.'

The crims were still kicking their doors. A minute later a voice cut through the block. It was the wing screw. 'Shut up you bastards. I fucking slam the lot of you up ya don't bloody cut it.'

'Right up here,' shouted the other screw.

The wing screw walks deliberately up to the second tier, and cracks the door. He must have swung a torch into the smokey cell, and his voice was a little too stagey when he said, 'Ah shit have a look at that.'

The junior screw for some reason went back down the stairs, got a bucket of water, and threw it in the cell. Maybe it was still smouldering.

It worked something like this: the orderly was called in, and the screws carried it over to the prison infirmary, where it was bandaged, or rather, swaddled. It must have been breathing. The next morning, the Governor came in to have a look, and didn't even bother to roar the wing screw for not waking him. He just rang a doctor. The doctor came a couple hours later, and sent it to Maitland hospital. The hospital called air ambulance, and it was DOA at a Sydney hospital. The air ambulance bit made about two paragraphs in the paper, and the papers printed the words 'believed to have been smoking in bed.'

The story, of course, was cut out of the newspapers allowed into the prisons. Zimmer heard of that later. In fact, most of the details he pieced together later. Once again, he was defensive about his feelings; he didn't seem to have any.

What impressed Zimmer most about Glaister's entire existence was how it had changed almost nothing in anyone else's life, except for the fact that Glaister had cost Zimmer his job in the library.

1974

BEV ROBERTS

Poem for Our Fifth Year

This will be
this is
the poem that has
for so long
refused to form,
the poem about water
the poem about love
like water, shapeless until contained,
resisting shape,
slipping through my words.

Sea people, our years have been spent
walking the coast of the world,
silent except for a hand touch,
heading always for that far point
at the end of the beach curve.

How can these things
be fixed in words
while our own fleshy tides
still sound the rhythms
of all those seas,
while we hold in our eyes
that moment when
above us the peak of the rearing wave
begins its white curl.

How can I do more than note
the components of delight:
the orange tent,
insignificant as a dropped handkerchief
in the space between the night-still lake
and its high starry lid.

The flotilla of swans
that sailed in slow motion
over rippling moon silver
to some other shore
and returned with the dawn
to their daytime place.
The boat with one light
coming silently to haven
and hovering in our darkness
like a dream.

'Come out of the water!'
they called from the shade
of their big umbrellas.
'Come out now or ... '
(some threat that didn't work).
'Real water babies' they said
as, burnt and bleached,
scratchy dry as sand,
we fretted through that long hour
after meals.

We did not know each other then
but later found
we spent our summers
in the same sea,
ran on the same beach,
turned the same rocks,
looking for crabs.
Today we stand on that beach
together
with the same old pictures
in our heads,
sharing history.

A child in sandy bathers
is picking shivery grass
is hiding, in ti-tree scrub
is rolling down dunes
is feeling the weathered wood
of a derelict kiosk
is listening to seedpods crack
through the hot silence
of an infinite afternoon.

And still the sea
here, high on the beach,
then there, far past the drying sand ribs.
Still two views each day
of the reefs edged with spray slaps,
the caves and weedy canyons.
Good flat skimmer stones
thrown now from a higher arm
follow the same three-four-skip line
into waves.
Hard old feet wincing over rocks
send messages of childhood lightness,
indifference to pain.

In Williamstown
we have made our home on an island.
Ships glide past the end of the street,
shifting winds add salt
to the garden scents.
On wild nights the sea
sounds through our windows;
hearing it in sleep
we are restless as beached mermaids.

This is the poem about five years
of love and its element
the water.
This is the poem
that still slips out of words.

1991

SANDRA SHOTLANDER

From *Is That You Nancy?*

(COLLECTED PHONECALLS OF GERTRUDE STEIN AND OTHERS)
Telephone Medley

The stage contains STEIN'S *chair and telephone table on one side and* PATSY
O'BRIEN'S *chair and telephone table on the other. Both tables have trumpet lilies in
vases on them.* PATSY *has a telephone, but* STEIN *uses two trumpet lilies throughout
the play as her telephone.* PATSY *finally uses lilies to connect with* STEIN *at the end.*

. . .

*One actor in a spot begins 'Look What You've Done'. She is joined by the second
actor. They have skirts, leotards and ruffles. The skirts are removed after the number.*
PATSY *has a basic costume underneath,* STEIN *has a velvet gown. Hear a reprise of
'Look What You've Done', music only to enter into the dialogue.*

OPERATOR: Directory, what city are you calling?
PATSY: Paris, France.
OPERATOR: Name?
PATSY: Stein.
OPERATOR: Initial?
PATSY: G—Gertrude.
OPERATOR: Address?
PATSY: Rue de Fleurus—27.
OPERATOR: I'm sorry, that number is no longer available.

PATSY: I'm trying to find Miss Gertrude Stein for an interview. Could you help me contact Miss Stein? My name is Patsy O'Brien. I'm calling from Australia.

STEIN: (*looking up*) Miss Stein is not available.

PATSY: Could I call again? Could you give me a time when I could call her?

STEIN: Miss Stein is busy, busy, busy, planning a dinner party.

(*A collage of telephone and electronic sounds.*)

. . .

(STEIN *sits at her table and addresses the audience.*)

STEIN: [. . .] Telephone calls can leave a bitter taste. And so can dinner parties. Alice and I were at a dinner party last week. I didn't know neither did Alice know and had we known we would not have been there.

(PATSY *is also lit.*)

PATSY: Uh ha, um, yes, oh ... just a minute. Is that the Cathy of Cathy and Trish or Cathy and Joy? The other Cathy, not Cathy and Trish or Cathy and Joy—oh, Cathy and Jane, the Jane who used to live with Barb, Barb of Susie and Barb. Susie was Jenny's ex-lover. Yes, I know Jenny of Jenny, Terry and Patti, yes and Patti and Fay and Fay and Cathy. Yes the same Cathy, no not the Cathy of Cathy and Trish or Cathy and Joy, the Cathy of Cathy and Jane who used to live with Barb of Susie and Barb. Susie was Jenny's lover, the Jenny of Jenny, Terry and Patti before Patti was with Fay and Fay and Cathy and Fay and Jane and Fay and Barb.

STEIN: One thinks one knows one's friends, but we didn't know such people existed as were at that table. Who was that man I asked Alice and what was he doing there? That Australian man with a wife in blue and the name of an Egyptian river. What was his name?

PATSY: That's definitely right Faye and Jane, the Jane of Cathy and Jane, who used to live with Barb da da da da Susie Jenny etc. Oh and Faye and Barb. What do you mean they weren't? Fay wasn't ever Barb's lover, they were just co-counsellors? Yes I know Barb changed her name to Rose Ella, when she went to the hills, and Cathy of Cathy and Trish is Autumn River, and Trish is Lightning Ridge now, didn't you know? And then Jenny, Terry and Pat are Calliope, Terpischore and Urania after the three muses, and Cathy and Joy have gone Celtic, and Fay's Morgan le Fay since she became a witch, and Susie can't make up her mind. Did you know, she's thinking of changing again. She's calling herself Susie Cambio which means Susie Changing in Italian. All those names. It ruins the flow of a good telephone conversation.

STEIN: I'm thinking of a river, an Egyptian river. Some public servant, Alice said, some travelling salesman, some bureaucrat in a clerical collar. He must have been from a sanitation department. Alice and I could hardly understand a word, a word he said. He wanted to cleanse the city, he wanted to clear people off the streets, so as to sterilise the city. His city was a sewer he said. A sewer because of the people. Blood tests he shouted they should all have blood tests. Alice went very pale. Alice has never had, nor would she ever have a blood test.

PATSY: Anyway what did the naturopath say? You didn't go. You went to what? An orthomolecular specialist. What's that? Oh allergies. And what have you got? Dust, grasses, yes, pollens, flowers, cat's fur, that's bad, tomatoes, avocadoes, strawberries, stone fruit, dairy, wheat flour, detergents, Germicidal Dot, boot polish and burnt toast. There's not much left really is there? I mean it's hardly worth living. And the tests can be negative, but you're still allergic. Why do you have the tests then? I see, so you can have them again if they turn up negative.

STEIN: I do not like crowds myself unless they are in New York. One doesn't usually clear people off the streets in order to clean them unless unless unless they are a certain sort of people and a certain sort of person is hauling his spiritual vacuum cleaner into the streets for the cleansing. What sort of people I asked are Australians if they are fouling the streets and if they aren't on the streets where are they doing it?

PATSY: You sound very elsewhere. Aren't I, I'm not the only one who's commented. Who've you been talking to? Is that the Cathy of Cathy and Trish or Cathy and ...? It doesn't matter. You know that's the third time you've mentioned Cathy. There isn't anything, I mean I know it's absolutely none of my business, since we became ex-lovers, since we have transcended our sexual ties and taken our space. I just thought we were both into celibacy, radical celibates.

STEIN: Homosexuals he said are fouling the streets, transvestites and prostitutes. The streets are sewers. It is the homosexuals and lesbians parading on the streets. The room was silent, absolutely silent except for the shaking of Alice's spoon against the side of her bowl.

PATSY: I know Cassie, I do understand, you've told me six hundred times. It's good for me to be on my own and I do meditate a lot on my trolloping around in my past lives. It's just that I'm alive now and you're on the other end of this thin wire connecting us and you seem to be in another world. Not even a thin wire. You're on the cordless phone. You know, Fay, that is Morgan le Fay, rang me the other day. Asked me if I'd ever had a sexual experience where you went out of your body. Have you? No, I haven't either. She has, but then she's not in this world very much at any time. You do sound elsewhere. What are you doing? I can hear purring. You're giving the cat reiki massage on her broken tail. I see the energy you put out comes right back. Well that's certainly an improvement on having relationships. No, really I'd like to try it, I would on my broken parts, but, you see, I'm really hoping to get to that place in meditation, where I don't need touch. I could become a socialist feminist and give up emotion altogether.

STEIN: I leant over gently gently gently and took the spoon from her whereupon he got up to make a call to Australia. They were going to have an election 'god can only go so far' he said. 'He can't fill in the ballot paper but we'll be praying.' A call to god. He couldn't get through. No-one was answering.

PATSY: Who told you that? No I didn't. I did not. I didn't cry on anyone's shoulder. I wish you wouldn't say things like that. You know all the cancer in my chart makes me vulnerable. She told you did she? She would. She's beyond help. She's not, she's straight. She'd wash a man's feet and dry them with that long hair of hers. Just grovels. I'll bet she's in a self-devised drama. Her life's one big self-devised drama, if you ask me. Look I know you think the only drama in the world is self devised, whatever that means. Anyway what's this got to do with healing? Did you notice the full moon last night? You were pre-menstrual. No, I'm not due till the third quarter. I guess we've stopped cycling together since we became ex—since we've transcended … taken our space.

STEIN: I wasn't surprised. I wasn't at all surprised and neither was Alice. She did look pale. She simply said said 'With a name like an Egyptian river one thinks of Cleopatra'. Alice was always a romantic.

PATSY: Why don't you pop over for a bit of brown rice and lentils or a hunk of chocolate cake if you like, and you can show me the reiki massage. Funny, you'll have to get rid of the cat now they've told you you're allergic to it. And speaking about separating, did you hear about Margaret and Teena? Well are they or aren't they? I mean they were together at Susie's party and apart at the women's ball. Yes, what about Fiona and Paula and Rainbow and …

STEIN: (*to the audience*) Identity is funny being yourself is funny as you are never yourself to yourself, except as you remember yourself and then of course you do not believe yourself.

PATSY: Bye for now. (*Puts down the receiver.*)

STEIN: (*to the audience*) Bye, bye for now, see you soon, so long, keep in touch, bye, bye. Telephone calls can leave a bitter taste and so can dinner parties.

(*We hear a collage of telephone sounds and electronic noises.*)

. . .

(*Silence—light up on* STEIN.)

STEIN: (*to the audience*) At the end of Hitler's war, the German army was made up of boy-soldiers on women's bicycles. Oh yes, they would burn and shoot and loot, the bully boys, the children sent in to menace on women's bicycles, taken along the way. It was unbelievable. One could not believe one's eyes and then I came home one day and there were about 100 boy-soldiers in the garden, in the house, all over the place. Poor Basket, my dog, sat and shivered in my bedroom all night, too horrified to bark. He has hardly barked since. They shot a dog in the village because she barked, a beautiful black labrador. I am trying to induce Basket to bark again. It is not right that a dog should be silent. It is not right to be silent. Who sends the bully boys in now? From where do they, I wonder, from where do they get their menace?

(*We hear a beat of a drum—a military beat, soft and haunting and a hint of menace. It fades out and* STEIN *begins* 'Would you?')

STEIN: Would you?
Would I what?
Would you? Would you?
Would I? Would I what?
Would you like? (*Begins a soft shoe.*)
Would I? Would I?
What would you
Like
Sweet sweet sweet sweet sweet tea
Alice B (*As the rhythm takes over she continues the soft shoe, moving about.*)
Sweet, sweet sweet sweet sweet tea
Alice B.
Would you?
Would I what?
Would you? Would you?
Would I? Would I what?
Would you mind?
Would I? Would I
Mind? (*Continues movements with the words.*)
Splashes splashes of jelly

Splashes of jelly
Splashes splashes of jelly
Splashes of jelly
Would you? Would you?
Like (*Goes to the coffee table down centre.*)
(*As she recites she dances and sits on the table, rolls back legs in the air, etc.*)
Soft brown eggs
Two dipped pears
Hot chocolate fudge Sunday
Thick custard
Toasted almonds
Rum ba bas
Brandy snaps
Licorice straps
Water melon, melon pink
Turkish delight
Would you? Would you want?
Vanilla kisses
Crystal glasses
Tangy, saucy, saucy, pie
Piece of cheese cake, cheesy, cheesy, cheesy tart
Spicy, spicy, spicy, buns
Hot hot hot chocolate
Whipped cream
No clotted cream
No, scalded cream
Cream whipped and scalded, whipped and scalded
Hm!
S & M?
Roast potatoes boiled dumpling
greasy chips
Greasy chips?
Buttered rum, honey drop, melting moment. Bags of feathers.
Rose petals. Pot pourri.
My Alice B. (*Stands behind the coffee table, arms extended in an open embrace.*)

1990

NIGEL KRAUTH

From *JF Was Here*

John could not eat breakfast. He had had a bad night, and he knew the sips of chardonnay were the catalyst. He wondered whether the agony was comparable to that of a gut full of shrapnel in Vietnam. He supposed it was. My private Vietnam. All the way with being gay. Ha.

He remembered telling Francis about the fist-fucking on stage at the Dungeon, off Oxford Street in Sydney. That's where he had misspent too many annual leave periods. Ten years in a row he flew to Sydney from Port Moresby. Flew in like the jet-setting boys from California. Ah, California boys, bronzed and oiled and shorn smooth. They stopped going to Vietnam and came to Sydney. 'Nobody told us what Vietnam would be like. No, sir. Nobody told us we would die.' He had groped with them at the Dungeon, had danced at parties. And nobody told them love was more dangerous than war. *Ah, California boys, dancing to their deaths.* Funny. Francis never believed my stories about fist-fucking at the Dungeon. Yet Francis believed in Taxi Number 33. *Kaposi's sarcoma. It sounded like a Tolai dance step. Or at least a Tolai name.* Francis Kaposi Sakoma Tapukai. *Oh, Jesus.*

Sitting in the wastes of the Hydro Majestic dining room among the museum pieces with bare toast and little air-tight packets of butter and Vegemite and marmalade staring up at him, John tried to avoid imagining his own bowels. Inside, in the dark there, those fucking nodules were swelling and swelling. Like the tiny bodies of dead boys in dark car boots. Bloating up. Dark brown secrets which his body hadn't been game to show to the world. One of his friends in Sydney had had the blotches on the outside, on his legs and chest, but John had got them on the secret skin of his gut.

. . .

By the end of his first year (it was 1972) John was convinced that life in Moresby suited him perfectly. Goffett's prediction about big fish in a small pool was correct: it was easy to make a mark as a town planner in a stone-age country hellbent on modernisation. In his social life too John was finding satisfaction. A regular round of weekend parties in glorious tropical settings (the bays, the islands, the mountains around the town) introduced him to the tight-knit community of public servants, journalists and teachers who had come to Moresby in circumstances similar to his own.

He loved being in the air and sunshine of Moresby. Their zest and clarity quickened him. Then in the wet season he loved the madness of the sudden downpours—rain which fell in exuberant warm curtains and could be happily walked through. It drenched then dried off rapidly with the returning sun. And after the rain he loved the rich leafy odours, the wild celery fragrance of the kunai grass beside the red dirt roads, the pig grease and woodfire smells emanating from rambling shacks in the local suburbs and settlements.

Moresby became his stage. He discovered a part to play which matched his sense of self. He delighted in the weekend group of friends who drank and swam and idled together, but who cared for each other as family. On weekdays he threw himself into his work where Goffett gave him a free hand in several major projects. To celebrate his new-found confidence he conceived the idea of affecting a bow tie at official functions (not the whirring version which came a little later), feeling certain that he was the only man in the entire tropics who was mad enough to wear a bow tie, making that his trade mark.

In his work he found amusement and challenge in the ironies of white men planning towns for a ten-thousand-year-old culture. He and Goffett had the task of assessing the social impact of the government's proposed showpiece—a new town called Waigani to be built on grasslands on the outskirts of Moresby in time for Independence. It would feature at its centre a Parliament House shaped like an upturned boat, an Australian Embassy taller than every other building, a Prime Ministerial office block resembling a giant pineapple wearing a plastic hat, and a six-lane super highway, to be called Independence Drive, which would run for a kilometre and stop abruptly. The proposed town was all for show. It was meant to make the statement: 'Look how far Papua New Guinea has come to gain independence'. But as John perceived, it said something quite different. It showed the country's new *dependence* on the twentieth century, on international politics and macroeconomics, on aid and pressures from outside, on concrete and plastic.

John devoted himself to the Waigani plan because he saw it was also very Papua New Guinean. It was a mad, tinsel-wreathed dance of buildings. It was bombast in a new architectural language. It was the new elite's big-time squatter settlement showing off muscles of steel.

On a typical weekend John drove down to Bugandi Bay for a party on a converted twin-hulled canoe. There were seven men present. They motored out across the broad reef-mottled bay, past Tatana Island, to the farthest reaches of the harbour where the mountains swept up from inlets, their grass-covered slopes rippling like velvet in the seasonal breeze. The men took off their clothes and swam in the pearly water among corals and rainbow-coloured fish.

On the deck, sunbathing and drinking, the men delighted in talk about Moresby—how shocking, how primitive, how logical a town it was. The flies on the unrefrigerated wallaby carcasses at Koki market, and the village couple who tried to sell a smoked baby there before the authorities confiscated it; the dangers of 'payback' reprisals if a European driver knocked down a local pedestrian, and how the Papua New Guineans ranked the car a deadlier weapon than the spear and did not subscribe to the notion that every time a car ran into something it was an accident; the story which had appeared in the papers during the week of a man who had fallen gravely ill after tearing up a Bible for a dare and, having been rushed to hospital by ambulance, turned into a python in the hospital bed, as reported by visiting relatives; the arrest of the self-styled Kung Fu Man who had attacked the Burns Philp Freezer windows with his bare hands in front of a crowd and lifted his bleeding palms to take the applause.

Lying back in a plastic chair on the boat deck with alcohol in his head and the sun in the recesses of his body, John felt the stories of Moresby enter his brain like a stirring drug. Port Moresby was *his* village, he was certain. He felt comfortably at home. And when two of the friends floated off the foredeck to enjoy sex in the drumming sunshine the talk did not miss a beat.

At the beginning of his second year John was given an assistant. His name was Francis Tapukai. He was a graduate from the university, and a Tolai. He was brilliant, shifty, handsome. During work hours he was gentle and charming. Outside work hours he was a monstrous drinker and betelnut addict. He arrived late in the office every morning with the reddest blood-shot eyes John ever saw. He was erratic in his work, but his brilliance far outweighed his faults. His understanding of the impact of modern pressures on Papua New Guineans, his articulation of those pressures, and his suggestions for acceptable solutions, formed the basis for most of the plans that John's office produced prior to Independence Day. There was no doubt that Francis Tapukai had a bright future: he took to town planning like a crocodile to water. Yet his village orientation did not seem to waver.

During Francis' first week in the office, while the two were poring over plans together, John asked him about the Tolai *warbat*.

Francis smiled coyly. 'You know about *warbat*, John?'

'I've heard of it.'

The *warbat* was one of the titillating topics John's friends discussed. When a Tolai man wanted a particular woman to fall in love with him he engaged the services of a *warbat* singer. By chanting *warbat* love charms the singer would draw the chosen woman from the hut where she slept and lead her, by song, to the lover waiting in the jungle.

'It's top secret magic, John.'

'Tell me about it then.'

Francis looked down at the plan spread out on the table in front of them. It was, of all things, the design for a public convenience to be placed near Independence Drive. Francis ran his finger along the lines of the plan. 'Shouldn't we be discussing Waigani?'

John shook his head. 'I want to know about *warbat*.'

'I have some songs on tape. Would you like to hear them?'

John went to Francis' place that night. Francis lived in Boroko, another Moresby suburb, in a small flat provided by the government. It was the first time John had been in a Papua New Guinean's home. He felt awkward. The flat was barewalled, mattress-strewn, lit by naked bulbs.

It smelt of sweat and sleep. But Francis was a capable, if uncomplicated, host. He pulled out beers from the fridge (proud of their coldness) and switched on the small Japanese cassette player. The *warbat* singing came into the room.

'Tolai women are scared of it,' Francis laughed. 'Even those who go to the university.'

John had to admit immediately that there was something powerful about the songs, something hypnotic even to a sceptical European.

'Do they work on white women?' he asked.

Francis smiled coyly again. 'Haven't you heard about my reputation?' He laughed with his face tilted downwards.

The singing was by marvellous male voices, falsetto and gravelly at once, punctuated by a bamboo xylophone. The song seemed to come in pulsating waves. John drank beer and closed his eyes. He felt the singing vibrate in his chest and spine. Was it the earth singing? It seemed like voices coming from wood, from leaves, from soil and falling water. He could hear the singers' breathing, could feel the closeness of them, of the song's intimacy, coming from inside himself now; yet, at the same time, the song shifted, built and vanished, like faraway cloud churning. Immobile in his chair, he felt he travelled through transparent membranes, one vista opening upon another. As the singing paused and surged he went with it, dreading and loving it, falling and climbing with an irresistible momentum, tumbling into the gulfs of the song, soaring up the mountainsides of the song.

The music stopped. 'I'm stoned,' John said, opening his eyes.

Frances sat in the chair opposite with his head thrown back and his smooth neck exposed. His Adam's apple was rising and falling gently. '*Liu liu liu*,' he sang, echoing the song.

After a few more beers and much laughter, John drove home through the squatter settlement beyond Boroko and Badili. He stopped the car at no place in particular and got out simply to experience the rich night air, the tropic sky rattling with stars, the overhanging trees with their pendant darknesses, the warmth rising from ditches beside the roadway, and the dark house yards screened by banana plants out of which came low laughter or talk or arguments, all carried on in darkness except for the pink glow of embers and the occasional garish pressure lamp. He breathed in the wood smoke, the tang of tropical blossoms, the exhalations of humid earth. Willingly, he opened his consciousness to the shadows and murmurs and dark fragrances surrounding him, and felt a subtle rearrangement inside, as if the suburbs of his soul were being invaded and taken over by new inhabitants.

The next Saturday John invited Francis to go with him to the swimming pool. It was a calculated move, he knew, and he did not wish to examine his motives too closely. He fully expected that Francis would decline, but after hesitating for a moment, as if he had another engagement which he was deciding to cancel, Francis said he would like to go.

It was the Saturday after a pay-day Friday. On the verges of Sir Hubert Murray Drive lay the occasional car wreck, as was normal following the pay-night spree. Drunkenness was endemic in Moresby on a fortnightly basis. John paid for Francis' admission into the pool and they found a patch of grass down by the cyclone wire fence, away from the European families and the talkative locals. Francis did not bring a towel. Expecting this, John had brought two of them which he spread out on the grass.

John tried not to look too directly at Francis' body as he stripped down to a pair of Speedo swimming trunks. During the week John had taken note whenever Francis hinted at his sexual prowess among women. John had no expectations and no definite evidence regarding Francis' preferences, but he did have an instinct. His radar was working. In any case, he could not resist the sight of a taut, handsome body under any circumstances. Perhaps fortunately, a pair of drunken highlanders arrived and clung to the outside of the wire fence to watch the antics of those who could afford admission to the pool. Their shirts were undone, their trousers awry. They provided a distraction.

'A big night on the road last night,' John commented awkwardly.

Francis lay down on the towel. 'Yes, plenty of parties. Drunkenness is a sacred state here.'

John knew that was true. Some parties were held in the middle of main roads, with the cartons of stubbies piled up on the double white lines. Drivers had to manoeuvre around the seated drinkers until the police came to remove them.

'You get sent to gaol for it in Australia.'

Francis frowned. 'Oh, drunkenness is your best excuse for anything here. If you roll your car off the road because you are drunk, well, that is your defence, isn't it? You were drunk, so it happened. You should not be punished again by being sent to gaol.'

John snorted. 'You don't subscribe to that, do you?'

'It is the unofficial view, I think.'

The two drunks still clung happily to the fence. John was reminded of the zoo; but was disturbed by the knowledge that he was on the enclosed side of the cage fence. The drunks grinned, and he smiled back at them. One of them, he noticed, wore a grubby T-shirt which had printed on it: 'I am Independent. I don't need to drink.'

'Oh, and another thing, John. Never laugh at someone who is drunk. A drunk man cannot help the way he looks.' Then Francis burst into a fit of high-pitched laughter. 'I am only pulling your leg, mate,' he spluttered.

John felt a strange vulnerability to Francis. There was something about the black man that struck at him deep down. He felt a stirring desperation to please Francis, to 'pleasure' him was perhaps the word. He wanted to impress him, and somehow to support him.

They swam languidly together in the pool, but found the splashing and screeching of the surrounding children a nuisance. They hauled themselves out and sat for a while in the sun on the pool's edge. John saw the suave shape of Francis' penis moulded in his wet swimmers and felt a sort of drunkenness pass through him.

When they went back to their towels the clinging highlanders had gone.

After just a month of working side by side with Francis Tapukai, John knew that his developing inverted racism had become focused towards the Tolai. He was turning into a Tolai culture buff, and a Gazelle Peninsula supporter. The Mataungans could do no wrong. Francis Tapukai could do no wrong. When Francis failed to present his work on time, John finished it for him. When Francis lied about goofing off in work time, John provided the alibis. When stories were told about Francis' affairs with white women, John was jealous.

During their first weeks of friendship Francis introduced John to the Boroko Hotel beer garden. The place was notorious for its brawls which the hotel management had to clear with high-pressure hoses. John got a kick out of drinking there. His Australian colleagues called it the Snake Pit. They told him stories about highlanders dragging broken stubbie bottles through the soft white throats of expatriates who entered there. But John discovered such stories to be nonsense. Certainly it was a black men's enclave, but he went there regularly with Francis and survived. And he knew why. He did not emanate prejudice and hatred. Prejudice was like sweat, he thought. You could smell it.

John and Francis were there together one evening, drinking at a concrete table under the rubber trees. Francis was moody, a little uncommunicative, as was common. John happened to look up and saw three brawny Australians come out of the pub lounge and into the beer garden. These men *did* stink of prejudice. The babble of the fifty or so Papua New Guineans drinking on the concrete seats dried up immediately. The three big whites came down the aisle between the concrete tables in an aggressive phalanx. John innocently wondered whether these fellows were newcomers in Moresby. He speculated as to whether they could be drivers of the giant bulldozers on the Bougainville Copper Project. Meanwhile, the three monsters were coming straight towards John and Francis' table. Before John properly knew what had happened, one of the three had sent his fist flying into Francis' face, knocking him sprawling on the concrete paving. The other two delivered full-blooded kicks to Francis' kidneys and head via steel-toed work boots. Then they walked out.

There was no eruption in the Snake Pit. The servery gates were not hurriedly rolled down, nor were the fire hoses manned by the hotel staff, as usually happened at the first hint of a brawl. Instead, Francis lay bleeding from the nose on the concrete while a crowd of black faces stared at him, immobile.

John bent down and tried to lift him under the shoulders. 'Jesus, Francis. Let's go.'

Francis allowed himself to be hauled to his feet. Then he sat again, shakily, at the table.

'I'll bring the car around to the gate.'

Francis shook his head. 'Stay and drink, *poro*.' He was forcing a laugh, holding his hands over his hurt face.

John protested, but it was no use. He went to the servery for more beer. *Perhaps he has to show his countrymen that he is a man. Damned Tolai pride.* John brought the open bottles back to the table. Francis edged one towards his bleeding mouth.

'I met her in the bar last night.' Francis spoke softly. 'I just met her and she asked me to come to the room upstairs. I couldn't help it.'

'Who, Francis? Who are you talking about?'

'That fellow's wife. The one who hit me.'

'Jesus Christ. You must be mad.'

Francis smiled. Freeman saw the blood and beer froth swimming over his teeth.

'European women fall in love with me like that,' Francis said.

They drank until the beer garden closed. Then John insisted on taking Francis back home with him. As they drove past the Burns Philp supermarket they heard the cascading shatter of the plate glass. Ahead of them highlanders spilt across the road. They charged about, picking up the rocks lining the trampled garden beds in the park opposite, using them to smash the windows of the Chinese shop fronts along Tabari Place.

'It's starting,' Francis said.

He was slumped in the bucket seat beside John, his head against the side window. He didn't turn to look as John threaded the car through the wild movement of men.

'What's starting?'

The car received several thumps along its side. A rock came through the back window on John's side, shattering the glass which spilt into the back seat.

'Independence is starting.'

They drove out of Boroko along Sir Hubert Murray Drive, over the hill and down into Badili. The sound of the riot reverberated behind them. *There are currents beneath the surface which I am disqualified from seeing.* John's thinking was a maze of vulnerabilities, but at the centre of it was something hard and selfish—an inexorable lust. He drove home quickly and parked the car right outside his front steps.

In the bathroom John sponged dried blood from Francis' face. Francis took off his shirt. He twisted to look in the mirror at the bruises from the kicking in his side and back. In the quavering fluorescent light John could see the swelling under the shinier patches of dark skin. Francis was disarmingly cheerful about the sight of his own injuries. He admired them for a time. Then he turned to John and laughed. 'I need a hot shower for the bruises.' He stripped the rest of his clothes off.

An exhibition. A seduction. A sudden view in a disturbing mirror.

Through the bathroom louvres the haunting sound of the riot pulsed across the hill from Boroko.

Francis took John's soap, shampoo, and toothbrush into the shower recess and turned the hot water to full blast without drawing the curtain. John went and sat in the lounge room, excited, hearing the riot far off, a wavering blur of sound in the night and, close by, through the walls, heard Francis singing a pained-sounding Tolai song, brushing his teeth at the same time.

It is one of those songs. The warbat. Liu liu liu.

When Francis came into the lounge room, dripping, laughing, saying, 'Hey, John. Will you go and bring me a towel?' John was gone, plummeting, unsavable. Under the clattering fan in the dark bedroom they did what they could not possibly avoid doing, with the riotous night receding outside open louvre windows.

In the early hours of the morning John drove Francis to his flat. The streets were still. It seemed as if the riot had dispersed, although a police wagon sped by them at one intersection and vanished into the night.

Turning into Francis' street they heard a thumping. It grew louder as they neared his place.

'The stewardesses,' Francis laughed. 'They have parties every night. Even a riot cannot stop them.'

Parking in Francis' drive John could hear clearly the words of the amplified music (the Rolling Stones singing 'Brown Sugar') and the punctuating rumpus of party abandon.

'The Air Niugini dormitory,' Francis explained.

Through the intervening cyclone wire fence John could see a riot of floral-coloured lap-laps, of strewn brown bodies and beer bottles under an outdoor spotlight. He had to admit there was an amusing, tawdry glamour about it all. These crazy drunks kept the aeroplanes flying! A bottle sailed through the air and smashed against a wall.

'Do they keep you awake?' John asked.

'Oh, no. Not really.'

'Do you ever go and join them?'

'Of course not. They are not the kind of women I am interested in. I think they prefer white men.'

Standing in the dark garden beside the tall wire fence, John felt a sudden urge to reassert his claim on territory. Another bottle soared and plummeted beyond the spotlight and John turned and caressed Francis through his shorts.

'You want to fuck again, mate?'

The Rolling Stones came to the end of the song. Some drunken hand in the night skidded the needle back to the start and the record began all over again.

'Brown sugar ...'

. . .

In the two years leading up to Independence, work in the planning office became hectic and the tensions grew. Goffett made it known that he had no interest in remaining in the country beyond Independence, and left most of the work to John and Francis. Together they shared an ironic appreciation of the incongruities of the job. Much of their professional time they spent imagining and discussing what life would be like for post-Independence Papua New Guineans who, typically, would have been born in a primitive village, would have mediocre education, would make family homes in shanty towns on the outskirts of Moresby, would commute to work in open trucks, and would have their workplace among skyscrapers.

But the difficulties of building lifestyle quality into the plan for Waigani were as nothing, in John's mind, to the difficulties of building a relationship with Francis. John did not expect loyal devotion, and he certainly did not get it, but Francis' affections and availability were so erratic, so prone to every sort of pressure, John often wondered what it was that motivated him. Francis exercised his charm on one white woman after another, yet he kept coming back to John, apparently unable to help himself. John suspected that in the depths of Francis there lay not a great capacity for sex, but a great capacity for resentment. Francis seemed to need sex with whites as a drug, but also as a way of revenge, an act of anti-colonialism. Yet thinking these thoughts, John knew how hypocritical it was to ascribe base motives to Francis. If Francis was using John for some deep-seated and confused psychological satisfaction, he at least was not abusing him. In bed together they showed each other a wonderful generosity. Francis never attempted the monstrosities he afflicted on his female admirers.

It was only in his lowest moments that John thought this way. He knew that no relationship in the world was found faultless in such analysis of its dark depths. He and Francis had marvellous times together—John easily recognised them as the best times of his life. Francis was his inspiration and his delight, and even in the arms of other men in Sydney or, occasionally, in Moresby, John's love for Francis grew and endured.

To escape the pressures of the planning office, John and Francis went on trips together around the country by car and plane, and on foot. 'Exploring,' they called it. *We were exploring each other, our relationship, as much as the land.* They drove out of Moresby (east, north and west) until the roads petered out. They went with male friends on drunken, twin-hulled canoe trips towards the Gulf, and in the direction of Samarai. They flew to the cool highlands where they bought English potatoes at markets nestled under pine trees and sipped hot fresh coffee in the evenings by log fires with the potatoes roasting. To Madang where the idyllic scenery of the coastal inlets eclipsed even the most romantic tropical travel brochures. And to Rabaul where volcanoes could pop out of the bay overnight and where nothing was left on open shelves because of the regular earthquakes. *In each place we fucked. It was like claiming the country together.* In his own village, out from Rabaul, Francis arranged an evening of dances especially for John's entertainment, and after the Whip Dance (where young blond-haired Tolai men leapt about and thrashed each other's ankles with long canes) a mild earthquake hit while John and Francis were making love in a thatched palm cottage *and we kept on fucking*.

But it was their walking of the Kokoda Trail that John remembered as the greatest exploration. They flew to Kokoda early one morning. There were six in the party (four Australians and two Papua New Guineans), all public servants, all male. John had been in training for weeks, climbing up and down Burns Peak each evening, lugging a haversack which contained an increasing number of heavy stones. He had also studied the maps of the trail. On the plan maps the track appeared as a twisting dotted line linking village to village half way across Papua—a long way to walk but not too forbidding. On the elevation maps however the trail was shown as the progress of an ant up and down the teeth of a comb. In total the trail from Kokoda back to the outskirts of Moresby rose and fell 29 000 feet (equivalent to climbing up and down Mount Everest from sea level) and it wriggled for 93 kilometres. They intended to do it in five days. That was the most time available to one member of the party, who had to return to work for a conference. Their Islander plane took off eastwards from Moresby airport and climbed into the grey dawn. Above Kokoda the plane dipped down into the valley through a wispy hole in the early morning cloud lying thickly over the airstrip.

The dotted lines on the maps gave little clue to the actual terrain they would enter. John found that the Kokoda Trail was even worse than he had imagined or seen in Parer's horror photographs and Johnston's *New Guinea Diary*. Even without the Japanese the Kokoda Trail was a nightmare: the constant draining battles against the tyranny of gravity up the sheer ridges where the knees faltered and the breath died in the chest; then the slippery, hellish descents where the ankles gave and the toes were crushed maddeningly in the boots. *Dante's descent through Hell was a stroll by comparison.* On the first night they slept in a village above the Kokoda Gap, at 5000 feet, and in the morning looked out on a level with light planes flying above the clouds. Later that day John stood on a ridge beyond Templeton's Crossing and turned full circle. What a scene! Myriad mountain tops, a countless crowd of craning green heads, serried and jostling to a serrated horizon. Giants dwarfing other giants.

Topography gone troppo. (Troppography?) Mad nodules eruptive on the earth's skin, a rash of mountains, seven, ten, fourteen thousand feet high. *But beside my hand, on a leaf shaped like a green trumpet blast, the most exquisite blue butterfly, giant, and frail as gauze.*

In a rushing stream at the foot of the ridge they lay together out of sight of the others with the spangled water whirring around them.

On the third day one of the Australians tossed his boots over a cliff and sat down in the middle of the track. He wept. 'I can't do it,' he repeated. He lay back on his unremoved pack and covered his eyes with the palms of his hands. They had to tie a rope around his waist and drag him along. 'We can't just leave you here, Geoff.' He shuffled, bare-footed. That evening in the thatched guest house in Nauro village, Francis took off his own boots and emptied his toenails out of his socks. His toes were a pulp of blisters. 'You should have trained, you mad bastard,' John told him. They filled his socks with antibiotic powder the next day, and lightened his pack. He hobbled on in agony. *Dear God. And it wasn't even war time.*

Along the Kokoda Trail, John consciously recognised history. In the jungle on either side of the track, in the *chiaroscuro* of light dripping through myriad leaves, he could make out the camouflaged faces of soldiers. In the torrid silences of moss forests he could hear the stealthy foot-falls, and the club-club of fearful hearts. Coming up to a rise in the track, a false crest, he noticed the depression in the mulch where a foxhole would have been and where a gun would have clattered at him. There were bullet cases and the occasional helmet or bayonet still able to be discovered in the tangle of undergrowth beside the track. John wondered how far he needed to stray from the dotted line of the trail before he came across dead bodies, skeletons by now. They were there; they had to be. He could feel that they were. A *live* Japanese soldier had been discovered that year in the jungle on the north coast. He had been bloody glad to hear that the war had ended, even though it happened thirty years before.

They slogged on to the finish. At Ower's Corner in the mountains at the Moresby end of the trail, the party was met by a friend with a car-load of beer and champagne. *Dear Christ, the stuff never tasted so good.* John and Francis toasted each other, poured it over each other. The whole group joined in, bathed in froth and alcohol. The man with the rope around his waist was liberated. (The rope had been unnecessary on the fourth day—his spirits had risen once the end of the ordeal was in sight, but he had worn it just the same, as a self-imposed badge of shame, it seemed.) They took photographs of each other smiling with their arms about each other's shoulders. *We were magnificent creatures. We had survived.*

To John the survival of the Kokoda Trail seemed tantamount to passing through a torrid initiation rite; he and Francis were clan mates. Later that night, down on the coast in hot Moresby, under the *chopper-chopper* of the bedroom fan, he and Francis celebrated again, feeling the incredible tautness of their track-tuned bodies, the hardness of their calf muscles, the leanness of their buttocks. 'Just don't touch my bloody toes,' Francis wailed.

It wasn't long before they were laughing about the entire Kokoda Trail experience.
'You didn't walk the Kokoda Trail, mate. You hobbled it.'
'The Cock-odour Trail?'
'The Cock-ardour Trail.'
'Cock harder?'
'What about when the cigarette papers ran out and we rolled them in toilet paper?'
'And bandaids.'
'Or that bloody bottle of pink-and-white humbugs.'
'With one black-and-white one at the bottom.'
They rewarded themselves with a boiled sweet at each ridge. Everyone was thinking about who would get the prize of the black one.
'Then bloody Alan disappeared for a while, just before Ua-Ulle Creek.'
'We thought he was having a shit.'
'And at the next ridge—Imita Ridge, it was—the black-and-white one had gone.'
'We nearly killed the bastard.'
'I really did want to kill him. I premeditated his murder.'
John had been lowered by the physical agony and mental torture of the trail to a baser, simpler plane of logic; he didn't care about the morals or the consequences of killing. He had come down the Golden Staircase choking with rage. Then he had waded neck-deep in a creek holding his haversack above his head and had plotted the murder of an Australian colleague because he had eaten a humbug.
'We were going mad, *poro*.'
'You might have been, with your toes falling off. I was perfectly sane. *War-sane*.'
When they reached Ower's Corner and the road which stretched down to Moresby, all the madness had dissipated.
'We did it, mate. We survived.'

In spite of the traumas, or perhaps because of them, John internalised the map of the Kokoda Trail. He carried it inside his head—a determined dotted line across the jagged centre of an unforgiving land. Unforgiving, yes. But not unpredictable. Papua New Guinea was a constant, a wilderness which reproduced itself over and over, celebrated itself in immutable growth, self-regeneration. It was a powerhouse with no interest in progress or change. It did not wish to be or produce other than it was. It was satisfied with its own perfection. Men, like occasional ants, walked on dotted lines over it, and it shrugged them off. Especially town planners. In John's mind the map of the trail became the blueprint and contract of his relationship with Francis. They had shared an incredible experience. An ascent into Hell. A topological reversal. It bound him to Francis and to the country. He felt he knew something of the heart of them both, and something of his own heart.

'You know what the soldiers called the stairs they dug into the side of Imita Ridge in the war? The Golden Staircase. Golden because it ran golden with the diarrhoea of thousands of sick Australian soldiers.' He couldn't get that out of his head. *Shitting their hearts out.*

But for Francis the conquest of the trail was only partly a binding. He resented the loss of his toenails. 'The trail turned me into a woman,' he complained. 'To match my arse.' He was very touchy about the blackness of his buttocks. 'Sitting on a bloody seat does it to you. Studying does it. Every student at the University has an arse blacker than the rest of his body. Every public servant has too. From rubbing on seats all day. That's what we get from Western culture. Black, black arses. Like village women who sit all the time.'

When he was drunk with John he would go floppy as a cloth doll, the sinews seeming to collapse in him. He would lie around on furniture or on the floor, happily defeated by drink, by the world, smilingly careless about his own submission. But in the company of women he was different. He had a reputation for getting drunk then beating them.

'I can't help it. I *have* to beat them.'

Always white women. Women who could not resist him.

'Your cock is a Moresby legend, mate,' John would say, hurt.

And Francis would smile with such charm. 'I'm a tragic victim of culture clash, *poro*. That's my excuse.'

John indulged Francis, and in doing so indulged himself. Some of his white friends were of the opinion that he was heading for trouble. He ignored their quiet warnings.

. . .

Ah, those long Papuan days. Driving in the early morning cool. That wild celery smell in large-leafed, long-leafed groves beside the roadway. Remember the smell? Fecund. That was the word I always thought of. Then bouncing rides along swampy tracks, through tangles of mangroves to out-of-the-way beaches. Remember Bootless Inlet? Taurama? The photographs? You floating naked. You bending over the camp-fire naked. You showing off, Tolai spear at the ready. God, I loved you. Was lost and found in you. Gaped and burnt for you, ached to disappear in you, to be buried and born in you, to take you and burn with you, wearing perspiration and clinging sand, the sun in my eyes and throat, the searing caress, lifting my head and howling at the blue. Liu liu liu.

. . .

Soon after the golfing match with Bunani, John's relationship with Francis took a turn for the worse. It was the 22nd of December, 1984.

John remembered the date because it was impossible to forget what he went and did on the Christmas Day after it. The 22nd was the eve of his departure for leave in Sydney. He had a bottle of Glenfiddich and an exquisite carving of coupling snakes for Francis' Christmas present. He also had a shell money necklace for Jill.

Jill was yet another Australian woman Francis had attracted by *warbat* or whatever means to live with Francis in his Hohola house. She too, or so it seemed to John, was a fervent inverted racist like himself. She had changed her name to Jill Warwarup (from Jill Hall) after Independence. She had an official white husband who was an anthropologist at the University, but maritally-speaking, Jill had opted for some original research of her own.

She hurt me, as they all did, but I was determined not to be a bitch about it. What right had I?

John turned off Hohola Road into the dirt road which led to Francis' place. He knew something was wrong the minute he turned into the drive. There was a crowd of people in the front yard, standing among the hibiscus bushes and traveller's palms looking up at the lighted windows. It wasn't until John stopped the car motor that he heard the crashing and screaming.

John had long known that any sort of domestic argument attracted a crowd of neighbours in Moresby. And it was usually a vocal, amused crowd. But this one wasn't. They were not used to a mixed-race melee where a black man was beating up a white woman. White man on black woman, yes. But not the reverse.

John rushed up the stairs to the balcony. If the argument had been black on black the door would have been open, the woman would have arranged it that way to ensure maximum publicity for the injustice she suffered. But the door was shut. He banged on it several times. There was no let up in the fracas inside. He had to break the fly screen wire beside the door to get his hand through the louvres and around to the inside door knob.

When John finally broke in he found Jill Warwarup in the bedroom, tied to the bed while Francis thrashed her with a belt.

On the floor in all rooms, like detritus left after a tidal wave, was a carpet of empty bottles, empty wine casks, empty cigarette packets, empty betelnut husks. Francis was paralytically drunk; clinically, John imagined, he should not have been able to stand. Jill too was practically unconscious. She did not have the awareness to rearrange her sarong as he pushed Francis away and untied the twine on her wrists and ankles. She grunted as he wiped at the vomit on the bed around her head, and at the mat of vomit in her hair. He asked her if she was all right, and seeing the terrible welts on her stomach and face, he turned on Francis.

Francis was leaning against the door post, not watching him, just looking unsteadily at the ceiling with his chin wavering up and down and his head against the jamb. He had a drunken, self-satisfied smile on his face, and John had the idea that there was a piece of music going through his mind, and that he was loving listening to it. His head nodded, swivelling on the fulcrum of his long neck, and John saw the Adam's apple beautifully defined in profile and hit it with his fist as hard as he could. He had never hit anyone like that before. He was impressed with how much it hurt his hand.

Francis fell down. In amazement he looked back at John from the floor. On his back, raised on his elbows, he slithered backwards, pushing through the party flotsam. When he was far enough off to feel safe he struggled to his feet. 'You colonialist bastard,' he slurred thickly, and crashed his way through the wire screen door.

John later decided that his biggest mistake that night was made when, at that point, he turned back to Jill. Not out of concern for her condition (he would regretfully admit to himself) but because he was fascinated— obscenely excited was closer to the truth—by the sight of her body: forked, dishevelled, entirely gaping with a worn, wet look about it. Francis had used her, had turned loose his private riot onto her. It made John feel sick, and terribly jealous.

The sound of the car motor did not register in his consciousness until it was well started and on its way. He ran out to the balcony and saw the neighbours peering down the road. Some of them looked back up at him with amused pity on their faces. The Papua New Guinean had escaped in the Australian husband's car! That lifted the domestic row to a more comical level for them.

But Francis did not get far. At a corner just before the Hohola shops he ran into a child crossing the road under a street light. She bounced off the car and into the gutter.

. . .

Francis spent six months in the Bomana gaol. During that time John arranged the compensation payment for the Hohola people. It was an expensive broken leg. The girl's group tripled their claim when they heard that a white man was paying it, which made Francis furious.

'Don't pay,' he said. 'It's the twentieth century, isn't it? I'll do my payback in gaol.'

Francis had no money in any case, and John preferred the depletion in his own savings to the thought that Francis could be hunted on his release. By paying the compensation he thought Francis would be fairly safe. The one thing in Francis' favour was that the Hohola group knew he was drunk on the night of the accident. At least he had some excuse.

John visited Francis each weekend. He drove out to Bomana in the dust and in the rain. Most weekends Jill accompanied him, but she let him go alone now and then—on purpose, he supposed, so that Francis could be entirely his.

They met in a bare compound along with a hundred other prisoners and visitors. They shook hands and found themselves a space where they could talk, up against the cyclone wire fence.

'What have you brought me, *poro*?'

'A sponge cake. Watch out for the wire cutters inside.'
Francis opened the bag. It was full of betelnut, as usual.
'Thank you, *poro*.'
'How have you been?'
'All right. Things don't change much. A Chimbu was beaten this week.'
'By a warder?'
'Yes. Another Chimbu. Village life goes on here.'
They leant against the wire. Beside them two highlanders held hands unselfconsciously, participating in the traditional custom of male friendship.
'Jill sends her love.'
'Thank you, *poro*.'
'Do you miss her?'
'Yes. And you.'
John smiled. 'Bullshit artist.'
'Why bullshit? I need both of you. That's my Independence. I wish we were having parties. Don't you?'
'Yes. I wish we were.'
'When I get out, we'll have a big party. Okay? Just you and me. We'll have an orgy. Like your Sydney orgies.'
'Not like my Sydney orgies.'
'Better than your Sydney orgies. We'll go crazy.'
They held hands secretly against the wire. The talk smouldered on in fifty languages across the compound. Someone in the crowd laughed. At the touch of Francis' skin John felt the blood marshalling in his groin and at the same time he felt the futility of it.
'One of us has the wrong colour skin, mate.'
'Perhaps both of us have the wrong colour skin, *poro*.'
Francis' hand tightened its grip. John felt the sleek bones inside the smooth, dry fingers.
'I love you, *poro*,' John whispered.
'Time's up,' the warders shouted.

On the weekend of Francis' release they drove out of town along the red dirt road to Bootless Inlet. They had the windows open, wanting the early morning air to rush at them and pummel them with fragrances. They turned down a hot bumpy track they knew well, wound through car-high savannah grass and screw-palms, and came out at last at the isolated beach which looked across a reef-strewn bay to crouching, sun-struck islands.
They tumbled out of the car, out of their clothes. Out of their minds with delight and passion they ran on the smooth dark sand. Drunk with freedom, they hit the water and plunged, grappled, sank, turned each other over, wallowed with the water whelming round them, chest-to-chest, clasped and crushed each other, desperate for the depths within to weld. Then on the hot sand, kiss-crazed, laved in saliva and suntan lotion, love-whipped, they rode each other, reckless cowboys, bolted

and bucked, till the skin broke and their bloods exchanged curses beyond their knowing.

The next week, worried about diarrhoea which he thought might be amoebic dysentery, John saw a doctor in Boroko. He was a wise young medic, as it turned out, for although John's was the first case he had seen, the first of its kind in the country, he suggested he go South for tests.

He said goodbye to no one. He stayed late after work then walked across to the executive building where he slipped his letter of resignation under the locked door to the Minister's office. He drove home and parked his car in the garage, leaving the keys in the ignition. Then he went into the house and packed his suitcase. The music cassettes, the novelty bow tie ... those were memories enough. He could think of nothing more he needed so he closed the case. He sat in the lounge room without the lights on and opened a new bottle of Glenfiddich. He drank straight from the bottle, and waited for the taxi.

On the way to the airport he asked the driver, 'Is this Taxi Number 33?'

The driver's head turned around, grinning. 'Nogat, masta. Em i namba twandi-paib tasol.'

The driver thought it was a great joke.

1990

MICHAEL DRANSFIELD

Is this how whales?

for Garth

is this how whales fuck? great
meat lying light rolling
over and over in their deep bed the sea
touching with faint dissident hands
in the deep night all green with waters
far and around   high drift through hours
and oceans   is that
what they do?
we have been here forever
the sea is nothing to us it is night only
we know night that we dive and swim through night
that voids our open eyes of all but shadow turning
now it is the furthest hour from light now while
we collide and gently play hit and miss games
breathing each other's indistinguishable smell
instinct leads
and the present is this wedded and welded
darts and weaves entering spinning fine
webs on me with his eleven fingers

1987

Assignation

we will meet
where we always do
go where we go
we will talk and he will
undress me then himself
he will touch me everywhere
with his sea hands
our two mouths wed
burst inside each other
lie late together
we will part
where we always do

1987

NICHOLAS JOSE

A Game of Go

A pair of bicyles couple against the wall. Under the bridge two men shelter from the rain, the penis of one thickening between the thighs of the other, who flutters like a moth. The water is black and sluggish until a passing carlight makes confetti of a swathe of rain and casts shadows over the house fronts. The couple under the bridge casts no shadow. There is only a head of luminous white hair that the darkness will not quite extinguish, and within the dark are always eyes.

The Professor stood out with his big pink nose and scratchy white moustache, the only foreigner in the foyer. The performer, materialising beside him after the show, had the sheen of cold cream along his hairline and eyebrows that wriggled like caterpillars. The Professor extended his business card at once, and later the same night he was thrusting between Princie's thighs.

The Shanghainese, who fear water, live in rubber boots, raincapes and umbrellas. In Shanghai, the moistest city in the world, it rains every day for three months. The city is a sponge, a water creature. Damp permeates floors and walls, bedding, clothing, pores and lungs. Sometimes the saturated roads crumble apart to reveal the old canals and drains under the surface.

The rain came on during the performance and the Professor could not get home on his bicycle without getting wet. He sat over coffee with the performer who revealed that his name was Princie. Prince, Princeling. Looking at the tendrils of white hair climbing between impressive breasts from his companion's shirtfront, Princie coined a title for the Professor in turn. White-Haired Pig.

Professor Theo Weiss, Ming Philosophy, was on his last study leave before retirement. Soon there would be no more embarrassing questions about that doctorate of long ago, written on Master Mo, court sage of the Ming, who argued that the universe was kept in balance by equal and opposing forces of darkness and light. Just when Theo was ready to submit his thesis, the library in Geneva discovered a hoax in the oriental collection. A good many of the papers on which Theo had based his research were fake. Master Mo, in particular, turned out to be an element in some nineteenth-century swindle. Master Mo had never existed. On a merciful legalism Theo was granted the degree, on condition that he sought employment elsewhere. He took a job in Melbourne and salvaged a career. Being a churchgoer, he gave thanks. Solid, celibate Professor Theo Weiss—about that he was honest—would not be fooled again by an illusionist of Master Mo's ilk.

'White-Haired Pig's a complete rice queen,' Princie would joke with his friends later.

They took the lower way to the river bank where tarpaulin-covered barges were tightly moored. The Pig stood blinking as the rain ran into his whiskers. Princie made to wipe the Pig's face with his t-shirt, baring his chest. As the Pig tried to push him away, Princie grabbed the man's baggy scrotum and pulled him in under the bridge. The opera school had trained Princie well. Working his thighs, he was able to milk the White-Haired Pig lovingly, to squeeze the flesh as if every ounce were gold. He longed for gold rings to put through those tough old nipples. As if he were a court vizier, the Pig peered back at the Ming Prince, whose face was a hairless smudge, a dim evocation of a dream, in the darkness under the bridge. The rain fell in fine drops, like the hairs of a brush. Gasping, Princie flicked his own silver droplets onto the rank ground. He knew the place. It was risky. He told the Pig of the risk he was taking. Three years in a labour camp his friend had got for being caught with a Spaniard. And there were all sorts of diseases you could get from foreigners. The sheer mass of the Pig's flesh repelled him even as it excited him. It was silver and gold. What medicine did the Pig eat? His penis was as coarse as an animal's, when most Chinese were like champignons, and what Chinese was still doing it at that age, except the top-ranking state leaders, stuffed full of rhinoceros horn?

The Professor hung his head. 'What can I do for *you*?'

Princie jerked his head to one side and sucked his teeth.

'I want to do something for *you*,' the Pig repeated. 'Please?' Theo stood in helpless craving.

'Being human is hard. Take the umbrella. Go,' said Princie. 'Just go!'

Like a clown on a slack wire, holding the open umbrella in one hand, the White-Haired Pig wobbled through the furry rain on his bicycle.

Princie filled the hollow of his cheek with spittle and aimed it at the black river.

2

Theo Weiss sat doodling at his desk. The day had begun with pale clarity as he worked with steady satisfaction through the marginalia in a scholarly edition of a Ming legalist text. Theo was sufficiently Calvinist to need work as justification for the modest privileges of his existence. Work paid the moral rent. If he ran his hand over his noble paunch, or anticipated the long lunch break, or even a good night's sleep mercifully unbroken by another's snoring, Theo would feel compelled to put in another couple of hours to pay for it. In this way he had maintained an academic career, publishing, administering, counselling, without fuss. Prudently he always kept the amount owed ahead of the privileges he had already used up. When the books were balanced on retirement, he would have a significant amount of desert up his sleeve; so his moral accountancy told him. But he doodled, thinking with irritated precision about what he wanted, and not for the first time since meeting Princie.

The boy had written a tender effusive letter declaring his wish to become the Professor's friend. Then he telephoned to check that the letter had arrived and they arranged another meeting, at a temple, and as the incense was lit, Princie said that the White-Haired Pig would have been a Holy Master in another life because he had Buddha's earlobes.

Theo's nostrils flared. 'As it is, I've been reincarnated as a foreign devil.'

When they reached the last courtyard, convinced that his friend was a good man, Princie asked the Pig to exchange some US dollars for him.

'In a few days,' the Pig replied.

'We can exchange,' confirmed Princie with enthusiasm.

'Indeed we can. I should like you to teach me the movements of Chinese opera. It's one area I have never adequately explored. Demonstrate to me, I mean,' said Theo with a pink-lipped smile.

Doodling at his desk, he wrote the character *mei* for 'beauty', which also means 'American', and the figure 200. Two hundred pieces of beautiful gold.

In the afternoon, when he called for the lesson, Princie had to register at the front desk of the residence building before he was allowed up to Professor Weiss's rooms. By then a gushing cloudburst had obscured the windows and rain came dribbling in through the cracks. Princie, in shorts, t-shirt and plastic sandals, was spattered with mud. When he saw that the White-Haired Pig's bathroom had hot water during the afternoon, he asked immediately if he could take a bath. He turned on the light, shut the door and steamed up the room. Theo's tea grew cold as he sat outside waiting, watching the steam rise from under the door.

'Are you all right?' he knocked at last. He opened the door to find Princie up to his neck in a tub of near-scalding rust-brown water.

'I can dream here,' said Princie blinking. 'It's beautiful. It's much better than the bathhouse.'

'Did you find the soap?'

Theo took a fresh cake of his duty-free soap, dipped it in the steaming water, and made the boy stand to be lathered. The body was a flat hard board, with two brown rings for nipples and a sleek black rose of hair between the legs. Theo worked up a white foamy lather to make the rose grow. Then he turned Princie round and soaped him from behind, until he came to a tight little rosebud that the soap would not enter. Princie reached round and pressed the stiff front of Theo's pants with a wet hand print. All of a sudden Theo was clambering free of his clothes and climbing into the bath, splashing hot waves over the sides of the tub.

Princie gasped as the White-Haired Pig poked at him with the soap. It was so tight. He said he had never done it that way before. He told the Pig to go slowly and to get a condom. But Theo bent Princie's head down to the side of the bath tub so his chin was in the water, and, grasping Princie's thighs to achieve unimpeded aim, pushed the head of his penis hard against the tight soapy hole until he felt something go in. Princie yelped, resisting with all his lean strength, wriggling and withdrawing himself. He allowed the Pig an inch and no more.

Theo was excited. He slipped and climaxed outside the hole in a lather of soap and cum.

Princie rinsed himself fastidiously.

The overflowing tub had wet their clothes. Theo put on fresh ones. Princie sat in the armchair in his underpants and sandals while he waited for his shirt and shorts to dry. He cupped a mug of hot tea.

Theo draped a blanket around the boy's slight shoulders.

'You're so good to me,' said Princie.

'I don't mean to hurt you.'

Princie demonstrated some slow turns from Chinese opera. His eyes flashed like black-and-white marbles. He raised one knee as high as his chest. Theo clapped, and rose to his feet to imitate the movement. He was like a drugged elephant, limbs in the air, offering prayer.

'Oh, the money.' It was time for Princie to go. 'Two hundred dollars. Thank you.'

Princie rode down the lane without a glance over his shoulder at Theo, who watched from the upstairs window. Theo sat at his desk to continue deciphering the marginalia. Instead of doodling, he started playing with himself. When his penis was erect, he took it out. He looked at it. He measured between thumb and forefinger the length it had entered Princie's body and calibrated that length against a ruler. No more than an inch. According to his calculations he was owed more than that.

3

Massive, pink, reassuring, the White-Haired Pig gave Princie a feeling of stability. They talked for hours. Princie related how his father had strangled himself with an electric flex in the cancer ward, how his brother had been picked up for brawling, how his sister couldn't get a husband. Princie was the bread-winner. How could you ever win enough bread in China? He admired the huge belly that eating bread and butter had given the Pig.

'You are my big brother,' he said. 'Meeting you has changed my life. You are my special foreign friend and I am your special Chinese friend.'

Master Mo had attempted to refute the Confucian Great Harmony. He did not believe that harmony could eliminate all the disharmonious elements, nor did he believe that disharmony was an aberration from the due order of things. Harmony and disharmony were separate poles, acting as a counterweight to one another, like a see-saw, to keep the universe moving. Black was black and white was white. To deny that was to be left with a frustrating grey. Theo's research had drawn attention to the affinities between Master Mo's position and the Manichean heresy in Christianity, the view that good and evil exist autonomously, that ultimately neither is able to overcome the other. It was like a game of Go. The two players have equal numbers of counters, one white, the other black. The game proceeds step by step. Black may dominate white, then in a single deft move the situation is reversed, and white surrounds black. Eventually one player must win, of course, but the game is only part of a series. As soon as one game finishes, the next game commences ...

When Princie came for the next lesson in Chinese opera, the sun was out. The door opened and there amidst the shabby furniture, in a square of sunlight that fell across the floorboards, stood the White-Haired Pig in a splendid opera robe of embroidered black silk brocade.

'Ah ha!' grinned Theo, tweaking each wing of his moustache in an operatic flourish. 'What do you think?'

'Who gave it to you?'

'I bought it.'

'How much.'

'Never you mind!'

Examining the braid, Princie found a few loose gold threads. He was suspicious and resentful that he had not been the one to find such a thing for his friend.

'I may never be able to move like an opera performer, but I can at least look the part.'

'You look like Judge Bao.'

'My back aches, Princie. Will you rub it?'

Theo carefully folded back the heavy robe from his shoulders and laid it on the chair. He was naked underneath. He lay on his stomach while Princie pummelled his spine.

'Turn!' commanded Princie.

'You're hot. You're sweating. Take off your shirt,' frowned Theo, preparing for the more delicate frontal rub.

He had the boy on top of him, and when he was aroused he began to thrust.

'No condom,' protested Princie.

Theo ground his teeth. 'You don't need to worry with an old man like me.' He was in two inches, but even as he rammed harder Princie had some knack of resisting. Once again Theo was denied complete satisfaction.

Princie lay on the Pig's chest. 'I love you,' he said, tears filling his eyes. 'I give you everything. I don't want you to leave.'

Tears watered Theo's eyes in turn. He ached to get in all the way. 'Baby,' he gasped, fingering Princie's hairless navel.

Next time all the way in, no condom, no money, and Theo Weiss would leave Shanghai satisfied.

4

The drizzle resumed, heavy, light. Theo was planning his departure. Princie didn't call, and Theo had no way of reaching him. He called at the opera theatre, he walked under the bridge. As days passed he became more and more frustrated. He heaved bundles of books about his rooms, needing someone to help him. Angrily, on his last evening, he sat on his bulging suitcase. He cursed at the damage he had done to his back and huffed as the rain continued without cease. The gates of the compound would soon be locked for the night. He had made scholarly progress during his time in China, but, as Master Mo would have understood, his achievements existed in a different realm from, and did not compensate for, the irritation he felt.

Theo was pushing his weight down heavily on the suitcase that refused to close when there was a light knocking at the door.

Princie stood there, smiling, with a large package. He looked sheepish. 'I have come to say my farewell. I will never forget you.'

'Where have you been?'

'I don't want you to go.'

Theo clutched him in a bearhug. 'Ah!'

'A little souvenir,' said Princie. He ceremoniously presented the parcel, wrapped in red paper.

'You shouldn't give gifts. No!' protested Theo. It was a carved jade incense burner. Coyly, as a way of offering an exchange, he suggested tea.

'Don't stand on ceremony,' replied Princie, and squeezed the stomach of the White-Haired Pig.

With a snort and a giggle, Theo had Princie on the bed, and Princie was able to take the Pig's hard, deep penetration, channelling the man's surges of passion with acrobatic conviction.

'Ai-ya!' cried Princie, losing his breath, smarting with pain.

'Oh! Oh! Oh!' In a mounting, prolonged convulsion, his heart shuddering, sweat running through white ringlets over his golden tits, Theo dug his nails into Princie's tight thighs, and at last collapsed on the flat Chinese body like a carcass whose last life was twitching away.

Still the rain poured. In a matter of hours the plane was leaving. Theo lay holding Princie, free-falling in bottomless satisfaction. He had cut in ecstasy through a veil to hold the fantasy it had taken his whole life to fulfil.

Princie wiped himself—he was bleeding—and composed himself to make an exit before the escort party arrived to take Professor Weiss to the airport.

'Please write to me,' Princie begged.

Princie stood outside in the rain below the window and gave the White-Haired Pig a Chinese opera salute of goodbye. Theo clapped, eyes bulging. By the time he stopped clapping, the boy was gone, and Theo had begun to tremble at what comes after satisfaction.

5

After completeness came craving. After satisfaction came the need to repay gratitude. Professor Theo Weiss lit incense in the jade burner that stood on the mantelpiece of his house in suburban Melbourne. He had just finished reviewing the last lecture he would give before retirement. The topic concerned how foreign economic exploitation of China gave rise to a philosophy of national renewal through communism. Communism, he argued, recognised that the exploiter's greatest power lay in the readiness of others to be exploited. The craving to have. The lust to be had. Master Mo would have laughed. In church on Sunday Theo prayed to have Princie again, have Princie spit in his face and call him imperialist scum.

6

Retired Professor Theo Weiss had to adapt to new ways after the papers came through and Princie arrived in Melbourne. Princie took over the spare room and it was soon understood that Theo would not go in without knocking. Sometimes Princie had other Chinese friends over. The study, which housed Theo's library, was surrendered to the video equipment and karaoke set Princie wanted for his birthday. Princie did the shopping and cooking, and Theo's French cooking ware was sacrificed to drunken prawns and stir-fried chicken gizzards. Princie would only eat Chinese food.

If he wanted to read or write, Theo had to retreat to his bedroom. Otherwise the garden in the back courtyard was his domain. Or else he was in the laundry doing the washing for both of them since Princie couldn't get the hang of the machine or the different washing products.

The first cheque Theo had written was to the language school in which he enrolled Princie. The second had been to the airline for the ticket from China—a return ticket since the Immigration Department insisted on the fiction that Princie was visiting Australia as a temporary resident. There was a money transfer to Shanghai to enable Princie to give what was necessary in bribes to procure documents. There was a cheque to a College of Business Administration in Melbourne to enable Princie to extend his visa. There were regular remittances to the family in China.

Princie persuaded Theo to trade in his old car on a flashier model that Princie could learn to drive to work. Princie saw no point in sitting around. He doubted the value of wasting time in a classroom as against hours spent earning dollars. Skimping school attendance, he managed to fit in two, sometimes three, jobs a week. Theo never asked how much money Princie had in the bank, but it was Theo who paid the health insurance for both of them. Theo suspended his retirement travel plans. He had to be careful with his superannuation. He sat at home at night wondering when Princie's key would turn in the lock.

Theo was proud of the splendid camellias and azaleas he grew in the courtyard at the back. In the morning, when he did the watering, he would glimpse Princie slipping in and out of the bathroom getting ready for work, the slim flat body, shapely torso and glossy coal hair, and he would smile in disbelief, as he hosed the leaves, at the exotic in his house.

Princie no longer let Theo touch him. There was no need. It was Theo in the end who wrote the long letters home to Shanghai and corresponded with the Immigration Department. It was Theo who rang his former university colleagues to solicit favours regarding the academic progress of Princie and his mates. Theo preferred the more matter-of-fact business of ironing Princie's shirts. The ingratitude was the same in either case. There was sufficient cause of pain for Theo to feel noble.

He sprayed the shrubs and moved the pots around to vary their exposure to darkness and light. He decided to move a favourite indoors, where it would go well with the black-and-white chequerboard tiles of the kitchen floor. Theo was in the habit of wearing the Chinese opera robe at home. Disinclined to change out of it he would often not leave the house all day. He put up the ironing-board and took Princie's jeans out of the dryer. Princie had not been in since the evening before. After ironing the jeans, Theo flopped down in his armchair and began to review one of the old Ming texts. He had come to believe that Master Mo existed after all, despite what they said in Geneva.

Nodding off, wrapped in his robe, the Professor dreamed that Master Mo winked at him. The illusionist did exist after all.

Princie came home in the evening with a new mobile phone he had bought. He found Theo snoring in the armchair.

'Lazy White-Haired Pig!' laughed Princie. He gave the fat, slack-jawed face a resounding slap. 'Wake up!'

(1993)

A f t e r w o r d s

MICHAEL DRANSFIELD

Memoirs of a velvet urinal

he turns his back to dress; i've lost him
already. after inevitability took our
hands and made us play, we talked
for hours in the slow
warm dark, touched each other. his body
is red like a fox, i had seen him before,
although he is sandpaper rough, not furry
like his kind. i love all poets; there is
no private self: as, if he needs me,
i go to him. the habit
forms, that we lie together
each time. when he touches me, it is true, a small
space turned in my belly; but
often he starts by brushing his red
fingers through my long, downy hair,
or kisses me. in the next bedroom
our host sleeps in electrified blankets,
wifeless through this and summer when
it comes to his cold province; he guesses
nothing, but would not care.

1987

DAVID MALOUF

Difficult Letter

And what should I write to you across
five oceans, who to me were nearer
once than my own breath? If you were set
at distance of mere enmity, I
might with casual phrases, cold politeness bridge the gap; but what dark words can
scrawl these oceans now that flow like time
between us? What can I say to you,
my neither enemy nor friend, when
once, between our lips, were printed wordless psalms of praise, when once I signed
my scribbles in the ocean of your blood?

1962

Hotel Room Revisited

It is there; though with a lover's
presumption I had thought
the street too must be down and those bare
walls where we made love
be hanging like our broken
vows above the square.

And still, as between four walls of an abandoned
dream, stands the real,
the solid furniture:
table, chairs, the iron
bed that was, we thought, quite incidental
to the affair.

They have survived; and sitting
among them now, I am
shaken with dry laughter;
hearing two shadows speak
eternal promises, in a room that we
had rented for an hour.

1962

PETER ROSE

Memorabilia

So, finally, what have I kept of yours,
what buried to remember you by?
For a start, philosophic ditties
of doubtful provenance,
boxfuls of old, elusive letters,
a morose photograph of you as Hamlet.
(You stayed up all night to develop it.)
Wrapped in our sheet,
absolutely cheerless and profound,
those lips might be cankered I have kissed,
the proud mouth a slash of desolation.
Cryptic Anno Dominis follow,
taunting the bearer of the key-shaped card:
Hitler's rise or a Happy Majority?
More prized, a pea-soupy edition of *La Nausée*,
next to Volume Two of de Beauvoir's memoirs,
Sartre's longiloquent love.
I remember, you stole them for me
at an English bookshop near the Spanish Steps.
Coward that I am, I watched you stuff them
down walking boot and trouser leg,
petrified and thrilled.
Hopelessly nobbled by Nietzsche,
you hobbled past a purblind creature,
reached the Steps—and shook!
Great literature flew from you like doves.
Humbled by such munificence
I led you back to our hotel
and now, when young colleagues
wish to borrow my *Prime of Life*,
I warn them, 'Mind you bring it back.
It was stolen for me by a great friend.'

1990

SUSAN HAMPTON

Lace

give me some relaxing drug I said
to no-one, to the piece of Spanish lace
i'd washed and dropped in the sand
in this small area where i was making
a circular brick paving so i could sit
and enjoy my lot. and all morning my guts
had been griping for no other reason
than a terrible sense of unfairness
ssdf Ass ;asd as j s df;lkjsjda;dlskadajks
grdujkl; asdfjkl; asdfjkl; finmcnvmb benim beni
on this page someone has typed a whole lot
of letters, words that don't quite look like
gradual, or circumvent, it's the kid who
lives here, he's a good boy and who could blame him
for using the typewriter to practise his keyboard skills
because he dropped out of biology
but it's fate i raise my hand against
and say it's typical, letters already on the page,
there's something dreadfully typical about it
so you hardly even notice but go on anyway,
incorporating those words into what you thought
you were going to say and howling stupid tears into
the Olivetti
you know the kind of day i mean there's no real need
to go on but i will anyway you can always leave the room
it's the twentieth century and freedom's in the air
i tell myself but what is it that gives men the right
to immunity from pre-menstrual tension do they have
and hide crocodile tears to the extent of the rivers
we create? the boring oceans?
but back to the lace. i was hanging it out
hoping the weather would clear and dry it
for a bedspread because soon she's arriving
and she likes white things in the night.
at her place there's a day garden
with cornflowers and lavender and those bright
orange california poppies and out the back
in a shady place there's a night garden
full of white so at twilight you sit there
watching things get intense as dusk falls
it's a good idea but right now i'm too angry
to think about such things with any tender feelings

and dropping the lace was the last straw
having to wash it again and howling in frustration
like a dog chained to its hormones
the kind of day when you think i'll go to my room
and work, only work will cure this nasty aspect
of biology, and except for the great love you feel
for your typewriter you would bash the letters
senseless
if she came in right now offering sympathy
and warm arms for my stupid pain
i'd only want to turn around and kick the wall
it's not the kind of relationship where someone
props you through a bad day i mean
she lives eight hundred miles away and that's
how we like it though things may get closer
who can say. all morning i've thought
how badly burned we are and wary of being
committed whatever that's supposed to mean
beyond a kind of copying neurosis. i don't know
anyone who wants to live together though i hear
rumours there are still people of this type around
and i certainly hope their well of happiness
keeps full from the underground spring they say exists.
i have nothing against couples as long as i don't
have to spend a lot of time with them while they're
together
but where does it get you in the end?
back on the street as we know, searching
with voracious eyes for the next one while
using your head to deny their possible existence
busily mopping up the pain from the last one
with any old T-shirts you left in the car
and thinking, always thinking that liberty
is better than this useless collection of scars.
and then the sun comes out and before you noticed
it's spring or it seems to be, and your hormones
are doing the opposite thing, sending you on the rampage
and love,,,,,, seems like a dirty word but a nice idea
and what would it be like to touch someone again
bring them home to bed put your arms around
someone else's breasts instead of your own
so you go to the party and look around
with your arrogant eye at what configuration
of skin on bone will turn you on and getting drunk
to calm the nerves of making out with some
mysterious stranger just off the street herself
bits of wet T-shirt hanging from her jeans pocket

at least you're in the same boat and cynical together
mentioning in passing as you speak of other things
how you aren't interested in falling in love
and neither is she, 'falling', you both scoff,
brandishing your bruised knees which prevent you
from dancing with too much abandon though getting drunk
helps. however it's not a night for talking
everyone's been celibate for too long
and even in the taxi you can't leave each other alone
so a wonderful night passes exploring a new body
in this language which has no words and is never
written about with any degree of unselfconsciousness
though theoretically your chances are doubled
with four pairs of lips in the bed speaking
their swollen secrets
and next morning you can hardly walk
but it's a good idea, and out you go, talking
about the past and explaining the bits of your scars
you're prepared to show—the trophies of ancient
desires from other delusional states with women
from interstate who appeared with mouthfuls
of independence and a secret cave in the heart
longing for the entry of its one true love.
so of course you are wary this person too
will be a believer, she'll think that someone somewhere
was made for her and maybe it's you
and the undercurrent of everything you say serves
to rob her of this notion should she hold it.
romantically enough she pulls something from a tree
and hands it to you, the powerful scent of orange blossom
momentarily drowns the traffic, and having been married
once years ago you might recognise it as the plant
they engrave on wedding rings, maybe they still do,
the last time you passed a wedding your guts griped
and you turned a corner, you wouldn't know,
but you hold the plant to your nose breathing it in
for dear life it's the first thing she ever gave you
you remember months later when it turns out
she wasn't a one-night stand though that was an option
you both kept open in case she wanted more
than you could give.
a desire to live in the same town would have thrown
you off your beat but that didn't happen
and things as they are, are OK, it's just
you've had a bad day
what with the lace dropping in the sand

1989

BEVERLEY FARMER

From *Alone*

My scrapheap bicycle was stolen one day from beside the gully trap in the yard. In its place, a pile of faeces heaped under the lamp. I am a snooper on foot now, much given to peering in at inhabited windows and doorways. I have always been outside, an onlooker. She was the only person to ever love me.

. . .

I pull off my clothes and lie down in my tangled bed, pulling the sheet and the grey blanket up over me. My watch has stopped again, must have stopped hours ago, at ten. I had just come out of the Library at ten. The night is half over. She can't be coming now. Perhaps it is not too late. If I just lie down, taking care not to fall asleep. I want to just lie and watch how candlelight flickers and flows over my still room, over the watery glass of the mirror and the glowing pane. Candlelight gilds me. I unplait my long hair to spread it over my throat and shoulders.

A sweaty stench emanates from the cabbage drooping flaccid leaves over the dressing table.

I have been burning papers with matches again, misbehaving at my own birthday party. Flames and gusts of black smoke have burst up to the ceiling, gutting the kitchen, burning the children alive. I have run out of the back door into the cold front yard. At last I see green flames waving in the cracked glass of the front door. I bang in frenzy at Mum's curtained window. She pulls the curtain aside, beaming and nodding inside the thick pane. I scream, plead, hammer the glass. The house is on fire, it's going to burn down, Mummy, come out. Slowly smiling, she turns away, smoothing her rolled grey hair, and walks into a wall of fire.

I awake shaking, whimpering as always, bathed in bland candlelight, alone.

I have been having the same dream half my life. Fully awake I can never quite recall with just the same precision the splintered planks of the verandah, the white-washed balustrade, the dingy double casement, the damask folds of my mother's curtain.

. . .

I must remember to burn what's left of my papers. I don't want anyone to read them. Papers screwed up one by one into multifoliate balls burn like black roses. The flame is roses. Am I repeating something I have said before?

I get out of bed. It is still dark beyond the golden pane. I wonder how long to daybreak. I pull on my bathrobe and flap in cold sandals to the bathroom, squat wincing on paper on the stinking toilet to piss, wash my hands in cold water at the cracked basin. I cup my hands and drink. My red palms, huge and wrinkled, glow under shaking water. I gulp cold bright water and wipe my cold hands on my robe. A moth clambers outside on the lamplit pane, her belly trembling above her frail legs. I turn out the light and creep back along the passage to my glowing doorway.

She is not there. I knew that all the time. Of course I knew she wouldn't be there all the time.

I hang up my bathrobe and insert my bony, numb, gawky, cold grey flesh between the rumpled sheets. The other bed, her bed, is a skeleton now, a mess of rusty springs. The very day she left me the landlady came and took the mattress and bedclothes off to another room. The candle flame flickering weaves a mesh of dusty gold under her bed.

Shall I at least set my affairs in order?

I, Shirley Iris Nunn, being of sound mind and body, do hearby bequeath what little I have to whomsoever might be able to make some use of it.

Let me therefore enumerate my worldly goods.

Item, one camera, lens shattered, shutter beyond repair, I'm sorry to say, miss, not worth fixing, it isn't.

Item, two rows of dusty books along the skirting board, some in good order, I leave to anyone who wants them, and much good may they do you.

Item, one flabby, rotten, yellow cabbage.

Item, sundry groceries.

Item, sundry articles of black clothing, well worn, but they've worn well.

Item, two amber earrings, glowing tawnily.

Item, one body, hardly used, one owner, but, regrettably, inanimate. Even when alive. Cold, cold, my girl. Included, sundry organs of more or less academic interest, which I hearby bequeath to the University for the purpose of research: or, failing that, to feed poor cats and dogs, or homeless riverbank rats.

Item, one sheep's skull, damaged, jaw missing.

Item, one empty purse, no money left at all. What little I managed to save from my pittance at the café has all gone now. Nothing left. I have taken no for an answer. Give me my due, admit it. Given no for an answer, too.

She must be coming to see me tomorrow. Oh, darling! Come here. I thought we would love each other for ever. She said so, too. She probably wants to avoid a scene by coming in the daytime. She knows that I'm going to kill myself tomorrow. I said so in my letter. She knows I mean it. How, I didn't mention, not having decided yet.

I am golden in the dark, in the light of mirrors and candles, on my narrow bed. As if any sure, disdainful goldenness in mirrors could erase the sight of me crawling naked, goose-pimpled, fluffed, bum-first from underneath her bed.

I never listen to music now. I hardly ever speak. When I do, the words come out sluggish and rusty, disconcertingly off-key. I strike a false note.

I overpunctuate with too eager, too compliant nods and grins, only to lapse into anguished silences. I have already said all I wanted to say, and all to no avail. I even get my hullos and goodbyes subtly wrong. People recoil. In the street I pass people I used to know with glazed distant eyes or an assumed frown of preoccupation.

One of her friends stopped me once.

Hullo!

Oh, hullo!

You are Shirley, aren't you?

Yes. Of course.

Thought so. How are you these days?

Oh, fine, thanks. How about you?

And so on. As I turned away she added:

Where are you living now, Shirley?

Oh, same place.

Oh, yes? Doesn't it get you down?

No, not really.

Pretty squalid, though, isn't it?

Interesting, though.

How the other half lives!

How I live.

I gather it's more or less an amateur whore-house.

Well, you could call it that, I suppose.

Right up your alley! Well, I must be off. 'Bye!

So evidently she thinks that I'm an amateur whore. Or maybe just that I have a depraved appetite for squalor, among other things, and that I thrive on vicarious lusts.

. . .

I only look backward. I have been muffled insidiously by despair and silence, like a slow burial in snow. There is no contact to be made, no one to communicate with, no one to write for. The whole city is empty. If it is madness, then madness is one of the forms reality takes. Am I mad, not that it matters? I am surprised that mad people renounce their validity and submit to being taken to pieces by psychiatrists. Is it just to stay alive on any terms? Everyone will die. There is a certain shabby dignity, integrity at least, in choosing when and how. There are ways enough. I'll know when the time comes. By this time tomorrow I'll be dead.

What will I say when she comes? What will she? I thought of killing her once, grasping her by her rough hair and stabbing deep. *Odi et amo.* Then hacking up her body and disposing of it in suitcases. The woman at the ruined hut. The tufty bog, the river of moored ships, the wide black sea. Who would ever have found out?

I never could have done it. I love you. I could never harm one hair of your head. I never did.

. . .

A cat shrieks. Behind the high rope of leaves at the open window my room is dark and cool. The hot grapes in the bowl have seeds in their deep green globes. I am alone. It is the Sunday of my eighteenth birthday. I have slept in.

I can hear the voices of children singing. *Chantant dans la coupole.*

I lift the warm sheet and shadows begin to move over me and lie in bony hollows of my hips and between my breasts. Brown hairs curl in my armpits and about and above the long closed lips between my thighs.

Licence my roving hands, and let them go,

Before, behind, between, above, below.

At the funeral home they must wash you there, wash you all over. They stop up the orifices. There was a phenol stench where Grandpa's body lay mounted in the coffin to be viewed. A casket is dearer, madam. The knotted throat was sewn into a calico shroud, the yellow mouth glued shut. They had plucked the fierce white hairs out of its ears and nose, and powdered its domed old pate. I kissed the cold mask over the skull bone. Death, I said. Death, this is me.

My watch has stopped. They were all expecting me home today to celebrate my birthday in the bosom of the family. Dad sunk brooding in his armchair. Mum drooling smoke, a cold eye cocked at the mantel clock. Val flouncing.

She's still not here. I'm waiting here. I'm waiting, too.

On the dull mahogany of the dressing-table among books and pots and pans the sheep's skull from the brown hill stares back with jewelled sockets in its splintered, yellow-toothed muzzle. The ribbed leaves of the cabbage, a give-away at sixpence, come on, lucky to get it, the lucky last at this price, yours for sixpence, miss, curl and cling in a pallid ball. In a dish of vinegar water lie two gutted, sequinned fish with torn gold-leaf eyes. The tilted oval of the mirrored sky is laced with leaves. Every mirror is a fragment of the one. A cat squalls.

Just tell me what you get out of living in this squalid old dump, she said once. Tell me, why should we live here? Is it another one of your penances or something? Like drudging round in that filthy café?

I can write here.

Oh, fine. You never seem to, though, do you?

I'm gathering the raw material.

Raw's right. If squalor's all you want to write about.

Where are you? Where were you last night? When the Library closed everyone, but not you, came shuffling and coughing away from its musty, high, echoing circles of books and its green-coned lamps down the marble staircases and the stone stairs in the lawns on to the thronged streets gaudy with warm rain. But not you. Where are you? Down on the Yarra Bank? With your freaks and cranks and fanatics. Afterwards we walked to watch the black ships on the sliding sunset river.

> The river glints
> Slime and oil
> Gulls prance
> In the sludge tread
> A rat's corpse
> Bled
> The red sun sinks in eddy and coil.

Pastiche, intones Miss Jones, is something of a misapplication of your undoubted intelligence.

At the market, in the crowds jostling over the cobbles—blood glinted in the noon glare—I was sure I would find you. I bought my sodden mullets. From a yelling Chinaman I bought furry peaches, the very last cabbage and a ripe pineapple. I munched a sugared doughnut, walking in the sun, amber drops burning on my ears.

Yesterday evening on the north bank of the tumid river black-robed hags were clambering to pick great bunches of those feathery tall stems that smell of aniseed. You remember. Their houses were black blocks patched with the yellow glowing out of window-frames and doorways, under the red sky. Outside one with a vine over the lintel people sat among fallen golden leaves and the shadows of other leaves above them. The bridge lamps were lit, swaying in the red water. The hill was leafy and dark. There were no lights on in your house.

On my last birthday we were sitting together with the family in our hot shiny cyclamen kitchen over the good tablecloth and the good dinner set, gorged on roast lamb and gravy and mint sauce, roast potato, sweet potato, three potato, four, pumpkin and parsnip and grated carrot raw. You'll come again soon won't you dear, we'd love to have you. I'm always at Shirl to bring her school friends home, aren't I Dad?

Shall this flesh live? shall this

Flesh live?

I rubbed and sloshed with the rank grey dishmop gravy-clogged plates and knives and forks and the slimy black baking tin. You wiped up. In my own room behind the golden falling fingers of the fig you lay reading *The Cocktail Party*. In the hot bar of sun on the lino I squatted to brush my drying hair over my face, the sun a small glitter in my iridescent fell of hair, the lit brush flashing amethyst, emerald, opal on to my lap. Sunlit, my eyes are green-speckled. In the old brown radio, crackle and boom, the *Pastoral Symphony*.

My hair is falling out.

Now it would be time—'Shir-irl, the iron's hot, Shirl'—to go and iron the same old striped, stained hankies and tea-towels and pillow-cases on the cleared kitchen table, dark by now under the lace curtain limp over grey palings.

I push a shiny wrinkled hand under the cool pillow. My silent watch shows ten. I never listen to music now. I pull out and unfold rustling the copy of my last letter with your lock of bright hair inside and a pencil sketch over the thick carbon words of my hand cupping a candle flame.

Darling,

It's six months today since I came home to find you gone. You shun me. You treated me as a stranger when we met in the street. I still love you and nothing else means a thing to me. What can I do now? While you loved me too I could brave any humiliation. Since I have known that you really don't love me any more I just stay shut in here all day and skulk around the city, night after night. It's not true that I'll find a man and get over it, as you said. I can't bear a man to touch me. I think I might be mad. I'll never go to the University now, nor go to Asia, to Europe, nor even be a writer, nor have a child. I never listen to music now. I am an object of scorn. Next Sunday week, on my eighteenth birthday, I am going to kill myself. You did love me once, didn't you? I would like to see you once more before I die.

There was, of course, no need for any signature. I thrust the letter back. I posted the original days ago. She might still come. Day after day I have crossed off. Oh, darling, come here, she said. Sullen, I hung back. Now she has gone forever. If she doesn't come, or if she does, soon I'll know if all bonds are broken and I am at a loose end.

A tram trundles past. In the yard a cat howls. Thrice the brindled cat hath mewed. On bare arched feet I stalk to the window, plucking the dusty green curtain across to cover me. On the landlady's bony black puss, ringed by bristling toms, one tabby leaps snarling and claws her down and rapes her, squalling, inside the intent still circle.

> Oh, Mrs O'Toole,
> It's bloody croole.
> There's poor Puss Cat
> Impaled, squashed flat
> By a brute like that
> While a dozen more droole,
> Mrs O'Toole.

Catherine was raped. She told me all about it, or all that could be told. As we lay coiled, golden by candlelight, in each other's arms she would ask, Is your body happy? Now and then, half asleep, I would feel her suddenly kick and jerk against me.

What's wrong?

Nothing, why?

You were kicking me in your sleep.

Was I? Oh, I sometimes do. It's nothing. Cramps.

It's as if you were repulsing me somehow. Don't you want me with you? Don't you love me?

Of course I do, silly. You know I do.

She would kiss me, smiling, gentle, golden all over, and hot and damp: I watched her fall asleep in my cool arms. I know now why she kicked and jerked. Much good it does me. I've never felt like that. I realized at last what it was when I went with the boy who used to sit staring at me in the café, and he did it too, and cried out. Before that all I knew was that it's what you have in mind when you dream of climbing stairs, according to Freud. I didn't think women could do it.

We climbed up dark stairs to his dark, dusty room. Too shy to speak, we kept glancing at each other and looking hastily away. He turned on a lamp on the dressing table, pulled down the blind behind the torn lace curtain, gave me his towel and took me down to the bathroom. If only it had been her with me instead.

I stood in a grimed tub, water glittering, mantling me, a gilded moth fluttering on the pane. I sat naked by lamplight in front of the mirror and peeled an orange for him, an orange for me, peeling glowing segments of veined cold oranges. My fingers burned scarlet against the lamp. His room was on the top floor of another old, dank slum, but the one window looked to seaward, its lace curtain breathing salt air.

It's sour, I said, after the rum.

Here's some honey, then. Have some honey.

We coiled and fed each other spoonfuls of the thick honey. He squatted, kindling a coal fire in a cracked grate. He turned his back to undress and stumbled to me, darker still by lamplight, his pale-palmed hands cupping his groin. Loose, my hair lay flickering over my breasts. I was golden, insolent, superb on his rumpled bed. I had smeared between my thighs with cold cream. By then we had drunk between us half a bottle of burning rum. He clambered clinging on top of me, clamped his hard mouth over mine.

Have you ever done it before?

No, I gasped. Haven't you?

No. Help me put it in.

No, I can't. Oh, don't, you're hurting. Don't!

Hold me!

No! No!

He flung away. A warm trickle ran down my rigid thigh, and he sagged, sobbing, against me. I held his rough head.

Don't cry.

I hurt you.

I lost my nerve. Don't cry, please.

Will we try again?

Oh, no. Not now. In the morning.

When I came back from the bathroom he lay turned to the wall, firelight wrinkling and sliding on his bare back. I lay down behind him and pulled the sheet up over us. I lay awake for hours listening to the fire, to the sea. The curtain woke me, breathing loudly in the dawn wind. On the morning sea the sun flashed and tracked, looped. Golden light filled the room, tarnishing the lit lamp: the fire lay in ashes in the dim grate. The silent street below was still deep in shadow.

I was alone.

As I crept past I saw him in the dark bathroom. He was sitting on the rim of the lion-pawed, grimy tub, rubbing his black hair with a towel. I vanished, leaving no addresses.

I never went back to the café again, not even for my pay. Perhaps he tried to find me there, perhaps not. It was a night to put in a poem, not deep and real, not love.

. . .

The sky deepens over the row of little yellow shops. Inside the cascading pane of the fish shop 'H KRHTH' the pewter fish gape with leaking, tarnished eyes, morwong, salmon trout, garfish. One red crayfish huddles, the rubbery petals under her belly spread open in a fan and showing her cluster of eggs. A tufted hand grabs her. I turn and drag open the door of the telephone box hot and rank with stale smoke and sweat. Beetles batter on yellow glass walls.

I prop my pennies in the slot and dial Mum. Engaged. Time passes. How time flies. A heavy moth slithering and flapping has black eyes painted on her wide wings. I could ring. I must have spent hours in this hot, bright box mouthing into the mouthpiece words that can never be said again, the dialling tone burring in my ear, a hail of moths and beetles battering. Will I ring? I flick the tattered directory open.

If, rather than die tonight, I let slow time carry me past all this, years and years on? I might never see her again, anywhere, ever. I might meet her again one day ten or twenty years from now, in some café or other, blood shaking my heart. A dim lamp to tangle that harsh hair.

Hullo, Catherine.

Do you know me?

I used to.

Where from?

We were at school together.

Oh, yes! Now I remember! I remember.

That's not worth living for. I've spoilt my life. There are no new starts, no new leaves. Palimpsests. I am a palimpsest of purple prose. I dial again.

'Hullo?'

Jangle clank. Home, with the hall light burning in the leaded green glass on the front door. Squat behind the hedge, a sagging weatherboard villa with daisies in the couch grass, a stained giant clam shell under the dripping garden tap, a black spider under the cover of the water meter, and lantana under the brown-blinded bow window.

I love a sunburnt country,
A land of stunted brains,
Of endless vapid villas
And clotted, leaking drains.

'Hullo, Mum. It's me.'

Did I drag you away from the TV? Or was it the latest Digest? Or were you getting Dad his tea? Bubble and squeak and a lean rasher of a Sunday night, or baked beans on toast, all slack and cosy in your dressing gown, your brindled hair slipping out of your French roll.

'Hullo? Hullo?'

'Hullo. It's me, Mum.'

'Hullo?'

'It's me, Mum. Can you hear me now?'

'Is that you, is it, Shirl? Happy birthday, darl! Well, and about time too! You caught me in the bath!'

'Oh. Sorry.'

You laid your furrowed rump in surging swirls of water, raising bony knees. On your curled pubic hair bubbles glowed bronze, and at the base of your sounding white belly, a white island gold-rippled, and about the pursy bivalve between your thighs.

I soaped your back. You were moaning in pain. The suds rippled down into your shaven armpits and down your loose thighs, scumming and shadowing the water, weaving laces of light shaking over aged flesh embalmed in honey. After such knowledge, what forgiveness?

'Never mind. I'm in my dressing gown. You're late, dear. On your way out, now, are you?'

'I'm sorry, Mum. I can't make it.'

'You mean you're not coming at all?'

'I can't. I'm sorry.'

'But it's your birthday! I've been looking forward. You know you said you'd be coming Home!'

'I can't make it, though. I'm sorry.'

'Oh, Shirl. How thoughtless can you get. Here's me going to all the trouble of doing a roast dinner, a whole leg and four vegies, we'll take a week to get through it all, and I didn't dish out till three, I was sure you'd be here. Why didn't you ring?'

I don't think of Home as it is now that you've had it done up. When I was little there was an alcove with a gas stove on legs, a kookaburra painted on the door, Early Kooka. There was an ice-chest in the darkest corner, a copper and a long pole and troughs for washday, a yellow jug of boiling water for hands and faces before breakfast. Porridge with the names scribbled in golden syrup. Milk with its blue-beaded net.

'What? I forgot it was my birthday.'

'There are some cards for you. Mrs Mac popped over a while ago with a plate of her shortbreads she baked for the occasion, Aunti Eth just rang to wish you many happies . . .'

I'm never coming Home again. We'll never see each other again. You've never seen my room with its glowing grapes and cabbages and sodden, gilded fish. A skull stares at the sun-slit wall. I have a mirror, and a candle, and deep port wine. Don't come tomorrow when they notify you. What would be the point?

'You there, Shirl?'

'Yes.'

'Where are you ringing from, darl?'

'The phone outside the café. I'm on my tea break.'

I quite liked being a waitress. It paid the rent. Men kept trying to pick me up. Are you all woman? one snarled. I went home with the black boy. Rum, honey, sour oranges. He cried, and slept.

'Oh well, I suppose that settles it, then. If you can't, you can't. I did try to get on to you last night, did the lady tell you? What was her name again?'

'Mrs O'Toole. Yes, she did.'

'She sounds such a nice person over the phone. We had quite a chat. You're not having too many late nights, are you, dear?'

'No. I just walked home from the Library.'

'Not alone?'

'Alone. Yes.' A woman runs a terrible risk.

At the hot, blinded window on summer afternoons we children lay in wait for the ice-cart. The horse stamped and twitched, fly-bitten: masses of brown shit bulged from its brown rump plop on the soft asphalt of our road. Sullen, the ice-man jabbed with his pick. Fragments of ice fell glittering. We stood around and sucked the stinging ice, watching the cart lurch clip clop away and blowflies swarm.

Birthday, deathday. The University is next to the great graveyard's jagged marbles and dry grass.

'Your Dad and myself wouldn't want you to think of us as spoilsports or anything like that, you know, dear, but we do worry. When'll you be down to see us now?'

'I can't say for sure. You see, I'm flat out all day at the café. By the time I knock off I've simply had it ...'

I cry, much of the day, and go out in the evening. I flick the tattered directory open at Catherine's number. It is there. I am embalmed in amber glass.

'You're quite a stranger. All summer we hardly set eyes on you from one week to the next, what with exams and then you taking it into you head to go hitchhiking all over the place goodness only knows where and then leaving Home. How time flies! It must be well over six months now since you moved into your flat and in all that time you haven't been to see us once.'

'I'll try.'

Two children peer at me with golden goggling faces.

'If it wasn't so awkward for me to get out and about since Dad's op I could of popped up to see you. I miss you, you know, Shirl ...'

'Well, I miss you, too. Of course.'

For years of safe Sunday nights I knelt on the faded floral carpet by the hoarse gas fire, baggy in Aunt Eth's old chenille dressing gown, daubing water-colours for school with the radio on full, the Hit Parade, Daddy and Paddy, Crosbie Morrison. I rode your ancient bike, the huge shadow of its basket lurching all around me, up our gold-patched street to the Greek's for four pieces of flake and two bob of chips, please, for you to pop wrapped in the newspaper, into the hot oven, reeking of dripping and vinegar and printer's ink, the times you didn't feel like beans or bubble and squeak. Pop up to the fish shop for us will you, Shirl, I just don't feel up to cooking tea tonight, there's a good girl.

'I hope it's not because of those things Dad said, Shirl.'

'Oh, no. No.'

'All right then, dear. I just thought I'd ask. I know it isn't like you to bear a grudge.'

'How is Dad?' I have dropped my voice, too.

'Oh. You know how it is. He has his good and his bad days. Mustn't grumble, you know.'

'I see.'

'He took it pretty hard, of course. He had his heart set on you going to University and all that. And when you broke it to him that you weren't going on, well it was quite a blow, you have to admit.'

'I gathered that.'

'And you didn't so much as send a get well card when he was in the hospital, Shirl.'

'He'd have torn it up.'

'It's hard to say. He might have. For show, he might. It's hard to tell with Dad. Deep down in his heart of hearts ...'

Plump, pompous, ponderous, prosy, parsimonious, pious, patronizing Podsnap. His red nape abristle over his stiff collar, his bald pate glooming over the financial pages. Picture of a stockbroker with a heart of hearts.

'How's your flatmate, what's her name again, starts with K — '

'Catherine.'

'Remember us to her, won't you. It's lovely to know you've got a nice friend like that. We all took quite a liking to her. You need someone to bring you out of your shell. Or your ivory tower, which is it? You always were a mite antisocial from a little girl.'

A dusty, red-eyed moth flutters, thumping the hot panes. She stayed that night in my room. She came to my bed by candlelight. Naked to naked. I remember our yellow flickering bodies, her nipple in my mouth, and her unbelievable wet secret lips bared for the first time.

A pacing shadow looms on the dusty pane.

'Are you there, Shirl? Hullo?'

'Mum, I think there's someone waiting for the phone.'

'Oh. Better make it snappy then. Well, remember, don't work too hard, dear. I still can't see why you have to work in a café when you've got your Leaving. You could just as soon find an easier job. What do you get out of being a waitress, anyway? You could get a nice job in a bank.'

'Look, Mum—'

'Oh, I know we've been through all this before. I can't help hoping you'll see reason one day. Val's fine, by the way. She's gone to some Church do. She came top of the class in the last test, isn't that marvellous, a hundred out of a hundred for Science. She was that disappointed you didn't turn up today.'

I bet she was.

'Give her my love.'

Sudden headlights jerking over the empty road flash on the panes. Shadows slide on the footpath. A black-thatched head squat on shoulder pads stares in at the door, blandly smiling.

''Ullo,' it grins, yellow-toothed.

Shaking, I push the slow door shut and jam it shut with my foot and shoulder.

'Mum—'

'Yes, all right, then, dear. Oh, yes, by the way, before I forget, it's Auntie Eth's birthday next Friday, did you remember? Your birthday's five days before hers. Poor soul, she's been that lonely since your Uncle Bill passed on.'

'I'll send her a card.'

'Shirl, there's someone at the door, hang on a sec, will you.'

Her footsteps tap away in my ear. The two golden children saunter out of the fish shop, probing avid fingers into their torn newspaper parcel, yelping, licking them. They goggle at me in the thick glass, then scamper off, singing:

> 'Oh ma darlun, oh ma darlun,
> Oh ma darlun Clementine,
> Makes yer realise kids are lucky
> To live in nineteen fifty-nine.'

Ten years ago I sang that. To live in nineteen forty-nine. Time passes. The faint moth spreads her painted eyes on the glass. Once Catherine stood in a telephone box and dialled Mum's number. I picked up the phone.

Hullo, is that you? she said. I've just been raped.

The long river lay at our feet, wrinkled, gold-ruffled under the lamps of its arched bridges. A train flashed mirrored across. Gulls squalled. A rat on the muddy bank below leapt into the long grass. The black image of a man padding along the cycle path stopped, fumbled, and sent his bright arch of piss hissing over the coiling water.

'There, Shirl? Only the Salvos taking up a collection. What was I saying? Oh, Auntie Eth's birthday.'

'I'll send her a card.'

'Will you, dear? I knew you'd want to. A nice card's just the very thing to cheer her up a bit.' The slow shadow slides off the pane. 'You always were her favourite niece, you know.'

'Yes, well, Mum, I really have to go, they're tapping on the door, so give Dad and Val my love, won't you—'

'Come out and see us soon. Bye bye dear.'

'Bye. Mum.'

I hang up. And that's that, as you'd say. Pull your cosy gown tighter around you and go and have a bit of a warm by the fire. Sit trickling smoke between your lips to furl the frilly golden lamps and fray the warm shadows in corners.

I shove the door open and step into the cool street. He is still there, dark against the ripples of the fish shop window, lit smoke trailing from his lips and nostrils. A tram is clanking up the street, its long rod hopping and flashing along the netted wires. Two rows of streetlamps shake gold rings on the asphalt. His hand falls, yellow-furred, on my shoulder. I clutch my bag. I feel his thigh against my buttock, and gasp.

'You don't frighten! You comun 'ome wiff me, darlun?'

His hand strokes my plait.

'Don't.'

I jerk his hand off me, and step on to the road, under the high lamp. Darling. The green and gold tram lurches up and stops.

'Give yer five quid,' he mutters after me. I shake my head, leaping aboard.

'Oo yer keepun ut for?'

1980

VAL VALLIS

Arachne

Out of your body you have spun this web
That folds me in a silence. Strand of smile,
Of lip and thigh and casual embrace
Cast from your origin of flesh you ply
Till I am shrouded in your body's art,
Stung by its sharp delight, then laid aside
In a forgotten corner, where to sleep
Within your tangled darkness of neglect
Seems greater joy than light or motion knew;
For there one thought spills sunlight in my blood,
That you must come again to feast on me!

1961

NOTES ON AUTHORS

ADAMSON, ROBERT (1943–) b. Sydney. Adamson is a distinguished poet (*The Clean Dark* has won three major poetry awards), editor and publisher. He was one of the founders of the modernist *New Poetry* magazine and has written an autobiographical novella entitled *Wards of the State*. He lives on the Hawkesbury River north of Sydney.

ALTMAN, DENNIS (1943–) b. Sydney. Altman is Australia's most prominent writer on homosexuality and society, and AIDS. His best-known works are *Homosexual: Oppression and Liberation* and *AIDS and the New Puritanism*. His first novel, *The Comfort of Men*, was published 1993. He lives in Melbourne.

BIARUJIA, JAVANT (1955–) b. Melbourne. Of mixed Celtic and Mediterranean descent, Biarujia lived in Indonesia in the late 1970s. He is the author of several chapbooks of poetry and has been published widely in magazines and anthologies in Australia and overseas. He lives in Melbourne.

BRERETON, JOHN LE GAY (1871–1933) b. Sydney. Brereton was the Professor of English Literature at Sydney University and a friend of Henry Lawson and Christopher Brennan. His lyric poetry (*The Song of Brotherhood, Sea and Sky, Swags Up!*) and collections of essays and reminiscences (*Landlopers* and *Knocking Around*) are now not held in particularly high literary regard, although he has an honoured place in Australian literary history.

CIANTAR, BENEDICT (1964–) b. Sydney. Ciantar is of English-Maltese descent. *Distractions* is his first novel. He lives in Melbourne.

DRANSFIELD, MICHAEL (1948–73) b. Sydney. Dransfield first published in underground magazines and became a cult-figure among champions of alternative life-styles after his early death. He published three volumes of poetry (*Streets of the Long Voyage, The Inspector of Tides, Drug Poems*) and 600 other poems were posthumously collated and edited by Rodney Hall into two volumes (*Voyage into Solitude* and *The Second Month of Spring*).

ELLIOTT, SUMNER LOCKE (1917–91) b. Sydney. Elliott wrote plays for the Independent Theatre in Sydney, including his most famous, *Rusty Bugles* (1948), based on his experience at a remote army camp in the Northern Territory during the Second World War. He left Australia permanently for the USA in 1948. Elliott wrote over fifty television plays and ten novels, including *Careful, He Might Hear You, Edens Lost* and *Water Under the Bridge*. He lived latterly in New York City and New Hampshire, USA.

FALLON, MARY (1951–) b. Queensland, grew up in Brisbane. Her books include *Explosion/Implosion*, *Sexuality of Illusion* and the prize-winning novel *Working Hot*. She has worked in and written for theatre in Sydney and published widely in anthologies and journals. She lives in Hobart.

FARMER, BEVERLEY (1941–) b. Melbourne. Farmer lived for three years in a Greek village with her Greek husband and began writing her first novel *Alone* there. Her first collections of stories, *Milk* and *Home Time*, came from that experience. Other works include *A Body of Water* (the writer's notebook interspersed with poems and stories) and the novel *The Seal Woman*. She lives at Point Lonsdale, Victoria.

FRIEND, DONALD (1915–89) b. Moree, New South Wales. One of Australia's most eminent painters, Friend is scarcely known at all for his writing, except *Bumbooziana*. He travelled widely, living in England, Ceylon, Bali and Australia.

GARNER, HELEN (1942–) b. Geelong, Victoria. One of Australia's best-known and most highly acclaimed writers, Garner is the author of *Monkey Grip*, *The Children's Bach*, *Cosmo Cosmolino* and the short-story collection *Postcards from Surfers*. She lives in Melbourne.

HAMPTON, SUSAN (1949–) b. Inverell, New South Wales. Hampton has published two books of poetry, *Costumes* and *White Dog Sonnets*. She co-edited *The Penguin Book of Australian Women Poets*. Her book *Surly Girls* is a collection of performance pieces, monologues, poems, stories and fables from contemporary women's culture. She lives in country Victoria.

HANFORD, BRUCE (1946–) b. Boise, Idaho, USA. Hanford emigrated to Australia in 1966. He has worked as a journalist, written some fiction, and held a variety of jobs in the media. He lives in Canberra.

HARFORD, LESBIA (1891–1927) b. Melbourne. An art teacher and social researcher, Harford had connections with the Communist Party. Some of her lyrical poetry was collected after her death by Nettie Palmer (*The Poems of Lesbia Harford*). There is some interest in her work now from feminist critics, but she is still not widely known.

HARWOOD, GWEN (1920–) b. Brisbane. Harwood has been publishing her poetry to widespread popular and critical acclaim for three decades. She has also written opera libretti. Her collections include *Poems*, *Poems: Volume Two* and *The Lion's Bride*. She shows some preference for conventional forms. Harwood lives in Tasmania.

HERBERT, TIM (1959–) b. Sydney. Herbert has published short fiction in many Australian gay magazines and journals, such as *Outrage* and *Cargo*, and one book of short stories, *Angel Tails*. He is currently editing a collection on taboo sex called *Love Cries*. Herbert lives in Sydney.

HERKT, DAVID (1955–) b. New Zealand. Herkt's publications include *The Body of Man* and *Satires*, for which he shared the 1990 Wesley Michel Wright Poetry Prize with John Tranter (1989). He lives in Melbourne.

JOLLEY, ELIZABETH (1923–) b. Birmingham, England. Jolley was born into a German-speaking family. She arrived in Australia in 1959 and is the internationally acclaimed author of numerous short stories and prize-winning novels, including *Mr Scobie's Riddle*, *The Well*, *My Father's Moon* and *Palomino* (which has a central lesbian theme). Jolley lives with her family in Perth.

JONES, RAE DESMOND (1941–   ) b. Broken Hill, New South Wales. Jones' published work includes three books of verse in the 1970s (*Orpheus with a Tuba*, *The Mad Vibe*, *Shakti*), *The Palace of Art* in 1982 and one short-story collection, *Walking the Line*. He was the founding editor of the modern poetry journal *Your Friendly Fascist* and lives with his family in Sydney.

JOSE, NICHOLAS (1952–   ) b. England, grew up in Australia. Jose studied at Oxford and has served as Cultural Counsellor at the Australian Embassy in Beijing. He has published several short-story collections and novels, including *The Possession of Amber*, *Feathers or Lead* and *Avenue of Eternal Peace*. He lives in Sydney.

KRAUTH, NIGEL (1949–   ) b. Sydney. Krauth is an award-winning novelist whose novels include *Matilda*, *My Darling* and *The Bathing Machine Called the Twentieth Century*. He lives with his family at Mt Tamborine, Queensland.

MACKENZIE, KENNETH 'SEAFORTH' (1913–55) b. Perth. Mackenzie published four novels, including *Dead Men Rising*, which was based on the outbreak of Japanese POWs at Cowra where he served during the war, and four collections of poetry (two posthumous). He is little known today outside literary circles.

MALOUF, DAVID (1934–   ) b. Brisbane. Malouf is recognised as one of Australia's most gifted contemporary poets and novelists. His novels include *Johnno*, *An Imaginary Life*, *Fly Away Peter*, *The Great World* and *Remembering Babylon*. He lives partly in Tuscany and partly in Sydney.

MAYNARD, DON (1937–   ) b. Rockhampton, Queensland. Maynard worked with the Australian administration in Papua New Guinea in cultural areas. He has been published in the Papuan Poets series, anthologies and magazines. He lives in Sydney.

MOORHEAD, FINOLA (1947–   ) b. Melbourne. Moorhead is a playwright, poet and contributor to many fiction anthologies including *Room to Move* and *Frictions*. Her latest novel is the prize-winning detective novel *Still Murder*. She lives in Sydney.

MOORHOUSE, FRANK (1938–   ) b. Nowra, New South Wales. Moorhouse's reputation as the leading exponent of short fiction in Australia was established with *The Americans, Baby* (1972). His innovative narrative methods include 'new journalism' techniques. He is identified with the 'Balmain' writers (left-wing, sexually explicit writers in 1960s and 1970s in Sydney). His best-known collections are *Conference-ville*, *Tales of Mystery and Romance*, *The Everlasting Secret Family* and *Days of Wine and Rage*. He has published two novels, *Forty-Seventeen* and *A Woman of High Direction*. Moorhouse lives in France.

PAGE, TONY (1952–   ) b. Melbourne. Page has lived and taught in the USA, South-East Asia, Portugal and Australia. He has published widely in Australian literary and poetry magazines and has two volumes of poetry, *They're Knocking at My Door* and *Satellite Link*. Page lives in Melbourne.

PAUSACKER, JENNY (1948–   ) b. Adelaide. Pausacker is a well-known writer for children and young adults. Her novels include *What are Ya?* and *Can*

You Keep a Secret? Her short stories have been widely anthologised and she co-edited *Moments of Desire* with Susan Hawthorne. She lives in Melbourne.

PAYNE, SIMON (1950–) b. England, brought up in Alice Springs, Northern Territory. Payne graduated from Flinders University, Adelaide, and began writing fiction and plays in Melbourne. *The Beat* was his first novel. He lives in Melbourne.

PORTER, DOROTHY (1954–) b. Sydney. Porter is best-known as a poet, although she also writes fiction. Her collections include *The Night Parrot* and *Driving Too Fast*. She teaches writing at the University of Technology, Sydney, and lives at Mt Victoria, New South Wales.

PORTER, HAL (1911–84) b. Melbourne. Porter was a poet, playwright, novelist and short-story writer and was described by A.D. Hope as Australia's 'most distinctive and perhaps . . . most distinguished writer of short stories'. He is best-known for his autobiography *The Watcher on the Cast-Iron Balcony* and the novels *A Handful of Pennies* and *The Tilted Cross*. Porter was essentially a regional writer, but also set works in Europe and Japan.

RICHARDSON, HENRY HANDEL (1870–1946) b. Melbourne. Richardson is one of Australia's most esteemed writers and was nominated for the Nobel Prize in 1932. She left Australia permanently in 1888 to study at Leipzig Conservatorium. Although her most celebrated works are set either in Australia (*The Fortunes of Richard Mahony* and *The Getting of Wisdom*) or in Germany (*Maurice Guest* and *The Young Cosima*), she lived most of her life in England.

RILEY, ELIZABETH (1946–) b. Gippsland, Victoria. *All That False Instruction*, Riley's only published work, was one of the earliest examples of overtly lesbian fiction in Australian literature. Yet to receive serious critical attention, it nevertheless won Riley the first Angus & Robertson Writers' Fellowship in 1972. Riley lives in country NSW.

ROBERTS, BEV (1939–) b. Adelaide. Roberts is a poet who has published widely in Australian poetry and literary magazines. She has had two collections published, *The Transvestite Next Door* and *The Exorcism Trip*. She has worked extensively in areas promoting literature (as a literary editor and community writing activist). Roberts lives at Breamlea, Victoria.

ROSE, PETER (1955–) b. Melbourne, grew up in Wangaratta, Victoria. Rose began publishing poetry in magazines in 1985. He has had two poetry collections published, *The House of Vitriol* and *The Catullan Rag*. Rose lives in Melbourne.

SHAPCOTT, THOMAS (1935–) b. Ipswich, Queensland. Shapcott is one of Australia's most eminent poets with many collections, often innovative in technique, published over three decades. He has also published novels, including *White Stag of Exile* and *Hotel Bellevue*, and short stories. He was Director of the Literature Board of the Australia Council from 1983 to 1990. Shapcott lives with his family in Melbourne.

SHOTLANDER, SANDRA (1941–) b. Melbourne. Shotlander's plays and monologues have been performed in the USA and throughout Australia at theatres such as the Universal and the Malthouse in Melbourne and Belvoir St in Sydney. Her best-known works are *Framework, Blind Salome* and *Angels of Power*. She lives in Melbourne.

SOLDATOW, SASHA (1947–   ) b. Germany. Soldatow is of Russian descent. In the 1970s he was connected with libertarian-anarchist circles in Sydney. He has published widely in magazines and anthologies and performed one-man theatre pieces, including the burlesque *Rock-n-Roll Sally*. He has also published two full-length works of fiction, *Private—Do Not Open* and *Mayakovsky in Bondi*. He lives in Sydney.

SPEARS, STEVE J., (1951–   ) b. Adelaide. Spears is the author of numerous plays (including *Young Mo, When They Send Me Three and Fourpence* and *Froggie*), performance pieces, film, radio and television scripts (including some for 'Neighbours' and 'A Country Practice'). *The Elocution of Benjamin Franklin* has been staged in over a dozen countries in Europe, North and South America. He lives in Sydney.

VALLIS, VAL (1916–   ) b. Gladstone, Queensland. Vallis taught at the University of Queensland and has published two collections of poems, *Songs of the East Coast* (1947) and *Dark Wind Blowing* (1961). He lives in Brisbane.

WALKER, KATE (1950–   ) b. Newcastle, New South Wales. Walker is the author of several acclaimed children's books, including *Marty Moves to the Country* and *Peter*. She lives in Newcastle, New South Wales.

WHITE, PATRICK (1912–90) b. London, England. Australia's most celebrated novelist, White was winner of the 1973 Nobel Prize for Literature (for *The Eye of the Storm*). His best-known novels are *The Tree of Man, Voss, Riders in the Chariot* and *A Fringe of Leaves*. His other work includes the plays *The Ham Funeral, The Season at Sarsparilla* and *The Night the Prowler*; the short-story collections *The Burnt Ones* and *The Cockatoos*; and an autobiography *Flaws in the Glass*.

ACKNOWLEDGEMENTS

The editor and publisher thank copyright holders for granting permission to reproduce the following material:

Adamson, Robert and Hanford, Bruce: excerpt from *Zimmer's Essay*, Wild and Woolley, 1974.

Altman, Dennis: excerpt from *The Comfort of Men* by Dennis Altman published by William Heinemann Aust. a division of Reed Books Australia.

Archer, Robyn: 'A Musical Interlude' from 'Poor Joanna' in *Heroines* edited by Dale Spender, Penguin Books Australia Ltd, 1991.

Biarujia, Javant: 'Hamid'. Reproduced by permission of the author.

Ciantar, Benedict: excerpt from *Distractions*, BlackWattle Press, 1991.

Dransfield, Michael: 'Is this how whales?', 'Assignation' and 'Memoirs of a velvet urinal' from *Michael Dransfield: Collected Poems* edited by Rodney Hall, University of Queensland Press, 1987.

Elliott, Sumner Locke: excerpt from *Fairyland*, © 1990 by Sumner Locke Elliott. Reprinted by permission of The Helen Brann Agency Inc.

Fallon, Mary: 'Peaches—Peaches and Cream' from *Working Hot*, published by Sybylla Co-operative Press and Publications Ltd, 1989.

Farmer, Beverley: excerpt from *Alone*. First published 1980 by Sisters Publishing Ltd. Republished 1984 by McPhee Gribble Publishers.

Friend, Donald: excerpt from *Save Me from the Shark*, HarperCollins Publishers Ltd, 1973.

Garner, Helen: 'La Chance Existe' from *Postcards from Surfers*, McPhee Gribble Publishers, 1985.

Hampton, Susan: 'Lace' and excerpt from *Surly Girls*, Angus & Robertson, 1989.

Harford, Lesbia: 'I can't feel the sunshine' and 'Lie-a-bed' from *The Poems of Lesbia Harford* edited by Drusilla Modjeska and Marjorie Pizer, Angus & Robertson, 1985.

Harwood, Gwen: 'Ganymede'. Originally published in *Poems*, Angus & Robertson, 1963 and then in *Selected Poems*, Angus & Robertson, 1990.

Herbert, Tim: 'Pumpkin Max' from *Angel Tails*, BlackWattle Press, 1986.

Herkt, David: 'Satires' from *Satires*. © David Herkt 1987.

Jolley, Elizabeth: excerpt from *Miss Peabody's Inheritance*, published by University of Queensland Press, 1983.

Jones, Rae Desmond: 'Dawn' and 'The El Paso Restaurant' from *Shakti*, Makar Press, 1977.

Jose, Nicholas: 'A Game of Go'. © Nicholas Jose.

Krauth, Nigel: excerpt from *JF Was Here*, Allen & Unwin, Sydney, 1990.

Mackenzie, Kennth 'Seaforth': excerpt from *The Young Desire It*, Angus & Robertson, 1972. First published by Jonathan Cape, 1937.

Malouf, David: 'Unholding Here', 'Dark Destroyer', 'Difficult Letter', 'Stars', 'Hearing you read the poems', 'Poem', 'Hotel Room Revisited' from *David Malouf: Poems 1959–89*, University of Queensland Press, 1992. 'Night Training' first published in the *Sydney Morning Herald*.

Maynard, Don: 'Athlete' from *Four Poets*, Cheshire (Melbourne and London), 1962.

Moorhead, Finola: 'Frances and Sophie' from *Remember the Tarantella*. © Finola Moorhead. First published by Primavera Press, 1987. Second edition published by the Women's Press, London, 1994.

Moorhouse, Frank: *The Everlasting Secret Family*, Angus & Robertson, 1980.

Page, Tony: 'Passion at Byron Bay', 'Monster in the Park' and 'Dialogue' from *Satellite Link*, Jacaranda Wiley, 1992.

Pausacker, Jenny: 'Graffiti' from *The Exploding Frangipani* edited by Cathie Dunsford and Susan Hawthorne. © Jenny Pausacker.

Payne, Simon: excerpt from *The Beat*, published by Gay Men's Press, London, 1984.

Porter, Dorothy: 'Sauce', 'My Sleeping Brother', 'Lies and Tin', 'Little Brother', 'Smenkhkare's Wedding', 'Just to Talk', 'All Touch' and 'The New Temple' from *Akhenaten*, University of Queensland Press, 1992.

Porter, Hal: 'The Dream' from *A Bachelor's Children*, Angus & Robertson, 1962. © Jack Porter, Bairnsdale.

Richardson, Henry Handel: 'The Wrong Turning' and 'Two Hanged Women' from *The End of Childhood*, 1934. Reproduced by permission of the copyright holder c/- Curtis Brown (Aust) Pty Ltd.

Riley, Elizabeth: excerpts from *All That False Instruction*, Angus & Robertson, 1975.

Roberts, Bev: 'Poem For Our Fifth Year' from *The Exorcism Trip*, Pariah Press, 1991.

Rose, Peter: 'Obscure Figure' and 'Memorabilia' from *The House of Vitriol*, Picador, 1990. 'Aviator' from *The Catullan Rag*, Picador, 1993.

Shapcott, Thomas: 'Elegy for a Bachelor Uncle' and 'Young Men's Bodies' from *Thomas Shapcott: Selected Poems 1956–1988*, University of Queensland Press, 1989.

Shotlander, Sandra: excerpt from *Is That You Nancy?* (collected phone calls of Gertrude Stein and others), written for and produced by the Sydney Mardi Gras 1990.

Soldatow, Sasha: 'Requiem' from *Travelling on Love in a Time of Uncertainty* edited by Gary Dunne, BlackWattle Press, 1991.

Spears, Steve J.: The permission of Currency Press to use this extract from 'The Elocution of Benjamin Franklin' is gratefully acknowledged.

Vallis, Val: 'Arachne' from *Dark Wind Blowing*, Jacaranda Wiley, 1961.

Walker, Kate: excerpt from *Peter*, Omnibus Books, 1991.

White, Patrick: excerpt from *The Twyborn Affair*. Copyright © 1979 by Patrick White. Used by permission of Viking Penguin, a division of Penguin Books USA Inc., and Random Century Group, London.

Every effort has been made to trace the original source of all material contained in this book. Where the attempt has been unsuccessful, the editor and publisher would be pleased to hear from the copyright holder concerned to rectify any error or omission.

INDEX OF AUTHORS AND TITLES